Carmen Ulrich (Hg.)
Dialog und Dialogizität
– interdisziplinär, interkulturell, international

Carmen Ulrich (Hg.)

Dialog und Dialogizität
– interdisziplinär, interkulturell, international

iudicium

Herausgegeben von Carmen Ulrich
Beiträge der IPIW-Konferenz – international promovieren in Wuppertal –
im Fachbereich Geistes- und Kulturwissenschaften an der
Bergischen Universität Wuppertal, 7.–11. November 2016
Der vorliegende Band wurde finanziert vom Deutschen Akademischen Austauschdienst (DAAD), dem Bundesministerium für Bildung und Forschung (BMBF) und der Bergischen Universität Wuppertal.

Titelbild: Christiane Kern

**Bibliografische Information
der Deutschen Nationalbibliothek**

Die Deutsche Nationalbibliothek verzeichnet diese Publikation in der
Deutschen Nationalbibliografie; detaillierte bibliografische Daten sind im Internet
über
http://dnb.d-nb.de abrufbar.

ISBN 978-3-86205-508-1

© IUDICIUM Verlag GmbH München 2017
Alle Rechte vorbehalten
Druck: ROSCH-BUCH Druckerei GmbH, Scheßlitz
Printed in Germany

www.iudicium.de

Inhaltsverzeichnis

Carmen Ulrich
Vorwort   7

Ursula Kocher
Dialog und Dialogizität – zur Einführung   13

Literaturwissenschaft

Sven Hanuschek
„Die Undine kennt Jeder von uns erementaschen hier." Dialogizität in Arno Schmidts Erzählung *Brand's Haide* (1951)   26

Robert Moscaliuc
Belligerent Dialogues? A Dialogical Approach to Fictional and Non-Fictional Representations of the American 'War on Terror'   46

Pia Martin
Adaption as Intercultural Dialogue: August von Kotzebue on the British Stage   60

Lisa-Marie Teubler
Literature and Democracy: Dialogue and Persuasion in Charles Dickens's Novels   79

Hannah Tischmann
Zur gesellschaftlich engagierten Literatur als dialogisches Genre   90

Myriam Dätwyler
Dialog und Dialogizität im *Taugenichts* von Robert Walser   109

Drishti Magoo
Interacting Selves in the *Diaries* of Franz Kafka   127

Johanna-Helene Linnemann
‚Bluhmen-Discurse' in Johann Rists *Jahreszeitengesprächen*: Figuren, Texte und epistemische Ordnungen im Dialog   145

Klassische Philologie

Valerio Petrucci
Hellenization and Romanization. The Dialogue between the Greek and Roman Cultures in the 1st and 2nd Centuries   160

Martin Schmidt
Der Dialog der Philosophen in Laktanz' *Divinae Institutiones* — 176

Georges Tilly
An early modern Conception of Dialogism: Giovanni Pontano and the Neapolitan Academy (1476–1503) — 190

Geschichte

Andrew Smith
Pope Leo IX: Three Letters containing Dialogues and Decisions in 1049 and 1050 — 207

Caterina Cappuccio
Die päpstlichen Subdiakone als Mittel der Kommunikation zwischen Rom und der Lombardei (1198–1216) — 216

Ricardo Márquez García
Das kamerunische Grasland und der ‚Afroatlantische Dialog' — 232

Philosophie

Martina Di Stefano
The Risk of Homogenization in the Dialogue between the Disciplines: the Case of Foucault's Reuse of Ancient Philosophy — 246

Valeria Fernandez Blanco
Der ununterbrochene Dialog zwischen Jorge Luis Borges und Michel Foucault — 266

Sprachwissenschaft

Janina Beutler
Topic Drop and Coherence in Dialogue — 276

Benjamin Richarz
Die dialogische Funktion des Höflichkeitskonjunktivs — 290

Die Beiträgerinnen und Beiträger — 310

Vorwort

Carmen Ulrich

Der vorliegende Band präsentiert einen Großteil der Vorträge, die auf der IPIW-Konferenz, vom 7. bis 11. November 2016, an der Bergischen Universität Wuppertal gehalten wurden. IPIW – international promovieren in Wuppertal – ist ein vom Deutschen Akademischen Austauschdienst (DAAD) und vom Bundesministerium für Bildung und Forschung (BMBF) gefördertes Programm zur Internationalisierung der Promotionsphase. Unter der Leitung von Prof. Dr. Ursula Kocher unterstützt IPIW interdisziplinäre und internationale Forschungsprojekte sowie die weltweite Vernetzung der Promovierenden.

Zu dem Tagungsthema „Dialog und Dialogizität – interdisziplinär, interkulturell, international" versammelten sich Doktorandinnen und Doktoranden aus 14 Ländern und verschiedenen geistes- und kulturwissenschaftlichen Fächern, um ihre aktuellen Forschungen einem Fachpublikum vorzustellen und mit Hochschullehrerinnen und -lehrern der Bergischen Universität Wuppertal und der Ludwig-Maximilians-Universität München zu diskutieren.

Der so häufig verwendete Begriff des Dialogs lud zu einer genaueren Bestimmung der Bedeutung und Zielsetzung ein, die in einer gemeinsamen Entscheidungsfindung, Sinngebung oder auch im wechselseitigen Anerkennungsverhältnis bestehen können. Diskutiert wurden Phänomene der Dialogizität in literarischen, philosophischen und historischen Werken, in theologischen Schriften und wissenschaftlichen Abhandlungen aus unterschiedlichen kulturellen Räumen, gesellschaftlichen Ordnungen und Epochen. Im Fokus standen daher auch politische und gesellschaftsbildende Funktionen des Dialogs – seine Struktur des Aushandelns allgemeingültiger Werte und Normen, seine Rolle innerhalb der Wissenschaftsgeschichte, zwischen Wissensvermittlung und Wissensproduktion, wie auch diskursspezifische Dialogformen und Dialogpartner.

Dialoge und Phänomene der Dialogizität konnten innerhalb verschiedener Themenfelder in fachspezifischer Verortung wie auch in verbindenden

Strukturmerkmalen ausgemacht werden. Wechselwirkungen zwischen verschiedenen Kontexten, Standpunkten, Horizonten und (sozialen) Sprachen ließen sich sowohl in älteren Schriften, durch Rekonstruktion der Prozesse der Kanonisierung, wie auch in gegenwärtigen Textkorpora der jeweiligen Geistes- und Kulturwissenschaften erkennen und freilegen.

In ihrer *Einführung* sondiert Ursula Kocher das weite Feld der Begriffe „Dialog und Dialogizität", indem sie nach dem Wesen und der Funktion des Dialogs fragt, ihn als sprachliches Phänomen in den Blick nimmt und differenziert von dem literaturtheoretischen Konzept der Dialogizität.

Die Sektion *Literaturwissenschaft* eröffnet Sven Hanuschek mit der Suche nach Spuren von Dialogizität in Arno Schmidts Erzählung *Brand's Haide* (1951) und findet – entgegen landläufigen Erwartungen an einen schmidt-typischen monologisierenden Erzähler – weit mehr als nur verstreute Spuren, indessen markante Grenzüberschreitungen zwischen verschiedenen Welten, zwischen fiktiven und faktischen Wirklichkeiten, in die das eigene Wirklichkeits-Erleben problemlos zwischengeschoben werden kann, ohne sich angleichen, verändern oder gar auflösen zu müssen und doch oder gerade deshalb in einem Maße irritiert wird, wie vielleicht nur der Dialog es vermag.

Robert Moscaliuc zeigt in seinem Artikel „Belligerent Dialogues?", wie verschiedene historische Ereignisse – der Untergang des Zivilschiffs *General Slocum* vor der Küste New Yorks (1904), der Angriff japanischer Streitkräfte auf eine amerikanische Pazifikflotte am Stützpunkt *Pearl Harbor* (1941) und der Terroranschlag auf das World Trade Center, kurz *9/11* (2011) – in fiktionalen und nicht-fiktionalen Repräsentationen miteinander verknüpft werden, so dass durch die Medialisierung vergangener und gegenwärtiger Diskurse eine dialogische Simultaneität entsteht.

Als einen interkulturellen Dialog beschreibt Pia Martin die englische Adaption zweier Dramen August von Kotzebues (*Lovers' Vows*, dt.: *Das Kind der Liebe* und *Pizarro*, dt.: *Die Spanier in Peru*), indem sie die Abweichungen vom deutschen Quellentext nach deren Funktionen befragt und sowohl moralische, politische wie auch kulturelle Intentionen ausmacht. Unter Adaption versteht Martin auch den Prozess der Interpretation eines Textes in Bezug auf das neue Publikum, changierend zwischen Gesten der Vermittlung und Gesten der Überlegenheit.

Indessen geht Lisa-Marie Teubler davon aus, dass Literatur einen echten Dialog generieren kann, d. h. einen demokratischen Austausch zwischen

Autor, Text und Leser, durch den neues Wissen und eine erweiterte Teilhaberschaft am Wissen entstehen. Bei genauerer Analyse von Charles Dickens Novellen lassen sich allerdings leserlenkende Textfunktionen erkennen, die den demokratischen Gehalt der populären Erzählungen in Frage stellen.

Hannah Tischmann reflektiert in ihrem Beitrag „Zur gesellschaftlich engagierten Literatur als dialogisches Genre" die Interaktionen zwischen Autor, Text, Leser und Literaturindustrie. Dialoge mit der außertextuellen Welt lassen sich hier vor allem in gesellschaftlich engagierten Werken finden, in denen soziale Ungleichheiten und gesellschaftsrelevante Fragen verhandelt werden.

In Robert Walsers *Taugenichts* setzt sich die Figur vor allem mit sich selbst auseinander, stellt Myriam Dätwyler fest, mit sich und seiner Eichendorff'schen Vorläuferfigur, und zwar vor allem in jenen Monologen, die, laut Bachtin, sämtliche Anzeichen der Dialogizität aufweisen, während die formal dialogischen Passagen im Dramolett auffallend monologische Züge tragen.

Verschiedene Stimmen – ein schreibendes Ich und ein geschriebenes Ich, ein Autor und ein Tagebuchschreiber und noch mindestens ein Anderer mit dem Namen ‚Ich' – markiert Drishti Magoo in Franz Kafkas *Tagebüchern* (1909–1923). Diese unterschiedlichen Stimmen interagieren aber nicht nur miteinander, sie konstituieren vielmehr – in ihrer Gesamtheit betrachtet – ein neues Textverständnis, das über die bisherige autobiographische Lesart hinausgeht.

Johanna-Helene Linnemann untersucht die Lehrer-Schüler-Gespräche in Johann Rists *Jahreszeitengesprächen* – die äußere Form der gemeinsamen Gartenspaziergänge wie auch die innere Form der textuellen Gliederung – und vermag in dem allseitigen Streben nach Erkenntnis dialogische Strukturen sowohl auf der Ebene der Figuren und Textpassagen wie auch der epistemischen Ordnungen aufzuzeigen.

In der Sektion *Klassische Philologie* widmet sich Valerio Petrucci dem Dialog zwischen der Griechischen und der Römischen Kultur im ersten und zweiten Jahrhundert, unter Einbeziehung verschiedener Modelle des interkulturellen Dialogs. Der Beitrag wirft Licht auf wesentliche Aspekte, Gründe und Funktionsweisen der Romanisierung und Hellenisierung – die politische Romanisierung der Griechen infolge der Vorherrschaft der Römer einerseits, die kulturelle Hellenisierung der Römer durch die griechische Bildungselite andererseits.

Martin Schmidt behandelt den Dialog der Philosophen in Laktanz' *Divinae Institutiones*. Laktanz' postulierte Wahrheitssuche erweist sich, bei genauerem Hinsehen, als höchst konstruierte Argumentation, die nicht nur der Verbreitung des Christentums und der Lehre christlichen Lebens dient, sondern auch – bei aller Kritik an den Philosophen – den Stellenwert der geistigen Auseinandersetzung hervorhebt.

Konzepte des Dialogs untersucht Georges Tilly im Kontext der Neapolitanischen Akademie bei Giovanni Pontano (1476–1503). Dabei richtet sich der Fokus auf die sozialen Beziehungen, die sich mit den neuen dialogischen Kommunikationsformen entwickelten. Anhand ausgewählter philologischer Quellen reflektiert Tilly den Dialog als wesentlichen Bestandteil des humanistischen Ideals.

In der Sektion *Geschichte* geben drei Briefe von Papst Leo IX. Auskunft über die Bedeutung des Dialogs in den kirchlichen Synoden Mitte des 11. Jahrhunderts. Andrew Smith hebt das kollegiale Miteinander bei den kollektiven Entscheidungsfindungsprozessen unter dem Pontifikat Leos IX. hervor, der seine päpstliche Macht und Autorität auch dazu nutzte, den Dialog als eine wichtige Kommunikationsform zu etablieren.

Caterina Cappuccio reflektiert die Beziehungen zwischen Papst Innozenz III. und den Regionen in der Lombardei (1198–1216), indem sie die päpstlichen Subdiakone als Mittel der Kommunikation voraussetzt. Der Beitrag behandelt zum einen die päpstliche Kapelle und ihre Aufgaben, zum anderen die Lebensläufe zweier päpstlicher Subdiakone, Aliprand Visconti und Wilhelm Balbo.

Am ‚Afroatlantischen Dialog' im kamerunischen Grasland sind, Ricardo Márquez García zufolge, verschiedene Akteure beteiligt, die auch den transatlantischen Sklavenhandel unterstützten. Interdisziplinär und globalgeschichtlich betrachtet, erweist sich Migration – im Hinblick auf die kulturellen Transformationen in den Herkunfts- und Ankunftsorten und entlang der Transportwege zum Atlantik – als Katalysator für den künstlerischen, religiösen und politischen Austausch mehrerer Regionen.

In der Sektion *Philosophie* diskutiert Martina Di Stefano Foucaults Rezeption und Verwendung der antiken Philosophie am Beispiel seiner Ausführungen zum Pastorat. Bei textgenauer Betrachtung von Foucaults Adaption der griechischen Quellen zeigt sich eine Tendenz zur Homogenisierung unterschiedlicher Konzepte – betreffend den Kulturraum, die Entstehungszeit und den jeweiligen semantischen Kontext –, welche das prekäre

Verhältnis von Diskurs und Macht innerhalb der Wissenschaften widerspiegelt.

Valeria Fernandez Blanco präsentiert eingangs eine Form des Dialogs zwischen Derrida und Gadamer, bei der einer der Dialogpartner abwesend ist, woraus sich die Frage ableitet: Was sind die Voraussetzungen für einen Dialog – wie präsent müssen beide Gesprächspartner sein, um als Teilhaber eines Dialogs gelten zu können? Unter der Prämisse besonderer Lektüreerfahrungen entwirft Blanco die These eines ununterbrochenen Dialogs zwischen Jorge Luis Borges und Michel Foucault.

In der Sektion *Sprachwissenschaft* beleuchtet Janina Beutler in ihrem Beitrag „Topic Drop and Coherence in Dialogue" unsere Alltagssprache. Darin unterscheidet sie zwischen dem empirischen Dialog und dem idealen Dialog, demzufolge alle Gesprächsteilnehmer über ein gemeinsames Wissen verfügen, sich der Dialogsituation bewusst sind und bestimmten Kommunikationsregeln folgen.

Benjamin Richarz analysiert das soziale Phänomen der Höflichkeit in seiner sprachlichen Kodierung. In den grammatischen Eigenschaften des Konjunktivs liegen Möglichkeiten der Verschiebung, infolge derer die Integrität von Sprecher und Hörer gewahrt bleibt und die Entscheidungsverantwortung gemeinsam übernommen wird.

Fragt man angesichts der vielfältigen Beiträge – zum politischen Dialog, zu Konstruktionen kollektiver Erinnerung und Geschichtsdeutung, zu philosophischen Theorien, zur linguistischen Dialoganalyse und Narrativität – nach Gemeinsamkeiten, Parallelen oder sogar nach einem übergreifenden Prinzip, welches die verschiedenen Fachdisziplinen miteinander verbindet, so stößt man auf Denkfiguren, die Entwicklungen, Verhältnisse und Perspektiven reflektieren.

Während sich selbst in faktualen Texten Reden und Gegenreden nicht immer klar ausmachen ließen aufgrund rhetorischer Stilmittel, temporärer oder lokaler Verschiebungen, erforderten fiktionale Texte – will man innerhalb dieser nicht nur intertextuelle Spurensuche betreiben, sondern tatsächlich dialogische Strukturen ausmachen – mitunter eine doppelbödige Präzisierung der Begrifflichkeiten. Denn ein Erzähler in narrativen Texten geht – selbst wenn er seine Rede explizit an einen Hörer richtet, unterschiedliche Perspektiven und Positionen gegenüberstellt oder sich sogar an Formen eines offenen Dialogs versucht – über die Grenzen des Erzählerbewusstseins, in der Regel, nicht hinaus. Doch selbst wenn das Gegenüber imaginiert, der Dialog inszeniert ist und es sich eher um einen ‚dialogisierten Monolog' handelt, so ist doch eines nicht übersehbar: Seine narrative Funktion, die darin besteht, eine Geschichte zu erzählen, die uns, im besten Fall, anzusprechen vermag, vor allem dann, wenn sie uns, die Leser, zu provozieren versteht. Wenn wir herausgefordert werden, die Alterität des Textes – oder gar unsere eigene Alterität – zu erkennen und Position zu beziehen, das heißt, in Dialog zu treten, haben wir, im Zusammenspiel der Alteritäten, womöglich schon die Distanz gegenüber dem Text überwunden und ziehen vielleicht sogar Vergnügen aus den zuweilen paradox erscheinenden Phänomenen des Dialogischen.

Wuppertal, im Juni 2017

Dialog und Dialogizität
– zur Einführung

Ursula Kocher

Der Dialog, von griechisch *dialégesthai* (sich mit jemandem auseinandersetzen), ist als Grundform des Gesprächs höchstwahrscheinlich existent, seitdem Menschen miteinander kommunizieren. Daher weist er vielfältige Erscheinungsformen auf und ist Untersuchungsgegenstand unterschiedlicher geistes- und sozialwissenschaftlicher Disziplinen. Vom philosophischen Dialog der Antike über die Dialogliteratur der Renaissance bis zum Dialog als (historisches) Ereignis des Aushandelns in der Politik tritt er einem in den unterschiedlichsten Formen gegenüber. Es ist daher unmöglich, alles auf wenigen Seiten zu erfassen, aber es ist durchaus möglich, einen Eindruck von eben dieser Vielfalt zu bieten. Und genau das soll im Folgenden versucht werden. Darüber hinaus gilt es, die Begriffe Dialog und Dialogizität voneinander zu trennen.

1. Über das Gespräch zur Erkenntnis – der Dialog in der Philosophie

„Der literarische Dialog gehörte in der Antike zu den zentralen Gattungen der Philosophie wie des theoretischen Diskurses im Allgemeinen."[1] Dabei liegen die Anfänge des Dialogs als literarische Gattung – falls er denn überhaupt eine eigenständige Gattung darstellt – im Dunkeln und sind nicht allein in der griechischen Antike zu finden. Vittorio Hösle verweist in seiner Monographie zum philosophischen Dialog auf Ägypten, Mesopotamien, Indien, China und Israel und stellt fest: „Der philosophische Dialog

---

[1] Föllinger, Sabine / Gernot Michael Müller (Hg.): Der Dialog in der Antike. Formen und Funktionen einer literarischen Gattung zwischen Philosophie, Wissensvermittlung und dramatischer Inszenierung. Berlin, Boston: de Gruyter 2013, Einleitung der Hg., S. 1–22, hier S. 1.

ist keine Schöpfung der Griechen."² Das würde auch verwundern, ist doch der Dialog, vor allem in seiner Form als Gespräch zwischen Lehrern und Schülern (oder Meistern und Jüngern), seit jeher die wichtigste Methode der Wissensvermittlung. Noch dazu ist es eine, die auf einen gemeinsamen Gewinn von Erkenntnis angelegt ist – der Dialogpartner, aber ebenso der Rezipienten, die bei der Lektüre aktiv an einem Prozess der Verständnisgewinnung beteiligt werden. „Trotz der vielen Dialoge in anderen Kulturen lässt sich dennoch behaupten, daß es den Griechen gelungen ist, das Genre auf ein neues Niveau zu heben, u. a. weil Alternativen zum Lehrer-Schüler-Dialog gefunden wurden."³

Man dürfte mit der Vermutung nicht falsch liegen, dass – trotz der erwähnten Dialoge anderer Hochkulturen – die erste Hochphase dieser Textform wohl mit der Blütezeit der attischen Demokratie und ihrer künstlerischen Ausprägungen zusammenhängt, in der sie an einer Reihe von Orten zu finden war (v. a. im Theater). Laut Aristoteles soll Alexamenes von Teos, über den man sonst nichts weiß, der Erste gewesen sein, der Dialoge als Methode der Erkenntnisgewinnung eingesetzt hat. Berühmt wurde indessen der sogenannte ‚Sokratische Dialog', benannt nach einem der größten Philosophen der Antike. Er gilt daher gemeinhin als Begründer des philosophischen Dialogs. Dieser hat zum Ziel, den Menschen zum Nachdenken über sein Leben, sein Handeln und seine Werte anzuregen. Es geht also nicht um rhetorische Wettkämpfe (wie bei den Sophisten zum Teil üblich), sondern um eine Vorgehensweise, die es ermöglicht, den Logos zur eigenen Lebensführung einzusetzen. Überliefert wurden die sokratischen Dialoge bekanntlich in erster Linie durch Platon, der sie für die Nachwelt festgehalten und zugleich genutzt hat, um eigene philosophische Ideen in quasi anonymer Weise zu vermitteln. Hierbei geht er in gewisser Weise literarisch vor und lässt die Dialogpartner mitunter ausführlich erzählen, sodass seine Dialoge teilweise nicht als „Dialoge im formalen Sinn"⁴ gelten, sondern fast schon narra-

---

[2] Hösle, Vittorio: Der philosophische Dialog. Eine Poetik und Hermeneutik. München: C. H. Beck 2006, S. 79.
[3] Ebd., S. 81.
[4] Erler, Michael: „Nur das Gründliche (ist) wahrhaft unterhaltend" (Thomas Mann). Zum Verhältnis lebensweltlicher und philosophischer Wirklichkeit in Platons Dialogen. In: Föllinger/Müller (Hg.): Der Dialog in der Antike (Anm. 1), S. 367–382, hier S. 368.

tive Passagen beinhalten. „Dabei wird deutlich, dass Platon theoretisch und in praktischer Anwendung sich einerseits auf eine Tradition bezieht, diese aber wie in anderen Fällen auch nicht einfach übernimmt, sondern sie transformiert und literarisch wirksam werden lässt."[5] Er nutzt, wie viele nach ihm, den Dialog als Medium der Unmittelbarkeit, der allein durch seine Simulation des Gleichzeitigen und Mündlichen eine hohe Authentizität für sich beansprucht.[6]

Damit sind wesentliche Vorzüge des Dialogs benannt: Er hat eine unmittelbare Wirkung, weil er durch fingierte Mündlichkeit Gegenwärtigkeit suggeriert. Dadurch folgt der Rezipient einem Erkenntnisprozess nicht nur, sondern vollzieht ihn mit. Auf diese Weise kann er belehrt werden, ohne dies unangenehm als Belehrung auffassen zu müssen – vordergründig wird schließlich nicht er, sondern derjenige unterrichtet, der im Text aktiv an dem Dialog beteiligt ist.[7]

2. Der Dialog als Mittel der Verständigung

Dialoge sind bekanntermaßen weder ausschließlich eine Angelegenheit der Philosophie noch der Literatur. Sie begegnen einem tagtäglich in diversen Situationen. Dabei dienen sie stets ein und demselben Zweck: Es geht darum, mittels Zeichen Verständigung herbeizuführen. Ein Dialog ist Teil eines Aushandlungsprozesses, der voraussetzt, dass Individuen in gesellschaftlichen Verbünden in der Lage sind, über die eigene Position hinaus mit anderen zu kooperieren:

> Zur Festlegung der Situation im Schnittpunkt von Ortsachse und Zeitachse bedarf es eines reflexiven Organismus, der von der Egozentrizität des jeweiligen hic et nunc (im Sinne Plessners) zu abstrahieren

---

[5] Ebd., S. 369.
[6] Vergleiche weitere Details zur formalen Gestaltung in: Szlezák, Thomas Alexander: Gespräche unter Ungleichen. Zur Struktur und Zielsetzung der platonischen Dialoge. In: Gottfried Gabriel / Christiane Schildknecht (Hg.): Literarische Formen der Philosophie. Stuttgart: Metzler 1990, S. 40–61.
[7] Vgl. Föllinger, Sabine: Lehren im Gespräch: Der literarische Dialog als Medium antiker Wissensvermittlung. In: Gymnasium 113 (2006), S. 455–470.

vermag, also eines personalen Subjekts, das als Teil eines offenen Systems von Co-Subjekten Situationen als solche (im Sinne Stegmüllers) ‚definiert'.[8]

Dialoge sind aus diesem Grund immer Hinweise auf eine offene Gesprächsatmosphäre im Kleinen und demokratische Gesellschaften im Großen. Genau deshalb setzt Michail Bachtins Theorie an eben dieser Stelle an (s. u.). Sie gehören zunächst in den Kompetenzbereich der Rhetorik, die sich allerdings nicht allzu sehr um sie gekümmert hat. Die Rede einer Person und folglich die monologische Form standen sehr viel mehr im Zentrum rhetorischer Lehren. Eine Ausnahme bilden die Dialoge Ciceros, die sicherstellen sollen, dass ein Gesprächsgegenstand von mindestens zwei Seiten beleuchtet wird. Damit soll, so wird in *De oratore* (55 v. Chr.) deutlich, rhetorische mit philosophischer Kompetenz verbunden werden. Zugleich stellt dieser Dialog über den Redner eine generelle Bestandsaufnahme der rhetorischen Lehre zu Ciceros Zeit dar, sodass die Aufnahme der Textform durch Tacitus mehr als 100 Jahre später (*Dialogus de oratoribus*, Datierung unsicher) nicht nur als Reminiszenz an Cicero zu verstehen ist, sondern als Hinweis auf die Funktion des Gesprächs selbst: Tacitus scheint

> ganz bewusst zwei Gespräche aufeinander beziehen zu wollen, um auf diese Weise weniger den Zustand der Beredsamkeit in seiner Epoche zu thematisieren, denn eher die Art des Umgangs mit diesem Problemfeld im Kreise einschlägiger Experten. Inszeniert Cicero den Beginn eines theoretischen Diskurses über die Beredsamkeit im Kreise philosophisch gebildeter Vertreter der spätrepublikanischen Oberschicht, thematisiert Tacitus dessen mühsame Reetablierung in einer Zeit, in der durch ein allgemeines Klima des Misstrauens und der Denunziation die Bereitschaft des offenen Meinungsaustauschs sogar im privaten Bereich Schaden genommen hat.[9]

---

[8] Hess-Lüttich, Ernest W. B.: Textproduktion und Textrezeption. Ein dialoganalytisches Modell. In: Klaus Neumann / Michael Charlton (Hg.): Spracherwerb und Mediengebrauch. Tübingen: G. Narr 1990, S. 45–68; hier S. 54.

[9] Müller, Gernot Michael: „Si mihi mea sententia proferenda ac non disertissimorum, ut nostris temporibus, hominum sermo repetendus esset". Zur Funktion der Gesprächshandlung in Tacitus' Dialogus de oratoribus. In: Föllinger/Müller (Hg.): Der Dialog in der Antike (Anm. 1), S. 327–363, hier S. 331.

Tacitus' Text tritt allein durch diese Bezugnahme, die bereits durch den Titel des Werks deutlich wird, in einen Dialog mit Ciceros *De oratoribus*. Dazu unten mehr.

Der Dialog dient dementsprechend der Aushandlung einer Sache, indem der Prozess des Aushandelns nachvollziehbar abgebildet wird, wodurch alle Gesichtspunkte unterschiedlicher Parteien offen zutage treten. Dieses Charakteristikum macht den Dialog in zweierlei Hinsicht tauglich für den Unterricht: Erstens kann man durch einen Dialog das Auffinden von Argumenten und damit das *officium* der *inventio* trainieren. Zweitens lässt sich auf diese Weise trefflich das Durchsetzen eigener Argumente und mithin der eigenen Position und Meinung üben, was vor allem in einer Stegreifdisputation besonders herausfordernd werden kann. In dieser Form war der Dialog insbesondere im Mittelalter beliebt.[10] Wenn es darum geht, über einen Gegenstand in Fragen und Antworten zu verhandeln, findet dies, vor allem innerhalb der Scholastik, im Rahmen der sogenannten *Quaestiones* statt.

Aber auch heutzutage sind derartige Kompetenzen wichtig und werden in Gesprächstrainings vermittelt.

> Offenbar wird in unserer Kommunikations- und Informationsgesellschaft der individuelle Erfolg zunehmend daran gemessen und werden entsprechende Gratifikationen danach vergeben, wie geschickt und sprachlich angemessen man sich in Gesprächen zu verhalten vermag, mit anderen kooperieren, andere beeinflussen, mit anderen gemeinsam relevante Resultate erzielen kann.[11]

Derartige Fähigkeiten sind allerdings nicht nur im Berufsleben eines einzelnen Menschen wichtig. Verständigung bzw. der Dialog mit oder zwi-

---

[10] Vgl. zum Dialog im Mittelalter vor allem die Schriften von Peter von Moos: Rhetorik, Kommunikation und Medialität. Gesammelte Studien zum Mittelalter. Bd. 2. Hg. von Gert Melville. Berlin: LIT 2006; Jacobi, Klaus (Hg.): Gespräche lesen. Philosophische Dialoge im Mittelalter. Tübingen: G. Narr 1999 (= Script Oralia 115); Strohschneider, Peter: Dialogischer Agon. In: Der Dialog im Diskursfeld seiner Zeit. Von der Antike bis zur Aufklärung. Hg. von Klaus W. Hempfer / Anita Traninger. Stuttgart: F. Steiner 2010, S. 95–117.

[11] Hess-Lüttich, Ernest W. B.: Dialog. In: Historisches Wörterbuch der Rhetorik. Hg. von Gert Ueding. Bd. 2. Tübingen: Niemeyer 1994, Sp. 606–621, hier Sp. 619.

schen etwas bzw. Personen sind zu Schlüsselbegriffen geworden. Kulturen stehen regelmäßig oder sogar dauerhaft ebenso miteinander im Dialog wie Religionen.

3. Eine eigenständige Gattung?

Wie bei allen Textformen, die sich im Alltag als Versatzstücke der Kommunikation, als Teile von Gattungen (hier das Drama) oder als ausgewiesene Textsorte finden lassen, stellt sich die Frage, ob und ab wann man tatsächlich von einer Gattung sprechen kann. Im Falle des Dialogs wird immer wieder festgestellt, dass eigentlich nur die dem platonischen Muster entsprechenden als ‚echte' Dialoge zu gelten haben. Damit scheint verbunden zu sein, dass man lediglich die Dialoge gelten lassen möchte, bei denen der Autor im Hintergrund bleibt, seine Ansichten aber über die Äußerungen der präsentierten Gesprächspartner sichtbar werden, wie es bei den platonischen Dialogen beobachtet werden kann. Diese Vorstellung widerspricht allerdings den dialogischen Formen der Frühen Neuzeit, bei denen es mitunter gerade darum geht, dass eine klare Botschaft nicht auf den ersten Blick zu ermitteln ist.

Da der Dialog allein durch seine Existenz Realitätsstatus beansprucht – schließlich findet er eben gerade im Lesegeschehen statt –, steht er in Konkurrenz zu ähnlichen Textformen oder Gattungen:

> Die besonderen Merkmale und Möglichkeiten des Dialogs gewinnen ihr deutliches Profil vor dem Hintergrund anderer, potentiell konkurrierender Gattungen des theoretischen Diskurses, also etwa des Traktats, des Kommentars, des discorso oder discours, schließlich auch des Essays in seinen verschiedenen, entweder dem Montaigneschen oder dem Baconschen Modell folgenden Ausprägungen. Während sich diese vergleichsweise konturschwachen Textformen untereinander ausschließlich durch ihre Diktion sowie durch mehr oder weniger strenge Systematizitätsansprüche und Gliederungsprinzipien unterscheiden und auch leicht ineinander konvertierbar sind, ist der Dialog in diesem Ensemble darin unverwechselbar, daß mit ihm die Theoriebildung im Modus der Fiktion erfolgt: Im Unterschied zu jenen anderen Gattungen kommunizieren Dialoge nicht unmittelbar die mehr

oder weniger komplexe Aussage eines auktorialen Subjekts über die Welt oder über einzelne Aspekte der Welt, in der dieses Subjekt und seine Adressaten, die Leser, existieren; stattdessen kommunizieren sie die Darstellung einer Welt, deren Identität oder Äquivalenz mit der ‚textexternen' Welt keineswegs vorausgesetzt werden kann und die ihrerseits zum Gegenstand oppositiver oder komplementärer Aussagen wird, die zwei oder mehr Redesubjekte, die in dieser Welt ‚existieren', über sie machen. Die unmittelbaren Adressaten dieser Aussagen sind ebenfalls Teil der ‚textinternen' Welt und nicht die Leser des Dialogtextes.[12]

Diese Theoriebildung durch Gespräch stellt in der Tat eine Besonderheit des Dialogs dar und könnte als Gattungsmerkmal ausreichen. Die unterschiedlichen Verwendungs- und Einbindungsformen des Dialogs wären dann lediglich als modale Ausprägungen derselben Textsorte zu sehen, die durch ihr hohes dramatisches Potential eben besonders im Drama zur Anwendung kommt. In jedem Fall wird die Performativität, die dem Dialog per se eignet, als entscheidendes Gattungsmerkmal genutzt. Also: ja, eine Gattung.

Das ist besonders, wie bereits angedeutet, für die Frühe Neuzeit festzustellen, in der der Dialog an Bedeutung gewinnt. Er eignet sich besonders für Verfasser der Renaissance, da er einerseits auf antike Formen Bezug nimmt, andererseits einem Verständnis entgegenkommt, das ‚Wahrheit' für eine noch zu verhandelnde Sache hält. Dieses Gespräch zum Zwecke einer Wahrheitsfindung gerät manchmal unter der Hand zu einer Art Spiel – zu beobachten in italienischen Texten wie dem *Cortegiano* von Baldassare Castiglione (1528) oder den *Gesprächsspielen* Georg Philipp Harsdörffers (ab 1644). Darüber hinaus wird in den Dialogen, darauf verweist das oben angeführte Zitat Häsners, über literarisches Schreiben und den Status des Fiktionalen nachgedacht, woraus sich eine weitere Analogie zu den antiken rhetorischen Dialogen ergibt.[13] Zudem findet sich ebenfalls der didaktische Dialog, der Wissensvermittlung mit Unterhaltung verbindet.

---

[12] Häsner, Bernd: Der Dialog: Strukturelemente einer Gattung zwischen Fiktion und Theoriebildung. In: Klaus W. Hempfer (Hg.): Poetik des Dialogs. Aktuelle Theorie und rinascimentales Selbstverständnis. Stuttgart 2004, S. 13–65; hier S. 19f.

[13] Vgl. zu diesem Komplex Hempfer, Klaus W.: Die Poetik des Dialogs im Cinquecento und die neuere Dialogtheorie. Zum historischen Fundament aktueller Theorie. In: Ders. (Hg.): Poetik des Dialogs (Anm. 12), S. 67–96.

4. Der Dialog als sprachliches Phänomen

Eben weil der Dialog sowohl ein häufiges Text- als auch Alltagsphänomen ist, hat sich innerhalb der Linguistik ein gesonderter Forschungszweig herausgebildet. Hess-Lüttich setzt den Beginn dieser Untersuchungen mit der „kommunikativ-pragmatischen Wende in den siebziger Jahren" an.[14] „In zahllosen Forschungsprojekten, die sich in den achtziger Jahren z. T. als soziolinguistische, z. T. als pragmalinguistische profilierten, wurden wichtige Erkenntnisse über den Aufbau und den Ablauf natürlicher D. auf den verschiedenen Strukturebenen gewonnen."[15]

Zeugnis davon gibt das *Handbuch der Dialoganalyse* von 1994, das Konzepte, Theorien und Anwendungsbereiche vorstellt.[16] In ihrer Einführung verweisen die Herausgeber darauf, dass es sich um ein Gebiet handle, das gerade in besonderem Maße wachse, weshalb ihr Band auch nur „ein Zwischenbericht über die Entwicklung eines lebhaft expandierenden Forschungsfeldes" sein könne.[17] Dass sich der Bereich inzwischen weiterentwickelt hat, zeigt eine Vielzahl an Monographien, Sammelbänden und Aufsätzen. Leider kam es, obwohl sich immer wieder interdisziplinäre Verweise erkennen lassen, zu einer disziplinären Spezialisierung. Dabei wäre die Dialoganalyse ein Gegenstand, der sich in höchstem Maße zu interdisziplinärer Forschung eignen würde, von der einige Disziplinen enorm profitieren könnten. Ob es wirklich daran liegt, dass die Fächer nicht auf die Linguistinnen und Linguisten zugehen?[18] In jedem Fall wäre ein Bemühen aller Seiten um mehr Interdisziplinarität wünschenswert.

---

[14] Hess-Lüttich: Dialog (Anm. 11), Sp. 613.
[15] Ebd., Sp. 614.
[16] Fritz, Gerd / Franz Hundsnurscher: Handbuch der Dialoganalyse. Tübingen: Niemeyer 1994.
[17] Ebd., Einleitung S. IX.
[18] „Vielleicht aus Enttäuschung darüber, dass sie nicht gefragt werden, machen Linguistinnen und Linguisten dann auch lieber alles selbst; sie untersuchen Politikergespräche, Unterrichtsgespräche, literarische Dialoge und historisch überlieferte Gespräche, auch wenn sie dabei manchmal das Unbehagen überfällt, dass selbst ein Zauberbuch mit allem gesammelten Wissen der Dialogforschung nur zur wissenschaftlichen Beschreibung und verstehenden Erklärung des Gesprächs leiten, dessen letzte Geheimnisse aber doch nicht entdecken wird." Kilian, Jörg: Alkmenes „Ach!". Die germanistische Linguistik entdeckt die dialogische Sprache. In:

5. Dialogizität als literaturtheoretisches Konzept

In der Literaturwissenschaft spielen Dialoge vor allem über ihre jeweiligen Realisierungen als Texte oder Teile von Texten eine Rolle. Darüber hinaus aber bereicherte das in den 1960er Jahren wiederentdeckte Konzept der Dialogizität Michail Bachtins die literaturtheoretische Diskussion und schärfte den Blick für die Möglichkeiten der dialogischen Struktur. Ursprünglich an der karnevalesken Lachkultur des Mittelalters entwickelt, betrachtet Bachtin Dialogizität als eine Eigenschaft des literarischen Textes, vor allem des Romans, der sich durch Polyphonie auszeichnet. Im Gegensatz zur monologischen, dogmatisch-konservativen Sprache zeichnet sich eine dialogische durch Offenheit, Polyvalenz und Hybridität aus, und eben durch diese Eigenschaften wird alles in einem literarischen Text mit anderen Texten und deren Elementen ins Verhältnis gesetzt. Genauer gesagt, verknüpft der Leser die unterschiedlichen ‚Stimmen' miteinander und setzt sich beim Lesen ins Verhältnis zu den ‚Helden' des Geschehens – ein Vorgang ästhetischer Aktivität. Der ist nur möglich, wenn der Text, der gelesen wird, nicht monologisch-einsinnig, sondern vielstimmig und in die Tiefe gehend ist.

Das Konzept der Dialogizität ist daher gerade nicht an die Gattung ‚Dialog' geknüpft, sondern eher im Roman zu suchen. Dennoch ist der Begriff des Dialogischen nicht irreführend. Wenn Bachtin nämlich annimmt, dass ein Wort Ereignischarakter haben kann, dann bedeutet dies, dass es im Rezeptionsprozess einen dialogischen Prozess entfaltet:

> Das Wort ist kein Ding, sondern das ewig bewegte, sich ewig verändernde Medium des dialogischen Umgangs. Ein einzelnes Bewußtsein, eine einzelne Stimme ist ihm niemals genug. Das Leben des Wortes besteht im Übergang von Mund zu Mund, von Kontext zu Kontext, von Kollektiv zu Kollektiv, von Generation zu Generation. Dabei bleibt das Wort seines Weges eingedenk.[19]

Jedes Wort beinhaltet folglich alle Kontexte und Texte, in das es jemals gestellt wurde und erweist sich daher in mehrfacher Hinsicht als dialogisch. Es

---

Germanistische Linguistik: Konturen eines Faches. Hg. von Helmut Henne / Horst Sitta / Herbert Ernst Wiegand. Tübingen: Niemeyer 2003, S. 159–183, hier S. 179.

[19] Bachtin, Michail: Literatur und Karneval. Zur Romantheorie und Lachkultur. Frankfurt/Main: Fischer 1990, S. 129.

steht in permanentem Dialog mit sich selbst, mit dem Kontext, in dem es sich aktuell befindet und mit dem Leser, der es mit Bedeutung versieht. Wie sehr sich allerdings dieser dialogische Prozess entfalten kann, hängt von der Gestalt des Textes ab, weshalb Bachtin in erster Linie den Roman mit seiner Vielzahl an vorkommenden und sprechenden Personen im Sinn hatte.

Im Zuge der Rezeption des Bachtin'schen Konzepts zeigen sich unterschiedliche Versuche, selbiges auszuweiten, was analytische Zugriffe erschwert bzw. geradezu unmöglich gemacht hat. So übertrug Julia Kristeva beispielsweise die Vorstellung vom dialogischen Wort auf den Text und entwickelte ihre Idee der Intertextualität, bei der sich Texte stets in einem Dialog mit anderen Texten befinden.[20] Verwässert wurde dadurch ein Kerngedanke, der sich durch alle Betrachtungen von Dialogen und Dialogizität zieht: Der Dialog lebt davon, dass er intersubjektiv ist, es ist die einer Person zuweisbare Stimme, die sich mit einer anderen Stimme auseinandersetzt. Diese Stimme bleibt auch in der Schrift einzigartig. Aus diesem Grund wird ein Dialog stets mindestens zweistimmig und daher vielsinnig sein, und Literatur ist, sofern sie Dialoge zulässt, in jedem Fall polyphon. Tatsächlich spricht im oben ausgeführten Fall des Dialogs von Tacitus nicht der Text mit demjenigen Ciceros, sondern der Autor Tacitus über sein Werk und dessen Aussage mit Cicero selbst, der zwar nicht in eigener Gestalt, aber durch seinen Text darauf reagieren kann, indem der spätere Autor darin Antworten auf die aktuell gestellten Fragen findet.

Dialogizität bezeichnet demzufolge die besonderen Charakteristika von Dialogen, die sich stets durch eine gewisse Unbestimmtheit in der Aussage auszeichnen. Weiterhin ist festzuhalten, dass sie nicht nur Interaktion vorführen, sie erzählen zugleich eine Geschichte.

Der Geschehens und Handlungszusammenhang, der die ‚Geschichte' des Dialogs ausmacht, mag oft eine nur rudimentäre Detaillierung und Dynamik aufweisen, er ist aber in jedem Fall vorausgesetzt, und sei es als bloße formale Bedingung einer Gesprächssituation. Im übrigen ist er, wie die Ausdifferenzierung der Gattung insgesamt belegen kann, prinzipiell expandierbar. Tatsächlich ließe sich

---

[20] Kristeva, Julia: Bachtin, das Wort, der Dialog und der Roman. In: Literaturwissenschaft und Linguistik. Ergebnisse und Perspektiven. Bd. 3: Zur linguistischen Basis der Literaturwissenschaft II. Hg. von Jens Ihwe. Frankfurt/Main: Suhrkamp 1972, S. 345–375.

das Genus des Dialogs nach Maßgabe der jeweiligen Reduktion bzw. Expansion der ‚Geschichte' typologisch auffächern und skalieren: Während einerseits seine ‚Geschichte' gegen Null tendieren und der Dialog sich damit dem Traktat annähern kann, gibt es andererseits Gattungsexemplare, deren ‚Geschichte' sie, zumindest optional, als Komödien oder Novellen rezipierbar macht.[21]

Jenseits des Literarischen verweist der Dialog zudem auf eine historische Situation, in der ein Aushandeln durch Gespräch von besonderer Bedeutung war und mithin in den Gegenstandsbereich der Geschichtswissenschaft fällt.

6. Zur Aktualität des Dialogs

Je krisenhafter die Welt, umso mehr wird der Dialog beschworen. Es verwundert daher nicht, dass er gerade jetzt wieder im wahrsten Sinn des Wortes in aller Munde ist. Für Theologen wie George Augustin ist in einer säkularen Welt „der Dialog zwischen Glaube und Kultur von zentraler Bedeutung".[22] Für manche Theologen ist der Dialog geradezu der Kern religiöser Haltung. Martin Buber beispielsweise ist und war für sein ‚dialogisches Prinzip' bekannt – wobei er mit Dialog weniger das menschliche Zwiegespräch meint, sondern vielmehr die Auseinandersetzung des Einzelnen mit anderen Personen, Gegenständen, vor allem aber mit Gott. Dafür bedarf es einer Reihe von Gesprächen, die einem Menschen erst dazu verhelfen, mit anderen in Dialog zu treten. Um dies nämlich tun zu können, muss er sich selbst erkennen.

Im 21. Jahrhundert hat das Wort ‚Interreligiöser Dialog' eine neue Bedeutung erhalten, da terroristische Akte oftmals im Namen einer Religion verübt werden und religiöse Differenzen zu politischen Verwicklungen und Streitigkeiten führen. Interreligiöse Gespräche sind inzwischen stark institutionalisiert und ritualisiert. Dazu gehört beispielsweise die Deut-

---

[21] Häsner: Der Dialog (Anm. 12), S. 28.
[22] Augustin SAC, George: Religion im säkularen Zeitalter. Das Phänomen der Säkularisierung und der Dialog mit den Kulturen. In: Ders. / Sonja Sailer-Pfister / Klaus Vellguth (Hg.): Christentum im Dialog. Perspektiven christlicher Identität in einer pluralen Gesellschaft. Freiburg: Herder 2014, S. 145–167, hier S. 167.

sche Islamkonferenz, deren Plenum einmal jährlich zusammentritt, um die Ergebnisse der kontinuierlichen Arbeit in Gruppen zu diskutieren. Selbstverständlich gibt es ähnliche Gesprächskreise auch zwischen anderen religiösen Gruppen. In Deutschland kommt der interkonfessionelle Dialog hinzu, der gerade im Reformationsjahr 2017 Auftrieb erhalten hat. 1982 bereits bemühte sich Hans Küng um den Dialog des Christentums mit drei anderen Weltreligionen. In einer Vorlesung an der Universität Tübingen wurden pro Sitzung zwei Vorträge direkt hintereinander gehalten, in denen zunächst Perspektiven des Islams, Hinduismus oder Buddhismus vorgestellt wurden, auf die anschließend eine christliche Antwort folgte. Aus diesem Experiment entstand schließlich ein Buch, das Hans Küng als „Zwischenbilanz des Gesprächs – als Anregung zur weiteren Diskussion" betrachtete.[23] All diese Bemühungen zeigen allerdings vor allem eines: ein eher geringes Streben um theoretische Klarheit. Für gewöhnlich werden Gespräch, Dialog, Diskussion usw. synonym gebraucht.

Wenn von ‚Dialog der Religionen' die Rede ist, wird darin zumeist auch der ‚interkulturelle Dialog' miteingeschlossen. Nähere Ausführungen wären an dieser Stelle – unter anderem wegen der inzwischen unüberschaubaren Menge an Forschung diverser Fachrichtungen – nicht zielführend. Zumal der Begriff, nach Meinung vieler, mittlerweile zu einem Schlagwort ohne Inhalt verkommen ist, wie bereits 2006 von Hendryk M. Broder festgestellt wurde:

> Ein Dialog also, wohin man schaut. Jeder redet mit jedem, als wäre die Ringparabel von G. E. Lessing Wirklichkeit geworden, mit Nathan, Saladin und dem Tempelherren als Moderatoren des großen interkulturellen Palavers. Wer heute nicht für einen ‚Dialog der Kulturen' eintritt, der ist ein Reaktionär, der die Zeichen der Zeit nicht erkennen will. Und wer sich am ‚Dialog der Kulturen' beteiligt, der steht automatisch auf der richtigen Seite der Geschichte, und wenn er nur regelmäßig zu seinem ‚Türken' geht, um dort einen Döner zu bestellen.[24]

---

[23] Küng, Hans / Josef van Ess / Heinrich Stietencron / Heinz Bechert: Christentum und Weltreligionen. Hinführung zum Dialog mit Islam, Hinduismus und Buddhismus. München, Zürich: Piper 1984, S. 17.

[24] http://www.spiegel.de/kultur/gesellschaft/kulturdebatte-dialog-nein-danke-a-403133.html vom 25.2.2006 (5.6.2017).

In der Tat gilt auch in diesem Fall: Die Begriffe werden nur selten klar definiert und abgegrenzt. Dennoch: Schlagwort oder nicht – hinter all diesen Aufrufen, Forderungen, Wünschen und konkreten Aktionen steht die Überlegung, dass allein Dialoge zu wechselseitigem Verständnis führen können.

Die Gattung ‚Dialog' ist, wie man sehen konnte, in ihren Erscheinungsformen vielfältig und in ihren modalen Präsentationen multifunktional. Das macht sie äußerst ergiebig für die unterschiedlichsten Forschungsbereiche, wovon die Beiträge dieses Bandes zeugen.

„Die Undine kennt Jeder von uns erementaschen hier." Dialogizität in Arno Schmidts Erzählung *Brand's Haide* (1951)

Sven Hanuschek

1.

Arno Schmidt ist nicht gerade der erste Autor, der einem zum Schlagwort *Dialogizität* einfällt. Zumal im frühen Werk (eigentlich ist das erst in den letzten Romanen anders, in *Schule der Atheisten*, 1972, und *Abend mit Goldrand*, 1975) gibt es stets einen Ich-Erzähler, besser wohl: Reflekteur, an dessen Gedankengänge und Wahrnehmungen wir als Leserinnen und Leser angeschlossen sind, eine sehr dominante Ich-Figur, die sich anscheinend prächtig im eigenen Kopf mit sich selbst und ihren literarischen Vorlieben amüsieren kann.

Und Dialogizität würde ja bedeuten, wenn ich Wolf Schmids Präzisierungen, vielleicht auch: Radikalisierungen des Begriffs aufgreife, dass wir keinen literarischen Monolog haben dürften – keine „Rede eines Sprechers, der nicht intendiert, eine sprachliche Replik eines realen, seinsautonomen Gegenübers auszulösen".[1] Zum Dialog gehöre vielmehr „die sprachlich oder kontextuell objektivierte Intention des Sprechers, eine fremde Rede auszulösen" sowie eine „echte, nicht nur imaginierte oder inszenierte Alterität des Gegenübers".[2] Gegen die beliebte Auffassung von Dialogizität, nach der ohnehin alles dialogisch ist, nach der man gar nicht heraus kann aus dem Dialogischen und den Verhandlungen der Diskurse und Texte untereinander, setzt Wolf Schmid eine weit strengere Auffas-

---

[1] Schmid, Wolf: „Dialogizität" in der narrativen „Kommunikation". In: Ingunn Lunde (Hg.): Dialogue and Rhetoric. Communication Strategies in Russian Text and Theory. Bergen: Department of Foreign Languages 1999, S. 9–23; zit. nach der Online-Ausgabe unter https://www.icn.uni-hamburg.de/sites/default/files/download/publications/schmid_dialogizitaet.pdf, S. 1–13 (19.3.2017), hier S. 2.
[2] Ebd., S. 3.

sung. Mit der Dialogizität in literarischen Texten sähe es demnach ohnehin nicht gut aus: Schließlich folgten Erzähltexte immer den Plänen ihrer Verfasser; auch eine Kommunikation zwischen Figuren oder zwischen Texten würde immer den „Intentionen des Autors" folgen, und darin würde eine latente „Monologisierung des Dialogs" stecken.[3] Eine dialogische Haltung könnte der Autor daher nur seinem Publikum gegenüber einnehmen – der konkrete Autor gegenüber seinem wirklichen Publikum, indem er z. B. versuchen würde, es zu beeindrucken, zu beeinflussen, zu provozieren, zu beschimpfen; oder er kann mit bestimmten Zeitgenossen in Verbindung treten, indem er sie konkret anspricht, zum Beispiel also Schriftsteller-Kollegen kommentiert, angreift, zitiert etc., und auf eine Reaktion hofft.

Nun war bekanntlich eine von Arno Schmidts Maximen, alle Dichter und Schriftsteller, auch die längst verstorbenen, immer als mit-lebend zu behandeln; ebenso bekannt ist, dass er eine polemische und provozierende Ader hatte, die sich in seinen Texten frei austoben konnte. Diese Art von Dialogizität dem Publikum gegenüber will ich im Folgenden eher nicht behandeln, wenn es um *Brand's Haide* (1951) geht, sondern schon den Text selber und seine Binnenbeziehungen schärfer ansehen. Nach all den Klischees, die über Schmidt kursieren, wäre zu erwarten, dass es keine ‚echte' Alterität in seinen Texten geben kann. Das wäre übrigens kein ästhetischer Einwand, wenn überhaupt ein Einwand, dann allenfalls ein sozialer. Ein bisschen geht es dabei auch um die Frage, wie eigentlich ‚Welt' in literarische Texte kommt, wie eine ‚andere' Welt, wie Alterität, hier nun in Arno Schmidts Text. Wir werden sehen, ob sich die populären Schmidt-Schlagwörter bestätigen lassen oder ob hier doch etwas ganz anderes geboten wird. Ich stelle kurz die Erzählung vor, vor allem den Nicht-Arno Schmidt-Lesern (2.); skizziere die Autobiographica und sogenannte Wirklichkeitspartikel in *Brand's Haide* (3.); skizziere (sehr knapp) einige Beispiele herkömmlicher Intertextualität, die ja zeitweilig umstandslos als Dialogizität gerechnet wird (4.). Im Anschluss geht es um eine unkonventionellere Intertextualität, die man nun schon Dialogizität nennen könnte, mit einiger Vorsicht und einigen Überraschungen (5.); schließlich diskutiere ich weitere Wirklichkeitsebenen des Textes wie Mythos und Traum (6.) und ziehe ein kurzes Fazit (7.).

---

[3] Ebd., S. 5.

2.

Brand's Haide ist im Erstdruck 1951 ein Text von 150 Seiten, hier wird er auch auf dem Deckblatt als „Erzählung" bezeichnet; in der *Bargfelder Ausgabe*, der gültigen Schmidt-Werkausgabe, sind das 80 Druckseiten, hier wird *Brand's Haide* als gattungsloser Text gedruckt, weder Roman noch Erzählung; gemessen an anderen frühen Schmidt-Texten ginge er vielleicht noch als Kurzroman durch. Schmidt hat nach einem ersten Einfall am 31.3./1.4.1949 die Erzählung vom Januar bis September 1950 niedergeschrieben, 1951 ist sie bei Rowohlt erschienen.

Der Text hat drei Teile, ein Triptychon sozusagen: Im ersten Teil, *Blakenhof oder die Überlebenden*, kommt der aus englischer Kriegsgefangenschaft entlassene Unteroffizier Schmidt in dem niedersächsischen Dorf Blakenhof an (ein fiktiver Ortsname). Es ist der 21. März 1946. Ein älterer Mann am Ortseingang, der erstaunlicherweise den Romantiker Friedrich de la Motte Fouqué kennt, schickt ihn zur Dorflehrerin, deren Sohn zeigt ihm den Schuppen, der ihm zugewiesen worden ist. Er lernt seine Nachbarinnen kennen, Lore und Grete, Flüchtlinge aus Schlesien wie er, 32 Jahre alt wie er, die ihm keinen Besen und Kehrblech leihen, die kriegt er wieder von dem Alten. Es wird beschrieben, wie der Protagonist Schmidt die Frauen in den nächsten Tagen besser kennenlernt, wir erfahren, dass er fast nichts hat – Grete schenkt ihm eine leere Heringsbüchse, die er als Tasse verwenden kann –, und dass er an einer Biographie Fouqués arbeitet. Es zeigt sich auch, dass „Schorsch", der Sohn der Dorflehrerin, Interesse an Lore hat, der Ich-Erzähler versteht ihn als Nebenbuhler. Es gibt Gespräche mit ihm, mit dem Pfarrer (Schmidt spielt Schach gegen ihn und will die Kirchenbücher einsehen), erneut mit dem Alten. Schmidt versucht, Lore wie Grete als Mitarbeiterinnen über seinen Fouqué-Materialien zu gewinnen. Die Freundschaft zwischen den dreien wird enger, die Frauen waschen seine armselige Wäsche mit. Als ein Care-Paket von seiner Schwester aus den USA kommt, vereinbaren sie, Teile des Pakets einzutauschen gegen die notdürftigste Ausstattung für Schmidts Bruchbude.

Im zweiten Teil, *Lore oder das spielende Licht*, sind wir ein paar Monate weiter, im Hochsommer, datiert auf den 26.7.1946. Im Wald, beim Pilze sammeln, funkt es zwischen Schmidt und Lore. Der Pfarrer hat endlich die Kirchenbücher „rausgerückt", mit Hilfe von Grete und Lore kann Schmidt seine gesuchten Fouqué-Details nachsehen; er sucht nach dem ersten

„*Die Undine kennt Jeder von uns erementaschen hier.*"

Hauslehrer des romantischen Dichters, Wilhelm Heinrich Albrecht Fricke. Dessen Großvater ist der Gärtner Johann Wilhelm Auen, einige seltsame Ereignisse um 1730 in dem Waldstück „Brand's Haide", direkt vor dem Dorf, scheinen mit Auen zu tun zu haben, es gibt darüber einen Bericht des damaligen Dorfpfarrers Overbeck in den Kirchenbüchern. Am folgenden Tag streitet Schmidt sich mit dem Lehrer und dem Pfarrer, als er die Kirchenbücher zurückbringt; Lore geht nun nicht mehr mit dem Lehrer (oder der Dorfjugend) tanzen, sie bleibt bei Schmidt, nachts gehen die beiden Äpfel stehlen, wieder treffen sie den Alten. Schmidt hat sich eine Erkältung eingefangen, er kuriert sie einigermaßen mit Schnaps vom Bauern Apel, dem sogenannten Großen Kuhfürsten (28 Kühe); er kann in der folgenden Nacht schon wieder mit den beiden Frauen Holz stehlen gehen. *Krumau oder willst Du mich noch einmal sehen*, der dritte Teil, spielt Ende Oktober/Anfang November 1946; Schmidt liest Lore und Grete Fouqué vor, nach einigen unguten Ankündigungen, die der Ich-Erzähler nicht versteht, beichtet ihm Lore, dass sie zu ihrem Cousin nach Mexiko gehen wird – ein materiell sicheres Leben, das sie dem Leben mit ihrer großen Liebe Schmidt vorzieht, obwohl er eigentlich der ‚einzige' sei, wie sie beteuert. Er bringt sie zum Zug und bleibt mit Grete zurück, künftig, so der Entwurf, wird er als Dichter/Schriftsteller mehr oder minder entsagungsvoll für sein Werk leben.

3.

Es handelt sich um einen Text mit einem Ich-Erzähler bzw. Reflekteur, der soweit das eingangs erwähnte Schmidt-Klischee bestätigt: Er monologisiert, und Schmidt erscheint einmal mehr als ein Autor, der als ‚Realist' die ‚Nessel Wirklichkeit' packen will, wie es in *Aus dem Leben eines Fauns* (1953) heißt, einer der meistzitierten Schmidt-Sätze. Zu allem Überfluss *heißt* das reflektierende Ich in *Brand's Haide* auch noch „Schmidt", es ist der einzige der frühen Texte, in dem das der Fall ist. Dass Autoren in ihren eigenen Texten herumgeistern, mag man mehr mit Thomas Meinecke, Walter Moers und Michel Houellebecq verbinden und dem, was eine Zeit lang Postmoderne genannt wurde, in diesem Aspekt jedenfalls ganz zu Unrecht. Solche metafiktionalen Scherze gibt es vermutlich so lange, wie es Literatur gibt, sicher schon im mittelalterlichen Epos, bei Chaucer und Cervantes, nicht erst bei Borges und Flann O'Brien, Erich Kästner und Calvino. In Schmidts Text heißt nicht nur der Protagonist Schmidt, er hat auch eine Menge Schmidtscher Autobiographica aufgebürdet bekommen; die Geburtsadresse im Hamburger Rumpffsweg ist genannt, „ich als Hamburger",[4] Kindheitserinnerungen, einzelne Mitschüler werden erwähnt (die das zeitgenössische Publikum der fünfziger Jahre natürlich nicht kennen konnte, wie viele der anderen privaten Details ebenso). Schmidts eigener Arbeitspass ist mit exakter Nummer angegeben;[5] seine Flüchtlingsnöte, die Armut der Figur dürfte der eigenen entsprechen, auch die britische Kriegsgefangenschaft ist authentisch. Zwar heißt keiner seiner Einquartierungsorte „Blakenhof", aber das Dorf ist eine Zusammenziehung der Wohnorte Benefeld und Cordingen, es sind sogar Nachbarn aus Cordingen im literarischen Werk genannt. Die Schwester Lucie Kiesler wird namentlich erwähnt, sie ist die Senderin der Care-Pakete, die im wirklichen Leben von Arno und Alice Schmidt eine ähnlich große Rolle spielten wie im Leben des Erzählungs-Schmidts und seiner beiden Nachbarinnen. Der Reflekteur arbeitet an einer Fouqué-Biographie, wie Arno Schmidt in diesen Jahren – sie wird erst 1958 erscheinen –, und er hat bereits einiges geschrieben, Texte, die *Leviathan, Alexander, Kosmas, Massenbach* heißen, alle in *Brand's Haide* erwähnt, ob veröffentlicht oder nicht, in Anspielungen sogar auch einige Juvenilia, die erst 1986, sieben Jahre nach dem Tod des Autors erschienen sind. Auch hier konnten die zeitgenössischen Leserinnen und Leser also gar nicht ermessen, wie nah die Figur Schmidt dem Autor Schmidt stand.

Von den Autobiographica ganz abgesehen, erhält der Text natürlich auch Verweise auf andere Realien, wie stets bei Schmidt und wie verschärft in seinen frühen Arbeiten. *Brand's Haide* zeigt tatsächlich ein ergreifendes Bild der Mangel-Jahre nach dem verlorenen Krieg, der Flüchtlinge und Vertriebenen zumal; die Beschreibung des Hab & Guts liest sich ein bisschen wie Günter Eichs Gedicht *Inventur* (1945):

---

[4] Schmidt, Arno: Brand's Haide. In: Ders.: Bargfelder Ausgabe. Werkgruppe I. Romane, Erzählungen, Gedichte, Juvenilia: Band I: Enthymesis. Leviathan. Gadir. Alexander. Brand's Haide. Schwarze Spiegel. Umsiedler. Faun. Pocahontas. Kosmas. Eine Edition der Arno Schmidt Stiftung. Zürich: Haffmans 1987, S. 115–199, hier S. 154.
[5] Ebd., S. 121.

Ich räumte meine Kiste aus: 3 Zeltbahnen [...], eine ganze Decke, ein winkliger rötlicher Rest. Dann richtete ich sie als Speisekammer ein: in einer Ecke das Brot; pedantisch daneben die Käse, die Margarine; auf die andere Seite der Brotbeutel am Strick, den Aluminiumlöffel darauf [...][6]

Das Essen auf Lebensmittelmarken, das sehnsüchtige Warten auf Care-Pakete von den wenigen, die sie bekamen, gibt ebenso ein Bild wie die Episode um die Blechbüchse, die Grete wegwerfen will und die der Protagonist ihr abschwatzt, nach Überwindung seiner Scham –

‚ich brauch nur was zum Trinken und so.' (‚Und so' war gut! Aber warum soll gerade ich immer Bedeutendes äußern?). ‚O Gott', sagte sie [...] und da hielt sie mir endlich das Ding hin: ‚Es sind Fischgräten drin', erklärte sie schüchtern: es hat Zuteilung gegeben.'; ‚Danke schön!' und weg war ich. Mitsamt der Fischgräten; bin dann nochmal rausgegangen und hab die weggeschüttet.[7]

Dass die Erzählung kurz nach dem Krieg in einem besetzten Land spielt, zeigt eine kleine Episode, in der sich ein durchfahrender „Tommy"-Soldat bei der Figur Schmidt nach dem Weg erkundigt – „Schmidt" zeigt ihm seinen Pass und tut so, als verstehe er kein Englisch. (Später gibt er allerdings zu verstehen, dass er die Besatzung für einen Segen hält und hofft, sie halte noch 50 Jahre an.[8]) Die politischen Kommentare sind gegenüber anderen Werken sparsamer ausgefallen, auf die Bauern, die im allgemeinen Mangel wie die Maden im Speck leben, gibt es gehässige Tiraden wie üblich bei Schmidt, der stets auf Bauern nicht gut zu sprechen war. Die bitteren Lebensumstände erzeugen auch erst einen wesentlichen Teil der Handlungsdramaturgie: Dass Lore schließlich der Armut entflieht, indem sie ihren Vetter aus Lateinamerika heiraten will, ist schon auch ein derber Zeitkommentar – wer Deutschland verlassen kann, der tut's!, auch nach dem Ende der NS-Diktatur.

Dass in der schriftlich niedergelegten Erzählung *Brand's Haide* kaum interagiert wird, sondern dass ein wahrnehmendes Ich die ganzen fixierten Partikel wahrnimmt, zeigt, darstellt – und dass wir (anscheinend) auch noch

---

[6] Ebd., S. 124.
[7] Ebd.
[8] Ebd., S. 168.

einigermaßen wissen, wer dieses Ich ist, nämlich „Schmidt" –, ist deutlich. So sehr der Protagonist seiner widrigen Wirklichkeit ausgesetzt sein mag, wir sind an sein ‚Gehirn' angeschlossen, wir nehmen als Leserinnen und Leser seine Wirklichkeit wahr, die uns kanalisiert und dirigiert überreicht wird; der Stoßseufzer des Protagonisten, auch einer der bekanntesten Schmidt-Sätze, ist also durchaus eingelöst: „*Warum* kann man andere Menschen nicht an sein Gehirn anschließen, daß sie dieselben Bilder, Erinnerungsbilder, sehen, wie man selbst? (Es gibt aber auch Lumpen, die dann)"[9]

4.

Intertextualität ist als Weiterführung des Konzeptes der Dialogizität verstanden worden; danach interagieren Texte immer mit Texten, sie sind sozusagen immer schon Intertexte. Dieses Verständnis von Dialogizität ist mir immer ein bisschen zu weit gegangen, mit Wolf Schmid würde ich eher behaupten, dass die Rede vom „Dialog der Texte" stets „hochmetaphorisch" ist. Wolf Schmid meint, in der Regel sei intertextuelle Dialogizität eine „Einbahnstraße. Der fremde Text kann nicht nur nicht antworten, er kann sich nicht einmal provozieren lassen. Er ist stumm und taub."[10] Dennoch soll dieser oft untersuchte Spezialfall kurz eingespielt werden, der zeigen will, wie poetische Texte auf andere poetische Texte reagieren; denn natürlich gibt es diese Art literarischer Intertextualität wie immer bei Schmidt reichlich. Das können isolierte Anspielungen auf einzelne Sätze sein, Jean Pauls Werk etwa ist auf diese Weise bei Schmidt immer präsent, ohne dass sich daraus dramaturgische oder anders weiterführende Momente ergeben würden. Wenn der Protagonist angesichts schlecht trocknender Wäsche denkt: „never say die", ist das eine Redewendung aus Charles Dickens *Pickwick Papers* (1836/37) im Sinn von ‚sag niemals nie' – vielleicht wird die Wäsche ja doch noch trocken.[11] Als er vor seiner Behau-

---

[9] Ebd., S. 130.
[10] Schmid: Dialogizität (Anm. 1), S. 8.
[11] Schmidt: Brand's Haide (Anm. 4), S. 153. – Diese Erläuterungen sind Heinrich Schwiers Handbuch sehr verpflichtet, vgl. H. S.: Lore, Grete & Schmidt. Ein kommentierendes Handbuch zu Arno Schmidts Roman ‚Brand's Haide'. München: edition text + kritik 2000, hier S. 148.

sung auf einem Hocker in der Sonne arbeitet, in der Hoffnung, Lore zu sehen, und sich sein Konkurrent neben ihn setzt, müssen sie beide nebeneinander ausharren, beide mit demselben Ziel. Dazu fällt dem Protagonisten ein Merseburger Zauberspruch ein, „eiris sazun idisi", die ‚Idisen' (eine Art Nornen) setzten sich einst nieder, und es geht in dem Zauberspruch um kriegerische Auseinandersetzungen; mehr oder weniger also ein Element, das die Beziehung wie die Situation der beiden Wartenden unterstreicht.[12]

Solche Assoziationen können auch scherzhafter Natur sein, wenn mit „Polvo di Bacco" etwa Backpulver gemeint sein soll (wörtlich ein ‚Bacchuspulver').[13] Beim unverhofften Luxus des Teetrinkens mit Rohrzucker, beides aus dem Carepaket, muss ‚Schmidt' an *Les mille et une nuits* denken, mit der Notiz „Galland war ein großer Mann; nicht der Flieger, sondern der alte Literat 1646–1715"; das ist ein kleiner Seitenhieb gegen die automatischen Assoziationen der Zeitgenossen der Fünfziger – der Jagdflieger und Luftwaffengeneral Adolf Galland war damals weit bekannter als der Orientalist Antoine Galland, der die erste Übersetzung von *Tausendundeine Nacht* in eine europäische Sprache vorgelegt hat.[14] Grete wird einmal als *Little Dorrit* bezeichnet, auch dies ein Roman von Charles Dickens; diese Anspielung könnte nicht ganz so harmlos sein, die gutwillige, sanfte Dorrit hält durch alle Widrigkeiten zu der männlichen Hauptfigur des Romans und wird ihn am Ende heiraten. Nachdem in *Brand's Haide* die geliebte Lore verschwunden ist, bleibt Grete zurück; die literarische Anspielung könnte also auf eine Zukunft sozusagen nach dem Abschluss der erzählten Fiktion verweisen.[15] Auf eines der Grundthemen des Textes hingegen verweist die Nennung von Grillparzers *Armem Spielmann* (1848, „da sieht man, was Grillparzer konnte, dämonisch! Jedenfalls mehr als ich") – wie der Schmidt in *Brand's Haide* muss sich der Spielmann zwischen Kunst und Leben entscheiden.[16] Nicht auf das Thema, sondern auf den Aufbau von Schmidts Erzählung verweist ein Zitat aus Vergils IV. Ekloge, einem Hirtengedicht, *magnus nascitur*

---

[12] Schmidt: Brand's Haide (Anm. 4), S. 130; Schwier: Handbuch (Anm. 11), S. 88.
[13] Schmidt: Brand's Haide (Anm. 4), S. 140; Schwier: Handbuch (Anm. 11), S. 118.
[14] Schmidt: Brand's Haide (Anm. 4), S. 149; Schwier: Handbuch (Anm. 11), S. 136.
[15] Schmidt: Brand's Haide (Anm. 4), S. 148; Schwier: Handbuch (Anm. 11), S. 132.
[16] Schmidt: Brand's Haide (Anm. 4), S. 128; Schwier: Handbuch (Anm. 11), S. 69.

ordo,[17] in etwa ‚der große Kreislauf hebt von Neuem an' – der Weltenlauf ist gemeint –, es gibt auch noch zwei, drei andere Verweise auf Vergil. Schmidttypisch fällt diese Assoziation beim ersten Mal Rührkartoffeln seit Jahren, also mit der gehörigen Fallhöhe; aber *Brand's Haide* hat einen ganz ähnlichen Aufbau wie die IV. Ekloge: Im ersten Teil „als Darstellung der Welt nach der Katastrophe", hier nach dem Zweiten Weltkrieg; im zweiten Teil die „trügerische Wiederherstellung des Paradieses samt Sündenfall", das Liebespaar kommt bei Schmidt zusammen, im Waldstück Brand's Haide; im dritten Teil „als Inszenierung des Abstiegs in eine Höllenwelt" mit Schmidt und Lore als Orpheus und Eurydike, ihre Abfahrt mit dem Zug (und anderes) ist als Höllenfahrt instrumentiert.[18]

Es gibt einige ‚weltanschauliche' Zitate, die immer wieder durch Schmidts Werk geistern, so auch durch *Brand's Haide*; dazu gehört etwa „Und siehe, es war alles gut", höhnisch-ironisch hervorgebracht. Schmidt hatte ein ziemlich geschlossenes gnostisches Weltbild (auch die Valentinianer, eine gnostische Richtung, sind ausdrücklich in *Brand's Haide* erwähnt), die Welt als Schöpfung eines bösen Leviathan; dem alttestamentarischen Satz ist angesichts des Leides in der Welt nur mit Spott oder gar Hass zu begegnen, dagegen werden die großen Skeptiker des 18. Jahrhunderts, Voltaire mit seinem *Candide* (1759) und Swift mit *Gulliver's Travels* (1726), immer wieder als Kronzeugen für die These bemüht, dass wir in einer heillosen Welt leben.

Schmidt verwendet also ein großes Repertoire an Stilhöhen, Texten, Funktionen; Bildungsgut ebenso wie Albernheiten, die als solches instrumentiert werden (das Geraune etwa um einen „Fritz Viereck" entpuppt sich als das Lob einer Rumsorte[19]); all die Ausrufe, Flüche, Schlager-Zeilen können Komik transportieren ebenso wie sie schwarzgallig ernst sein können. Ein schönes Beispiel dafür ist ein angeblicher Schlagertext, den der Erzähler vorspricht („Leben ist ein Hauch nur / ein verhall'nder Sang / und wir sind das auch nur / und es währt nicht lang"), sein Konkurrent fängt tatsächlich an, damit herumspielend zu singen; der Text entpuppt sich als

---

[17] Schmidt: Brand's Haide (Anm. 4), S. 149.
[18] Schwier: Handbuch (Anm. 11), S. 133.
[19] Schmidt: Brand's Haide (Anm. 4), S. 175; Schwier: Handbuch (Anm. 11), S. 224.

Fouqué-Gedicht aus einem unveröffentlichten Drama, das Schmidt in Auszügen der Fouqué-Biographie mitteilen wird.[20]

Diese Auswahl aus dem reichen Spektrum von Einzelstellen-Erläuterungen und Verweisen mag erst einmal ausreichen; dank Heinrich Schwiers Handbuch zu *Brand's Haide* (2000) können dergleichen Entschlüsselungen in großer Vollständigkeit nachgelesen werden. Zu jedem oder doch mindestens jedem zweiten Satz könnte man solche Erläuterungen abgeben, die Faktur von Schmidts Texten ist sehr dicht; Schwier braucht 300 Seiten, um die Erzählung in dieser Weise zu erläutern. Dass Schmidt hier immer mit Prätexten spielt, sie integriert, auf sie anspielt, Eigenes damit macht, sollte deutlich geworden sein; aber es geht mir doch noch um einen anderen Begriff von Dialogizität.

5.

Denn diese genannten Beispiele sind mehr oder weniger amalgamiert, Schmidts Sprachduktus kann sehr viele solcher Details, Anspielungen, auch Sprachbrüche, fremdsprachlicher Partikel aufnehmen, dennoch wissen seine Leser nach spätestens zwei Zeilen, dass es sich eben um einen Schmidt-Text handelt. Eine ungleich stärkere Form von Dialogizität, eine wirkliche Polyphonie entsteht meines Erachtens, wenn eingefügte Texte einem ganz anderen sprachlichen Duktus folgen; wenn also Literatur Anderer in einer Weise eingebaut wird, dass sie als Anspielung oder gar in ihrer Funktion für den Text, der sie rahmt, nicht mehr unbedingt sichtbar ist – sozusagen Haupttexte, die weiter reichen als einfache Anspielungen oder Scherze im Detail. Für *Brand's Haide* speziell wichtig sind der *Don Sylvio* von Wieland (1764), überhaupt eines der Haupt-Bücher für Schmidt, er soll ein Exemplar im Krieg fast immer bei sich gehabt haben. Der vollständige Titel lautet: *Der Sieg der Natur über die Schwärmerey, oder Die Abentheuer des*

---

[20] Schmidt: Brand's Haide (Anm. 4), S. 131; Schwier: Handbuch (Anm. 11), S. 89. Schmidt hat die Verse aus dem Drama *Griechisches Feuer* im Anhang seiner Fouqué-Biographie veröffentlicht, vgl. Arno Schmidt: Fouqué und einige seiner Zeitgenossen. In: Ders.: Bargfelder Ausgabe. Werkgruppe III. Essays und Biografisches. Band I. Eine Edition der Arno Schmidt Stiftung. Zürich: Haffmans 1993, S. 646.

Don Sylvio von Rosalva. Eine Geschichte worinn alles Wunderbare natürlich zugeht. Der Untertitel könnte auch für *Brand's Haide* gelten, und eine Charakterisierung des Protagonisten ebenso für den „Schmidt" der Erzählung:

> Solcher Gestalt schob sich die poetische und bezauberte Welt in seinem Kopf an die Stelle der wirklichen, und die Gestirne, die elementarischen Geister, die Zauberer und Feen waren in seinem System eben so gewiß die Beweger der Natur, als es die Schwere, die Anziehungskraft, die Elasticität, das elektrische Feuer, und andere natürliche Ursachen in dem System eines heutigen Weltweisen sind.[21]

So wichtig Wieland ist, auch er ist eher in Anspielungen präsent und allenfalls auffällig, wenn man seinen Roman kennt. Breiteren Raum nimmt Johann Gottfried Schnabels *Insel Felsenburg* ein, ein anderes Lieblingsbuch Schmidts, hier gibt es eine Episode, ein *Insel Felsenburg*-Triptychon sozusagen, in dem es um das Sich-Weg-Träumen aus der belastenden Gegenwart geht und sich der Protagonist nach einer neuen Fahrt zur Insel sehnt, ein Utopia, von dem aus ab und an per Schiff einzelne Leidende eingesammelt werden. Auch diese Episode übergehe ich, es handelt sich um keinen Fremdtext, sondern um einen vom Protagonisten geträumten Schnabel, wenn auch mit ein paar Realien aus dessen Leben.

In *Brand's Haide* gibt es aber fünf lange Texte, deren sprachlicher Duktus und deren Erzählweise deutlich herausfallen. Zwei davon stammen von Fouqué – er ist sicher der wichtigste ‚dialogische' Partner in dieser Erzählung, obwohl er bereits 1843 verstorben ist – wie gesagt, verehrte Kollegen sind als immer mit-lebend zu behandeln. Beide Texte sind im Wesentlichen wörtlich eingefügt, zwei Ausschnitte aus dem Roman *Alethes von Lindenstein* (1817), jeweils etwa 4 Druckseiten der Werkausgabe lang; der erste Ausschnitt beschreibt eine beklemmende Szene zwischen einem jungen Ritter bei einem wahnsinnigen Alten in dessen Wohnhöhle, die noch einen offenbar höllischen Untergrund hat, den der junge Mann dauerhaft verriegelt – nutzlos, wie ihm der Alte mitteilt, die Geister seien durch eine Tür nicht zu stoppen. Der Alte hält den Ritter für seinen Schüler, der er aber nicht ist, nur deshalb bleibt er freundlich.[22] Die zweite Passage schildert

---

[21] Schmidt: Brand's Haide (Anm. 4), S. 164; Schwier: Handbuch (Anm. 11), S. 187f.; Wieland hier zit. n. Schwier, ebd.
[22] Schmidt: Brand's Haide (Anm. 4), S. 181–184.

die Höllenfahrt der schönen jungen Mathilde, sie wird mühsam von einem Priester mit allerlei Zauberformeln wieder an die Oberfläche geholt, ist aber schon der Hölle verfallen, sie verspottet die entsetzte Gesellschaft und fährt wieder in den Untergrund, wo sie bleiben will.[23] Beide Episoden weisen Hohlwelten auf, einen unterirdischen Höllen-Raum, damit lassen sie sich auf Lores Abreise beziehen; auch sie wird in die (heiße) Hölle Lateinamerikas reisen und dem Protagonisten nicht mehr erreichbar sein, und sie will das auch; der zweite Fouqué-Text, durch die Mathilden-Figur, verdüstert das Bild der geliebten Lore, wenn man beide aufeinander beziehen wollte – aber man muss es selber tun, der Erzähler vermeidet diese Explizitheit. Allein der Umfang und der Detailreichtum der Fouqué-Episoden sprengt die motivische Funktionalität allemal; ein großer Anteil dieser Fouqué-Texte kann deren eigener Logik folgen. Nebenher finden sich zahlreiche weitere Fouqué-Bezüge, vor allem zur *Undine* (1811), auch hier ein Mann zwischen zwei Frauen, ein Text der Elementargeister und ein düsteres Ende; Teil II., *Lore oder das spielende Licht*, beinhaltet eine weitere Fouqué-Anspielung, diesmal auf den *Zauberring*, ein sogenannter Ritterroman, demzufolge das spielende Licht in den Augen ein Kennzeichen von Elfen sein soll – Lore selbst wird also als Elementargeist, einmal auch als Pflanzengeist mit spitziger Rosenzunge apostrophiert.[24]

Einer der einmontierten Texte stammt aus den Erinnerungen der Suzanne de Robillard, *Kurtze Nachricht von meiner Flucht aus Frankreich*. Hier erzählt eine Hugenottin von ihrer gelungenen Flucht aus Frankreich 1687, sie wurde mit den Ihren im Frachtraum eines Schiffes versteckt. Obwohl eigentlich nur fünf Personen hätten mitkommen können, ließ sich der Kapitän erweichen, auch noch ihre kleine Schwester mitzunehmen.[25] Suzanne de Robillard der Champagné (1670–1740) ist Fouqués Urgroßmutter – nicht, dass das in *Brand's Haide* erwähnt würde![26] Ihr Bericht steht isoliert ohne ausdrückliche Bezüge zur Erzählung, man kann sich überlegen, ob man ihn einer Schnabelschen Fluchtphantasie zuordnen will, hier mit einer

---

[23] Ebd., S. 190–194.
[24] Vgl. Schwier: Handbuch (Anm. 11), passim – auch die hier genannten Details stellen nur eine kleine Auswahl dar.
[25] Schmidt: Brand's Haide (Anm. 4), S. 133–135; Schwier: Handbuch (Anm. 11), S. 97f.
[26] Schmidt: Fouqué (Anm. 20), S. 17f., 472, 579.

ausbleibenden Trennung von einer nahestehenden Person; dennoch bleibt der Text etwas erratisch, wieder müssen sich die Lesenden selbst überlegen, ob sie eine Verbindung zu *Brand's Haide* entdecken.

Weit befremdlicher ist dann wieder der „Bericht des Predigers Overbeck vom 11.10.1742", den die drei Kirchenbuch-Leserinnen und -leser dort finden und sich gegenseitig vortragen. Dieser Text hat nun eine eminent wichtige Funktion, er erklärt, warum die Dorfbewohner bis zum Jahr der Handlung 1946 das Waldstück Brand's Haide unheimlich finden. Hier muss nun doch wenigstens ein kleiner Ausschnitt eingerückt werden:

> Unterschiedliche Bauern instruiereten mich, daß man am heutigen Abend in Brands-Haide viele Lichter sehe, auch Stimmen hören könne, so daß gar das liebe Vieh in den Ställen unruhig sey und sich Kinder und Mägdgen nicht aus den Häusern traueten. Ich verfügte mich in Begleitung des adjuncti, Hrn. von Bock, sogleich auf den Kirchturm, wohin mir auch besagte Bauern mit Laternen und Dusacken folgeten, um den casum zu untersuchen. Die Nacht war ungemein windstill, kühl, und, zumal über Brands-haide voll einiger Nebel, so aber die Sicht nicht sonderlich störeten: so observiereten wir in Richtung Krumau viele schweifende Lichter im Forst, deren Anzahl wir auf circa Fünf-Hundert ästimieren mußten; doch konnte selbst der v. Bock, so sich mit einem guten Dollond versehen hatte, nichts Näheres eruieren.[27]

Der Pfarrer meint, es müsse sich um Irrlichter handeln; in der Folge wird noch von einer Art Teufelserscheinung berichtet und von einem Knecht, der die Erscheinung in den Wald verfolgt hat und nie wiedergekehrt ist. Dieser Text stammt nun nicht vom Prediger Overbeck aus einem (z. B.) Cordinger Kirchenbuch, es handelt sich um einen Fake – auch er ist reiner Schmidt, zusammengesetzt aus alten Chroniken, Fouqué, Cooper, Schnabel, Storm, Sagen, Märchen und anderem;[28] der große Gestus des Authentischen will uns also gerade eine Fälschung andrehen, allerdings scheint es ein Waldstück mit dem Namen „Brand's Haide" tatsächlich gegeben zu haben, jedenfalls Schmidts *Fouqué*-Biographie zufolge, eine dichte Waldung „im damals noch sehr öden Fleming", in der sich Schmuggler- und

---

[27] Schmidt: Brand's Haide (Anm. 4), S. 160.
[28] Schwier: Handbuch (Anm. 11), S. 174f.

Raubgesindel aufgehalten habe, und auch „im Frost irrende Lichter" seien in diesem Grenzgebiet manchmal zu sehen gewesen.[29] Der Fläming (!) ist ein Höhenzug an der Grenze von Brandenburg und Sachsen-Anhalt, das Waldstück scheint allerdings nicht – oder nicht mehr unter dem Namen Brand's Haide – zu existieren.

Der letzte große abweichende Text nun, der *Öreland*-Traum, wird mit dem Satz eingeleitet: „Dies hab ich am 22.3. gegen Morgen get[...]räumt; kein Wort verstellt! (Wie auch die andern Träume im Leviathan! Bin ein Bardur in dieser Hinsicht.)"[30] Hier lässt der Autor Schmidt also seine Figur Schmidt auf den 1946 geschriebenen Erstling *Leviathan* des Autors Schmidt verweisen und behauptet, der Traum sei authentisch, ein Satz, der zudem den autobiographischen Pakt schließt und behauptet, Figur und Autor seien identisch. (Bardur ist erneut eine Fouqué-Figur, einer, der „allzuviel auf Träume gab", aus *Saga von dem Gunlaugur, genannt Drachenzunge und Rafn dem Skalden*, 1826.[31]) Nach den Erfahrungen mit dem Herrn Overbeck stinkt das nun ein bisschen gegen den Wind; wenn jemand so laut behauptet, etwas sei authentisch, ist es das bestimmt nicht. Zudem passt der Traum auch motivisch einfach zu gut in *Brand's Haide* hinein: Es ist ein Text, der atmosphärisch an Hebbels *Kannitverstan* (1808) erinnert, nur dass immer das Wort *Öreland* fällt; es geht um einen Neuanfang nach einer Sintflut (ähnlich dem Neuanfang der *Brand's Haide*-Figuren nach dem Krieg), es gibt einen Alten wie in *Brand's Haide* und in Fouqués *Undine* und obendrein noch einen möglichen Tagesrest des Protagonisten, am Ende will sich die Traumfigur Werkzeug beim Nachbarn borgen und hofft, ein paar Nägel geschenkt zu kriegen, die uns flugs an Handfeger und Schaufel zu Beginn von *Brand's Haide* erinnern.[32] Bernd Rauschenbach hat für das Bibliothek Suhrkamp-Bändchen *Traumflausn* (2008) mit einigen Traumprotokollen Schmidts nachrecherchiert: Schmidt hat den Öreland-Traum am 29.12.1947 um 7 Uhr notiert, zweieinhalb Jahre vor dem Beginn der Arbeit an *Brand's Haide*; im Typoskript der Erzählung *fehlt* der Öreland-Traum, er ist als separates Manuskript der Druckvorlage beigelegt worden, auch in anderer Papierqualität; und Alice Schmidt notiert in ihrem Tagebuch, ihr

---

[29] Schmidt: Fouqué (Anm. 20), S. 49.
[30] Schmidt: Brand's Haide (Anm. 4), S. 124.
[31] Schwier: Handbuch (Anm. 11), S. 61.
[32] Schmidt: Brand's Haide (Anm. 4), S. 127.

Mann habe von einem Traum erzählt, den er vor Jahren geträumt habe und der „so rein paßt als ob er extra dafür erfunden wäre ,So sehr paßt er, daß es mir geradezu peinlich ist'".[33] Offenbar ist nun gerade der Traum, gerade der unwahrscheinlichste der eingefügten Texte, tatsächlich ein authentischer ‚Fremd'-Text wie der von Suzanne de Robillard – von einem früheren Ich des Verfassers geträumt und in das fertige Typoskript nachträglich eingefügt. Träume bei Schmidt sind ein großes Thema; es gibt auch noch ein Blatt *Brand's Haide*, datiert auf den 31.3./1.4.1949, aus dem hervorgeht, dass der erste Einfall für die ganze Erzählung ein Traum gewesen ist, nun wieder ein anderer.

6.

Wenn wir auf dieses allererste Entwurfs-Blatt zurückgehen, zeigt sich dort auch eine Figurenliste mit ein paar Merkwürdigkeiten:[34] Außer den Flüchtlingen, dem Bäcker im Ort und dem Prediger Overbeck wird eine „Nymphe Cannae" erwähnt; ein Waldgänger, „der hinein kann"; der Gärtner Auen; Wege, die sich im Wald verändern: wir sind im titelgebenden Waldstück *Brand's Haide* angekommen. Es geht hier offenbar nicht mit rechten Dingen zu, „Der Elfenwald" steht in der Überschrift. Kinder, die Steine hineinwerfen, werden geschreckt, ein Knecht gibt einem Ast die Hand (der sie im fertigen Werk nicht mehr loslässt, er schneidet sie ab und rennt mit dem blutenden Stummel durchs Dorf), eine ganze Reihe von Märchen- und Schauerromantik-Motiven.

Brand's Haide ist offenbar auch ein Elementargeist-Roman, ein Roman von Nichtmenschlichen, die in dem titelgebenden Waldstück leben. Prominent ist hier ein Herr Auen, der auch mit Fouqué zu tun hat: Der Großvater seines ersten Hauslehrers trug den Namen Johann Wilhelm Auen. Gleich auf der ersten Seite zeigen sich Ungewöhnlichkeiten, die man zunächst

---

[33] Alice Schmidt zit. n. Bernd Rauschenbach: Ein Bardur. In: Arno Schmidt: Traumflausn. Gesammelt und mit einem Nachwort versehen von B. R. Frankfurt/Main: Suhrkamp 2008, S. 93–118, hier S. 93f.

[34] Die erste Skizze zu *Brand's Haide*, skizziert nach einem Traum in der Nacht vom 31.3./1.4.1949, ist faksimiliert und transkribiert in Arno Schmidt: Bargfelder Ausgabe. Supplemente. Bd. 1: Fragmente. Prosa, Dialoge, Essays, Autobiographisches. Frankfurt/Main: Suhrkamp 2003, S. 26f.

überliest: Der Alte, den das Ich ständig trifft, scheint auf den zweiten Blick nicht recht menschlich, und wenn er beifällig dem Ich recht gibt und sagt: „Es hat viel zu viel auf der Welt: Menschen",[35] klingt das ganz anders, als wenn man einen menschlichen Sprecher annimmt. Er kommt und verschwindet blitzartig; er leiht ‚Schmidt' Besen und Schaufel, die markant wieder abgeholt werden: der Protagonist soll sie an einen bestimmten Wacholder stellen: „Ich ging, langsam, mit queren Querulantenaugen […] Sah wieder zurück: klein lehnte es am zufriedenen Busch. Auf der Straße. […] Wieder den Kopf rum: – weg war es! Da kann man fertig sein."[36] Der Erzähler bekennt sozusagen seine Begrenztheit gegenüber dem Alten, an dieser Stelle (und an anderen) entspricht er keineswegs dem Klischee vom allwissenden Schmidt-Protagonisten (das ohnehin meist nicht mehr als ein Klischee ist). Der Alte verteilt Blätter im Waldstück, statt sie einzusammeln, hängt schon auch mal ein Blatt an einen Nadelbaum, er ist offenbar für die Natur an diesem Ort, für *Brand's Haide* zuständig, ein Gärtner eben. Und er wünscht dem Protagonisten für die Kirchenbuch-Lektüre „viel S-paß noch für den Herrn Auen",[37] eine Bemerkung, die sich der Erzähler nicht erklären kann, schließlich hatte er selbst den Namen noch gar nicht erwähnt! Der Alte unterstützt den Erzähler, er weiß schon, als Lore und Schmidt zusammengehen, dass sie ihn im Oktober verlassen wird; seine ‚Kunstwerke' sind vorbildlich, „meisterhaft, meisterhaft", kommentiert der Erzähler ein Ahornblatt aus dem Karren, das er gegen das Licht hält: „Und welche Verschwendung! Der muß es dicke haben!"[38] Unter der Ägide des Alten wird der Protagonist tatsächlich vom Flüchtling und Fouqué-Biographen zum Poeten, zum Orpheus. Und der Alte *kennt* Fouqué und Undine, den historischen Autor wie die erfundene Figur, nicht als Text, sondern die Personen! Schließlich ist sie, Undine, auch ein Elementargeist, und die kennen sich eben untereinander – „die Undine kennt jeder von uns erementaschen hier".[39] Der Hörfehler des Protagonisten erklärt sich auf diese Weise: jeder von ‚uns Elementarischen hier' (plus die Eremitage vielleicht noch, man lebt für sich im Wald, getrennt von den Men-

---

[35] Schmidt: Brand's Haide (Anm. 4), S. 117.
[36] Ebd., S. 123.
[37] Ebd., S. 142.
[38] Ebd., S. 117.
[39] Ebd., S. 118.

schen). Es gibt neben dem Alten noch eine Reihe von Neben-Geistern wie einen Wetter-Geist und andere, zum Teil sehr kurz erwähnt; und der Alte weiß natürlich von dem Herrn Auen, weil der ein Elementargeist und Gärtner ist – er scheint *selbst* dieser Großvater von Fouqués Hauslehrer zu sein. Lore liest aus dem Kirchenbuch vor: „Johann Wilhelm Auen, Gärtner zu Amt Coldingen"; ‚Schmidt' ergänzt: „das ist der Großvater, der immer im Scherz behauptete, keinen Geburtstag zu haben."[40]

Johann Wilhelm Auen ist also, *Brand's Haide* und der Figur Schmidt zufolge, ein Elementargeist; das führt aber nun dazu, dass der Autor Schmidt in seiner Fouqué-Biographie, in der Auen natürlich vorkommt – der zitierte Großvater-Scherz nicht –, dessen Lebensdaten nicht nennt: Ein Elementargeist hat schließlich keine.[41] Und hier kommt die vielleicht radikalste Dialogizität ins Spiel, deshalb skizziere ich überhaupt diese Elementargeist-Ebene: Schmidt erzählt tatsächlich so, als seien alle Zeiten und Welten gleich unmittelbar vorhanden, die politische, geschichtliche Welt wie die der Geister, die historische wie die gegenwärtige, die Fouqués so wie seine eigene, die poetische wie die wirkliche. Der veritable doppelte Boden, der hier konsequent eingezogen ist, wird noch verstärkt durch Anspielungen auf den Mythos: Nach dem Sündenfall (der Aufnahme einer sexuellen Beziehung?) wird ‚Schmidt' zu Orpheus, Lore zu Eurydike, deshalb muss der dritte Teil fortlaufend Untergründe, Hohlwelten, Höllen benennen, und deshalb wird das Paar auch scheitern. Orpheus bleibt im Mythos bekanntlich allein, ein singender Kopf am Ende.

Damit radikalisiert Schmidt, was Fouqué mit seinem Nixenmärchen *Undine* erreicht hat, mindestens wenn ich mich dem Verständnis des Romantikers von Monika Schmitz-Emans anschließe: „Das Vertraute wird fremd, das Fremde und Befremdliche erweist sich als allgegenwärtig." Diese Erfahrung verbindet sich mit den Elementargeistern bei Fouqué, mit Undine selbst und ihrem vielgestaltigen Onkel Kühleborn, dem Wassergeist. Fouqués Erzählung tue „harmloser, als sie ist. Genau gelesen, erzählt sie von der Erschütterung des menschlichen Bewußtseins durch die Gegenwart und die Macht einer gänzlich fremden Welt, in der Mächte be-

---

[40] Ebd., S. 160.
[41] Schmidt: Fouqué (Anm. 20), S. 587; Auen ist nur über Frickes Stammbaum aufzufinden, er hat kein Lemma im Register.

stimmen, die der Mensch nicht einmal durchschaut, geschweige denn beherrscht."[42]

Genauer, erzähltheoretischer und für Arno Schmidt gesprochen, der ja nun in anderer Weise die „Überschreitung der Grenzen der Welt" darstellt:[43] Er erzählt konsequent metaleptisch, nichts anderes bedeutet die permanente Ebenen-Irritation in *Brand's Haide* – eine Strategie, die wiederum als typisch postmodern gilt, die es aber bereits in der Frühromantik, besonders im Werk von Ludwig Tieck gibt. Jorge Luis Borges hat am deutlichsten gesagt, was es mit den Metalepsen auf sich hat:

> Warum beunruhigt es uns, dass Don Quijote Leser des *Quichote*, Hamlet Zuschauer des *Hamlet* ist? Ich denke, die Ursache herausgefunden zu haben: solche Spiegelungen legen die Vermutung nahe, daß, sofern die Figuren einer Fiktion auch Leser und Zuschauer sein können, wir, ihre Leser oder Zuschauer, fiktiv sein können.[44]

Oder, um Schmidts Bild vom Ahornblatt aufzurufen, das „meisterhaft" geraten ist: Die Kunst des Autors besteht darin, wie sein Elementargeist die Blätter so zu verteilen, dass jeder Leser, jede Leserin ihre eigene Phantasie – und ihr eigenes Wirklichkeits-Erleben – dazwischen schieben kann, tatsächlich ‚in' diesen Texten lebt und so natürlich sein/ihr eigenes hinzutut, nicht zu knapp, und das Erleben des Textes nach draußen trägt.

Brand's Haide erzählt subjektiv und ad personam eine Schriftstellerwerdung, eine Initiationsgeschichte, die gerade durch die Mythologie- und Elementargeister-Schicht auch wieder geöffnet wird. Wir steigen durch die Zeiten (bis zurück zum Mythos und zu Märchen, Fouqué ist schließlich hier vor allem als Erzähler des Kunstmärchens *Undine* und des Märchenromans *Die wunderbaren Begebenheiten des Grafen Alethes von Lindenstein* präsent), von der Antike bis heute, und können auch unsre eigenen (Man-

---

[42] Schmitz-Emans, Monika: Wasserfrauen und Elementargeister als poetologische Chiffren. In: Hans-Georg Pott (Hg.): Liebe und Gesellschaft. Das Geschlecht der Musen. München: W. Fink 1997, S. 181–229, hier S. 197.

[43] Benz, Patrick: Friedrich Baron de la Motte Fouqué: Undine. In: Werkführer durch die utopisch-phantastische Literatur. Hg. von Franz Rottensteiner / Michael Koseler. Meitingen: Corian 2002, 36. Erg.-Lfg., S. 1–5, hier S. 3.

[44] Genette, Gérard: Metalepse. In: Ders.: Die Erzählung. Aus dem Französischen von Andreas Knop, mit einem Nachwort hg. von Jochen Vogt. München: W. Fink 1998, S. 167–169, hier S. 169.

gel-)Erfahrungen einhängen. Hier wird zwar der Mangel der Nachkriegszeit vergegenwärtigt; aber eben auch Kindheitserfahrungen, Einschränkungen anderer Art – und irgendeine Art von Mangel hatte vermutlich in Kindheitszeiten Jeder, Jede trägt ihre Einschränkungen mit sich herum, wir alle brauchen den Hallraum der Kunst, Musik, Literatur, um diese Defizite auszugleichen. Allerdings hinterlässt diese Schmidtsche Vision einen bitteren Nachgeschmack – die ‚Goldene Zeitalter'-Vision ist die Mitte des Triptychons, eine Vision vom Gelingenden Leben ist die Erzählung nicht gerade. Die Liebe scheitert, in der Kunst steht dieser Erzähler am Anfang, vielleicht begleitet von seiner *little Dorrit*.

7.

Ich hoffe, ich habe einigermaßen verständlich machen können, was ich mit Dialogizität meine. *Brand's Haide* hat weit mehr zu bieten als einen ergreifenden Ausschnitt aus den Armuts- und Kältejahren direkt nach dem Krieg, nicht weniger als die Allegorie einer Schriftstellerwerdung, ein düsteres Weltbild mit eigenen Raum- und Zeitbegriffen, und einer radikalen Statuierung von Kunst und Natur als Überlebenshilfen, zusammengefasst im Bild des Ahornblattes.

Dialogizität erhebt sich aus den großen eingeschobenen Texten, zum Teil wirkliche Fremdtexte, zum Teil Träume und Fälschungen – bei der Lektüre ohne Handbuch ein irritierender, gleichwohl höchst vergnüglicher und aufregender Wechsel von Text- und Stilebenen, die sich mit einiger Überlegung in den von der Erzählung etablierten Erzählmodus einfügen können – oder auch nicht.

Als Ausblick am Schluss: Echte Dialogizität zeigt sich bei Schmidt immer wieder in den Frauenporträts, auch hier. Denn Lore macht, was sie will, sie hört nicht auf das Ich: sie beginnt die Affäre, wenn *sie* will, sie beendet sie, wenn *sie* will, da mögen die süßen Liebesbeteuerungen noch so laut und deutlich ausfallen. Sie ist längst nicht so beeindruckbar wie Grete. Ihre Unabhängigkeit wird immer präsent gehalten: sie geht tanzen, mit den Bauernburschen, mit dem Lehrer, ‚Schmidts' Intimfeind; sie verlangt von ihm, dass er tanzen lernt. Lore „expects every man to do his duty", heißt es einmal; sie verschwindet auch gelegentlich aus der Erzählung, Besorgungen machen, zur Post gehen, sie bekommt Briefe, von denen der Erzähler lange nichts weiß; und sie geht schließlich und überlässt ihn seiner Kunst. Er muss in der Folge diese Alterität, die ihm nicht mehr zur Verfügung steht, ins Innere verlegen, obwohl er's lieber anders hätte; er *muss* Kunst schaffen, ‚mal lieblich, mal rabiat'; er muss Lore eine Konkurrentin erfinden, der sie nicht gewachsen ist – die literarische Lore; und er unterliegt einer Folge von Selbsttäuschungen, was Lore angeht, ein Aspekt, den besonders Hans-Edwin Friedrich herausgearbeitet hat.[45] Wir wissen also am Ende nicht, ob der erste Text dieses nun entschiedenen Künstlers ‚Schmidt' nicht der Text ist, den wir gerade gelesen haben: *Brand's Haide*.

---

[45] Friedrich, Hans-Edwin: Frommer Mann, Baron und Dichter. Zur Funktion Fouqués in *Brand's Haide*. In: Ders. (Hg.): Arno Schmidt und das 18. Jahrhundert. Göttingen: Wallstein 2017, S. 268–294 [im Erscheinen]. Einen ersten Fouqué-Durchgang hat unternommen: Peter Piontek: Zum Wald-Stück „Brand's Haide". In: Bargfelder Bote 71–72 (1983), S. 3–19.

Belligerent Dialogues?
A Dialogical Approach to Fictional and Non-Fictional Representations of the American 'War on Terror'

Robert Moscaliuc

When Liberty Island reopened to the public three months after the attacks of September 11, 2001, tourist information plaques on the island still needed to catch up with the altered Manhattan skyline. A vacancy had appeared where the Twin Towers of the World Trade Center stood. "Amid the glittering impassivity of the many building across the East River," John Updike wrote in *The New Yorker* a few days after the attacks, "an empty spot had appeared, as if by electronic command, beneath the sky that, but for the sulfurous cloud streaming south toward the ocean, was pure blue, rendered uncannily pristine by the absence of jet trails."[1] Even three months after the events, one of those tourist plaques, situated just at the edge of Liberty Island where visitors could get a breathtaking view of the tip of Manhattan, still featured the 'old' Manhattan skyline in which the two towers stood proudly intact.

The disparity between reality and representation was haunting. It placed the two instances, the old and the new, in a relation of simultaneity, of coexistence. This dialogic simultaneity between reality and its representation gave an ominous aura to 'that day', as 9/11 came to be called in its aftermath, and it reflected a state of mind. It was a showcase of 'before and after' akin to shampoo TV commercials or those 'brain-fitness puzzles' that ask players to spot the differences. Yet, it indicated something else as well, a shift not just in terms of landscape. The gap in the "glittering impassivity"[2] of Manhattan's skyline needed more than concrete and hard physical work to be sealed.

---

[1] Updike, John: Tuesday, and After. In: http://www.newyorker.com/magazine/2001/09/24/tuesday-and-after-talk-of-the-town (31.01.2017).

[2] Idem.

The plaque on Liberty Island was not the only one which proffers such uncanny commentary on the changing scenery. In November 2015, while I was staying in New York City, during one of my morning runs in Astoria Park I stumbled across a similarly ominous plaque. Situated on the sidewalk, approximately halfway between the Robert F. Kennedy Bridge and the Hell Gate Bridge, the green plaque faces the East River and, beyond it, Manhattan's skyline. It does not contain any images, yet the weather-beaten plaque tells the story of the 1904 *General Slocum Disaster*, which involved a steamboat that sunk in the East River along with its 1,300 people on board. Out of all those people on board only about 280 managed to survive. However, that was not the information that caught my eye as I was skimming the long commemorative text. What drew my attention was the last sentence of the first paragraph, which tells its readers that "prior to September 11, 2001, the burning of the *General Slocum* had the highest death toll of any disaster in New York City history."[3] Besides the seemingly innocuous comparison that this piece of information offers, which is most likely meant to help New Yorkers and tourists to get a sense of perspective with regards to the death toll and the importance of such an event, it appears to me that the plaque is incidentally much more about what happened on and in the aftermath of 9/11 than about the *General Slocum Disaster*.

The two events, akin to the two versions of Manhattan's skyline, were also placed in a dialogic simultaneity. Yet, in this case, the comparison was no longer about forceful changes in an otherwise recognizable landscape but rather about how certain events are 'dethroned' by culturally resounding ones in a city's cultural memory. It somehow chronicled the degree to which 9/11 turned into a 'watershed moment' in the city's history since most people will not remember a steamboat that sunk on a Sunday afternoon due to "organizational and leadership failings."[4] The comparison also offered 9/11 as a unit of measurement for the perception of that other disaster, as if the *General Slocum Disaster* could not have been understood without bringing 9/11 into the picture, and maybe even the other way around.

---

[3] New York City Department of Parks and Recreation: Astoria Park, General Slocum Disaster. In: https://www.nycgovparks.org/parks/astoria-park/highlights/19029 (05.02.2017).

[4] Idem.

Joan Didion, in *The Year of Magical Thinking*, was making a similar, albeit unconscious association while speaking about how violent events are almost always preceded by unremarkable circumstances; she brings together the "ordinary Sunday morning" of *Pearl Harbor* and the "ordinary beautiful September day" before *9/11* happened.[5] Yet, the mental levelling Didion succumbs to in her comparison is not far-fetched. Akin to *Pearl Harbor*, 9/11 was an act of unswerving aggression perpetrated on the homeland, and Didion was surely not the only one to shed light on the connection. David Ray Griffin, an American professor and political writer, declaratively entitled his book on the Bush Administration after 9/11 *The New Pearl Harbor*,[6] and in the days following the attack, politicians of all colors resorted to the same association in their public speeches. In this sense, it seems that there is a transfer of 'cultural weight' between these events placed in dialogic simultaneity: the *steamboat incident* offers the death toll, 9/11 offers the attitude and the solemnity the former somehow fails to trigger, while *Pearl Harbor* legitimizes a military response.

This transfer of 'cultural weight' could be easily explained and understood in psychological terms by invoking such notions as the 'availability heuristic'.[7] If applied, the notion would reveal that whoever conceived the text for the plaque offered readers a mental shortcut by relying on immediate examples that come to a given person's mind when evaluating, for instance, the death toll of the *General Slocum Disaster*. Yet, such an approach is limiting, to say the least. It reveals more about the authors and the readers of the text, as well as about the *post-9/11* atmosphere, than about the nature of the events themselves, if such nature could ever be graspable.

On this line of reasoning, it is my contention that this dialogic simultaneity indicates a modification in the world's 'primal scenes' and constitutes a symptom of how *9/11* and the ensuing wars have created a ripple effect from a cultural point of view. "Many people", George Packer argues in *The Assassins' Gate: America in Iraq*, "allowed historical analogies to do their

---

[5] Didion, Joan: The Year of Magical Thinking. New York: Vintage Books 2007, p. 4.

[6] Griffin, David Ray: The New Pearl Harbor: Disturbing questions about the Bush administration and 9/11. Massachusetts: Interlink Publishing Group 2004.

[7] Kelman, Mark: The Heuristics Debate. New York: Oxford University Press 2011.

thinking for them."[8] In the case of the 'war on terror', triggered by the events of September 11, the two 'primal scenes', or mental shortcuts, were the Second World War and the war in Vietnam and many people funneled their perception of the new wars along those lines. However, the *General Slocum* commemorative plaque indicates a further development in that mental process. The plaque seems to suggest that, in terms of casualties, 9/11 has become the 'primal scene' for the understanding of the *General Slocum Disaster* despite the chronological primacy of the latter.

By taking into consideration both fictional and non-fictional texts as well as other cultural artifacts coming from different fields, this paper looks at how culturally resonant occurrences such as the terrorist attacks of September 11 and the ensuing 'war on terror' tend to become 'selfish events'. As this paper will argue, this transformation is particularly fruitful when these artifacts enter processes of dialogic simultaneity with those artifacts that have "circulating signifiers"[9] and whose cultural frames could be exported to fit new contexts. To this purpose, by looking at Elliot Ackerman's novel *Green on Blue* as well as other texts pertaining to the discourse(s) of the 'war on terror', the paper tries to argue that such dialogues result in 'violent' interpretative intrusions not only at the level of succeeding cultural discourses but also at the level of preceding discourses. However, the notion of dialogue employed in my argument does not inherently imply intertextuality. Albeit their authors do acknowledge some writerly debt to other cultural artifacts and authors, the degree of influence is never stated specifically within the texts themselves. 'Dialogue' hereby implies simultaneity and is most observable when these texts and cultural artifacts are brought together in interpretative processes and their overlaps are pinpointed and discussed.

One way to go deeper into this process of transfer to understand it better would be to look for other instances in which this dialogic simultaneity and transfer of 'cultural weight' occur, and post-9/11 literature offers plenty of revelatory examples. One of these moments of cultural transfer is accurately documented, for instance, in Siri Hustvedt's novel *The Blazing*

---

[8] Packer, George: The Assassins' Gate: America in Iraq. London: Faber & Faber 2007, pp. 86f.

[9] Willis, Susan: Portents of the Real: A Primer for Post-9/11 America. London, New York: Verso 2005, p. 15.

World. In terms of narrative tactics, the novel strategically builds the story using different points of view thus permitting the reader to see the issue from dissimilar angles. After having lived for so long in the shadow of her art-connoisseur-dealer husband, Harriet Burden, the protagonist of the novel, decides to conduct an experiment by concealing her female identity behind three male artists who agree to present Burden's work as if it was their own. The purpose of the experiment, as explained by the protagonist herself in the many journal entries included in the novel, was to show the degree to which the art world was biased against female artists, the latter being portrayed as victims of a 'phallocentric' perception of art. What interests me most however, is the way in which one of Burden's art installations, titled suggestively *The Suffocation Rooms*, was perceived simply because it was mounted in the aftermath of 9/11:

> The show was mounted the spring after New York was attacked, and the little mutant that crawled out of the box had the haunting look of a damaged survivor or a new being born in the wreckage. It didn't matter that the work had been finished well before 9/11. The increasing heat in the rooms contributed to the interpretation; the last, hot room felt ominous. At the same time, my debut was an insignificant casualty of the falling towers.[10]

Yet, in Hustvedt's fragmented narrative, Burden's art installations are not the only ones that fall prey to the cultural violence of the 'falling towers'. The works of another artist, who goes by the name of Rune and who later becomes one of Burden's male fronts, are subjected to the same kind of interpretation with the only exception that his works are exhibited well before the events of September 11. The narrative thus chronicles how after 9/11 Rune's 'colored crosses' took on an entirely different meaning. "Modeled on the Red Cross symbol in different colors," one of the narrators explains, "they could have been an ironic reference to the whole history of Christianity or to the Crusades. After 9/11 they looked prescient: East-and-West conflict, civilizations at war. Or were they just a shape?"[11]

---

[10] Hustvedt, Siri: The Blazing World. New York: Simon & Schuster 2014, p. 129.
[11] Idem, p. 170.

In a similar vein, the novel also accounts how after 9/11 artists themselves felt compelled to change their own aesthetics. Culturally resounding events such as September 11, the novel seems to suggest, not only contaminate interpretation but also engender a need for aesthetic shift and a commitment on the part of the artist that transcends the boundaries of representation. They formulate an ethos of art production and perception, one that must necessarily acknowledge the presence of these events as regulatory 'primal scenes'. This double shift even became the topic of a 2012 exhibition at the Museum of Modern Art. Entitled *September 11*, the exhibition gathered a series of artworks, most of which were not necessarily connected to 9/11 but were close enough to force the audience to come to terms with the idea that while the works themselves had suffered no alterations in the meantime their perception had in fact changed in the aftermath of the events. "The exhibition", as Michael H. Miller notes in the *Observer*, "is more about how September 11, 2001 changed the experience of viewing art after the fact, and less about the day itself. This new kind of context gave certain works a more menacing appearance."[12]

A similarly striking example can be found in Don DeLillo's novel *Falling Man*, where a still life painting by Giorgio Morandi, showing a series of household items (boxes, biscuit tins, and bottles), appears to be weighed down by the same artistic prescience with regards to 9/11. It is worthwhile to note that Morandi's paintings, much like Rune's 'colored crosses' from Hustvedt's novel, had been conceived and exhibited more than fifty years before 9/11:

> Two of the taller items were dark and somber, with smoky marks and smudges, and one of them was partly concealed by a long-necked bottle. The bottle was a bottle, white. The two dark objects, too obscure to name, were the things that Martin was referring to. "What do you see?" he said. She saw what he saw. She saw the towers.[13]

The two dark objects in Morandi's painting could have been any two household objects as the series itself suggests. Yet, after September 11, their

---

[12] Miller, Michael H.: An Associative Trip at MoMA PS1's "September 11" Exhibition. In: http://observer.com/2011/09/an-associative-trip-at-moma-ps1s-september-11-exhibit (31.01.2017).

[13] DeLillo, Don: Falling Man. London: Picador 2011, p. 49.

obscurity and lack of a definite signifier take on a precise meaning. The mere resemblance to the Twin Towers makes them appear as representations of the towers themselves and the dark implications that come with that interpretation. In a similar manner, George Segal's sculpture titled *Woman on a Park Bench*, mounted as part of MoMA PS1's *September 11* exhibition, corroborates the same kind of interpretation process. When the show was mounted at MoMA in 2012 the artist had been dead for more than ten years, and his artwork first came to the light of day well before 9/11. Yet, the woman in the sculpture, of complete whiteness as if covered in white powder, could have been easily seen, akin to the 'little mutant' in Burden's art installation, as one of the survivors who had fled the clouds of dust coming from the falling towers.[14]

The same process of dialogic simultaneity becomes apparent even in the case of the discourse(s) surrounding the American 'war on terror'. To include even examples from popular culture, consider for instance the atmosphere of government surveillance portrayed in Netflix's original series *Stranger Things* released in July 2016. Though set in 1983 the audience of the series could only perceive this atmosphere from the point of view of the Edward Snowden leaks and the ensuing surveillance scandals that dominated the mass media immediately after. When Mr. Wheeler, the oblivious dad from *Stranger Things*, tells his wife to trust a pack of shady government officials because the government is always on their side, somehow that does not ring true anymore considering recent events. Much like the works of art in Hustvedt's and DeLillo's novels, these images become prescient and almost an admonition directed at those who, in their daily ignorance, 'had not seen it coming' even in the 1980s.

Now, taking these examples into consideration one might begin to see a connecting thread. Even though these representations do not make specific references to the events of September 11 or the ensuing 'war on terror' along with their subordinate discourses, they tend to have "circulating signifiers"[15] that can be easily exploited by a culturally dominating event or a 'selfish event' (following Richard Dawkins' notion

---

[14] Lehigh University Art Galleries: George Segal: Woman on a Park Bench, 1998. In: http://www.luag.org/event/george-segal-woman-on-park-bench-1998 (31.01.2017).

[15] Willis: Portents of the Real (note 9), p. 15.

of the "selfish gene"[16]). This interpretative intrusion occurs not only at the level of succeeding cultural discourses (consider, for instance, the examples from Hustvedt's novel) but also at the level of preceding cultural discourses (consider, for instance, the Morandi painting in DeLillo's novel), up to the point where even cultural artifacts, that previously bore no inherent connection to the events themselves, begin to gain new significance in the aftermath of the occurrence of those events. These become prescient in a bizarre kind of way.

Such was the case, for instance, of an episode from Van Partible's American animated television series *Johnny Bravo* that was aired on April 27, 2001, on Cartoon Network. Entitled *Chain Gang Johnny*, the episode innocuously shows in the background of one of its scenes a movie poster that features a burning tower. Ominously enough, the movie poster vaguely states that the burning tower is 'coming soon'. The movie featured in the poster does not have a title, which further fueled the imagination of conspiracy theorists around the world. The theory was later dismissed as mere coincidence.

Even more ominously and somehow ironically, on September 10, 2001, on a stage in Vegas, George Carlin, the comedian, performed a "red-hot closing bit he planned to use for his latest HBO special" in which he told his audience that he enjoys "fatal disasters with a lotta [sic] dead people."[17] It is worth noting that before this closing bit of the show Carlin had also joked about Osama bin Laden and airplane explosions due to excessive flatulence. The HBO special was released only fifteen years after its initial recording. Carlin had supposedly withheld the release on matters of taste. *The Quiet American*, a movie based on Graham Green's novel with the same title, "had been ready for distribution just after September 11, but Mira-

---

[16] In *The Selfish Gene*, Dawkins makes the argument that an individual, from an evolutionary point of view, ought to be treated as a "selfish machine, programmed to do whatever is best for its genes as a whole" and as such it will "stop at nothing" to preserve those genes (Dawkins, Richard: The Selfish Gene. Oxford: Oxford University Press 2006, p. 66).

[17] Edgers, Geoff: Fifteen years after 9/11, we can hear the only bit George Carlin ever cut for taste. In: https://www.washingtonpost.com/entertainment/fifteen-years-after-911-we-can-hear-the-only-bit-george-carlin-ever-cut-for-taste/2016/09/07/40e0312c-745c-11e6-8149-b8d05321db62_story.html?utm_term=.affe92c90513 (31.01.2017).

max's fears that the movie might be thought unpatriotic delayed the release for more than a year."[18] Like Burden's and Segal's works of art, these cultural artifacts would have become casualties of 'the falling towers' if they had been released on time.

To put it differently, culturally resounding events, such as these, have the capacity to 'contaminate' cultural artifacts that happen to be in their proximity and change the way they come to be interpreted by an interpretative community, a 'contamination' that is never unidirectional from a chronological point of view. When cultural artifacts with "circulating signifiers"[19] are placed in dialogic simultaneity, be it temporal or spatial, with these 'selfish events' they tend to be *absorbed* within the discourse of those events, especially when the events have not yet had the time to form a stable discourse of their own and they are still 'cultural stumps'. Like Dawkins' "selfish machines"[20] they will stop at nothing to preserve their cultural subsistence. To push the concept even further, one might say that such 'selfish events' ultimately perform a 'cultural appropriation' of sorts. Their 'cultural stump' enters a dialogue with fully formed cultural artifacts and they appropriate some of their features up to the point where they even contaminate those artifacts. By extension, and due to this ethos of appropriation that ultimately becomes the signature move of culturally selfish events, the cultural artifacts that further stem from this kind of events will tend to *replicate* that signature move. But cultural appropriation can be a tricky thing. To appropriate one cultural artifact or at least some of its features implies stepping away from one culture, shedding the characteristics that separate it from the others, and plunging into another. Such appropriation also infers that boundaries between cultures are always clearly set and 'accessible' by intellectual means.

This last assumption probably drove Elliot Ackerman, "whose five tours of duty in Iraq and Afghanistan left him highly decorated"[21], to write his first novel, titled suggestively *Green on Blue*.[22] Set in Afghanistan and told

---

[18] Packer: The Assassins' Gate (note 8), p. 89.
[19] Willis: Portents of the Real (note 9), p. 15.
[20] Dawkins: The Selfish Gene (note 16), p. 66.
[21] Bissell, Tom: Elliot Ackerman's 'Green on Blue'. In: https://www.nytimes.com/2015/03/01/books/review/elliot-ackermans-green-on-blue.html?_r=0 (31.01.2017).
[22] Ackerman, Elliot: Green on Blue. New York: Scribner 2015.

from the perspective of an Afghan soldier who desperately fights to maintain his wounded brother's manly dignity, Ackerman's novel has been repeatedly described by literary critics as performing an act of 'cultural appropriation', an audacious act unheard of at least in the genre of war writing. True, novels *about* the enemy are common in times of war, but Ackerman does more than that. *Green on Blue* lets readers linger, at least for the duration of the reading, in the very mind of the enemy, who, in the end, is not much of an enemy after all, but the peon caught in the vicious whirlpool of a war in which money has become a "weapons system", to use a phrase from Phil Klay's *Redeployment*.[23]

Yet, besides the typical reactions that a novel narrated from the perspective of the 'enemy' could ultimately trigger, and besides the ideology of the conqueror/winner lurking in the backstage of such denunciations of 'cultural appropriation', it is my contention that Ackerman's novel also offers precious insight precisely into how discourses surrounding such historical events as the terrorist attacks of September 11 and the 'war on terror' perform these interpretative intrusions by setting up a dialogue between two cultural artifacts. One way to assess the degree of this intrusion would be to bring two other cultural artifacts, one pertaining to and imbued with the culture of the one performing the 'cultural appropriation', namely Cormac McCarthy's novel *Blood Meridian*, and the other pertaining to the culture of the 'enemy', namely Hassan Blasim's collection of short stories, *The Corpse Exhibition: And Other Stories of Iraq*.

Though Ackerman explicitly stated that "while the American West wasn't 'front and center' in his mind while writing, 'the American counterinsurgency campaign was, and so by default, the Indian Wars became a layer in understanding how Americans behave in these types of war'."[24] Worth noting from this point of view are the novel's frequent covert references to the American West and the Indian Wars, which, besides being pertinent because of the similarities between the Afghan landscape and that of the American West, also attest to a cultural recognition of preexisting narratives. In fact, a great number of vets identify McCarthy's *Blood Meridian*

---

[23] Klay, Phil: Redeployment. New York: The Penguin Press 2014, p. 77.
[24] Castner, Brian: Afghanistan: A Stage Without a Play. In: https://lareviewofbooks.org/article/afghanistan-stage-without-play (31.01.2017).

as the novel that best describes Afghanistan for several reasons that are not as striking as they look.[25]

The resemblance is mostly visible in the way the landscape is described in Ackerman's and McCarthy's novels. On one of his first missions with the Special Lashkar, a military group supported with American money to maintain a balance of power and influence in the region, the narrator, Aziz, describes the Afghan mountains in animalistic terms, giving them the characteristics of a mouth that "swallows" the convoy, the ravine that "rolled out like a sloppy tongue"[26], descriptions that recall some of those present in McCarthy's *Blood Meridian*: "the cotton eye of the moon squatted at broad day in the throat of the mountains."[27] From this point of view, both Ackerman's *Green on Blue* and McCarthy's *Blood Meridian* seem to portray a geography whose constitution is imbued with fear, a feeling prompted by a nature that refuses to be something other than a stubborn force, that refuses to accommodate human presence. In both novels nature has its own impenetrable rhythms, it follows cycles and unwritten rules.

Along the roads travelled by the protagonists of the two novels, one can almost hear the same sounds, the same barking dogs, see the same "low mud houses"[28], and sometimes even encounter the same characters. Consider, for instance, the old hermit whom 'the kid' from *Blood Meridian* encounters towards the beginning of the novel, an old man who is so much like Mumtaz from *Green on Blue*, both offering comfort to the protagonists. "The family of itinerant musicians" who "were dressed in fools' costumes with stars and halfmoons embroidered on"[29] reemerge under a similar guise in Ackerman's novel as "travelling musicians looking for work."[30] There is even something in Aziz's demeanor that reflects the behavior of 'the kid' from *Blood Meridian*. Both protagonists are young and unknowing, and their education, or lack of it, is not aligned with the violently changing political environment, an aspect which in turn reinforces their malleability. Yet, the references to the American West are at their peak of visibility par-

---

[25] Idem.
[26] Ackerman: Green on Blue (note 22), p. 51.
[27] McCarthy, Cormac: Blood Meridian. London: Picador 2015, p. 81.
[28] Idem, p. 90.
[29] Idem, p. 82.
[30] Ackerman: Green on Blue (note 22), p. 96.

ticularly when the narrator tells how their military company had been divided into two groups with revealing names, the Tomahawks and the Comanches. The split, Aziz explains, had been done not only for strategic purposes but also because their American sponsor, the ghostly Mr. Jack, "had a great affection for the American West"[31].

Yet, it is my contention that this is the issue with Ackerman's attempt at 'cultural appropriation'. Though the novel is written from the perspective of an Afghan soldier, Aziz is still the beholder of an 'American gaze', or, to put it more bluntly, an 'Americanizing gaze'. Aziz inherits some parts of that myth of the self-made man. This is particularly visible towards the end of the novel, where Aziz emerges triumphant as a spy in an American spy movie, as someone who has reached a superior understanding, despite his limited education, of the very war he had been fighting in and of the forces that come into play. His 'Americanizing gaze' is also visible when he goes back to visit his maimed brother under the guise of deceit to tell him that he had been apprenticed to a merchant in Kabul and that he was doing the work of an honest man. Aziz acts like an American when, while still fighting for the Special Lashkar, he pounds on the top of the car to let the driver know that they are all ready to go. The gesture, somehow an awkward imitation of Hollywood action movies, has the same hollow ring as the scene in which 'the kid' from *Blood Meridian* enters a bar and all the men inside "quit talking when he entered"[32]. Most importantly, that presence of spirit is there when he tells his imagined readers that Mr. Jack wrongly assumed that they, Afghans, "did not understand what it meant to be named after the Indians of his country, but we understood. To us, it seemed a small but misguided sort of insult. For our tribes had never been conquered."[33] For an uneducated Afghan soldier, Aziz seems to know an awful lot about Native Americans.

Still, the novel's cultural appropriation works best particularly when members of the US occupation forces come to be portrayed throughout the novel. Besides the occasional American soldiers that appear in contrast with the Afghan soldiers due to the size and shape of their bodies, the only instance of American presence that somewhat strikes a chord is that of Mr.

---

[31] Idem, p. 51.
[32] McCarthy: Blood Meridian (note 27), p. 21.
[33] Ackerman: Green on Blue (note 22), p. 51.

Jack, whose ghostly presence matches in tone the almost carnivalesque appearance of the Comanches and the Apaches in McCarthy's *Blood Meridian*. Mysterious, coming and going only during the night in a pitch-dark vehicle, Mr. Jack stands out chiefly because of his blinding white teeth, his ridiculous wardrobe, "his shalwar kameez [that] still held the creases from where it'd been folded in plastic packaging,"[34] and his American way of speaking *Pashto*.

One way to test the accuracy of this instant of cultural appropriation would be to look for similar textual instances in narratives written by those within the culture that is being appropriated and see how they engage in dialogue with each other. The example that comes nearest to that of Mr. Jack is the representation of "the blonds"[35] in Hassan Blasim's short story *The Madman of Freedom Square*, included in *The Corpse Exhibition*.[36] Albeit the narrative does not specify overtly that the two blonds are American, their narrative seems to follow a prescribed structure: two blonds, most likely a reference to the color of their skin and hair, come to town and suddenly everyone is getting a raise, the town's infrastructure develops, the usual tropes of American financial support within the discourse of the 'war on terror'. Soon enough, akin to Mr. Jack with his blindingly white teeth and eyes drained of color, the blonds acquire a certain mythical aura around their presence. "The local women", the narrative goes,

> attributed to the baraka or spiritual power of the blonds the fact that their husbands, who worked sweeping the streets or as school janitors in the city center, had all received pay raises. The husbands, who had been skeptical about the baraka of the two men, soon stopped scoffing, when the government decided to install electricity at the beginning of winter.[37]

The very presence of these two men bears an uncanniness akin to the presence of Mr. Jack in Ackerman's *Green on Blue*. This mode of describing American presence, however, has apparently turned into a trope and is not

---

[34] Idem, p. 217.
[35] Blasim, Hassan: The Corpse Exhibition: And Other Stories of Iraq. New York: Penguin Group 2014, p. 81.
[36] Idem, p. 78.
[37] Blasim: The Corpse Exhibition (note 35), p. 83.

limited to fictional representations. In *The Assassins' Gate*, while describing a formal meeting between American officials and Iraqi exiles that took place at the London Hilton Metropole in 2002, George Packer resorts to the same vocabulary. "Sprinkled among them", Packer notes the contrast, "palely lurking, were the Americans. [...] These Americans moved through the throng of Iraqi exiles with the glowing and watchful fervor of missionaries among the converted."[38]

Going back to the notion of 'selfish events' and trying to give an answer to the question why interpretative intrusions such as these occur, it is my contention that any such event, due to the immediate effects of its occurrence, does not have the time and the cultural resources to create a discourse that could explain the complexity of that event, and as such it resorts to cultural artifacts that happen to be in its proximity so as to sustain its cultural presence at least until a separate discourse, of its own, has been created and culturally reinforced. This process is most visible, for instance, in the kind of comparisons that politicians, and other figures that retain high amounts of cultural capital, make in the immediate aftermath of violent and sudden events. Such is the case, just to give an example, of how the attacks of *September 11* were frequently compared to the attacks on *Pearl Harbor*. At that point in time, *9/11* lacked an eloquent discourse that could make it culturally sustainable and therefore it needed another, more eloquent discourse, to act as cultural scaffolding. And until the 'war on terror' does not form its own eloquent discourse it will keep resorting to other discourses for cultural sustenance. For the time being, it thrives only within this constant dialogue between cultural artifacts, images, ideas, texts.

---

[38] Packer: The Assassins' Gate (note 8), pp. 88f.

Adaptation as Intercultural Dialogue: August von Kotzebue on the British Stage

Pia Martin

Literary scholars of British Romanticism traditionally focused their research on poetic and novelistic works wherefore drama of the Romantic period remains a highly under-researched genre until today. This neglect stems from the fact that the majority of dramas produced during the Romantic period have to be categorized as popular literature and many of those plays indeed may be regarded to be of low aesthetic value due to their repetitive plots, stereotypical characters, reduced complexity and use of rather simple language. This applies to original compositions, but even more so to dramatic adaptations which suffered and still suffer from a dual neglect: as popular literature and as mere adaptations. As adaptive practice necessarily establishes overt and explicit connections between a source text and its adaptation, its dialogic potential renders dramatic adaptations of the Romantic period attractive for comparative studies, because contemporary adapters sought out inspiration across generic, linguistic, temporal, national and cultural boundaries.

Intercultural adaptations are especially interesting in the context of this collection because they require the adapter and potentially also the audience to engage with a different culture, enable the adapter to comment on both source and target culture and grant modern readers insights into the Romantics' understanding of foreign cultures. For a conclusive comprehension of the mechanisms of Romantic adaptations a short introduction to recent findings in adaptation theory will be provided in the following. Moreover, information will be given on German and British cultural history in order to contextualize the following analyses of the two most famous adaptations of August von Kotzebue's works – *Lovers' Vows* (1798) and *Pizarro* (1799). It will be shown how the adapters, Elizabeth Inchbald and Richard Brinsley Sheridan, appropriate elements from the German sources for the British audience, creating a new distinctly different work in a different context. However, as adaptations are "deliberate, announced, and extended revisitations of prior works"[1], the adapter not only creates a British end product but further initiates a dialogue between German sources and British adaptions. The reception of this dialogue is influenced by prejudices about German literature and the British audience's limited or often even non-existent first-hand knowledge of said German literature in general and Kotzebue's works in particular. Therefore, the adapters' strategies for ensuring that their productions are received as adaptations will be considered in order to shed light on the importance of cultural mediation in the context of adaptive practice.

The Processual Nature of Adaptations

The tools for a profitable investigation of Sheridan's and Inchbald's usage of the German source texts have been provided by recent developments in adaptation studies. Instead of placing value judgements and normative fidelity discussions in the centre of their research, theorists like Thomas Leitch, Julie Sanders, Linda Hutcheon and Patrick Cattrysse promote a target-oriented approach. Patrick Cattrysse for example argues that adaptations are phenomena which are situated in a specific place-time context and function in particular ways in this target context. For the purpose of this paper, this means that the adaptations by both Inchbald and Sheridan have to be read in the context of late eighteenth century Britain. However, in order to describe the position of an adaptation and its function in the target context it has to be acknowledged that the term 'adaptation' not only refers to a product but also to a process whose mechanisms should be understood as the result of the adapter's engagement with and interpretation of the source text. Referring to Romantic translation practices, Frederick Burwick points out:

> Translation for the theatre was shaped by a presumed need for cultural adaptation. [...] One tug-of-war in the process of translation was between the principle of fidelity to the original and the principle of cultural adaptation.[2]

---

[1] Hutcheon, Linda: A Theory of Adaptation. Oxon, New York: Routledge 2006, p. XIV.
[2] Burwick, Frederick: Romantic Theories of Translation. In: The Wordsworth Circle 39/3 (2008), pp. 68–74, here p. 69.

Burwick ascribes the necessity of catering for the requirements of the target culture to translation practices which increasingly applied to the process of adapting material for the British stage. Therefore, intercultural adapters had to omit or alter what was morally, politically or culturally uninteresting or inappropriate for their target audience. A conclusive reading of intercultural adaptations thus has to take into account not only the end product itself but must further strive to trace the adaptive production process by comparing source and target texts.

Furthermore, when dealing with adaptations, it is not only the production process and the resultant product that differ from original compositions, but also the reception process. In her influential book *A Theory of Adaptation*, Linda Hutcheon demonstrates that

> [f]or the reader, spectator, or listener, adaptation *as adaptation* is unavoidably a kind of intertextuality *if the receiver is acquainted with the adapted text*. It is an ongoing dialogical process, as Mikhail Bakhtin would have said, in which we compare the work we already know with the one we are experiencing [...].[3]

It is the readers' knowledge of both versions which initiates a dialogue between adaptation and source inevitably influencing each other. Therefore, in the following my focus will first be on the context from which the British versions emerge in order to argue that the plays can be read as *British* ones which are deeply embedded in the historical, political and socio-cultural context of *British* Romanticism. Ultimately, I will show how these anglicized adaptations can be understood as a reaction to the statements made in the source texts and how Inchbald and Sheridan make use of paratexts in order to influence the reception of this dialogic aspect of their adaptations. Although the two adapters follow different strategies, their intentions will be shown to be identical: to strengthen the cultural, moral and political superiority of the British and to promote adapters as important and even necessary mediators between cultures.

---

[3] Hutcheon: A Theory of Adaptation (note 1), p. 21. Emphasis in original.

The Reception of Kotzebue in Germany and England

August von Kotzebue was by far the most successful playwright of the late eighteenth and early nineteenth century, with 227 plays published during his lifetime or posthumously. Not surprisingly, DIE ZEIT recently explained: What is commonly understood to be the age of Goethe in Germany should rather be called the age of Kotzebue.[4] What differentiates the playwright from his esteemed contemporaries like Goethe and Schiller, however, is that he did not produce what is understood to be high literature but catered for popular tastes, which is the reason why his works have been banished from the German canon. Nevertheless, during his lifetime, Kotzebue's artistic flexibility rendered him extremely popular among theatre-goers. The impressive generic variety of his productions – including tragedy, comedy, historical and sentimental plays, travesties, operas, parodies, satires and melodramas – goes along with a plurality of topics portrayed by Kotzebue who made sure to meet the tastes of his multifaceted audience, for instance by staging types like the revolutionary, the bourgeois and the aristocrat – without preferring one over the other.[5]

Not all the topics addressed by Kotzebue, however, met complete public approval and August von Kotzebue himself as well as his works evoked critical reactions not only for aesthetical reasons but also for political ones. Indeed, Kotzebue's works often include characters or incidents which could easily be interpreted as politically subversive and whenever his plays critically dealt with current social, moral or political issues more than a few of his contemporaries excoriated him. At times of political turmoil caused by the French Revolution and Napoleon's quest to conquer Europe, his repeatedly critical depiction of aristocratic characters, for instance, was already enough to rise suspicion of the

---

[4] Vgl. Erenz, Benedikt: Im Uni-Himmel. In: DIE ZEIT, No. 1, 29.12.2016, p. 65.
[5] Karin Pendle similarly states: "He could seem to be revolutionary, reactionary, middle-class, aristocratic, sentimental, rational, or exotic without really committing himself to any one philosophy or outlook. [...] Thus everyone in the audience could respond to him with a nod of recognition." In: Pendle, Karin: August von Kotzebue, Librettist. In: The Journal of Musicology 3/2 (1984), pp. 196–213, here p. 213.

author's political tendencies.[6] Moreover, Kotzebue's characters did not always stay within the confines of propriety as illegitimacy; adultery and even polygamy often remain unpunished in his plays.

In England, Kotzebue and his works evoked similar reactions, and most contemporary critics and theatre-goers agreed that he had to be discredited as a popular dramatist who aimed at financial gain through mass production but was incapable of producing high literature. Thomas Dutton claims in the preface to a satirical poem about Kotzebue:

> The present degraded state of the English drama; the little encouragement held out to the native genius of the country – nay I ought rather to say the *actual conspiracy* formed against it by the extravagant and senseless patronage of German literature, to the neglect of our own – the infatuation for the incoherent rhapsodies of Kotzebue; [...] loudly demand the aid of honest satire, and the intervention of upright, dauntless criticism [...] to rescue genius from the contamination of false taste, and the tyranny of a foreign usurper.[7]

As Dutton's harsh criticism exemplifies, many critics were dissatisfied with the current quality of British drama – deeply regretting the absence of geniuses like Shakespeare among their nationals. They accused not only German pieces but also French plays flooding the British stages for the disparaged state of their theatrical culture and for threatening the position of their national literature, calling for more genuinely British productions.

As the political developments on the continent had caused what Mortensen terms 'Europhobia'[8] – a chronic suspicion of everything European – the British intellectual elite condemned Kotzebue's supposed political danger more harshly than their German contemporaries, fearing the

---

[6] The personal life of the playwright further led many of his contemporaries to doubt his loyalty towards his fatherland. The fact that he worked as a consul in Russia and was married to a Russian woman, for instance, generated rumours of him being a Russian spy. Also when he spent some time in Paris in the early 1790s after the death of his wife, heresy spread that he sympathized with France and revolutionary sentiments and in fact had joined the Jacobite movement.

[7] Dutton, Thomas: The Wise Man of the East; or, The Apparition of Zoroaster, the Son of Oromases, to the Theatrical Midwife of Leicester-Fields. A Satirical Poem. London: H. D. Symonds 1800, p. Vf. Emphasis in original.

[8] See Mortensen, Peter: British Romanticism and Continental Influences. Writing in an Age of Europhobia. Basingstoke: Palgrave Macmillan 2004, p. 9.

subversive influence his plays might have on the less-reflective audience at the theatres under the disguise of popular entertainment. Robert Southey, for instance, maintained in a letter to a friend that Kotzebue's plays "are so thoroughly Jacobinical in tendency, they create Jacobinical feelings – almost irresistibly – in every one that I have yet seen […] some old prejudice or old principle is attacked."[9] Therefore, in the anti-Jacobin climate of the 1790s, a strict censorship was advocated that should protect the British public. In fact, the British theatrical system was well equipped for controlling the repertoire of the theatres, because already the Licensing Act of 1737[10] granted the Lord Chamberlain, also called the Examiner of Plays, full power of licensing plays for the two patent theatres in London – Drury Lane and Covent Garden.[11] Although the Lord Chamberlain strictly rejected or censored plays, which were critical of the existing political, social, cultural or moral standards of Britain, many authors infused their plays with hidden allusions to reformatory ideas. As Romantic drama enabled them to reach the largest possible audience and readership of the largest possible variety, it was the perfect communication channel for spreading ideas contrary to the conservative standards.

Elizabeth Inchbald's Adaptation *Lovers' Vows*

With *Lovers' Vows*, an adaptation of Kotzebue's *Das Kind der Liebe* (1791), Elizabeth Inchbald provided her British audience with a version which, plot-wise, was rather close to the German source text. One of the two plot

---

[9] Southey, Robert: 395. Robert Southey to Charles Watkin Williams Wynn, 5 April 1799. In: https://www.rc.umd.edu/editions/southey_letters/Part_Two/HTML/letterEEd.26.395.html (09.09.2016).

[10] In Germany, in comparison, a similar censorship policy was not established until the Circular-Rescript of 1820.

[11] In 1660, after the Puritan Interregnum, Charles II had granted the exclusive right to the production of theatre in London to dramatists Thomas Killigrew and William Davenant. Over the centuries those patents became firmly associated with the staging of legitimate spoken word drama, namely tragedy and comedy, at the theatres royal, Drury Lane and Covent Garden. Other theatres were only allowed to show illegitimate forms without spoken dialogues like burletta, pantomime and later also melodrama.

lines presents Wilhelmine (Agatha in Inchbald), an impoverished social outcast who was several years earlier abandoned by Baron Wildenhaim when she was carrying their illegitimate child. Later in the play this child, Frederick, decides to beg for his starving mother and in the course of this attacks his father because he does not give as much money as Frederick would like to have. The Baron, however, pardons him and when he learns of Frederick's origin accepts him as his legitimate son and marries Wilhelmine. The second plot line deals with the Baron's daughter from a previous marriage, Amalie, who refuses a suitor approved by her father (Count von der Mulde) as a possible husband and wants to marry her tutor, a priest. After some objections from her father's side she finally is allowed to wed the man she loves.

Although some of Inchbald's changes at first glance appear to moderate potentially subversive elements for a British audience, a thorough analysis of *Lovers' Vows* reveals them to be part of a general tendency of turning from political issues to moral ones. The most interesting character in this context is Inchbald's version of Kotzebue's Count von der Mulde. In the German source, the Count is a superficial and ignorant representative of the upper-class who returned to Germany because he did not feel safe in Paris anymore: "*Gr.* [...] ich passire das Palais Royal, ich weiß von nichts – tout d'un Coup ich sehe mich umringt von einem Haufen Lumpengesindel, man stößt mich hier, man zwickt mich da [...]. Man prügelt mich, foi d'honette homme!"[12] The Count's account of how he was chased by a mob in Paris reveals that he lived in the French capital completely uninformed of and disinterested in the political developments in France in the wake of the Revolution. Moreover, his highly artificial German-French code-switching characterizes the Count as a mere figure of fun whose worries are restricted to his own well-being and reputation: "*Gr.* [...] aber dennoch [...] mein Savoir vivre, meine Formirung, der Pli den man an mir remarquirt, der ist ganz Französisch, ganz Parisisch."[13] As a wealthy aristocrat,

---

[12] Kotzebue, August von: Das Kind der Liebe. Ein Schauspiel in fünf Akten. Leipzig: Paul Gotthelf Kummer 1791, p. 130f. Transl.: "*Gr.* [...] I pass the Palais Royal, I don't know anything – suddenly I find myself surrounded by a bunch of riffraff, they prod me here, they pinch me there [...] They beat me, a reputable man!"

[13] Idem, p. 131. Transl.: "*Gr.* [...] Nevertheless [...] my sophistication, my character, the knack one observes in me, is completely French, completely Parisian."

the Count does not share the worries and desperate needs of the lower orders and has neither understanding nor sympathy for them nor is he inclined to use his more powerful position to fulfil his social duty to help them. Kotzebue's "Count is a *social* character and he stands for social ills, for the abuse of privileges that goes unpunished"[14], because in the prevailing hierarchical society the privileged people, like Count von der Mulde, do not fulfil their social duties towards the lower classes. The fact that he is portrayed as a highly ridiculous figure of fun can be read as an expression of sympathy with the revolution in France and the egalitarian values it promotes.

Inchbald's adaptation strips the original version of the Count off his representational function as an insensitive aristocrat and omits his allusions to the French Revolution as well as the code-switching which turned him into a rather ridiculous fob in Kotzebue's version. Christoph Bode points out that through her changes in this character "the political and critical dimension of the original play is much diminished."[15] However, while this certainly holds true for the political implications of the character, Inchbald does not delete the Count's critical potential but rather shifts its expressiveness from the political to the moral dimension. In fact, Inchbald's Count Cassel is an impertinent coxcomb who shares close affiliation with the type of the Restoration rake. While Kotzebue's Count leaves the Wildenhaims after he finds out that Amalie will not inherit her father's fortune, Inchbald has the Baron dismiss the Count as unfit for his daughter in an added scene,[16] in which Wildenhaim harshly

---

[14] Bode, Christoph: Unfit for an English Stage? Inchbald's *Lovers' Vows* and Kotzebue's *Das Kind der Liebe*. In: European Romantic Review 16/3 (2005), pp. 297–309, here p. 303.

[15] Idem, p. 303.

[16] "*Baron.* Amazing insensibility! And can you hold your head erect while you acknowledge perfidy [the betrayal of the other woman]? [...] / *Count.* [...] let me assure you, my Lord, that, although, from the extreme delicacy of your honor, you have ever through life shuddered at seduction; yet, there are constitutions, and there are circumstances, in which it can be palliated. / *Baron.* Never (*violently.*) / *Count.* Not in a grave, serious, reflecting man such as *you*, I grant. But in a gay, lively, inconsiderate, flimsy, frivolous coxcomb, such as myself, it is excusable [...]." In: Inchbald, Elizabeth: Lovers' Vows. A Play in Five Acts. Dublin: Thomas Burnside 1799, p. 43f. Emphasis in original.

criticizes the Count for having tricked another young woman into an intimate relationship with the promise of marriage which he never fulfilled. The Count, however, appears to be unconscious of any guilt which aggravates his immoral and reckless behaviour towards women. Where Kotzebue's Count ignores his political duties towards the needs of the lower classes, Inchbald's version refuses to fulfil his moral ones towards women he sexually engages with.

Another decisive alteration is a general change of focus in the adaptation, which turns away from presenting both couples – Wildenhaim and Agatha and Amelia and Anhalt – as happily joined in the end but gives prominence to the younger couple and Amelia's active role in their union. Although Kotzebue's Amalie declares her love to Anhalt in the most forward manner possible, exclaiming "Ich liebe Sie"[17], the original girl appears to be the more innocent one who can even be characterized as an example of "Rousseau's simple child of nature"[18]. In the German version, Amalie's ignorance towards love, matrimony and sexuality excuses her straightforward conduct. In Inchbald, in contrast, Amelia is presented as more mature and well-aware of the scandal a marriage between her and Anhalt would cause. She wants to marry the man she loves irrespective of social conventions and class differences. When she persuades Anhalt to forget the class issues possibly preventing a union of theirs, she promotes love instead convenience to be the deciding factor for marriage. Therefore, Inchbald's exemplary marriage is facilitated by the efforts of a daring woman who, in contrast to Kotzebue's innocent Rousseauean child, is the agent of her own happiness. In the case of Amelia, the authoress thus presents the British audience with a woman whose conduct towards marriage and class issues deviates farther from Britain's moral standards than the German source.

---

[17] Kotzebue: Das Kind der Liebe (note 12), p. 91.
[18] Bode, Christoph: August von Kotzebue. In: Frederick Burwick (Ed.): The Encyclopedia of Romantic Literature. Malden/Mass.: Wiley-Blackwell 2012, pp. 734–742, here p. 739.

Richard Brinsley Sheridan's Adaptation *Pizarro*

In *Pizarro*, an adaptation of Kotzebue's *Die Spanier in Peru* (1796),[19] Sheridan choses a completely different strategy from Inchbald by adopting the political implications of the play and even amplifying them for the British context. The play presents the story of the Spanish conquest of Peru. The main characters on the Spanish side are the cruel leader of the Spaniards, Pizarro, and his mistress Elvira who left her home and family to follow his ambitious campaign. Among the Peruvians the military leader Rolla is supported by his best friend Alonzo, who left his native Spanish people to support the enemy. During a major battle Alonzo is captivated but Rolla secretly replaces him aided by Elvira. When the Spanish captivate Alonzo's child, Rolla manages to escape with it but is injured on the flight and dies shortly after. Hence, Kotzebue's original is basically compatible with the historical facts of Pizarro's conquest of Peru by letting the Peruvians, who are portrayed as innocent, noble savages, be defeated by the gold-craving Spanish invaders.[20] The fact that Kotzebue's portrayal of the two nations clearly favours the innocent natives over the invaders suggests a reading of the play as a radical promotion of the suppressed. When considering the publication and reception context of Kotzebue's play in 1796, during Napoleon's extensive military conquest in Italy, the tragic ending raises sympathy for conquered peoples and criticizes recklessly invasive nations like the Spanish and the French. As it is Rolla who dies in the end and not Pizarro, however, Kotzebue does not relieve his audience with poetic justice. The fact that he refuses to sanction the conquering force, but only indirectly criticizes it, enables Kotzebue to avoid making his play a definite political statement.

Although Sheridan, like Inchbald, retains the majority of the original play's plot and thus adopts the parallel between the Spanish and the French from the German original, his adaptation cannot only be read in

---

[19] Kotzebue, August von: Die Spanier in Peru, oder Rollas Tod. Ein romantisches Trauerspiel in fünf Akten. Wien: Johann Baptist Wallishauser 1796.

[20] He remains true to historical facts in so far that the Spanish, led by Pizarro, invaded Peru, which was under the rule of Atahualpa (commonly written Ataliba), but adds fictitious characters like Rolla and Cora.

connection to the conflict between England and France but can be interpreted in the context of Britain's colonial endeavours as well. This dual reference potential results in a political ambivalence of *Pizarro*, which, depending on the context from which it is approached, can be read as either nationalistic or as a critique of British politics. As has been pointed out before, the German source was already interpretable as a comment on French politics. However, while it was acceptable to present the Spanish, symbolizing the French, as the victorious force on a German stage, because parts of the country were occupied by the French, it would have been unacceptable in an English context as France and Britain had been at war for years. On account of this, Sheridan's most decisive change of the German play is that he supplies poetic justice by adding a final combat between Alonzo and Pizarro in which Alonzo, with the help of Elvira, defeats Pizarro and forces the Spanish to surrender. A play which presents an innocent and virtuous people as the defeated party would probably not have passed censorship in Britain at a time when the threatening developments on the continent made nationalistic sentiment the major virtue to hold on to. Sheridan thus changed the historical facts in order to have the defeated Spanish forces under leadership of Pizarro represent the French while the victorious Peruvians stand for the triumphant British.

Sheridan further adds a speech of Rolla's which he gives to his army before the battle against the Spanish in order to emphasize the allusion to the conflict between France and Britain and the anti-revolutionary implications of his adaptation:

THEY, by a strange frenzy driven, fight for power, for plunder, and extended rule – WE, for our country, our altars, and our homes. – THEY follow an Adventurer whom they fear – and obey a power which they hate – WE serve a Monarch whom we love – a God whom we adore. […] They boast, they come but to improve our state, enlarge our thoughts, and free us from the yoke of error! – Yes – THEY will give enlightened freedom to *our* minds, who are themselves the slaves of passion, avarice, and pride. – They offer us their protection – Yes, such protection as vultures give to lambs – covering and devouring them! – […] Be our plain answer this: The throne WE honour is the PEOPLE'S CHOICE – […] Tell your invaders this, and tell them too, we seek no change; and, least of all, such changes as they would bring us.[21]

Rolla here tries to encourage his soldiers as well as his people in general by reminding them of the rightfulness of their cause. He condemns the Spanish invaders' motivation for their assault (greed for money and power) and for following the orders of their leader Pizarro (fear). Rolla further challenges their supposed moral, cultural and political superiority which they use as an excuse for subordinating the Peruvians. He describes the Peruvians in contrast to the Spanish, stressing that they fight for their nation, religion and family; they follow their monarch out of love and are in fact superior because they are not tainted by avarice and pride. Rolla's repeated reference to the throne and the king further makes his speech a plea not only for monarchy in general but for the British sovereign because it suggests that he is beloved by his subjects (in contrast to Luis XVI of France, who was dethroned by his dissatisfied people) which chime in with the nationalistic sentiments prevailing in Britain at the turn of the century.

The history of Rolla's speech, however, adds a political ambivalence to the play as it was not originally written for Sheridan's adaptation but is based on a speech which Sheridan himself had given in Westminster Hall on June 13, 1788, in the context of the Hastings Trail.[22] As a champion of human rights and liberty Sheridan vehemently spoke against Warren Hastings, the first Governor-general of India, because of his exploiting politics in India. The original reference point of the speech's criticism suggests

---

[21] Sheridan, Richard Brinsley: Pizarro. A Tragedy in Five Acts (1799). In: Cecil Price (Ed.): The Dramatic Works of Richards Brinsley Sheridan. Vol. 1. Oxford: Clarendon Press 1973, pp. 651–704, here p. 669. Emphasis in original.

[22] "This was British justice! this was British humanity! Mr Hastings ensures to the allies of the Company, in the strongest terms, their prosperity and his protection; the former he secures by sending an army to plunder them of their wealth, and to desolate their soil! His protection is fraught with a similar security, like that of a vulture to a lamb; grappling in its vitals! thirsting for its blood! scaring off each petty kite that hovers round; and then, with an insulting perversion of terms, calling sacrifice protection!" Sheridan, Richards Brinsley: In Support of the Impeachment of Warren Hastings, Esq., on the Second Charge. June 13, 1788. In: Modern Orator. The Speeches of the Right Honourable Richard Brinsley Sheridan. London: Aylott and Jones 1845, pp. 151–163, here p. 154.

that the Spanish in the play might also be seen as representing colonial Britain and its inhumane colonial politics. This is further emphasizes by the rhetoric Rolla uses for portraying the Peruvians as united by familial strings, believing in a natural deity and being a nation "untainted" by civilization. This description draws on the concept of the noble savage, a concept deeply embedded in colonial discourse, in order to establish a contrast between the innocent Peruvians and the Spanish invaders.

Therefore, the British context of Sheridan's adaptation adds another perspective to Kotzebue's already politically charged source text. Interestingly, while the original parallel to the French Revolution and Napoleon's conquest of Europe is highly critical of Britain's enemies and anticipates their inevitable defeat by the glorious British, the play's stance on colonial politics reverses the roles of protagonist and antagonist, passing criticism on the Empire and its exploiting politics in the colonies. Thus, as Dana van Kooy points out, "Sheridan provided his audience with two contradictory views of the British – as both victim and oppressor."[23] Taking into account the severe censorship politics in Britain at that time, the implied analogy between the two colonial powers of Spain and Britain and the resulting critical portrayal of British colonialism probably would not have been acceptable without the obvious analogy between the victorious Peruvians and the British. In any case, the political ambivalence of Sheridan's adaptation exceeds the original version's political dimension and thereby exposes the adaptation process not to be defined by a reduction or omission of the source's critical potential but by its amplification.

The Dialogic aspect of Adaptations

While the preceding analysis of the target-oriented production process has shown the adaptations of both Inchbald and Sheridan to be embedded in the political and socio-cultural context of their publications, a focus on the paratexts, which serve to direct the reception of the plays, can further grant insights into the dialogical mechanisms employed by both adapters. As

---

[23] Kooy, Dana van: Darkness Visible. The Early Melodrama of British Imperialism and the Commodification of History in Sheridan's *Pizarro*. In: Theatre Journal 64/2 (2012), pp. 179–195, here p. 194.

both plays have been shown to have critical potential in terms of their political (Sheridan) and moral (Inchbald) implications in the British target context, the fact that both adapters altered the source suggests a reading of the adaptations as critical comments on the German sources. In fact, both Inchbald and Sheridan made sure to raise their readership's awareness of their works' adaptive nature in the paratexts, which even included strategies of using their readerships knowledge or ignorance of the sources, in order to influence their reception of both original and adaptation, although the reception conditions of the two adaptations were rather dissimilar.

In the case of Inchbald, the majority of her contemporaries could not have known the original version of the play, which she compensated for by adding an extensive preface with explanatory comments on her alterations in *Lovers' Vows*, in which she encouraged a reception of the play as an intercultural adaptation by i) fashioning her adaptation as an evaluation of the source text and culture, ii) juxtaposing source and target culture and iii) promoting the importance of the adapter as a cultural mediator. In her preface Inchbald explicitly refers to her deleting the political dimension of the original Count Cassel: "the part of the Count, as in the original, would have inevitably condemned the whole play".[24] By alluding to the pro-revolutionary sentiments detectable in Kotzebue's Count von der Mulde, Inchbald activates wide-spread prejudices against Kotzebue and German drama as being radically subversive and thus implicitly contrasts German and English conventions. This also happens in the author's comments on the changes made to the character of Amelia:

> [T]he forward and unequivocal manner in which she announces her affection to her lover in the original, would have been revolting to an English audience [...]. I have endeavoured to attach the attention and sympathy of the audience, by whimsical insinuations, rather then coarse abruptness [...].[25]

Inchbald thus suggests that she has rendered Amelia a more moral character than in the original German version. However, a comparative reading

---

[24] Inchbald, Elizabeth: Preface on the First Publication of *Lovers' Vows*. In: Elizabeth Inchbald. The British Theatre; or, A Collection of Plays (1808). Vol. XXIII. Hildesheim/New York: Georg Olms Verlag 1970, pp. 3–6, here p. 3.

[25] Idem, p. 6.

of source and adaptation has revealed that Inchbald presents her audience with an even more daring woman than Kotzebue's innocent Rousseauean child. It seems that she hoped to avert criticism from her own Amelia by presenting her, in moral terms, as an improvement on Kotzebue's. Some of Inchbald's contemporaries, in fact, did not fall for this strategy but insisted on the moral deficiency of Inchbald's Amelia, despite of her endeavors to claim the contrary. A commentator in the *Porcupine*, for instance, writes that "Amelia, notwithstanding the pains which Mrs. Inchbald, the adapter of the play, has taken to polish her, still remains coarse, forward, and disgusting, and, we trust, will never be imitated by the British fair."[26] A reviewer of the *Anti-Jacobin Review* argues in a similar direction emphasising "that neither the taste of a British public will be improved, nor their morals meliorated" through the adaptation.[27]

Moreover, the question why Inchbald explicitly states in the preface to have improved Amelia's character, although she did not realize it in her adaptation, is further connected to the fact that the dialogic aspect of adaptations has to be understood as an *intercultural dialogue* in Inchbald's intercultural adaptation, which the author closely connects to mechanisms of identity construction. What Inchbald does in her preface is to evoke an image of the Germans as morally and politically degraded on the basis of their dramatic productions. When Inchbald states in her preface that German drama is "unfit [...] for an English stage"[28], the negative portrayal of the source culture functions as a counterpart to the British target culture, which is automatically perceived as superior. Although she explicitly only refers to the moral deficiencies of Kotzebue's original and only implicitly criticizes its political subversion, the overall impression her comments convey to the readers is that a divergence exists between German and British theatrical standards: What is acceptable on a German stage does not suffice the standards of British theatrical culture. In this context, the fact that Inchbald claims to have corrected Amalie's morals but actually presents her readers with a far

---

[26] Quoted in: Reitzel, William: Mansfield Park and Lovers' Vows. In: Review of English Studies 9/36 (1933), pp. 451–456, here p. 453.
[27] Anonymous: Review of *Lovers' Vows*. In: Anti-Jacobin Review and Magazine (1798), pp. 479–481, here p. 481.
[28] Inchbald: Preface on the First Publication of *Lovers' Vows* (note 24), p. 5.

more proactive female than the original character can be read as part of her strategy to reinforce British superiority over the Germans.

Elizabeth Inchbald's juxtaposition of German and British morals and culture not only praises her native culture but simultaneously legitimizes the role of the adapter as a necessary mediator between source and target culture. The quoted comments from her preface suggest that a mere translation of the German play would not have been appropriate for a British audience. On account of this, Inchbald presents herself as a mediator who deletes the dangerous and immoral tendencies of the continental plays and turns them into morally correct entertainment for the British public. The importance of the adapter is further emphasized in the prologue Inchbald adds to her adaptation, in which she explains that the play should not only entertain but that it also has moralizing implications, stating that *Lovers' Vows* is "[i]nten[ded] as well to cheer as to amend"[29]. Hence, preface and prologue suggest that the adapter, in order to achieve a satisfactory didactic effect for the British public, has to alter the German moral principle imprinted on the source text.

The role played by the adapter in the production process of intercultural adaptation became even more prominent in the discussion following the premiere of *Pizarro* and later the publication of Sheridan's authorized printed version. In fact, the substantial amount of material connected to Kotzebue's *Rolla* and Sheridan's *Pizarro*, which was accessible to the British public, initiated an extensive debate over the appropriateness of translations and adaptations. Already within the first week after *Pizarro* premiered at Drury Lane, two faithful translations by Thomas Dutton and Anne Plumptre,[30] which both stick closely to the German source text, were published. Therefore, the reception conditions of Sheridan's adaptation differed from Inchbald's as he was able to resort to a more knowledgeable audience and readership. The reactions to *Pizarro* can be traced in numerous articles published in newspapers and literary magazines which, like the following, portray the comparative endeavours of Sheridan's contemporaries.

---

[29] Inchbald: Lovers' Vows (note 16), p. 3.
[30] Dutton, Thomas: Pizarro in Peru, or the Death of Rolla. London: Printed for W. West 1799; Plumptre, Anne: Pizarro. The Spaniards in Peru; or, the Death of Rolla. London: Printed for R. Phillips 1799. Plumptre's translation was published May 29 and Dutton's June 3.

> We have carried with us to the theatre the translations [by Plumptre and Dutton], both jointly and severally, and found, that the passages, which delighted, affected, and instructed us the most, were not in either of the translations. The *body* may be Kotzebüe's, but the SOUL is Sheridan's.[31]

The quotation taken from the *Historical Magazine* of June 1799 shows that, on the one hand, critics focused on questions of fidelity, tracing the similarities and differences between source and adaptation with the help of the available literal translations. On the other hand, it points out that their reading did not assume a pre-existent hierarchical structure established on the basis of originality, which is suggested by the fact that the above-quoted reviewer of *Pizarro* praises Sheridan's alterations although his production is adaptive and not original.

In fact, Sheridan himself encouraged his readers to take part in the discussion on the merits of adaptation and translation by tracing the dialogue between the different versions of the story. In the advertisement to the first edition of *Pizarro*, Sheridan explains that because of the two already existing translations of Kotzebue's *Rolla*, "the Public are in possession of all the materials necessary to form a judgement on the merits and defects of the Play performed at Drury Lane Theatre."[32] Although Sheridan, in contrast to Inchbald, refuses to provide his readers with an extensive explanation of his changes, he nonetheless makes sure that his readers receive his play in connection with Kotzebue's original. Indeed, publications like John Britton's *Sheridan and Kotzebue*, which was published shortly after Sheridan's play and not only compares Kotzebue's and Sheridan's version but further provides information on the historical context of the plays as well as on Jean Françoise Marmontel's novel *Les Incas, ou la destruction de l'Empire du Pérou* (1777), which formed the basis for Kotzebue's German drama, testifies to a general awareness of *Pizarro's* adaptive nature. They prove Sheridan successful in his endeavours to encourage a comparative reading of his drama while simultaneously enabling his readers to detect the dialogic aspect of adaptive practice.

---

[31] Quoted in: Britton, John: Sheridan and Kotzebue. London: J. Fairburn 1799, p. 131. Emphasis in original.

[32] Sheridan: Pizarro (note 21), p. 652.

On the title page of the various editions of *Pizarro* the play is described as having been "taken from the German drama of Kotzebue"[33] which, on the one hand chimes in with Sheridan's encouragement of a comparative approach to his adaptation and, on the other hand, already hints at the fact that it is not *translated* but *taken* from Kotzebue's original. This is also emphasized by the additional information that the German play was "adapted to the English stage by Richard Brinsley Sheridan."[34] Thus, Sheridan suggests what Inchbald states explicitly: What is presented at the German theatres cannot be transferred to the British stages without alterations by a skillful adapter. In the context of the preceding comparative reading of *Rolla* and *Pizarro*, this reference to the source suggests two interpretations: First, it implies that a mere translation would not have been sufficient because the political implications of the source (leaving Pizarro/Napoleon unpunished) were unacceptable for the British readership and second, Sheridan, like Inchbald, promotes himself as an adapter who is a necessary mediator between the German and the British stages.

The preceding analysis has shown how adaptations cannot only be understood as entities fitting the requirements of their target context but also as explicit reactions to their sources. When literature crosses cultural boundaries, adaptive practice plays an important role in dialogic interactions not merely between texts but also between cultures. In this context, the focus on the text and paratext has revealed that intercultural adaptive practice is defined by a variety of factors influencing the resultant target text. The preceding investigation of *Lovers' Vows* and *Pizarro* has exemplified that British adapters like Inchbald and Sheridan made sure to raise their readers' awareness of the adaptive and thereby dialogical nature of their productions. While the former explained the production process explicitly, ensuring that those readers who did not know the German source text realized its moral inferiority and esteemed her endeavours not merely as an inexpert adapter but as a cultural mediator, the latter only pointed out his role as a necessary mediator but left the evaluation of *Rolla* and *Pizarro* to his readership, suggesting that the literal translations already at hand suffice to realize the superiority of his adaptation in the British context. Therefore, a dialogic perspective on adaptation grants fruitful insights

---

[33] Idem, p. 651.
[34] Idem.

into the complex structures of adaptive practice defined by the demands of the source and target readerships, the social and political situation of source and target culture, negotiations of authorship as well as the reception conditions of the adaptations.

Literature and Democracy: Dialogue and Persuasion in Charles Dickens's Novels

Lisa-Marie Teubler

This paper develops a few aspects of my doctoral dissertation work and discusses them in connection with the theme of the IPIW-Conference 2016: Dialogue. Specifically, the paper proposes a line of argumentation that the subject of dialogue allows scholars to adopt when discussing the rhetorical context of Charles Dickens's authorship, his works, and his readership. Dickens's works have been read and discussed for over a century. As they have inspired many communities of readers to engage with them, these works have sustained not only a dialogue with their readers but also a broader dialogue within the public sphere. In addition, Dickens actively fostered community amongst his readership, aided, among other things, by his public engagements, his readings, and his journalism. Before the paper can proceed any further, however, it is necessary to present the definition "dialogue" that informs the argumentation.

Although the term dialogue has come to mean a variety of things, this paper relies on the Greek origin of the term, which is διάλογος (dialogos). Plato is one of the first scholars who used the term which has its roots in διά (dia: through) and λόγος (logos: speech, reason). In her article "From Dialogos to Dialogue: The Use of the Term from Plato to the Second Century CE", Katarzyna Jazdzewska states that "[i]n Plato's works the word is associated with a particular type of conversation — an inquiry carried out by two interlocutors, shaped as an interchange of questions and answers".[1] Furthermore, she argues that it is because of its particular alignment to the Socratic form of dialogue that "in later tradition we find authors using διάλογος for 'dialectical argumentation'".[2] Importantly, this definition highlights dialogue as a conversation in which new knowledge is created.

---

[1] Jazdzewska, Katarzyna: From Dialogos to Dialogue: The Use of the Term from Plato to the Second Century CE. In: Greek, Roman, and Byzantine Studies 54 (2014), pp. 17–36, here p. 34.

[2] Idem, p. 18.

It assumes that this knowledge does not get carried into the discourse, but rather that it is created through a back and forth of questions and answers. In a similar vein, David Bohm highlights in his paper "On Dialogue" the democratic connotations of the term's original meaning:

> The picture of image that this derivation suggests is of a stream of meaning flowing among and through us and between us [sic]. This will make possible a flow of meaning in the whole group, out of which will emerge some new understanding. It's something new, which may not have been in the starting point at all. It's something creative. And this shared meaning is the 'glue' or 'cement' that holds people and societies together.[3]

The definition of dialogue in its original form is thus more than merely a conversation between a number of participants; it is a discourse in which knowledge is created dialectically.

This definition of dialogue can be useful for the study of literary texts when these are understood as rhetorical situations. Patricia Bizzell and Bruce Herzberg elaborate the connection between literature and rhetoric in their comprehensive work *The Rhetorical Tradition* and state:

> Both are concerned with ways of moving audiences by means of language. And even if, as many critics have argued, there is a distinction between the 'contemplative' goal of literature and the 'active' goal of rhetoric, literature frequently uses persuasion and argumentation.[4]

Any rhetorical situation incorporates author, text, reader, and context. In addition, any rhetorical situation has a purpose and functions toward achieving a certain goal. According to Bizzell and Herzberg, Wayne C. Booth suggests, "that all literature is discourse addressed to a reader",[5] and Kenneth Burke goes as far as to claim that literature is always a persuasive discourse.[6] These scholars assume similar starting points as the

---

[3] Bohm, David: On Dialogue. In: http://sprott.physics.wisc.edu/Chaos-Complexity/dialogue.pdf, p. 2 (12.12.2016).

[4] Bizzell, Patricia / Bruce Herzberg: The Rhetorical Tradition: Readings from Classical Times to the Present. Epping: Bedford Books 2000, p. 1193.

[5] Idem, p. 1194.

[6] Idem, p. 1193.

reader-response movement, which argues that "the reader has an active role in producing the meaning of the work."[7] While this understanding can be productive, a contemporary literary scholar might be weary of solely emphasizing the readers' reception of the text.

Terry Eagleton, quoted in *The Rhetorical Tradition*, works with a more productive definition of the connection between literature and rhetoric, he states, "rhetoric [...] takes the most comprehensive view of the operations of discourse."[8] Connecting his theory to Stanley Fish's, Wayne C. Booth's, and Kenneth Burke's, Eagleton comprehends rhetoric as a useful tool for analyzing power relations in language and society. Following Eagleton's line of thought, this paper understands rhetoric as a useful tool to analyze power relations as established through literary dialogue, between reader and text but also among characters. Analyzing literature as a rhetorical situation thus allows literary scholars to take into consideration all parts of the rhetorical situation at once and draw from this a useful toolkit to examine the effect that literary texts have. To extend this line of thought, it is possible to see literature as dialogue in the original sense of that term: rhetorical situations in which ideas can come about and be probed and where knowledge is created between author, text, and reader.

This paper aligns itself with other contemporary scholars who argue that seeing literature as rhetorical situations makes it possible to apply a useful toolkit to the literary work, a way that allows scholars to understand literature as inviting communities. Roger D. Sell is one of these scholars; he sees literature as "one among other forms of communication".[9] He is not the first to do so, Ivor Armstrong Richards — one of the founding fathers of the discipline of English studies — for example, argued in his work *Practical Criticism* (1929) that poetry is communication.[10] Sell uses the concept of dialogue to describe the interaction between author, text and reader; specifically, he focuses on the dialogue between different communities of readers and the author, stating that "literature can be thought of as a dia-

---

[7] Idem, p. 1194.
[8] Idem, p. 1198.
[9] Sell, Roger D.: Communicational Criticism: Studies in Literature as Dialogue. Amsterdam: John Benjamins 2011, p. 6.
[10] Richards, Ivor Armstrong: Practical Criticism. Wilmington: Mariner Book 1956, p. 11.

logue between writers and their public: a kind of give-and-take which has both ethical entailments and communal consequences."[11] Working with this productive definition of literature makes it imperative to question the nature of dialogue in the literary works, both as a means of uncovering ethical entailments as well as a means of understanding the consequences that these might have for the communal experience of the texts.

According to Sell, in novels (e. g. Great Expectations), "fiction is a means by which a communicator can explore general or moral truths which go beyond the detail of particular empirical cases, or can probe feelings and opinions which have yet to be stabilized into constant attitudes."[12] While he makes an important claim, there is another side to this argument. An extensive corpus of work such as Dickens's begins to establish its own moral codes; if these are shared, embodied, and engaged with by large communities of readers, they can begin to function outside of the fictional works as well.

As mentioned briefly in the introduction, Dickens's own engagement in public readings and charitable endeavors (such as building a house for fallen women) further enforced communities based on the values and ideas that his novels express. The definition of modern Christmas spirit is one example in point. Dickens's *A Christmas Carol* both uses the kairos of Christmas time to make its point as well as it works toward establishing the very meaning of "Christmas time" that we perceive as traditional in large parts of Western culture today. Finally, Dickens's corpus and the readers' understanding of it served and still serve to strengthen Dickens's ethos and to create and maintain his brand.

Dickens's contemporaries were quite aware and even wary of the strength of novelistic representations and of the power and opportunity that reading and thinking entailed. In his article "Educating the Victorians", Patrick Brantlinger states that "[i]n the early 1800s some contended that the poor should not be taught to read, because it would make them discontented with their lot".[13] Dickens's texts suggest an acute awareness

---

[11] Sell: Communicational Criticism (note 9), p. 10.
[12] Idem, p. 13.
[13] Brantlinger, Patrick: Educating the Victorians. In: Holly Furneaux / Sally Ledger (Ed.): Charles Dickens in Context. Cambridge: Cambridge University Press 2013, pp. 219–226, here p. 219.

of this danger and of the danger of uproar in general (see *Hard Times*); however, they also show an acute awareness of social discrepancies and have been described as instrumental in driving political and social agendas forward. Sell asks how it is possible for Dickens to have become so successful and claims that "Dickens, though so often blamed for being intrusively manipulative [becomes] canonical thanks to a communicational genuineness that ran far deeper than any such appearances to the contrary."[14] According to Sell, 'genuine communication' is a kind of "communication in which different parties respect each other's human autonomy."[15] Moreover, "genuine communication involves seeing the other in light of the self, and the self in the light of the other."[16] Here, Sell's analysis and understanding of Dickens become problematic. Seeing one's self in 'the light of the other' requires empathy, a feeling 'with' the other. However, characters in Dickens's works tend to exhibit a top down kind of pity with others; this reinforces hierarchies rather than breaking them down. An example of this kind of pity can be found in *A Christmas Carol,* in which Scrooge quite literally looks down upon the Cratchit family; his journey with the ghosts teaches him how to feel for those in need.

It could be argued that Dickens's career and works invite dialogue and elicit public engagement, and both aspects are vital in sustaining democratic communities. However, if these works can be seen as having such an impact on the public sphere, then it becomes necessary to question the ways in which they engage with their readers. Ideally, when reading a novel, readers enter into a dialogue with it. The imagination engages with the text, forms opinions, sides with characters and distances itself from others. However, after close reading, it seems that Dickens' novels are filled with rhetorical functions that guide the readers' engagement with them. Rather than entering into a dialogue with the readers' imagination, the novels' rhetorical situations thus become persuasive or even seductive. James R. Kincaid makes an interesting point with regard to the seductive force of the novles by analyzing the rhetoric of laughter as guiding the readers' understanding of the novels. He shows convincingly that the use of comedy, irony and other laughter producing rhetorical devices evokes the readers respond to the

---

[14] Sell: Communicational Criticism (note 9), p. 24.
[15] Idem, p. 23.
[16] Idem, p. 207f.

text.[17] Instead of creating communities, they reinforce hierarchy. Problematically, some of the persuasive mechanisms of the novels are so subtle that in the process of reading the texts, readers might happily accept the ends of the persuasion without questioning them further.

The prefaces and the novel's narrators hold the most obvious persuasive functions of the text. In the prefaces, Dickens positions himself in connection to his text. That is, he states very clearly how he wishes his text to be understood and thereby frames the narrative, managing the perception as well as the reception of the novels. One representative set of prefaces can be found in the Oxford World Classic's version of *Martin Chuzzlewit*, which presents three prefaces and one postscript.[18] All four short pieces of text enter into a dialogue with the overall narrative. The first preface is from 1844, the year in which the serialization of the novel was concluded. It is the briefest of the three prefaces and also the least guiding in its declarations. At this point, Dickens does not take the reception of the overall work into much consideration.

He begins by stating that he does not have anything particular to say, but then he contradicts himself somewhat and makes an overall claim, stating that his purpose was to exhibit "in various aspects, the commonest of all the vices".[19] Notably, he does not add which vice this is, leaving it to the reader to draw their own conclusions. Moreover, he makes interesting points about the interpretive process, the dialogue between text and reader by suggesting that the readers' ability to recognize themselves or others in the characters is crucial to the reading process. Sell strikes the right point when he mentions literary works as eliciting empathy. Indeed, Dickens suggests that it is much easier to recognize others in a novel than oneself. Noteworthy enough, the readers are invited to identify with only very specific characters. This aspect will be addressed briefly in the next section.

Dickens's second preface, the "Preface to the Cheap Edition (1850)", is a bit more detailed than the first one, it takes the initial reactions to the text into consideration. It specifies a few aspects, for example "the commonest of all the vices", which were already mentioned in the earlier edition; now

---

[17] Kincaid, James R.: The Rhetoric of Laughter. Oxford: Oxford University Press 1971.

[18] Dickens, Charles: Martin Chuzzlewit. Oxford: Oxford World's Classics 2009.

[19] Idem, Preface (1844).

it states clearly that this vice is "selfishness".[20] In addition, Dickens offers a way of reading some of the novel's characters.

Jonas Chuzzlewit is not mentioned at all in the first preface; however, in the second preface Dickens spends an entire paragraph writing a defense of Jonas, one of the most criminal characters of the novel, and argues that Jonas's upbringing contributed to his behavior. Finally, Dickens states why he makes these comments:

> I make this comment on the character, and solicit the reader's attention to it in his or her consideration of this tale, because nothing is more common in real life than a want of profitable reflection on the causes of many vices and crimes that awaken the general horror [...]. As we sow, we reap.[21]

Highlighting the complicity of the readers in creating these characters, Dickens makes an important appeal to pathos that encourages the readers to pity even the most horrid characters. However, within the diegesis, this call for empathy is very often countered by clear mechanisms that distance the reader from certain characters.[22] Consequently, although the statements of the prefaces are important elements of the overall dialogue that the rhetorical situation of the novel sustains, they are not always consistent with the persuasive forces of the narrative.

In his final paragraph of the second preface, Dickens states that "in this cheap series, and in all [his] writings" he hopes to show the need for sanitary improvements in the dwellings of the poor.[23] He criticizes the hospitals of London specifically and deems them "noble Institutions" but "very defective".[24] He also presents his solution to all of these issues: "the Hospitals, with their means and funds, should have left it to private humanity

---

[20] Dickens, Charles: Preface to the Cheap Edition (1850). In: Dickens: Martin Chuzzlewit (note 18) Appendix A, p. 717–718.

[21] Idem.

[22] For a development of this line of argument see: Teubler, Lisa-Marie: Mollifying the Masses: Obscuring Class and Alleviating Inequalities in Charles Dickens's *David Copperfield, Great Expectations,* and *Little Dorrit.* In: http://lup.lub.lu.se/luur/download?func=downloadFile&recordOId=3814547&fileOId=3814991 (12.12.2016).

[23] Dickens: Preface to the Cheap Edition (note 20), p. 717f.

[24] Idem, p. 718.

and enterprise, in the year Eighteen Hundred and Forty-nine, to enter on an attempt to improve that class of persons."[25] Dickens proposed solution in *Martin Chuzzlewit*, but also in many of his other works, consists in private humanity. He does not trust the state's institutions to solve the problems of his time, so he argues that private humanity should aim to solve them. This is a declaration of purpose and can be found as underlying nearly all larger persuasive endeavors in Dickens's novels. Problematically, this solution reinforces hierarchies. While Dickens declares that he wants to ensure that everyone lives in decent circumstances, his novels do not support the systematic change that many of his contemporary political and economic theorists proposed as the way forward. The novels propose ways of alleviating the suffering of the poor but not the eradication of poverty.[26]

In the third and final preface, Dickens focuses specifically on the difference between truth and exaggeration, fact and fiction. He starts the preface by saying "what is exaggeration to one class of minds and perceptions, is plain truth to another."[27] He engages here in a direct manner with the idea of audience reception and with the differences in the readers' interpretations. The meta-dialogue continues when Dickens points to the judgement of Jonas Chuzzlewit which he describes as not just "a mere piece of poetical justice, but […] the extreme exposition of a direct truth."[28] Dickens invites the readers to judge the characters as if they were actual beings in a shared world. This allows the readers to see his works as part of a larger dialogue and not merely as self-referential.

The third preface develops the statements that Dickens made in the final sentence of the second preface. Now, he uses the past tense instead of the present tense, indicating that the situation has changed: "the Hospitals of London *were*, in many respects, noble Institutions; in others, very defective" and "Mrs. Betsy Prig *was* a fair specimen of the Hospital Nurse" (my emphasis).[29] The addition of a bit in the very end of the repeated sentence suggests that Dickens has a specific idea of how it was improved. He states

---

[25] Idem.
[26] See: Teubler: Mollifying the Masses (note 22).
[27] Dickens: Preface to the Charles Dickens Edition (1867). In: Dickens: Martin Chuzzlewit (note 18), Appendix A, p. 719–720.
[28] Idem, p. 719.
[29] Idem, p. 720.

that it was "since, greatly improved through the agency of good women."[30] This is a statement that Dickens did not make seventeen years earlier. Much has changed in that time, not least his own charitable engagement in private humanity and enterprise, for example, the opening of his house for fallen women which he began to work with in 1846.

How can the framing, Dickens engages in, be understood as a way of monitoring the narrative? Dickens determines several issues as important to deal with. Moreover, he presents the best solution, in his view: private humanity and enterprise. Finally, he refers to this way of solving the issues in his third preface as having been successful. Consequently, the readers' understanding of the text is guided by the prefaces but not only within the narratives; instead, Dickens invites the audience to see his fictional works as commenting on larger social issues and offers his perception of the best solution. The end of the novels' persuasion is thus declared and the means of it are left to be studied. However, they are no longer dialogical because they have a predetermined end.

The narrators of the texts have a second persuasive function whereas the ends are often less visible than in the prefaces. For example, in *Oliver Twist*, narrative commentaries and interjections are frequent. The comments and interjections made by a narrative voice often reach out of the narrative's diegesis, they build a bridge between the text and the reader, presenting one way of interpreting the overall events. The first comment of this kind refers to Oliver's birth when his mother passes away. The narrator presents the unfolding events through a clearly colored narrative:

> The hungry and destitute situation of the infant orphan was duly reported by the workhouse authorities to the parish authorities. The parish authorities inquired with dignity of the workhouse authorities, whether there was no female then domiciled in 'the house who was in a situation to impart to Oliver Twist, the consolation and nourishment of which he stood in need. The workhouse authorities replied with humility, that there was not. Upon this, the parish authorities magnanimously and humanely resolved, that Oliver should be 'farmed,' or, in other words, that he should be dispatched to a branch-workhouse some three miles off, where twenty or thirty other juve-

---

[30] Idem.

nile offenders against the poor-laws, rolled about the floor all day, without the inconvenience of too much food or too much clothing, under the parental superintendence of an elderly female, who received the culprits and for the consideration of sevenpence-halfpenny per small head per week.[31]

The contrast between the descriptive terms – "dignity", "humility", "magnanimously", "humanely" – and what is actually happening – namely Oliver's removal to a branch-workhouse to be "farmed" – creates an almost comical dissonance in the narrative. The narrator's presence, in particular in the beginning, is pervaded by ironical comments and snide remarks. The bulk of these ironic comments can be found in the representations of the 'system' of poor relief that was a result of the Poor Law Amendment Act of 1834.

The commentary betrays the reader clearly the characters to side with and the 'right' attitude towards the system that is in place to take care of orphaned children. Some characters in the foreground seem to be more trustworthy than others and influence the reading thereby. These two guiding functions within the novels influence the dialogue between reader and text significantly or turn it even into persuasion.

Several aspects impede the dialogue between text and reader as well as between the characters. One of these aspects, which is also highlighted in the above quotation from Oliver Twist, is irony. The message of the commentary is only comprehensible if the readers understand the irony that the narrator applies. In her work *Rhetorical Style*, Jeanne Fahnestock defines irony as one of four key tropes and states that "irony makes a claim by saying the opposite, with the further stipulation that the speaker uses this mode intentionally and expects the hearer to recognize it."[32] She describes a "primary effect" of irony, which lets the reader know that what is said is the opposite of what is meant; moreover, Fahnestock describes a "secondary effect" of irony, which pertains to "supporting the rhetor's argument and/or enhancing the rapport between rhetor and audience".[33] Most importantly, the primary effect of irony assumes that both speaker and reader

---

[31] Dickens, Charles: Oliver Twist. Oxford: Oxford World's Classics 1999, pp. 3–4.
[32] Fahnestock, Jeanne: Rhetorical Style: The Uses of Language in Persuasion. Oxford: Oxford University Press 2011, p. 111.
[33] Idem.

understand the statement as ironic. The narrator's message in *Oliver Twist* thus presupposes a certain audience, an audience that understands the social and political context in which the statement is placed as well as the stylistic task of decoding the opposite of the message. The two most important implications of using irony within the text are then: 1. the definite intention of the narrator because without intention there cannot be irony[34] and 2. a common ground of values and understandings that the reader must share with the narrator in order to be able to decode the text.

Irony works as a similarly exclusive mechanism on the character level. Only some characters can use irony and understand it; while for others it is impossible to decode a message that applies irony. Consequently, the use of irony makes genuine conversation impossible because it excludes all those who do not recognize it. Irony is only one of these exclusive mechanisms that the novels apply on all three levels: author-reader, reader-text, and character-character. Some of the other mechanisms include characters' accents, the inability to speak, the inability to make oneself understood, a lack of ethos, an overuse of pathos, and many more. Altogether, these phenomena obstruct the dialogue; the overall message becomes rather hierarchically than dialectically.

In conclusion, this paper proposes to understand novels as rhetorical situations – dialogues between author, text, and reader — and investigates these by focusing on Charles Dickens's oeuvre. When reading the novels and their paratexts carefully, it becomes clear that they are persuasive rather than dialogical. Combined with the overall approach of foregrounding persuasion over dialogue, Dickens's works become not only persuasive but also seductive – it is impossible for all readers to take in all information and to contribute to the communicative situations that the novels present. Democratic dialogue is not possible if some participants of the communication are not able to decode the messages that are sent. Consequently, Dickens's novels must be seen rather as sights of hierarchical persuasive discourse than as the democratic dialogic communities that Sell proposes.

---

[34] Idem, p. 114.

Zur gesellschaftlich engagierten Literatur als dialogisches Genre

Hannah Tischmann

Literatur und Gesellschaft stehen in einem reziproken Verhältnis: Zum einen können gesellschaftliche Verhältnisse die Produktion, die Form und den Inhalt sowie die Publikation und die Rezeption eines literarischen Werkes beeinflussen. Zum anderen besitzt das literarische Werk selbst ein gesellschaftsveränderndes Potential, wenn es beispielsweise den Fokus auf soziale Missstände richtet und/oder alternative Lebenswelten aufzeigt.

Literatur, welche Themen wie Klassenunterschiede oder soziale Ausgrenzungen behandelt und die Idee einer auf Gleichberechtigung und Freiheit basierenden Gesellschaft verfolgt, lässt sich als gesellschaftlich engagierte Lyrik, Dramatik oder Prosa bezeichnen. Die Vielfalt an Ausdrücken und thematischen Schwerpunkten solcher Texte erschwert jedoch eine allgemeingültige Definition dessen, was gesellschaftlich engagierte Literatur ist. Die Beschreibung des Inhalts alleine ist dabei nicht ausreichend, um den Zusatz „gesellschaftlich engagiert" zu definieren, der eine aktive Komponente besitzt und eine extratextuelle Verbindung suggeriert.

In den folgenden Ausführungen wird daher vorgeschlagen, gesellschaftlich engagierte Literatur im pragmatischen[1] Sinne als dialogische Literatur zu verstehen. Eine solche dialogorientierte Definition reflektiert den vielschichtigen und interaktiven Charakter dieser Literatur und umfasst, wie sich in den folgenden Ausführungen zeigen wird, sowohl intra- als auch extratextuelle Aspekte. Der Vorteil dieser Definition liegt darin, dass sie ihren Fokus weder auf Autorintentionen oder die Autonomie der Texte noch auf die Leserrezeption reduziert. Die Gefahr intentionaler und affektiver Fehlschlüsse in positivistischen und leserorientierten Ansätzen,

---

[1] „Pragmatisch" – und dementsprechend auch „Pragmatik" – wird hier als Terminus technicus für kontextabhängige Bedeutungen verstanden und nicht als im alltäglichen Sprachgebrauch vorherrschendes Synonym für „anwendungsbezogen" oder „sachbezogen".

auf die Vertreter des New Criticism hingewiesen haben,[2] wird dabei minimiert; ebenso wird die Position werkimmanenter Interpretationsansätze modifiziert, denen zufolge Bedeutung alleine im literarischen Text zu finden sei.[3]

Dieser Definitionsansatz entspricht dialogischen und pragmatischen Herangehensweisen an Leseprozesse und Bedeutungskonstruktionen, wie sie sich in den letzten Jahrzehnten entwickelt haben. So argumentiert beispielsweise der Kommunikationswissenschaftler W. John Harker, „that the process of reading literature is better approached through a notion of literary understanding which recognizes the interacting contributions of the author, the text, and the reader within a communicative framework"[4]. Willi Huntemann und Kai Hendrik Patri weisen in ihren Überlegungen zum Wesen engagierter Literatur in dieselbe Richtung, wenn sie betonen, dass sich „[d]as Engagement engagierter Literatur [...] zureichend nur im Viereck von Autor, Text, (literarischer) Öffentlichkeit und politischem Status quo erfassen"[5] lässt. Übersetzt man dieses nun in einen aktiven Vorgang, so sind am Prozess der Bedeutungsbildung immer mehrere Akteure beteiligt. Jeglicher Form des literarischen Engagements kann damit ein dialogischer Charakter zugeschrieben werden. Der literarische Text wird dabei zum Ausgangspunkt einer kommunikativen Situation, die soziale Ungleichheiten und gesellschaftsrelevante Fragen verhandelt.

Es wird sich allerdings zeigen, dass der dialogische Charakter eines gesellschaftlich engagierten literarischen Werkes weiterhin differenziert wer-

---

[2] Vgl. Wimsatt Jr., William K. / Monroe C. Beardsley: The Intentional Fallacy. In: The Sewanee Review 54 (1946), Nr. 3, S. 468–488; Wimsatt Jr., William K. / Monroe C. Beardsley: The Affective Fallacy. In: The Sewanee Review 57 (1949), Nr. 1, S. 31–55.

[3] Vgl. Gruber, Bettina: Werkimmanente Literaturwissenschaft/New Criticism. In: Jost Schneider (Hg.): Methodengeschichte der Germanistik. Berlin, New York: de Gruyter 2009, S. 763–776, hier S. 763–765.

[4] Harker, W. John: Literary Communication: The Author, the Reader, the Text. In: The Journal of Aesthetic Education 22 (1988), Nr. 2, S. 5–14, hier S. 6.

[5] Huntemann, Willi / Kai Hendrik Patri: Einleitung: Engagierte Literatur in Wendezeiten. In: Willi Huntemann / Małgorzata Klentak-Zabłocka / Fabian Lampart / Thomas Schmidt (Hg.): Engagierte Literatur in Wendezeiten. Würzburg: Königshausen & Neumann 2003, S. 9–48, hier S. 11f.

den muss, um Aussagen über seinen Zusammenhang mit der außerliterarischen Welt und seinen Einfluss auf diese treffen zu können. Zunächst stellt sich auf rein inhaltlicher Ebene die Frage nach dem Dialog zwischen Fakt und Fiktion beziehungsweise danach, in welcher Form und in welchem Ausmaß diese beiden Phänomene in einem literarischen Werk tatsächlich interagieren. Weiterhin lässt sich im rezeptionsgeschichtlichen Umfeld diskutieren, in welcher Form und zwischen welchen Akteuren im literarischen Feld eigentlich der Dialog stattfindet, der einen Text zu gesellschaftlich engagierter Literatur macht.

Nach einer kurzen Darstellung dessen, was den Begriff „gesellschaftlich engagierte Literatur" inhaltlich ausmacht, werde ich diesen also um eine dialogische Perspektive erweitern. Auf einen kurzen Überblick zu meinem an pragmatischen Ansätzen von Edda Weigand, Michael Macovski und Roger D. Sell orientierten Verständnis des Dialog-Begriffes folgt daher eine Auseinandersetzung mit den Phänomenen Fakt und Fiktion sowie den Akteuren Autor, Leser, Text und Literaturindustrie, um abschließend gesellschaftlich engagierte Literatur als dialogisches Genre definieren zu können. Eine Einbeziehung pragmatischer linguistischer Ansätze ist für die Definition gesellschaftlich engagierter Literatur von Vorteil, da sich mit ihrer Hilfe zeigen lässt, dass es sich bei gesellschaftlich engagierter Literatur um ein relationales Konzept handelt, welches in diversen Kommunikationssituationen innerhalb des literarischen Feldes entsteht und geprägt wird. Dabei ist es möglich, dass ein literarisches Werk nicht als ein gesellschaftlich engagiertes entsteht oder überliefert wird, sondern erst zu einem späteren Zeitpunkt zu einem solchen gemacht wird.

„Littérature engagée", politische Literatur und gesellschaftlich engagierte Literatur – eine erste inhaltliche Annäherung

Seitdem Jean-Paul Sartre in seinem 1948 veröffentlichten Essay *Qu'est-ce que la littérature*[6] eine „littérature engagée" gefordert hat, ist der Begriff „engagierte Literatur" ausführlich diskutiert worden. Was im Nachhinein als „engagierte Literatur" debattiert worden ist, entspricht allerdings nicht unbedingt Sartres existenzialistisch beeinflusster Idee einer „littérature en-

---

[6] Sartre, Jean-Paul: Qu'est-ce que la littérature? Paris: Gallimard 1948.

gagée".⁷ Wie „engagierte Literatur" ist auch der Begriff „politische Literatur" von verschiedenen Forschern im Kontext des literarischen Engagements definiert worden.⁸ Die Bezeichnung „gesellschaftlich engagierte Literatur" benötigt hingegen eine weitere Verdeutlichung, da sie oft ohne weitere Eingrenzung verwendet wird.

„Gesellschaftlich engagierte Literatur" verweist auf literarische Werke mit einem Fokus auf öffentliche Debatten und gesellschaftliche Fragen. In diesem Sinne behandelt sie kritisch die Beziehung zwischen Individuum und Kollektiv oder die Beziehung zwischen verschiedenen Kollektiven einer Gesellschaft. Laut Sartre ist eine „littérature engagée" antidiktatorisch.⁹ Dies ist in Bezug auf engagierte Literatur hinterfragt worden, indem man herausgestellt hat, dass Engagement im Sinne eines Willens zur Veränderung auch als Engagement gegen demokratische Prozesse verstanden werden kann.¹⁰ In der hier vertretenen Definition gesellschaftlich engagierter Literatur wird gesellschaftliches Engagement jedoch als Engagement für demokratische Ideale wie Würde, Freiheit und Gleichberechtigung verstanden. Gesellschaftlich engagierte Literatur verhandelt folglich sowohl Themen wie Menschenrechte und faire Arbeitsbedingungen als auch gesellschaftliche Exklusion und Tabus. Gesellschaftlich engagierte Literatur hebt hervor, hinterfragt, fordert heraus oder schlägt Alternativen vor. Daraus resultiert, dass manche gesellschaftlich engagierten literarischen Werke nicht nur den Fokus auf gesellschaftliche Debatten richten,

---

⁷ Vgl. z. B. Neuhaus, Stefan / Rolf Selbmann / Thorsten Unger: Engagierte Literatur zwischen den Weltkriegen. Ein Vorgespräch. In: Dies. (Hg.): Engagierte Literatur zwischen den Weltkriegen. Würzburg: Königshausen & Neumann 2002, S. 9–18, hier S. 10; Wechsel, Kirsten: Grenzüberschreitungen zwischen Realität und Fiktion. Engagierte Ästhetik bei Inger Christensen und Kjartan Fløgstad. Göttingen: Vandenhoeck & Ruprecht 2000, S. 13. Im Folgenden verweist „littérature engagée" daher explizit auf Sartres Konzept, während der Begriff „engagierte Literatur" ein Verständnis impliziert, das sich nicht ausschließlich auf Sartres Ideen bezieht. „Engagierte Literatur" ist also keine einfache Übersetzung von „littérature engagée".

⁸ Vgl. z. B. Howe, Irving: Politics and the Novel (1957). Chicago: Ivan R. Dee 2000; Wegmann, Nikolaus: Engagierte Literatur? Zur Poetik des Klartexts. In: Jürgen Fohrmann / Harro Müller (Hg.): Systemtheorie der Literatur. München: W. Fink 1996, S. 345–365 oder Huntemann/Patri: Engagierte Literatur (Anm. 5).

⁹ Vgl. Wechsel: Grenzüberschreitungen (Anm. 7), S. 12.

¹⁰ Vgl. die Diskussion bei Neuhaus/Selbmann/Unger: Engagierte Literatur (Anm. 7) und Huntemann/Patri: Engagierte Literatur (Anm. 5), S. 13.

sondern auch an diesen teilhaben können. Diese aktive Teilhabe ist jedoch, wie sich unten zeigen wird, keineswegs notwendig, um als gesellschaftlich engagiertes literarisches Werk gelesen zu werden. Ebenso wenig bedeutet dies, dass gesellschaftlich engagierte Literatur von Anfang an notwendigerweise politisch ist – auch wenn die häufige Verbindung von sozialem und politischem Engagement der Grund dafür ist, dass gesellschaftlich engagierte Literatur Staatsangelegenheiten oder Fragen der Demokratie verhandeln kann.[11] Durch die Bezeichnung „gesellschaftlich engagiert" werden die umfassenden Begriffe „politische Literatur" und „engagierte Literatur" differenziert: Werke, die sich vorwiegend mit dem Individuum oder dem Kollektiv in seinem sozialen Umfeld auseinandersetzen, müssen nicht notwendig politisch sein.

Im Gegensatz zu Sartres Konzept einer „littérature engagée", das sich ausschließlich auf Prosa bezieht, ist gesellschaftlich engagierte Literatur nicht an eine besondere literarische Gattung gebunden. Sie umfasst epische, dramatische und lyrische Texte, deren Inhalt den oben genannten Merkmalen entspricht. In diesem Sinne ist der Versuch, gesellschaftlich engagierte Literatur zu definieren, nicht der Versuch, durch die Betonung formaler Aspekte ein neues Genre zu bestimmen. Es ist vielmehr der Versuch, die Position eines Textes gegenüber außerliterarischen gesellschaftlichen Verhältnissen und die Einstellung der Rezipienten diesem Text gegenüber zu beschreiben. Hieraus ergibt sich auch die thematische Vielfalt gesellschaftlich engagierter Literatur, die unter anderem Arbeiterliteratur, feministische Literatur oder Literatur, die sich mit den Bedingungen von Migration auseinandersetzt, einschließt, insofern soziales Engagement beziehungsweise Engagement für demokratische Ideale erkennbar wird. Gleichzeitig wird deutlich, dass diese erste inhaltliche Annäherung an das Konzept einer gesellschaftlich engagierten Literatur zwar eine grundlegende thematische Richtung erkennen lässt, für sich alleine genommen aber noch nicht aussagekräftig genug ist, um ihre Position im literarischen Feld nachvollziehen zu können. Inwiefern gesellschaftliches Engagement erkennbar wird, lässt sich durch eine ergänzende dialogische Perspektive erfassen.

---

[11] Zu Demokratie, Diktatur und literarischem Engagement s. z. B. Johan Svedjedals Untersuchung zur schwedischen Protestliteratur: Ner med allt? Essäer om protestlitteraturen och demokratin, cirka 1965–1957. Stockholm: Wahlström & Widstrand 2014.

Dialog – eine pragmatische Perspektive

Der dialogische Charakter eines gesellschaftlich engagierten Werkes bezieht sich in diesen Überlegungen weder auf die Häufigkeit und die Art von Figurendialogen, die durch Sprecherwechsel charakterisiert sind, noch handelt es sich um eine einfache Übertragung des Wortes „dialogisch" im Bakhtinschen Sinne. Wie bereits erwähnt, liegt dem hier vertretenen Verständnis von „Dialog" und „dialogisch" in Bezug auf Literatur stattdessen ein pragmatischer Ansatz zugrunde, wie er sowohl von Vertretern der Linguistik als auch der Literaturwissenschaft repräsentiert wird. Die Grundlage dieses Ansatzes ist, dass die Bedeutung einer Äußerung kontextabhängig und damit nicht im Text selbst festgelegt ist.

Die Linguistin Edda Weigand beschreibt Dialoge als Verhandlungsprozesse, die auf der Folge von Aktion-Reaktion basieren.[12] Indem Weigand auch Sprache – definiert als „the natural phenomenon of language use"[13] – als dialogisches Konzept versteht,[14] ändert sich

> the traditional concept of a speech act from an independent separate act to a dialogically oriented, i. e. dependent one. The intrinsic dialogic criterion is constituted by the mutual dependency of every act being ultimately based on the insight that there is no single speech act which is communicatively autonomous. Every act either is making a pragmatic claim or fulfilling a claim thus being dependent on a subsequent or preceding act.[15]

Auf diesen Grundideen errichtet Weigand ihre Theorie der dialogischen Handlungsspiele. Handlungsspiele stellen kulturelle Einheiten dar, in deren Mittelpunkt Menschen mit ihren individuellen Erfahrungen und

---

[12] Vgl. Weigand, Edda: The Dialogic Action Game. In: Dies.: Language as Dialogue: From Rules to Principles of Probability. Amsterdam: John Benjamins Publishing Company 2009, S. 265–281, hier S. 274.

[13] Weigand, Edda: Discourse, Conversation, Dialogue. In: Dies.: Language as Dialogue (Anm. 12), S. 45–69, hier S. 65.

[14] „A dialogic concept of language rests on two basic assumptions: – Language is primarily used for communicative purposes. – Communication is always performed dialogically." (Weigand, Edda: The Dialogic Principle Revisited. Speech Acts and Mental States. In: Dies.: Language as Dialogue (Anm. 12), S. 21–44, hier S. 23).

[15] Weigand: Discourse, Conversation, Dialogue (Anm. 13), S. 64.

ihren jeweiligen kognitiven Voraussetzungen stehen.[16] Weigands Hervorhebung des dialogischen Charakters jeglicher Kommunikation bedeutet:

> every communicative action game will be dialogic not only when we have clearly dialogic forms. [...] These action games do not always require an interlocutor to be present or active; in some cases the reaction may be a mental one. Thus a sermon or a speech without the active participation of an audience as well as an action game in the written medium will be dialogic.[17]

Dieses ist möglich, da Weigand zwei Ebenen unterscheidet, denen unterschiedliche Konzepte des Dialogs entsprechen. Diese beiden Ebenen bezeichnet sie als funktionale Ebene (*functional level*) und als formale/situative Ebene (*formal/situational level*). Während dialogische Konversationen, bei denen Sprecherwechsel stattfinden, ebenso wie deren monologischer Gegensatz situationsbedingt und auf der formalen Ebene einzuordnen sind, gehören dialogische Handlungsspiele zur funktionalen Dialogebene. Sie müssen also keineswegs einen formalen Sprecherwechsel aufweisen, um dialogisch zu sein:[18]

> At the level of communicative function [...], dialogic action games are performed with monologic as well as dialogic forms. Speech at the level of function is always to be analysed as dialogic speech, every individual speech act can be considered as dialogically oriented [...].[19]

Literarische Werke erhalten ihren dialogischen Charakter folglich auf der funktionalen Ebene.[20] Auch der Literatur- und Kulturwissenschaftler Michael Macovski betont, dass Dialog in literaturwissenschaftlichen, philosophischen und linguistischen dialogischen Ansätzen das Ergebnis eines sozialen Aktes ist, welches unabhängige Autor- und Leserkategorien herausfordert:

---

[16] Vgl. Weigand: The Dialogic Action Game (Anm. 12), S. 270.
[17] Weigand: Discourse, Conversation, Dialogue (Anm. 13), S. 65.
[18] Ebd., S. 66.
[19] Weigand: The Dialogic Principle Revisited (Anm. 14), S. 22.
[20] Ebd., S. 25.

> [Dialogue] necessarily revises the prevalent postromantic concept of a single, originary writer and a designated, implied reader. For in this schema both the production and the interpretation of ostensibly original meaning become social acts: collaborative constructions derived from manifold viewpoints. In reconceiving the notion of literary voices, we speak not of a circumscribed artifact, but of a socially constituted action, a dynamic whose methods and objects are neither focal nor discrete, but processive, accretive, and multireferential.[21]

Für Macovski wird Bedeutung durch die Leser generiert und ergibt sich aus dem Zusammenspiel zahlreicher weiterer Komponenten:

> [T]he precepts of dialogue suggest that readers instantiate meaning in response not only to texts, but to a variety of other voices: extratextual and intertextual, oral and written, present and absent. As a result, linguistic meaning accrues not only in relation to a given reader, but in interaction with this polyphony of both literary and nonliterary voices. If reception theory focuses on the exchanges between a given text and its particular reader, dialogue redefines and extrapolates such interactions as necessarily multireferential and multivocal. Moreover, if such affectivist studies demonstrate how a given text necessarily implicates a reader — in, say, postlapsarian sin or misinterpretation – dialogism includes this implicating process among a plethora of readerly interactions: between text and reader, speaker and reader, reader and reader, and even text and text. The result is an image of an ultimately more eclectic reader, influenced by a wide spectrum of voices, whose affective responses are a product not only of the text that is read, but of other utterances as well, both textual and atextual.[22]

Interaktion ist ebenso die Grundlage des Konzepts „Mediating Criticism", das der Literaturwissenschaftler Roger D. Sell vertritt. Sell zielt hierbei auf die Interaktion zwischen Autor, Leser und Text und hebt damit „[t]he

---

[21] Macovski, Michael: Introduction: Textual Voices, Vocative Texts: Dialogue, Linguistics, and Critical Discourse. In: Ders. (Hg.): Dialogue and Critical Discourse. Language, Culture, Critical Theory. Oxford, New York: Oxford University Press 1997, S. 3–26, hier S. 4.

[22] Ebd., S. 5.

pragmatic conditions for literature as a genuine form of communication"[23] hervor. Jeder Kommunikation liegt nach Sell ein Kommunikationsdreieck zugrunde, indem zwei Kommunikationseinheiten über eine dritte, zum Beispiel einen literarischen Text, kommunizieren. Auch wenn sich diese kommunizierenden Einheiten in einem soziokulturellen Kontext befinden würden, so sei dieser nicht vollständig determinierend. Sell spricht vielmehr davon, dass neben dem soziokulturellen Kontext eine potentielle, ungebundene menschliche Vorstellungskraft existiert. Dieses begründet er damit, dass eine solche notwendig sei, um sich überhaupt in andere Situationen und Charaktere hineinversetzen zu können, was er als die Grundlage einer „zufriedenstellenden" Kommunikation sieht.[24]

Der Begriff „Dialog" übernimmt in Sells Pragmatik eine schwächere Funktion als bei Weigand und Macovski. Dennoch definiert auch Sell Literatur als Dialog, der sich zwischen Autor und Lesern entwickelt und beschreibt diesen als „a kind of give-and-take which has both ethical entailments and communal consequences"[25]. Auf den Leseprozess bezogen entwickelt Sell, ausgehend von seinem Verständnis von Kommunikation und seiner Idee von Literatur als Dialog, eine „historical yet non-historic pragmatics", um einen bestimmten Autor, einen bestimmten Entstehungskontext und die Rolle der einzelnen Leser mit ihren jeweiligen Lebenserfahrungen für den Prozess der Deutungsbildung sowie den Leseakt als Kommunikationsprozess hervorzuheben.[26] Abschließend fügt er hinzu:

> [D]espite the inevitable lack of correspondence between the author's sense of the work and any particular reader's sense of it, and despite the lack of a feed-back channel, the act of reading can nevertheless be experienced as part of a process of communication, sometimes giving rise to strong antagonism, or even to self-reassessment or personal change, which may ultimately lead to social change as well.[27]

---

[23] Sell, Roger D.: Literature as Communication. The Foundations of Mediating Criticism. Amsterdam: John Benjamins Publishing Company 2000, S. 1.
[24] Ebd., S. 2, 4, 7.
[25] Sell, Roger D.: Communicational Criticism. Amsterdam, Philadelphia: John Benjamins Publishing Company 2011, S. 10.
[26] Vgl. Sell: Literature as Communication (Anm. 23), S. 75.
[27] Ebd.

Dieser letzte Punkt, der auf mögliche Änderungen persönlicher oder kollektiver Verhältnisse im Anschluss an eine Textlektüre verweist, wird unten für die Definition gesellschaftlich engagierter Literatur wichtig werden.

Ausgehend davon, dass ein literarisches Werk immer einen Adressaten präsentiert oder zumindest impliziert, gegenüber welchem die realen Leser Position beziehen, steht in Sells Überlegungen vor allem das Verhältnis zwischen Autor und Leser im Mittelpunkt.[28] Dieses Verhältnis zwischen Autor und Leser werde ich im Folgenden nicht in den Vordergrund stellen, weil mich der Text als Schnittpunkt dieser beiden Akteure stärker interessiert. Sells Versuch, das „writerly there-and-then and some current readership's here-and-now"[29] zusammenzubringen, ist aber im Kontext des Verhältnisses von Autor, Text, Leser und Literaturindustrie interessant. Zunächst aber zum Verhältnis von Fakt und Fiktion.

Gesellschaftlich engagierte Literatur zwischen Fakt und Fiktion?

Auch wenn sich die Bezeichnung „gesellschaftlich engagierte Literatur" auf ein literarisches Werk bezieht, das Referenzen zur außertextuellen Welt aufweist, lässt sich diese Art von Literatur nicht über ihren Anteil an faktualen und fiktionalen Elementen definieren – und nicht nur, weil „viele literarische Texte [...] faktenreich [sind] und viele Texte, von denen man Fakten erwartet, [...] Fiktionen (etwa Wahlkampfreden)" liefern.[30] Zum einen ist das Ermitteln dieses Anteils nicht nur schwierig bis unmöglich. Ein solcher Definitionsmaßstab richtet sich auch gegen wesentliche Charakteristika des literarischen Textes: seine Varianz und seine Möglichkeit, dichotomes Denken zu hinterfragen. Aus diesem

---

[28] Vgl. Sell: Communicational Criticism (Anm. 25), S. 10, 14.
[29] Sell, Roger D.: Mediating Criticism. Literary Education Humanized. Amsterdam, Philadelphia: John Benjamins Publishing Company 2001, S. 26. Sell entwickelt den „Mediating Criticism" für die Analyse einzelner Werke und nicht für die Definition eines Genres. Dennoch sind wesentliche Ansätze für die individuelle Werkinterpretation auch für einen größeren Kontext gültig.
[30] Neuhaus/Selbmann/Unger: Engagierte Literatur (Anm. 7), S. 15.

Grund lässt sich ein literarisches Werk nicht in den Standardrahmen zwingen, den man konstruieren würde, um einen gemeinsamen Nenner für die Beziehung von Fakt und Fiktion zu finden. Auch wenn zum Beispiel ein explizit fiktionaler Erzähler die Beziehung von Fakt und Fiktion definieren würde, so würde seine Definition nur für diesen Text gelten. Andere Texte können eine ganz andere Haltung gegenüber der fiktionalen Verhandlung faktualer Elemente aufweisen. Neben Narration und reflektiertem Sprachgebrauch kann Literatur nämlich gerade durch Verfremdungen der Realität Analogien zu gesellschaftlichen Diskussionen schaffen.

Zum anderen ist dieser empirisch geprägte Ansatz wenig zielführend, wenn man sich dafür interessiert, *wieso* gewissen literarischen Werken zu einem bestimmten Zeitpunkt ein gesellschaftliches Engagement zugeschrieben werden kann. Darüber hinaus würde die Bevorzugung eines dieser Aspekte entweder über die Möglichkeit von Literatur, alternative Realitäten zu konstruieren, oder über ihren Ursprung in der nichtliterarischen Welt hinwegsehen. Sowohl fiktionale Elemente als auch faktuale Referenzen sind dieser Art von Literatur inhärent. Andernfalls würden wir ein literarisches Werk nicht als gesellschaftlich engagiert, das heißt als Kombination von Literatur und sozialem Engagement,[31] definieren. Denn ein gesellschaftlich engagiertes Werk steht trotz der Fragwürdigkeit einer auf faktualen und fiktionalen Anteilen basierenden Definition immer in einem Dialog mit der Wirklichkeit, in der sich der Rezipient zum Zeitpunkt der Lektüre befindet oder die dieser retrospektiv zu aktualisieren versucht. Dieses geschieht beispielsweise, wenn man Texten aus dem 19. Jahrhundert, wie Henrik Ibsens Dramen oder Charles Dickens' Romanen ein gesellschaftliches Engagement zuschreiben möchte.

Anders ausgedrückt, findet im Falle gesellschaftlich engagierter Literatur stets ein deutlich kontextuell beeinflusster Dialog in Form einer Interaktion zwischen dargestellter und außertextueller Welt statt, der die Basis für das zu Beginn erwähnte reziproke Verhältnis von Literatur und Gesellschaft bildet. Dieser Dialog zwischen fiktionalen Darstellungen gesellschaftlicher Verhältnisse und einer außertextuellen Welt kann vom Autor intendiert werden, muss letztlich aber im Text, das heißt in der intradiege-

---

[31] Ebd., S. 12.

tischen Welt, nachvollziehbar sein und vom individuellen Leser aktualisiert werden.[32] Dies leitet über zu dem nächsten Punkt: dem Dialog zwischen Autor, Text, Leser und Literaturindustrie.

Dialoge im literarischen Feld:
Autor – Text – Leser – Literaturindustrie

Genauso wenig zielführend wie die Definition faktualer und fiktionaler Anteile an gesellschaftlich engagierter Literatur ist der Versuch, gesellschaftlich engagierte Literatur über ihren Grad an sozialem Engagement zu definieren. Es gibt kein objektives Werkzeug, um das soziale Engagement eines literarischen Werkes zu messen. Die einzigen Hinweise, die wir als Leser haben, wenn wir entscheiden, dass Literatur gesellschaftlich engagiert ist, sind explizite oder implizite Verweise auf soziale, politische oder historische Gegebenheiten. Irving Howe definiert den politischen Roman als „a novel in which *we take to be dominant* political ideas or the political milieu, a novel which permits this assumption without thereby suffering any radical distortion and, it follows, with the possibility of some analytical profit."[33] Dies lässt sich auf gesellschaftlich engagierte Literatur übertragen. Wieder wird die Beziehung des Werkes zur Öffentlichkeit relevant, dieses Mal aber nicht in Bezug auf außertextuelle inhaltliche Aspekte, sondern mit dem Fokus auf die literarische Öffentlichkeit, den Leser. Nach Wittgenstein und dem, was als pragmatische Semantik bezeichnet wurde, besitzt ein Wort nur Bedeutung, wenn es gebraucht wird.[34] Analog dazu wird Literatur nur dann zu gesellschaftlich engagierter Literatur, wenn sie als solche verwendet beziehungsweise gelesen wird. Um den literarischen Text herum treten also mehrere Akteure in Erscheinung, durch deren Dialoge mit und über den Text gesellschaftlich engagierte Literatur konstruiert wird. Der Begriff „gesellschaftlich engagiert" beinhaltet

---

[32] Sell nennt den Schreibkontext, den intradiegetischen Kontext und den Lesekontext als wesentlich für die literarische Kommunikation. Vgl. Sell: Literature as Communication (Anm. 23), S. 61.
[33] Howe: Politics and the Novel (Anm. 8), S. 17.
[34] Vgl. Hættner Aurelius, Eva: Genrers rörlighet. Genredefinitionens dilemma sett i ett semantiskt perspektiv. In: Tidskrift för litteraturvetenskap 44 (2014), Nr. 3/4, S. 95–104, hier S. 99–102.

immer schon eine Interpretation, die sich aus einer komplexen Kommunikationskette ergibt.

Die übliche, in eine Richtung weisende literarische Kommunikationskette, die, dem Prinzip Sender-Empfänger entsprechend, kurzgefasst die Interaktion zwischen Autor und Leser via impliziten Autor und impliziten Leser beschreibt, muss daher in Bezug auf gesellschaftlich engagierte Literatur als dialogisches Genre um drei Interaktionsstränge erweitert werden. Der literarische Text inklusive seiner Paratexte steht dabei auch nach dieser Modifikation im Mittelpunkt der Kommunikationsketten. Er ist es, der die inhaltliche Grundlage für jegliche Form des literarischen Dialogs bietet.

Auch wenn Huntemann und Patri in dem obigen Zitat die Autorrolle nicht als einzigen Anhaltspunkt für engagierte Literatur betrachten, so betonen sie doch die Intention des historischen Autors, „erhebt er doch gerade den Anspruch einer politischen Meinungsäußerung, zumal er sich auch oft – wie alle prominenten Beispiele beweisen – publizistisch (nichtfiktional) mit Reden, Essays, Interviews usf. zu Wort meldet".[35] Dadurch ließe er sich „dem literarischen und dem politisch-publizistischen"[36] Diskurs zuordnen. Das Für und Wider einer Hervorhebung der Autorintention in Bezug auf engagierte Literatur ist bereits zuvor von Neuhaus, Selbmann und Unger kontrovers diskutiert worden.[37] Eine pragmatisch orientierte dialogische Perspektive umgeht die Notwendigkeit einer Entscheidung dafür oder dagegen, da sie auf den jeweiligen Lesekontext des literarischen Werkes Rücksicht nimmt. In diesem Kontext kann der historische Autor, nach Macovski, eine „Stimme"[38] im Prozess der Bedeutungsentstehung darstellen, muss aber nicht präsent sein. Diese Distanzierung von einer inhärenten Autorintention scheint mit Blick auf die Rolle der Rezipienten für die Konstruktion von gesellschaftlich engagierter Literatur sinnvoll.

Wie insbesondere in der rezeptionsästhetischen Forschung ausführlich diskutiert wurde, werden eventuelle Intentionen, zum Beispiel in Bezug auf das gesellschaftliche Engagement eines Textes, nicht unbedingt von den Lesern erkannt – oder werden von diesen anders gedeutet. Denn auch

---

[35] Huntemann/Patri: Engagierte Literatur (Anm. 5), S. 12.
[36] Ebd.
[37] Vgl. Neuhaus/Selbmann/Unger: Engagierte Literatur (Anm. 7), S. 12f., 15f.
[38] Vgl. Macovski: Introduction (Anm. 21), S. 4.

Leser und Text treten während des Rezeptionsprozesses ebenfalls in einen Dialog. In rezeptionsästhetischer Terminologie ausgedrückt, bringen sie ihre eigenen Erfahrungen und Erwartungshorizonte in diesen Dialog ein, um textuelle Leerstellen zu füllen. Roger D. Sell betont:

> [e]ven at its strongest, the role of [...] initiating participants can never be more decisive for how the communication actually turns out than the role of hearers, readers, receivers or narratees. Both kinds of role can be performed with either greater or lesser success, and the plain fact is that words can be taken in a very different way by one party from that intended by another. As speech-act theoreticians put it, perlocutionary effect may bear little relation to illocutionary act.[39]

Dementsprechend ist die Ergänzung der literarischen Kommunikationskette – vom Leser zum Text – insbesondere in Bezug auf gesellschaftlich engagierte Literatur notwendig.

Auch die Literaturindustrie kann auf die Rezeption eines Werkes einwirken. Paratextuelle Hinweise des Verlags, ob ein Text als gesellschaftlich engagiert gilt, können durchaus seine Rezeption beeinflussen oder auch eine Diskussion hervorrufen – beispielsweise wenn Kritiker, Literaturwissenschaftler oder Leser das vom Verlag beschriebene gesellschaftliche Engagement hinterfragen.

Schließlich kann die Kommunikationskette im Falle gesellschaftlich engagierter Literatur weitergeführt werden. Sobald in der Kontextualisierung von Text und Lektüre auf die Koordinaten und Debatten der außertextuellen Welt eingegangen wird, treten neue Optionen einer kritischen Rezeption hervor. Wie oben angedeutet, kann eine solche Bezugnahme natürlich ursprünglich vom historischen Autor intendiert sein. Dies lässt sich jedoch nicht eindeutig nachprüfen, und es ist auch kein notwendiges Kriterium für das Entstehen dieser dialogischen Situation, in der die Leser als Initiatoren auftreten.

Der literarische Text wird folglich durch ganz unterschiedliche pragmatische Dialogsituationen zur gesellschaftlich engagierten Literatur. In diesem Sinne ist er nicht als autonom zu betrachten, muss aber selbstverständlich gewisse intradiegetische Merkmale enthalten, die es dem individuellen Rezipienten ermöglichen, ihn als gesellschaftlich engagiert zu bestimmen.

---

[39] Sell: Literature as Communication (Anm. 23), S. 3.

Gesellschaftlich engagierte Literatur als dialogisches Genre

Die Beschreibung gesellschaftlich engagierter Literatur über den Begriff des Dialogs bietet sich an, da solche literarischen Werke aufgrund ihrer spezifischen Verhandlungen von außertextuellen Verhältnissen und der aktiven Rolle der individuellen Leser bei der Anerkennung gesellschaftlichen Engagements keinem eindeutig determinierten Genre angehören und ihre Zuweisung als gesellschaftlich engagiert erst in kommunikativen Situationen entsteht. Die Dialogizität gesellschaftlich engagierter Literatur beruht nicht auf einer durch Sprecherwechsel geprägten Konversation, sondern auf der Vielfalt der inter-, intra- und außertextuellen Stimmen, die die Leser bei der Produktion von Bedeutung miteinbeziehen (Macovski), auf der Dialogizität von literarischen Handlungsspielen (Weigand) und auf der von den Lesern wahrgenommenen Interaktion zwischen Faktum und Fiktion. Die Bezeichnung „dialogisches Genre" ist dabei keineswegs als ‚schwammig' zu interpretieren. Im Gegenteil, sie spiegelt das Potenzial dieses Genres auf eine selbstreflexive Art und Weise wider.

Für das Erkennen gesellschaftlicher Probleme und sozialer Ungleichheiten und ihre mögliche Verbesserung sind Interaktion, Empathie, Analysefähigkeiten und die Offenheit gegenüber anderen Lebenssituationen notwendig, um aus einem Text gesellschaftliches Engagement herauszulesen.[40] Hieran anknüpfen lässt sich die Frage nach dem Potenzial gesellschaftlich engagierter Literatur, soziale Verhältnisse zu verändern. Inwiefern Literatur gesellschaftlichen Wandel auslösen kann – inwieweit zum Beispiel Harriet Beecher Stowes Roman *Onkel Toms Hütte* (*Uncle Tom's Ca-*

---

[40] Beispielsweise haben zahlreiche Rezipienten die Sprache in Jonas Hassen Khemiris Roman *Das Kamel ohne Höcker* (*Ett öga rött*, 2003) als authentisches Einwandererschwedisch gelesen und den Roman als Einwandererliteratur definiert, während es sich um eine von Khemiri erfundene Sprache handelt. Ist man sich dessen bewusst, lässt sich *Das Kamel ohne Höcker* als gesellschaftlich engagierter Roman lesen, der stereotype Einwanderer-Zuschreibungen in Frage stellt. Vgl. z. B. Behschnitt, Wolfgang: ‚Willkommen im Vorort': Neue schwedische Literatur zwischen Einwanderer- und Nationalkultur. In: Karin Hoff (Hg.): Literatur der Migration – Migration der Literatur. Frankfurt/Main: P. Lang 2008, S. 35–48, hier S. 36f., 40f. Zur Rezeption von *Das Kamel ohne Höcker* vgl. Källström, Roger: ‚Flygande blattesvenska' – recensenter om språket i Ett öga rött. In: Svenskans beskrivning 28 (2006), S. 125–135.

bin, 1852) zur Abschaffung der Sklaverei in den Vereinigten Staaten beitrug –, darüber herrscht in der Literaturwissenschaft Uneinigkeit.[41] Betrachtet man gesellschaftlich engagierte Literatur als dialogisches Genre, wird allerdings deutlich, dass sie zunächst Denken und Einstellung der Rezipienten beeinflussen kann. Indem diese wiederum in einen Dialog mit gesellschaftlichen und/oder politischen Institutionen treten, können gesellschaftliche Veränderungen erwirkt werden: „[R]egardless of the precise way in which the communicational triangle happens to be realized, any change to the status quo will begin as a change in the communicants' perceptions and evaluations of this real, hypothetical or fictional entity under discussion."[42] Das gesellschaftsverändernde Potenzial dieser Literatur beruht also weniger auf ihrem Inhalt allein als auf ihrem dialogischen Charakter, der eine Kommunikation zwischen den verschiedenen Akteuren – Autor, Text, literarische Öffentlichkeit und auch gesellschaftliche Institutionen – generieren kann.

Literarische Werke als Stellungnahme zu sozialen und politischen Problemen zu lesen, erfordert dabei keine autobiographische oder autofiktionale Perspektive. Eine Fokussierung auf den Autor würde die Perspektive auf gesellschaftlich engagierte Literatur, die im Austausch von kontextuellen und textuellen Elementen entsteht, einschränken. Dieses soll am Beispiel von *April im Angehörigenschweden* (*April i Anhörigsverige*, 2015) der schwedischsprachigen Autorin Susanna Alakoski verdeutlicht werden. *April im Angehörigenschweden* ist ein Tagebuchroman über das Leben der Angehörigen von Suchtkranken und das eigene und gesellschaftliche Schweigen darüber. Dass Alakoski mit ihrem Buch, rückgreifend auf eigene Erlebnisse, auf die Situation der Angehörigen aufmerksam machen möchte, zeigen ihre bisherigen literarischen und kulturjournalistischen Veröffentlichungen sowie ihr aktives Auftreten in der schwedischen Öffentlichkeit. So klingt das Thema bereits in Alakoskis früheren Romanen wie *Bessere Zeiten* (*Svinalängorna*, 2006), *Ich hoffe, du fühlst dich wohl im Gefängnis* (*Håpas du trifs bra i fengelset*, 2010) oder *Oktober im Armutsschweden* (*Oktober i Fattigsverige*, 2012) an und wird bei ihren Lesungen diskutiert. Auf ihrer Homepage schreibt Su-

---

[41] Vgl. hierzu Birthe Sjöbergs einleitende Diskussion zur Macht der Literatur: Litteraturens makt – inledning. In: Birthe Sjöberg (Hg.): Litteraturens makt. Lund: Litteraturvetenskapliga institutionen 2000, S. 9–22.

[42] Sell: Literature as Communication (Anm. 23), S. 2f.

sanna Alakoski: „Ein Schriftsteller sollte einen literarischen Auftrag haben. Ein Schriftsteller muss kein Politiker sein, aber ein Schriftsteller muss Zusammenhänge offenlegen, die politische Konsequenzen haben können."[43] Diese gesellschaftlich engagierte Agenda von Autorinnenseite macht *April im Angehörigenschweden* jedoch noch nicht zu einem gesellschaftlich engagierten Werk. Zu diesem wird es erst durch die zuvor genannten literarischen Akteure. *April im Angehörigenschweden* ist eine Erzählung, deren Handlung und narrative Vermittlung Verlag, Kritiker und Leser dazu bewegen, ihr ein gesellschaftliches Engagement zuzusprechen – ungeachtet möglicher oder unmöglicher Autorintentionen. So schreibt Alakoskis schwedischer Verlag Albert Bonnier auf seiner Internetseite:

> Durch die Literaturgeschichte hindurch betrinken sich Männer meisterlich. Der Süchtige steht im Fokus. Die Frauen werden ungeachtet ihrer Klassenzugehörigkeit als co-abhängige Alkoholikerfrauen gestaltet. Aber jetzt treten Alkoholikerkinder und andere Angehörige in die literarische Arena ein und bezeugen ein vollständig unglamouröses Dasein. Wir, die mit mangelndem Vertrauen, Verleugnung, Angst, Grenzenlosigkeit und Unsicherheit gelebt haben. Chaos, Gewalt. Vermissen, Trauer. Scham.[44]

In den Rezensionen wird *April im Angehörigenschweden* als „wichtig"[45] bezeichnet, als ein Buch, das „ein großes Bedürfnis" erfüllt und „von großem Nutzen" sein wird[46]. Es wird als Lesetipp auf Internetseiten wie der des Nationalen Kompetenzzentrums für Angehörige geführt,[47] und Susanna

---

[43] http://susannaalakoski.se/om/ (07.01.2017). Meine Übersetzung aus dem Schwedischen.

[44] Albert Bonniers Verlag: http://www.albertbonniersforlag.se/Bocker/Svenskskonlitteratur/A/april-i-anhorigsverige/ (02.01.2017). Meine Übersetzung aus dem Schwedischen.

[45] Berg, Aase: Susanna Alakoski: ‚April i Anhörigsverige'. In: http://www.kristianstadsbladet.se/kultur-noje/susanna-alakoski-april-i-anhorigsverige/ (02.01.2017). Meine Übersetzung aus dem Schwedischen.

[46] Schottenius, Maria: Susanna Alakoski: ‚April i Anhörigsverige'. In: http://www.dn.se/dnbok/bokrecensioner/susanna-alakoski-april-i-anhorigsverige/ (02.01.2017). Meine Übersetzung aus dem Schwedischen.

[47] http://www.anhoriga.se/anhorigomraden/psykisk-ohalsa/boktips/9803/ (02.01.2017).

Alakoski berichtet davon, dass sie nach der Veröffentlichung eine außergewöhnliche Menge an Reaktionen und Angehörigenschilderungen erhalten habe.[48] *April im Angehörigenschweden* wird somit zum Mittelpunkt verschiedener dialogischer Situationen, in denen die Rezipienten die dargestellte und außertextuelle Welt in Beziehung setzen und dem Roman sein gesellschaftliches Engagement zusprechen beziehungsweise ein eventuell intendiertes Engagement aktualisieren.

Anhand der zentralen Rolle der Rezipienten wird deutlich, dass gesellschaftlich engagierte Literatur, wie oben erklärt, nicht notwendig ein aktiver Teil öffentlicher, politischer Debatten sein muss: Geht man davon aus, dass einem literarischen Werk sein gesellschaftliches Engagement im Leseakt zugesprochen oder bestätigt wird, kann dieses durchaus auf einem ‚privaten' Niveau geschehen. Leser können, basierend auf ihren eigenen Wahrnehmungen und Bedeutungszuschreibungen, ein literarisches Werk ganz individuell als gesellschaftlich engagierte Literatur lesen, ohne dass diese Deutung kollektive Gültigkeit besitzt oder gar zu einer öffentlichen Einflussnahme führt.

Die Aussagen bezüglich der Dialogizität von Literatur lassen sich selbstverständlich auf literarische Texte im Allgemeinen beziehen, insbesondere, wenn man Weigands Aussage folgt, dass „every individual speech act can be considered as dialogically oriented"[49]. Die Betonung von Dialogizität im Falle gesellschaftlich engagierter Literatur hat nichts mit einer künstlerischen oder thematischen Bewertung von literarischen Textvarianten zu tun, sondern allein damit, wie diese Werke inhaltlich und formal gestaltet sind und damit Potenzial für gesellschaftlich engagierte Interpretationen bieten.

Darüber hinaus wurde zu Beginn die Behauptung aufgestellt, dass eine Definition über inhaltliche Merkmale allein nicht ausreichend ist. Das gleiche gilt natürlich auch für eine Definition über den dialogischen Charakter allein. Dialogischer Charakter und inhaltliche Merkmale sind in einer Relation wechselseitiger Abhängigkeit zu betrachten, wodurch sich thematische und wirkungstechnische Unterschiede in literarischen Werken erkennen lassen.

---

[48] Vgl. Alakoski, Susanna: En oändlig ström av sorg på våra gator. In: http://arbetet.se/2015/05/22/en-oandlig-strom-av-sorg-pa-vara-gator/ (02.01.2017).
[49] Weigand: The Dialogic Principle Revisited (Anm. 14), S. 22.

In ihrem Vorgespräch zu dem Sammelband *Engagierte Literatur zwischen den Weltkriegen* (2002) definieren Stefan Neuhaus, Rolf Selbmann und Thorsten Unger engagierte Literatur nach bestimmten Kategorien wie Autor- oder Textintention oder ästhetischen Qualitäten. Dabei machen sie selbst deutlich, dass sie zu keinem Konsens gelangen.[50] Huntemann und Patri umgehen Entscheidungen, indem sie neben dem Autor sowohl den Text als auch die literarische Öffentlichkeit und den politischen Status quo als Referenzpunkte für engagierte Literatur anführen. In Bezug auf den Autor und die Autorintentionen ist für eine Modifikation argumentiert worden, die diese Aspekte nicht als notwendige Bedingungen für gesellschaftlich engagierte Literatur sieht. Eine einengende Festlegung dessen, was gesellschaftlich engagierte Literatur aus formaler oder inhaltlicher Perspektive ist, scheint angesichts ihres dialogischen Charakters, der aus pragmatischen Gründen immer individuelle Perspektiven und Momente situativer Kommunikation einbezieht, weder durchführbar noch erstrebenswert. Weder die Intentionalität von Autor respektive Text wird durch die Betonung der Dialogizität unangemessen in den Vordergrund gestellt noch die rezeptionshistorische Kontextualisierung als Alleinstellungsmerkmal hervorgehoben. Statt von einer „Wirkungsabsicht"[51] engagierter Literatur zu sprechen, die sich nach Selbmann auf die Intention eines Textes bezieht, bietet es sich daher an, den Zusatz „gesellschaftlich engagiert" zwar als inhaltliche und methodische Eingrenzung, aber vor allem als Positionsbestimmung eines Werkes im literarischen Feld zu verstehen.

---

[50] Vgl. Neuhaus/Selbmann/Unger: Engagierte Literatur (Anm. 7), S. 9.
[51] Ebd., S. 11, 15.

Dialog und Dialogizität im *Taugenichts* von Robert Walser

Myriam Dätwyler

1. Der Dialog im Drama nach 1900

Der Dialog zwischen den Figuren, den Robert Walser zu Beginn des 20. Jahrhunderts auf die Bühne bringt, funktioniert nicht reibungslos. Die Figuren reden aneinander vorbei und hören einander nicht zu.[1] Doch gerade das Experimentieren mit dem Dialog und das Hinterfragen seiner Voraussetzungen treibt die Arbeit Walsers produktiv voran. Allerdings schenken Walsers Zeitgenossen sowie die Forschungsliteratur zum Genre ‚Drama' dem Dialog weniger Aufmerksamkeit als anderen formalen und inhaltlichen Fragen. Maurice Maeterlinck zum Beispiel, welcher 1900 in der avantgardistischen Zeitschrift *Die Insel* einen Essay unter dem Titel *Das moderne Drama*[2] veröffentlicht, formuliert die Charakteristiken des „neuen Dramas", kommt jedoch nirgends auf den Dialog selbst

---

[1] Ein Beispiel dafür ist das *Schneewittchen*-Dramolett Walsers, das 1901 in der Zeitschrift *Die Insel* erscheint. Bei Peter Utz ist in Bezug darauf zu lesen, dass die Figuren „präzise aneinander vorbei" reden, vgl. ders.: Tanz auf den Rändern. Robert Walsers „Jetztzeitstil". Frankfurt/Main: Suhrkamp 1998, S. 289. Auch andere Schriftsteller problematisieren den Dialog und das gegenseitige Verstehen, beispielsweise Tschechow. In *Drei Schwestern* (1900) setzt der russische Schriftsteller dafür einen Schwerhörigen ein, in dessen Beisein allein die Figur Andrej sprechen kann, da er weiß, dass er nicht verstanden wird. Tschechow, Anton: Drei Schwestern. Übersetzt von Sigismund von Radecki. Stuttgart: Reclam 2011, S. 28. Vgl. dazu auch: Szondi, Peter: Theorie des modernen Dramas. Frankfurt/Main: Suhrkamp 1969, S. 37f., 77.

[2] Maeterlinck, Maurice: Das moderne Drama. In: Die Insel 1/2 (1899/1900), S. 48–60. Der Essay wurde von F. von Oppeln-Bronikowski übersetzt und war in Frankreich noch nicht erschienen.

zu sprechen.³ Das Drama befindet sich um die Jahrhundertwende in einer Umbruchphase, die später von Szondi als ‚Krise des Dramas' betitelt wird.⁴ Auch der Dialog ist dabei inbegriffen, wird aber selten explizit erläutert. Ebenso wurde die Analyse des Dialogs und seiner Funktionsweise in der Literaturwissenschaft vernachlässigt; es besteht ein Mangel an methodologischen Mitteln, welche die spezifischen Eigenschaften literarischer Dialoge berücksichtigen.

Der dramatische Dialog um die Jahrhundertwende, seine Struktur und das künstlerische Potential, das im Spiel mit den Bedingungen des Dialogs liegt, werden im ersten Teil dieses Beitrags am Beispiel des Dramoletts *Der Taugenichts* von Robert Walser thematisiert. Welche spezifischen Züge trägt dieses Stück hinsichtlich des Dialogs? Kann man überhaupt von Dialog sprechen? Wie lassen sich die Struktur und Funktionsweise des Dialogs analysieren? Im zweiten Teil soll das von Michail Bachtin stammende Konzept der Dialogizität adaptiert werden, um die Textur von Walsers Stück herauszuarbeiten. Die Metaphorizität des Begriffs, die Entwicklung, welcher er bei Bachtin selbst durchläuft, sowie die unterschiedlichen Aspekte, welche mit der Dialogizität zusammenhängen – unter anderem der Leser bzw. Zuschauer, die Intertextualität und die Gattungsfrage –, sind dabei zu berücksichtigen.

1.1. Zu den Methoden der Analyse des literarischen Dialogs

Zu Beginn ist es notwendig, den literarischen Dialog in Abgrenzung zum Alltagsdialog sowie die spezifischen Analysemethoden zu definieren. Die ‚klassischen' Ablaufbedingungen eines Alltags- und eines literarischen Dialogs sind grundsätzlich dieselben: die Beteiligung von mindestens zwei Personen/Figuren, das Alternieren von Sprecher- und Hörerrolle, die thematische Gebundenheit, d. h. das Sich-Aufeinander-Beziehen der Dialogpartner, sowie die Kommunikationssituation, welche implizit oder explizit Teil eines Dialogs ist. Im dramatischen Dialog allerdings modifiziert der Leser/Zuschauer diese Bedingungen. In einem natürlichen Gespräch teilen

---

[3] Genannt wird unter anderem die „Abschwächung und Lähmung der äußeren Handlung zu Gunsten der unverkennbaren Tendenz das menschliche Seelenleben tiefer zu erfassen […]." Ebd., S. 48.
[4] Szondi: Theorie des modernen Dramas (Anm. 1), S. 20.

die anwesenden Kommunikationspartner eine gemeinsame Sprechsituation und partiell auch das Vorwissen, auf das sie sich beziehen können. Dieses Vorwissen ist im Dialog impliziert. Im Drama dagegen „kommt es zu einem ‚Mehr' an Informationen, zu einer Explikation der pragmatischen Ebene, um dem Leser einen ‚sinngarantierenden Kontext' zu bieten".[5]

Es sind außerdem auf der syntaktischen und lexikalischen Ebene Unterschiede zwischen einem Alltags- und einem literarischen Dialog zu verzeichnen, wie dies auch bei der Unterscheidung von mündlichen und schriftlichen Texten der Fall ist, insofern ein schriftlicher Text nicht konzeptionell mündlich angelegt ist oder umgekehrt. Die dramatische Sprache ist in der Regel durch ein höheres Reflexionsniveau charakterisiert und orientiert sich an schriftsprachlichen Normen, selbst da, wo ein Autor in der Figurenrede Mündlichkeit fingiert.[6] In Bezug auf die Analyse des dramatischen Textes Walsers interessiert jedoch weniger das Verhältnis von Mündlichkeit und Schriftlichkeit als vielmehr das gegenseitige Verstehen und das Verhältnis der Figuren zueinander sowie die Handlungsbezogenheit der Rede, welche für den dramatischen Dialog konstitutiv ist. Diesbezüglich ist jedoch eine methodologische Lücke innerhalb der Literaturwissenschaft zu konstatieren.[7] Immer wieder wird in diesem Kontext auf das linguistische, spezifischer auf das textlinguistische Instrumentarium verwiesen.[8] Die Linguisten und Linguistinnen interessieren sich seit den 1980er Jahren insbesondere für den literarischen Dialog. Auf Seiten der Linguistik können die Herangehensweisen jedoch disparater nicht sein;

---

[5] Kiel, Ewald: Dialog und Handlung im Drama. Untersuchungen zur Theorie und Praxis einer sprachwissenschaftlichen Analyse literarischer Texte. Frankfurt/Main: P. Lang 1992, S. 20. Kiel zitiert hier: Ingenschay, Dieter: Sekundäre Konstruktionen. Überlegungen zum Verhältnis von Drama und Handlungstheorie. In: Poetica 12 (1980), S. 443–463.

[6] Kiel: Dialog und Handlung im Drama (Anm. 5), S. 23.

[7] Dies bestätigt beispielsweise auch Asmuth, Bernhard: Einführung in die Dramenanalyse. 5. aktual. Aufl. Stuttgart: Metzler 1997, S. 72.

[8] Beispielsweise Pfister, Manfred: Das Drama. Theorie und Analyse. München: W. Fink 1977, S. 204. Auch Ernest Hess-Lüttich schlägt zur Deskription des Dialogs unter anderem textlinguistische Verfahren vor: Hess-Lüttich, Ernest: Soziale Interaktion und literarischer Dialog. Zeichen und Schichten in Drama und Theater: Gerhart Hauptmanns ‚Ratten'. Berlin: E. Schmidt 1985, S. 150.

eine mehr oder weniger einheitliche Methode bezüglich der oben genannten Aspekte hat sich bislang nicht durchgesetzt.[9]

Wie lassen sich also das Verstehen, das Missverstehen oder das Nicht-Verstehen, das Miteinander- oder Aneinander-Vorbei-Reden sowie das Verhältnis der Figuren zueinander innerhalb der Dialogstrukturen in dramatischen Texten analysieren? Diese Fragen betreffen die Kohärenz und die Kohäsion des Dialogs. Es ist zu beschreiben, wie die Figurenaussagen thematisch bzw. inhaltlich miteinander verknüpft sind und wie die Verkettung der Aussagen auf der sprachlichen Ebene aussieht. „Lässt der Antwortende seinen Partner ausreden oder fällt er ihm ins Wort? Geht er auf den eigentlichen Sinn von dessen Äußerung – bestätigend oder zurechtweisend – ein, oder greift er einen Nebeninhalt heraus? Lässt er vielleicht, etwa in der Fortsetzung seiner eigenen letzten Worte, die des Partners ganz außer Acht?", fragt beispielsweise Asmuth.[10] Diese für Walsers dramati-

---

[9] Die Methodenvielfalt geht auf eine Diversität der Fragestellungen zurück, für den Redestil der Figuren aus sprachsoziologischer Sicht interessiert sich vor allem Hess-Lüttich: Soziale Interaktion und literarischer Dialog (Anm. 8). Verschiedene Herangehensweisen (beispielsweise eine Analyse von Interaktionspostulaten sowie der Grice'schen Kooperation und die der Intention der Gesprächsteilnehmer aus pragmatischer Sicht) sind versammelt in: Hess-Lüttich, Ernest (Hg.): Literatur und Konversation. Sprachsoziologie und Pragmatik in der Literaturwissenschaft. Wiesbaden: Atheneion 1980. In den 1980er Jahren setzt sich Edda Weigand eingehend mit dem dramatischen Dialog und der Zuordnung der jeweiligen Dialogteile bzw. Figurenaussagen zu Sprechakttypen auseinander: Weigand, Edda: Sprache als Dialog. Sprechakttaxonomie und kommunikative Grammatik. Tübingen: Niemeyer 1989. Franz Hundsnurscher konzentriert sich auf die kommunikative Intention des Sprechers, die Faktoren der Sprechsituation sowie die sprachlichen Regeln für Äußerungsformen mit hörerzentrierten Effekten. Hundsnurscher, Franz: Dialoganalyse und Literaturbetrachtung. In: Edda Weigand (Hg.): Concepts of Dialogue. Tübingen: Niemeyer 1994, S. 77–105. Näheres zu den Grice'schen Konversationsmaximen, dem Prinzip der kooperativen Kommunikation und der Implikatur vgl. Kiel: Dialog und Handlung im Drama (Anm. 5).

[10] Asmuth: Einführung in die Dramenanalyse (Anm. 7), S. 74. Pfister zufolge steht ebenfalls das textlinguistische Kriterium der Kohärenz der Aussagen (der einzelnen Figur, aber auch der aufeinander bezogenen Aussagen verschiedener Figuren) bei der Analyse der Dialogstruktur im Mittelpunkt. Pfister: Das Drama (Anm. 8), S. 204. Beide Einführungen sind inzwischen zwar schon älter, werden jedoch immer noch als aktuell angesehen, was sich in ihren Auflagen widerspiegelt.

sche Texte ergiebigen Ansätze und Fragen müssen für *Der Taugenichts* um die Frage nach dem Redeanteil und der Positionierung der Figuren sowie ihrer Funktion im Dialog ergänzt werden. Bereits diese relativ ‚simplen' Methoden erlauben es, die Dialogstruktur von Walsers Stück, welches im Folgenden eingeführt wird, näher zu beschreiben.

1.2. Walsers Dramolett *Der Taugenichts*

Der Schweizer Schriftsteller Robert Walser (1878–1956), von Robert Musil, Franz Kafka und Walter Benjamin gerne gelesen und oft als Schriftsteller für Schriftsteller betitelt, widmet sich seit Beginn seiner Tätigkeit der kleinen Form. Außer den drei großen Romanen aus der ‚Berliner Zeit', mit denen sein Bekanntheitsgrad beachtlich steigt, machen unzählige Feuilletons, Prosastücke und Kurzdramen wie das Dramolett, den Großteil seines Gesamtwerks aus. Seine Texte publiziert Walser in Buchform und in unterschiedlichen Periodika wie *Die Insel*, *Die Schaubühne*, später umbenannt in *Die Weltbühne*, die *Frankfurter Zeitung* oder das *Berliner Tageblatt*. Das Dramolett *Der Taugenichts* veröffentlicht Walser 1922 in der Schweizer Zeitschrift *Pro Helvetia*.

Der Titel nimmt es vorweg: Walsers Dramolett ist eine dramatisierte Version der Novelle Eichendorffs *Aus dem Leben eines Taugenichts* (1826). Das intermediale Übersetzen erlaubt es Walser – neben dem ironischen Umgang mit dem Stoff –, sich von der romantischen Novelle zu distanzieren und gleichzeitig gegen seine Etikettierung als (Neo-)Romantiker anzuschreiben.[11] Wenn Walser Eichendorffs Novelle in die dramatische Form übersetzt, versetzt er gleichzeitig auch dessen Figur in eine andere Epoche bzw. ändert deren Referenzrahmen. Walsers Taugenichts benötigt nun eine „Auf-

---

[11] Walsers *Poetenleben* (1917) hat viele Rezensenten, darunter Max Brod und Hermann Hesse, zu Vergleichen mit Eichendorff veranlasst. Hesse publiziert in der *Neuen Zürcher Zeitung* einen Artikel, in dem er zuerst *Aus dem Leben eines Taugenichts* zitiert und dessen Rezeptionsgeschichte darlegt und danach Walsers *Poetenleben* kommentiert. Hesse will Walser bei seinem Vergleich mit Eichendorff jedoch keinesfalls als „Romantiker oder ‚Neuromantiker'" verstanden wissen, der mit „Talent und Glück alte poetische Rezepte wieder verwende" (Neue Zürcher Zeitung, Nr. 2222 v. 25. Nov. 1917), stilisiert ihn dann aber implizit doch zu einem Dichter mit neoromantischen Zügen, worauf Walser brieflich reagiert.

enthaltsbewilligung"[12] um zu reisen – das Vagabundieren funktioniert nicht mehr so bequem und problemlos wie im fiktionalen Raum der Romantiker. Die Figur ist zudem mit ihrer eigenen Vorgeschichte bekannt, auf die immer wieder angespielt wird. Diese wird auch beim Leser/Zuschauer vorausgesetzt. Der moderne Taugenichts reist – anders als die Figur in der Novelle Eichendorffs – nach Berlin, sogar nach Venezuela und tritt in Salzburg als Schauspieler auf. Er fühlt sich nichtsdestotrotz „im eigenen Kleid [...] am wöhlsten"[13] und möchte „jene Taugenichtsstunden, die mit Bachesrauschen, Mühlradsklappern, [...] Schwalbenzwitschern, Fuhrmannspeitschenknallen und Wagenrollen eng verquickt sind",[14] noch einmal erleben. Eichendorffs Novelle ist im Hintergrund des Dramoletts Walsers demnach stets präsent, wird als Referenz immer wieder aufgerufen. Das Stück setzt überdies mit der Schlussszene aus Eichendorffs Novelle ein, d. h. mit der Wiederbegegnung mit der Geliebten. Walser geht es also nicht darum, die Geschichte neu zu erzählen, sondern vielmehr um das Spannungsverhältnis zwischen dem romantischen Taugenichts und seinem Auftritt in einer modernen Landschaft sowie um die Auseinandersetzung der Figur mit ihrer eigenen literarischen Existenz. Dies alles charakterisiert das Dramolett und fungiert als Motor des Dialogs.

1.2.1. Im Dialog mit sich selbst

Das Dramolett besteht aus zwei Monologteilen des Taugenichts, die am Anfang und am Ende angesiedelt sind, und aus einem Dialog, der sich hauptsächlich zwischen dem Taugenichts und der Geliebten, genannt die Zofe, abspielt. Dem Dialog geht eine metasprachliche Anmerkung der Hauptfigur voraus:

> Taugenichts: [...] Wenn sie dich etwas fragen, so antworte ihnen möglichst witzig; im übrigen gib gar nicht so sehr acht, was du sagst. Red' etwas, das Wie ist völlig gleich. Ich hab den größten Unsinn sprechen hören und kann schwören, dass die Wirkung und der Eindruck, der Effekt und der Erfolg geradezu berückend waren.[15]

---

[12] Walser, Robert: Der Taugenichts. In: Jochen Greven (Hg.): Komödie. Sämtliche Werke in Einzelausgaben. Bd. 14. Zürich, Frankfurt/Main: Suhrkamp 1986, S. 138.
[13] Ebd., S. 140.
[14] Ebd., S. 141.
[15] Ebd., S. 136.

Der Taugenichts legt den Akzent also auf die „Wirkung" seines Sprechens; Wahrheitsgehalt und Form treten in den Hintergrund. Der Inhalt und Sinn seiner Aussagen werden fragwürdig. Doch beschreibt der Taugenichts damit vor allem eine (sinnvolle) kommunikative Strategie, welche die Absicht verfolgt, beim Dialogpartner einen gewissen „Eindruck" und den gewünschten „Effekt" zu erzeugen. Unterstrichen wird dabei auch die Performativität des Sprechens. Die Hauptfigur erzählt ihre Vergangenheit und erdichtet dabei gleichzeitig ihr ‚Selbst' im Dialog. Von diesem ‚Selbst' handelt das Stück hauptsächlich. Denn so heißt es im Anfangsmonolog: „Die Taschen sind leer, ich kam arm nach Hause, hab' doch etwas mitgebracht: mich selbst."[16]

Betrachtet man die Struktur des Dialogs, in dem es hauptsächlich um die Erlebnisse des Taugenichts geht, so fällt vor allem die Funktion der Zofe ins Auge, nämlich die, ihrem Gegenüber Fragen zu stellen.

Taugenichts: […] Ich war in Italien.
Zofe: Du?
Taugenichts: Ganz gewiss!
Zofe: Und wo sonst noch?
Taugenichts: In Rom.
Zofe: So lautet die Hauptstadt dieses schönen Landes. Was tatest du dort?
Taugenichts: Nicht sehr viel. Ich tat überhaupt nie viel. Jedenfalls hab' ich mich nicht überanstrengt, würde das nicht für passend gefunden haben. Sind Menschen nicht zum Glück bestimmt?
Zofe: Einige meinen's, andere aber sind durchaus nicht dieser Ansicht.
Taugenichts: Sah dort einen wundervollen Springbrunnen in blendend heiterem Mondlicht. Schöneres gibt es nicht. O Juwel von einer Stunde! Auch du warst dort, obgleich du's leugnen wirst. […] Daraufhin –
Zofe: Was darauf?
Taugenichts: Packte mich einer und nannte mich unverdientermaßen einen Taugenichts, band mir mit einer an Frechheit grenzenden Flink-

---

[16] Ebd.

heit und mit einer an Zauberei erinnernden Dreistigkeit die Augen zu. Ich wurde in einen Wagen gehoben und abtransportiert.
Zofe: Wohin?
Taugenichts: Nach Venezuela.[17]

Die Figurenaussagen sind inhaltlich/thematisch eng miteinander verbunden, eine Kohärenz kann den aufeinanderfolgenden Repliken nicht abgesprochen werden. Doch ist der Redeanteil der Figuren unausgeglichen. Die Zofe nimmt dabei vorwiegend die Position einer Zuhörerin ein und fungiert so als Rückenfigur.[18] Sie will – wie der Leser/Zuschauer auch – wissen, wer dieser Taugenichts ist und ob es sich um den eichendorffschen Taugenichts handelt.

Der Dialog selbst besitzt eher die Charakteristik eines Monologes und dient der Selbstinszenierung des Taugenichts. Das Monologisieren der Figuren im dramatischen Dialog scheint symptomatisch für Walsers Epoche. Es sei die Tendenz der Figurendialoge um 1900, so Szondi, ins Monologische zu kippen.[19] Dem ist allerdings hinzuzufügen, dass der Dialog auf eine andere Ebene transportiert wird. In diesem Fall stehen der Dialog der literarischen Figur mit sich selbst sowie die Auseinandersetzung der Figur mit ihrem Auftritt in einem modernen Zeitalter im Vordergrund. Konkret ist dies an den Monologteilen des Stückes ablesbar, welche eine dialogische Struktur aufweisen. Der Taugenichts stellt sich Fragen, die er sich jeweils selbst beantwortet, dialogisiert also mit sich selbst: „Übereil dich nicht, mein Freund. Ein gewisses Quantum Leben steht dir wohl noch bevor."[20] Weiter heißt es im Selbstgespräch des Taugenichts: „Selige Minute, die mich glauben macht, alles sei nun in Ordnung und ich müsse glücklich werden. Warum glaub' ich das? Bin ich leichtgläubig? […] Trau' ich mir so

---

[17] Ebd., S. 137.
[18] Der Begriff ‚Rückenfigur' wird in Bezug auf die Malerei und die Fotographie verwendet. Er dient dazu, dem Zuschauer den Eintritt in die dargestellte Welt zu erleichtern, da ihm angeboten wird, sich mit der Rückenfigur zu identifizieren. Ähnlich ist in Walsers Dramolett die Rolle der Zofe angelegt. Sie hat primär die Rolle einer Zuhörerin und will mehr über den Taugenichts erfahren. Sie begünstigt damit die Einbindung des Lesers/Zuschauers in den Text, bewirkt also, anders ausgedrückt, eine Öffnung hin zum Rezipienten.
[19] Vgl. Szondi: Theorie des modernen Dramas (Anm. 1), S. 77.
[20] Walser: Der Taugenichts (Anm. 12), S. 135.

sehr?"[21] Die sich selbst gegebene Antwort lautet: „Ja, ich tu es und hoffe, dass das eine Stärke sei, wo nicht, so will ich schwach sein, tut auch nichts. Ein Mensch ist, wie er einmal geschaffen ist."[22] Es lässt sich demnach festhalten, dass der formal dialogische Teil des Stückes monologischen Charakter hat und die Monologteile, in denen sich der Taugenichts mit sich selbst auseinandersetzt, dialogischen Charakter besitzen.

2. Dialogizität in Walsers *Taugenichts*

Angesichts dessen, dass nicht der Dialog zwischen den Figuren, sondern vielmehr das Verhältnis der Taugenichts-Figur zu ihrer literarischen Vergangenheit sowie das Zusammenspiel des Textes mit dem Leser/Zuschauer in den Vordergrund rückt – gerade in den dialogisierten Monologteilen dient der Leser/Zuschauer als Gegenüber – eignet sich Michail Bachtins Konzept der Dialogizität als Beschreibungsinstrument. Dies soll im Folgenden erläutert und für eine literarische Analyse adaptiert werden.

2.1. Aspekte der Dialogizität

Bachtins Idee der Dialogizität oder des dialogischen Verhältnisses entwickelt sich in unterschiedlichen Phasen, die in der Literaturwissenschaft oft nicht berücksichtigt werden. Bereits im Werk *Probleme der Poetik Dostoevskijs* (1929) hebt Bachtin die Polyphonie hervor, die ihm zufolge aus der Kopräsenz der verschiedenen Stimmen eines Textes entsteht und zwar der Stimmen der (eigenständigen) Helden eines Romans oder von Held und Autor.[23] Dialogisch wird der Roman Dostojewskijs dadurch, dass die Helden und der Autor bzw. deren Bewusstsein miteinander interagieren, ohne

---

[21] Ebd., S. 135f.
[22] Ebd., S. 136.
[23] Bachtin, Michail: Probleme der Poetik Dostoevskijs (1929). Übersetzt von Adelheid Schramm. München: C. Hanser 1971, S. 10. Vgl. dazu Wutsdorff, Irina: Bachtin und der Prager Strukturalismus. Modelle poetischer Offenheit am Beispiel der tschechischen Avantgarde. München: W. Fink 2006, S. 39.

dass eine Stimme überhandnimmt.[24] Durch die Simultaneität der unterschiedlichen Stimmen im Wort manifestiert sich, laut Bachtin, das Dialogische im Roman, in dem die Stimmen immer aufeinander bezogen sind.[25] Der Begriff der Polyphonie bezeichnet dabei den Pluralismus und die Koexistenz der Stimmen, das Dialogische die Beziehungen der koexistierenden Kräfte zueinander, also ihre Wechselwirkung; beide Begriffe werden jedoch beinahe synonym verwendet.[26]

Zu dieser dialogischen Ausrichtung kommt noch hinzu, dass das Wort bei Dostojewskij, laut Bachtin, immer adressiert, d. h. nie definitiv ist.[27] Diese Poetik der Offenheit sowie das Adressiertsein des Textes machen das Dialogische eines Romans ebenfalls aus. Problematisch ist jedoch Bachtins fast vollständiger Verzicht auf Belegstellen für die Polyphonie und die dialogischen Verhältnisse im Werk Dostojewskijs. Eine konkrete Analyse literarischer Texte ist, wohl auch für Bachtin selbst, der Metaphorizität des Konzepts wegen schwierig und muss beispielsweise durch narratologische Konzepte ergänzt werden.[28]

---

[24] So heißt es bei Bachtin: „Das Wort des Helden über sich selbst und die Welt hat genau so viel Gewicht wie das gewöhnliche Autorenwort […]. Ihm kommt völlige Selbstständigkeit in der Struktur des Werkes zu, es erklingt *neben* dem Autorenwort und wird auf besondere Weise mit ihm und den vollwertigen Stimmen anderer Helden verbunden." Bachtin: Probleme der Poetik Dostoevskijs (Anm. 23), S. 11.

[25] Vgl. dazu: „Dostoevskijs Intentionen nach ist der Held Träger eines vollwertigen Wortes und nicht stummes, schweigsames Objekt des Autorenwortes. Der Autor konzipiert den Helden als *Wort*. Deshalb ist das Wort des Autors über den Helden ein Wort über ein anderes Wort. Es ist an dem Helden als an einem Wort orientiert und deshalb *dialogisch* an ihn *gerichtet*. Der ganze Roman ist so angelegt, dass der Autor nicht *über*, sondern *mit* dem Helden spricht." Ebd., S. 72.

[26] So auch Sasse, Sylvia: Michail Bachtin. Zur Einführung. Hamburg: Junius 2010, S. 84.

[27] „Das Moment der *Anrede* ist jedem Wort bei Dostoevskij eigen, dem Wort der Erzählung in gleichem Maße wie dem Helden." Bachtin: Probleme der Poetik Dostoevskijs (Anm. 23), S. 267. Vgl dazu auch: „Es gibt also in den Werken Dostoevskijs kein endgültiges, abschließendes, ein für allemal bestimmendes Wort." Ebd., S. 284.

[28] Eine Analyse der Romane Dostojewskis lässt sich mit dem Modell Bachtins nur schwer durchführen. Auch die Dialogizität tritt bei Dostojewski nicht in jenem Maße auf, wie Bachtin behauptet, vgl. Wutsdorff: Bachtin und der Prager Strukturalismus (Anm. 23), S. 26f. Die Schwierigkeit liegt darin, dass Bachtins Kon-

Eine weitere Etappe in der Arbeit Bachtins und des darin zentralen Konzepts der Dialogizität markiert der Text *Das Wort im Roman* aus den 1930er Jahren. Darin postuliert Bachtin eine dem „Wort" eigene, ontologische Dialogizität, welche kein ästhetisches Phänomen sei, sondern die Eigenschaft der Sprache an sich.[29] Die verschiedenen koexistierenden Kräfte bzw. Stimmen sind darin jedoch kaum lokalisierbar oder definierbar, das Konzept selbst noch abstrakter als in seiner Studie zu Dostojewskij. Oft ist nur von fremden Stimmen oder Worten die Rede.[30] Es sind dies die Stimmen der Epoche, der Tradition, des sozialen Umfelds und aller potentiell sprechenden Instanzen. Diese Stimmen bzw. die Dialogizität gelten Bachtin als Voraussetzung des Schreibens. Für den Prosaschriftsteller

> ist der Gegenstand eine Konzentration von in der Rede differenzierten Stimmen, unter denen auch seine eigene Stimme erklingen muss; die Stimmen bilden den notwendigen Hintergrund für seine Stimme, einen Hintergrund, ohne den die Nuancen seiner künstlerischen Prosa nicht wahrnehmbar sind, ‚nicht klingen'.[31]

Wie lässt sich dieses Konzept für eine literarische Analyse nutzen? Wiederum sind bei Bachtin selbst keine bzw. sehr wenige konkrete Beispiele dieser Form der Dialogizität ausfindig zu machen. Die Dialogizität bzw. die Stimmen sind eigentlich Metaphern in heuristischer Absicht.[32] Bachtin selbst spricht in den beiden Texten (*Probleme der Poetik Dostoevskijs* und *Das Wort im Roman*) unter anderem von den Stimmen des ‚Autors' und des ‚Helden', also

---

zept, literaturwissenschaftlich gesehen, nicht präzise genug ist, so Wutsdorff, um eine Analyse von Texten anhand seines Konzepts der offenen Poetik durchzuführen. Ebd., S. 183.

[29] Vgl. Sasse: Michail Bachtin (Anm. 26), S. 90. Dieses Phänomen nennt Bachtin auch Mikrodialog.

[30] „[Z]wischen Wort und Gegenstand, zwischen Wort und sprechender Person liegt die elastische und meist schwer zu durchdringende Sphäre der andern, fremden Wörter zu demselben Gegenstand, zum gleichen Thema." Bachtin, Michail: Das Wort im Roman. In: Ders.: Die Ästhetik des Wortes. Übersetzt von Rainer Grübel. Frankfurt/Main: Suhrkamp 1979, S. 169.

[31] Ebd., S. 171.

[32] Die Metaphorizität des Begriffs wird in Bezug auf Bachtins Konzept mehrmals erwähnt in: Blödorn, Andreas / Daniela Langer / Michael Scheffel (Hg.): Stimme(n) im Text. Narratologische Positionsbestimmungen. Berlin: de Gruyter 2006, S. 2, 9, 16, 53 u. a.

Textinstanzen, setzt aber auch die Begriffe ‚Intentionen', ‚Standpunkte', ‚Bewusstseine' und ‚Bedeutungstendenzen' ein, die in eine Wechselwirkung miteinander treten.[33] Die Unschärfe des Begriffs besitzt meines Erachtens jedoch folgenden Mehrwert: In der Stimmenmetaphorik ist die Flüchtigkeit einer Instanz, einer Intention sowie ihre potentielle Konturlosigkeit impliziert. Die Dialogizität erlaubt es zudem, das Phänomen der Überlagerung, die Pluralität von Stimmen zu erfassen.[34] Teil der Dialogizität ist auch die Adressiertheit an den Leser, welcher eine wichtige Konstituente im Text darstellt. Welche Rolle ihm in Bezug auf die Dialogizität zukommt, soll thematisiert werden. Eine weitere Facette bildet die Intertextualität, die Kristeva in den 1960er Jahren von Bachtin aus entwickelt und die es in einem weiter gefassten Begriff der Dialogizität ebenfalls zu berücksichtigen gilt. Die Intertextualität als Teil der Dialogizität zu betrachten, bedeutet jedoch nicht, zwei Texte stünden in einem direkten dialogischen Verhältnis zueinander.[35] Vielmehr kann ein Text als ‚Stimme' einen anderen Text mitkonstruieren und mit dessen ‚Stimmen' in eine Wechselbeziehung treten.

Bevor die Analyse der Dialogizität im *Taugenichts* Walsers durchgeführt wird, stellt sich allerdings die Frage nach der Gattung: Bachtin attribuiert die Dialogizität ausschließlich der Prosa. Ihm zufolge wird in den meisten poetischen Gattungen im engeren Sinn „die innere Dialogizität des Wortes nicht künstlerisch genutzt, sie findet in das ‚ästhetische Objekt' des Werkes keinen Eingang, wird im poetischen Wort unter gewissen Bedingungen gelöscht."[36] Lässt sich in Bezug auf Walsers Stück überhaupt von Dialogizität sprechen, oder wird die Gattungsfrage zum Problem?

---

[33] Vgl. Bachtin: Probleme der Poetik Dostoevskijs (Anm. 23), S. 205. Auch Wutsdorff spricht in diesem Zusammenhang von Standpunkten, die sich durch die jeweilige Positionierung verschiedener Bewusstseine artikulieren, vgl. Wutsdorff: Bachtin und der Prager Strukturalismus (Anm. 23), S. 39f. Els Jongeneel hält dafür, „plot, characters and space are presented dialogically, by means of the juxtaposition of conflicting events, attitudes and different spaces." Der Text sei dialogisch, da in ihm eine „heteroglossia of existing discourses, languages and texts" anzutreffen sei (Silencing the voice in narratology? A synopsis. In: Blödorn/Langer/Scheffel (Hg.): Stimme(n) im Text (Anm. 32), S. 9–30, hier S. 22).

[34] Blödorn/Langer/Scheffel (Hg.): Stimme(n) im Text (Anm. 32), S. 6.

[35] Es wäre höchstens unter Einbeziehung des Rezipienten denkbar, dass zwei Texte miteinander dialogisieren.

[36] Bachtin: Das Wort im Roman (Anm. 30), S. 176f.

2.2. „Bin ich diese dichterische Figur nicht selbst, obgleich ein anderer?"[37]

Der spiegelverkehrten Disposition von Dialog und Monolog fügt sich eine weitere Eigenschaft des Dramoletts Walsers hinzu, die vor allem die narratologische Struktur im Dialogteil betrifft. Der Taugenichts wird zum Erzähler seiner selbst und erdichtet sich dabei eine neue Vergangenheit; das Stück trägt also epische Züge. Dies erlaubt es, das Stück im Hinblick auf die Dialogizität im Sinne Bachtins zu untersuchen.

Zum einen vermittelt sich Dialogizität in Bezug auf die (erzählende) Figur des Taugenichts. Sie ist polyphon, denn in ihr klingen mehrere ‚Stimmen' nach: die ‚Stimme' des Taugenichts von Eichendorff, mit der sich die Figur identifiziert, von der sie sich aber auch distanziert. Auf die Frage der Zofe, wo es ihm am besten gefiel, antwortet er:

> Taugenichts: Dort, wo ich begann, d. h. dort im Grase, wie es uns Eichendorff so reizend schildert. Wie ich es fühlte und empfand, denn bin ich diese dichterische Figur nicht selbst, obgleich ein anderer?[38]

Der Taugenichts entpuppt sich einerseits als Leser Eichendorffs und identifiziert sich – als ein „anderer" – mit der Hauptfigur.[39] Andererseits ist er aber auch der Taugenichts, der den Blumen zuschaut, „wie sie sich mit stummer Wonne […] unter leisen Windstößen hin- und herbewegten"[40], bevor er sich auf die Reise begibt. Er erinnert sich an seine „Taugenichtsstunden", die nur er als Taugenichts verstehen kann: „nur er weiß, was es ist; denn nur er spricht aus Erfahrung."[41] Dass der Taugenichts in diesem Satz von sich selbst in der dritten Person spricht, kreiert allerdings wiederum eine Distanz der Figur zu sich selbst. Dieses Oszillieren bzw. die Simultaneität des ‚Selbst' und des ‚Anderen' lässt sich als Dialogizität bzw. Polyphonie beschreiben.

---

[37] Walser: Der Taugenichts (Anm. 11), S. 141.
[38] Ebd., S. 140f.
[39] Etliche seiner Reisestationen stimmen mit denen Eichendorffs nicht überein. Der Taugenichts Walsers war beispielsweise einige Jahre in Berlin, „demnach bin ich ein Weltmann", so heißt es. Ebd., S. 138f. Damit differenziert und distanziert er sich von Eichendorffs Figur.
[40] Walser: Der Taugenichts (Anm. 12), S. 141.
[41] Ebd.

Überdies kreiert den Taugenichts eine weitere ‚Stimme', nämlich die des Autors selbst. Einige autobiographische Elemente sind in das Stück eingestreut. Wie Robert Walser verbrachte die Figur einige Jahre in Berlin. Ebenso trat der Taugenichts auf seiner Reise in Salzburg – Walser in Stuttgart – als Schauspieler auf. Bekanntlich arbeitete Walser nach seiner Ausbildung einige Monate als Diener in einem Schloss in Oberschlesien. Dazu bemerkt der Taugenichts Folgendes: „Zeitweilig fuhr ich als Bedienter auf einem Kutscherbock, hab' aber den Herrn leider bald verloren."[42] Die Aussagen der Figur können also als mehrstimmig charakterisiert werden, in ihr kommen mehrere Erzählinstanzen und Referenzfiguren zusammen wie die der romantischen Figur, ihres modernen Abkömmlings und des Autors Robert Walser selbst.

Dass das Stück Walsers hochgradig dialogisch ist, lässt sich zum anderen an seiner Intertextualität bzw. am sprachlichen Material aufzeigen. Walsers Figur beginnt ihren Monolog mit folgenden Worten: „Sagt' ich es mir nicht immer, dass es mit mir gut kommt? Schon damals wusste ich's, als ich fortlief."[43] Indem das Ende der Novelle aufgerufen wird, ist der enge Bezug zum Prätext Eichendorffs explizit: „und es war alles, alles gut!"[44] Ein anderes Beispiel ist im Schlussmonolog zu finden, in dem Walsers Figur ihre Erinnerungen an die „Taugenichtsstunden" wieder aufleben lässt:

> Wie's in den Bäumen um die heiße und doch kühle Mittagszeit bezaubernd von Grün und Licht zitterte. Wenn sich's über mir wölbte, ich die Augen schloss und blind in ein Meer von Glanz blickte, sich mir ein Paar Augen entgegenwandten, nah und doch unsäglich fern, Augen die den deinen ähneln […].[45]

---

[42] Ebd., S. 139. Von den autobiographischen Elementen in Walsers *Taugenichts* auf eine Identifikation des Autors mit der Figur zu schließen, wäre jedoch ein Irrtum. Der Taugenichts – eine Künstlerfigur – lässt sich bei der Lektüre nicht einfach durch den Schriftsteller substituieren. Gerade die erfundenen Varianten der Geschichte und die Präsenz von unterschiedlichen Stimmen, die Teil des *Taugenichts* sind, schließen diesen Interpretationsansatz aus.

[43] Walser: Der Taugenichts (Anm. 12), S. 135.

[44] Eichendorff, Joseph von: Aus dem Leben eines Taugenichts (1826). Stuttgart: Reclam 2001, S. 101. Dadurch wird eine Abfolge generiert. Die Novelle wird damit sowohl der Figur (als deren erlebte Vergangenheit) als auch dem Dramolett vorangestellt.

[45] Walser: Der Taugenichts (Anm. 12), S. 141.

Bei Eichendorff heißt es im dritten Kapitel:

> Als ich eine Strecke so fortgewandert war, sah ich rechts von der Straße einen schönen Baumgarten, wo die Morgensonne so lustig zwischen den Stämmen und Wipfeln hindurchschimmerte, dass es aussah, als wäre der Rasen mit goldenen Teppichen belegt. [...] Ich war recht fröhlich im Herzen, die Vögel sangen über mir im Baume, ich dachte an meine Mühle und an den Garten der schönen gnädigen Frau, und wie das alles nun so weit weit lag – bis ich zuletzt einschlummerte. Da träumte mir, als käme die schöne Fraue aus der prächtigen Gegend unten zu mir gegangen oder eigentlich langsam geflogen zwischen den Glockenklängen mit langen weißen Schleiern, die im Morgenrote wehten. [...] und ich sah dabei ihr Bild in dem stillen Weiher, noch vieltausendmal schöner, aber mit sonderbaren großen Augen, die mich so starr ansahen, dass ich mich beinahe gefürchtet hätte.[46]

Während es bei Walser um die Mittagszeit von „Grün und Licht zitterte", „schimmerte" bei Eichendorff die Morgensonne „lustig zwischen den Stämmen und Wipfeln" hindurch. Der mit „goldenen Teppichen" belegte Rasen wird bei Walser zu einem „Meer von Glanz", als dieser, wie sein Vorgänger, sich unter einen Baum legt und die Augen schließt. Auch die Augen der „schönen gnädigen Fraue" finden sich in Walsers Dramolett wieder, nämlich „nah und doch unsäglich fern". Im Traum, wie ihn die Novelle schildert, befindet sich die Frau ebenfalls weit weg. Dann werden ihr Bild und besonders ihre „sonderbaren großen Augen" aus der Nähe beschrieben. Diese Passage bei Walser ist erstaunlich nah an Eichendorffs Schilderung orientiert und sie ist nicht die einzige. Walser flechtet bruchstückhaft Passagen aus der romantischen Novelle in sein Dramolett ein, so wird die Erzählstimme Eichendorffs Teil der Figur Walsers.

Ein weiteres im Stück zentrales Element der Dialogizität ist das Verhältnis, welches zum Leser/Zuschauer aufgebaut wird. Dieser externe, die romantische Vorlage miteinbeziehende Adressat wird in die Auseinandersetzung mit der Figur des Taugenichts und dem romantischen Gedankengut einbezogen. Gerade auch im Dialog mit sich selbst ist der Taugenichts

---

[46] Eichendorff: Aus dem Leben eines Taugenichts (Anm. 44), S. 28f.

auf ihn angewiesen. Der Text ist auf diesen externen Adressaten hin organisiert, er wird das kommunikative Handlungszentrum des Stückes. Auch die Ironie des Textes, welche durch die Vorkenntnis des Lesers/Zuschauers und die Differenz zwischen dem Prätext und der Inszenierung Walsers entsteht, setzt diesen externen Adressaten voraus. Konkret ist dieses vom Text produzierte, enge Verhältnis zum externen Adressaten – mit Bachtins Worten: die Adressiertheit des Textes – am Ende des Dramoletts ersichtlich:

> Taugenichts: Nun geh' ich zu meiner Mutter, sie sitzt im traulichen, lieben Stübchen, wo ich einst tagelang träge herausschaute. Gewiss wird sie sich über meine Ankunft freuen. Seht, wie's hell wird. Freut euch, klatscht in die Hände. [...] Lasst uns Türen und Fenster mit Kränzen schmücken und auf offenem Platze dann zusammen tanzen. Adieu einstweilen.[47]

Auf diese Art und Weise verabschiedet sich der Taugenichts nicht nur von den anderen Figuren, sondern auch vom anwesenden Dritten im Bunde. Überdies nehmen seine abschließenden Worte den eventuellen Applaus im Zuschauerraum vorweg („klatscht in die Hände"). Mit seiner Aufforderung, draußen „auf offenem Platze" zu tanzen, entlässt er die fiktiven Zuschauer aus dem Theatersaal. Das Ende des Stückes wird also im Stück selbst mit-inszeniert.[48] Der Taugenichts entwirft dabei ein utopisches Zusammensein aller Instanzen des Stückes, in das auch der Leser/Zuschauer miteinbezogen ist. Umso mehr ist dieser eine wichtige Konstituente des Stückes, als die verschiedenen Stimmen des Taugenichts bzw. des Textes in ihm konvergieren. Die Adressiertheit des Textes potenziert also nicht nur die Dialogizität, der externe Adressat ist auch ihre Voraussetzung.

---

[47] Walser: Der Taugenichts (Anm. 12), S. 142.
[48] Gleichzeitig weist das Stück auch über sein Ende hinaus bzw. geht nur provisorisch zu Ende. Die Schlussworte des Taugenichts „Adieu einstweilen" suggerieren, dass die Figur sich nur vorläufig verabschiedet; eine Wiederbegegnung mit ihr ist vorprogrammiert.

3. Schlusswort

Ein gelungener Dialog zwischen den Figuren kommt in Walsers *Taugenichts* nicht zustande. Zentral ist darin die Auseinandersetzung der Figur mit sich selbst, was sich unter anderem in den dialogisierten Monologteilen widerspiegelt. Indes ist das Stück dialogisch im Sinne Bachtins. Der dramatische Text produziert verschiedene Perspektiven auf die Figur des Taugenichts, aus der zugleich mehrere ‚Stimmen' sprechen. Sie ist als polyphone Figur zu charakterisieren. Das Stück ist also durch einen hohen Grad an Dialogizität bestimmt, die den Dialog zwischen den Figuren teilweise ersetzt. Dabei wird dem Leser/Zuschauer eine aktive Rolle zugeschrieben: er ist sowohl Element der Dialogizität als auch deren Bedingung.

Doch wie ist diese Polyphonie bzw. Dialogizität in Bezug auf Walsers Stück zu deuten? Sie kann einerseits als mehrstimmige Antwort auf die Frage gelesen werden, wer nun dieser Taugenichts ist und wozu er denn – auch in einem moderneren Kontext – noch taugt, eine Frage, welche der Text implizit und explizit aufwirft[49] und die sich unter den Schriftstellern nicht nur Walser stellt. Auch Gottfried Keller, Hermann Hesse und Thomas Mann haben sich mit dieser literarischen Figur beschäftigt.[50] In diesem Zusammenhang inszeniert Walser eine Figur, die nicht eindeutig fassbar ist und der mehrere Stimmen inhärent sind. Subversiv wird damit andererseits die einstimmige Erzählung Eichendorffs verhandelt. Die Polyphonie erlaubt es dem Text und der darin konstruierten Figur, sich von der romantischen Vor-Schrift zu emanzipieren. Der Taugenichts wird im Dra-

---

[49] Die Zofe stellt sich beispielsweise in der Mitte des Stückes, also an zentraler Stelle, die Frage, ob der Taugenichts überhaupt zum Ehemann tauge. Walser: Der Taugenichts (Anm. 12), S. 140.

[50] Gottfried Keller schreibt ein Gedicht mit dem Titel *Der Taugenichts*, das er 1851 in der Sammlung *Neuere Gedichte* publiziert. Auch Heinrich Lee, der Held des Romans *Der grüne Heinrich*, kann als Taugenichts bezeichnet werden. Dazu: Lüthi, Hans Jürg: Der Taugenichts. Versuche über Gestaltungen und Umgestaltungen einer poetischen Figur in der deutschen Literatur des 19. und 20. Jahrhunderts. Tübingen: Francke 1993, S. 33. 1915 erscheint *Knulp (Drei Geschichten aus dem Leben Knulps)* von Hermann Hesse bei S. Fischer. In seinem umstrittenen Werk *Betrachtung eines Unpolitischen* (entstanden zwischen 1915 und 1918) widmet sich auch Thomas Mann der romantischen Novelle.

molett zu einem mehrstimmigen Erzähler und bringt die festgeschriebene Geschichte damit wieder in Bewegung. So heißt es im Anfangsmonolog: „Um mich musste stets Beweglichkeit sein."[51] Diese „Beweglichkeit" kommt auch in der Figur des Tanzes, dem ein gewisses Verwandlungspotenzial zugeschrieben wird, am Ende des Stückes nochmals zum Ausdruck;[52] tanzend löst sich die Figur endgültig vom festgelegten Handlungsverlauf der Novelle. Die Dialogizität ist also, wie der Tanz bzw. das gemeinsame Tanzen am Ende, als Bewegungsfigur lesbar.

---

[51] Walser: Der Taugenichts (Anm. 12), S. 135.

[52] „Lasst uns […] auf offenem Platze dann zusammen tanzen", so der Taugenichts, bevor er sich verabschiedet. Ebd., S. 142. Der Tanz trägt um die Jahrhundertwende ein gewisses Verwandlungs- und Lebenspotential in sich, kann bei Walser jedoch unterschiedliche Funktionen annehmen. Vgl. dazu Utz: Tanz auf den Rändern (Anm. 1), S. 41.

Interacting Selves in the *Diaries* of Franz Kafka

Drishti Magoo

The *Diaries* of Franz Kafka (1909–1923) are not just the diaries containing Kafka's personal experiences. They have more to offer because in this viscous space the multifarious voices exist and these voices vigorously lead to the formation and recognition of new literary texts. The voices belong to the Writerly-Self, Author-Self and the Other-Self, and many other simultaneously evolving and dissolving Selves set in motion the phenomenon of dialogism. The cluster of the words taken out from the diary entries are put in a new form and this also recreates and redefines the speaker/the I in the text. The choice of words or cluster of words, termed by Roland Barthes as Lexia, is explained by him as follows:

> The tutor signifier will be cut up into a series of brief, contiguous fragments, which we shall call lexias, since they are units of reading. This cutting up, admittedly, will be arbitrary in the extreme; it will imply no methodological responsibility, since it will bear on the signifier, whereas the proposed analysis bears solely on the signified. The lexia will include sometimes a few words, sometimes several sentences; it will be a matter of convenience.[1]

While taking up the semiotic approach for understanding the metaphors and motifs of writing in the *Diaries* of Kafka, an attempt would be made to analyse the ever forming new literary texts in the *Diaries*. Keeping in mind the semiotic approach of Roland Barthes and Umberto Eco, the *Diaries* would be treated as such texts which are plural in nature. I will focus on the new writing motifs, which are derived through Peirce's idea of 'Unlimited Semiosis'. While the meaning keeps shifting throughout the process of reading, for the analysis, a definite moment of this meaning mechanism is

---

[1] Barthes, Roland: S/Z. Transl. by Richard Miller. New York: Hill and Wang 1974, p. 13.

caught, where the theme of writing and it's relation to the Writerly-Self are in the focus. The focus lies not on the biographical first person narrative but rather the *Diaries* would be analysed with respect to the Writerly-Self and the further interaction of the Writerly-Self with the other voices in the *Diaries*.

The subject in the *Diaries* of Franz Kafka is dealt at various levels and therefore, 'I' in the *Diaries* differs in every diary entry. Since 'I' is not defined by one theme and the *Diaries* contain myriad aspects, therefore, having one definite plot or a series of sequence is not possible. The *Diaries* represent open space which is put to experiment using the critique's projector. Critic is also one of the subjects. This subject is reader centric. What is being reflected through this projector is yet one way of looking at the text and there may exist more permutations and combinations of interpretative texts. The analysis is a product of the critic's perspective and it has the capability to reflect what the critic sees and not what the author intends to portray, therefore, an ahistorical approach would be used for understanding the *Diaries*. When the syntagmatic approach of reading is removed, then the *Diaries* of Kafka shall only carry the status of a primary text. The approach for analysis shall be explained in detail later on.

The *Diaries* were written by Kafka, not solely with the purpose of recording personal events, they also serve as a laboratory to experiment with the literature.[2] But even if the personal events are being written down in diaries, then writing them in a dialogue form offers an open space to examine the possible personal issues with a distant objective approach. The moment personal aspects in the text are approached by the reader objectively, it is no more read as a pragmatic text, rather it is read as a text which is having a non-pragmatic interpretative status. This reader could imagine the time of the author's writing and the dialogue of the writer with the Self helps in forming an unbiased opinion of the event.

The aim of this paper is to recognise and examine dialogic aspects in the *Diaries* of Franz Kafka. These dialogic aspects could be understood by observing the different voices which exist in an interactive relationship. They do not carry biographical traits.

---

[2] Rother, Andrea: Die Tagebücher von Franz Kafka. Ein literarisches Laboratorium. In https://depositonce.tu-berlin.de/handle/11303/1913?mode=full (01.06.2017), p. 12

Manfred Hornschuh offers the idea of Self in the *Diaries* of Franz Kafka in his work *Die Tagebücher Franz Kafkas: Funktionen – Formen – Kontraste*:[3] The Diary is treated as a literary form and the Selves categorised in his work are as follows: the Real-Self (Real-Ich), the Diary-Self (Tagebuch-Ich), the Writing-Self (Schreibendes Ich) and the Written-Self (Geschriebenes Ich). But this idea of categorisation does not offer solution because it covers the biographical issues during the analysis of the text in his work, where as I am aiming for a non-pragmatic result in the analysis. The categorisation of the Self to the extent of making detailed distinction of the act of writing on the temporal basis is commendable but still raises a few questions on the necessity and the relevance of two distinguished Selves, i. e. the Written- and the Writing/Writerly-Self. Hornschuh explains: "Das geschriebene Ich ist innerlich literarisch, das schreibende Ich ist ein Ort der Reflexion außer dem Immanenzzusammenhang und doch ihm angehörend."[4] This quote suggests, that the Writerly-Self represents the outer world and the Written-Self represents the inner world but the reason for this categorisation has not been explained. Hornschuh comments that the Writerly-Self manifests conscious level of the *Diaries* whereas the Written-Self is the conscious state within the *Diaries*. This categorisation does not seem crucial for understanding the Selves in the *Diaries*. The Selves, as per Hornschuh's categorisation, do not interact but clearly remain in their own defined spaces. To what extent the Writerly-Self differs from the Written-Self is never definite and how is the state of consciousness worth differentiating? This distinction is blurred, because the driving motivation behind writing cannot be measured with a yardstick, and hence, there is a possibility that the Written-Self could equally be the part of outer world and Writerly-Self could equally be the part of the inner world. According to me, the Self keeps oscillating between the outer and the inner world because writing is the main motive which keeps the Self in the tussle. Hence, the Written-Self (das Geschriebene-Ich) and the Writing-Self (das Schreibende-Ich) intermesh and overlap in each other's spaces.

In order to examine the dialogic, Bakhtin's theory of dialogism would be relevant here. The dialogic – as the term devised by Bakhtin – suggests

---

[3] Hornschuh, Manfred: Die Tagebücher Franz Kafkas: Funktionen – Formen – Kontraste. Frankfurt/Main: P. Lang 1987.

[4] Idem, pp. 23–24.

multifarious voices speaking against one monologic voice.[5] This voice is not necessarily dyadic nor in a binary relation with other voices. Although, the diary usually resonates with the voice of the diarist, but here, in these *Diaries*, the Self speaks differently in different diary entries, hence, numerous voices come into picture.

The alternative categorisation which breaks the tradition of reading the *Diaries* biographically and also creates more space for the new voices to exist, can be suggested as follows: The Writerly-Self, the Author-Self, the Diarist/Diarist-Self and the Other-Self. These Selves do not confine to their respective diary entries but rather interact and at times invade the spaces of each other. This ongoing interaction may not be noticed apparently but by using semiotic approach, it can be unravelled. This process suggests dialogic interaction in the diaries.

This paper shall also attempt to explore the possibilities of understanding various Selves and their interaction. Self has to be understood through relativity. Self is like a sign which has no absolute meaning in itself.[6] Thus, the meaning is derived in the *Diaries* through the utterances by various Selves. Utterance may be considered as a text which resonates with or without any purpose or motivation in any form, be it vocal or written. If one Self utters, it is understood always with respect to the Other-Self. At a semiotic level, every diary entry is an utterance which is in a dialogic relationship with another utterance. "Common point where dialogism and semiotics converge lies in utterance. Utterance is Bakhtin's central unit of analysis. He is concerned with how different embodied beings interact and not just with the relations between words and concepts."[7] Utterance is dialogic because one utterance leads to another. It is an interplay of what is being expected and what is delivered while uttering in the *Diaries*, and this chain is carried forward through dialogism. Hence, it could be said that the dialogic process of utterance is equivalent to the 'Unlimited Semiosis'[8].

---

[5] Robinson, Andrew: In Theory Bakhtin: Dialogism, Polyphony and Heteroglossia. In: https://ceasefiremagazine.co.uk/in-theory-bakhtin-1/ (01.06.2017).

[6] See: Holquist, Michael: Dialogism: Bakhtin and his World. New York: Routledge 2002.

[7] Leiman, Mikael: Toward Semiotic Dialogism: The Role of Sign Mediation in the Dialogical Self. In: Theory and Psychology 12/2 (2002), pp. 221–235, here p. 224.

[8] Eco, Umberto: A Theory of Semiotics. London: Indiana University Press 1976, p. 68.

This term has been used by Charles Peirce in order to explain that meaning is not absolute and it tends to shift till infinity.

The analysis of the Self in the *Diaries* is based on the principle: "The statement I love liquor does not mean that the subject of the utterance loves liquor. It means that there is somewhere somebody who loves liquor and who says that."[9] This rule indicates the approach which offers a way to create a rational divide between the person and the Self in the *Diaries* of Kafka. The moment this divide is approached, the signifier 'person' carries diachronic connotations and the 'Self' stands in an ahistorical space. The one who writes is not as important as what and how it is being written. Thereby, it makes the understanding of the *Diaries* more liberal. At the textual level different Selves are not prominently recognisable. They are spread through all the diary entries and also, they exist in the spatial order as per the dates and time when the diary entry is written down. But after the analysis and the following diagrams supporting them have been explained, the dynamics of Selves shall become clear.

The Selves mentioned above converge to a common binding point, i. e., all the Selves are striving for something. Due to a lurking dissatisfaction which is reflected in various dairy entries, it results in various literary forms with varied intensity in the write-ups. Through their interaction, these Selves thereby also try to compensate for each other. The dialogic mechanism in the *Diaries* of Kafka can be understood at multiple levels. The lurking dissatisfaction for the Author-Self lies in the inability to write a worth publishing article. For the Writerly-Self, the inability to write at all results in dissatisfaction. The Other-Self is in itself the result of a dissatisfied Author and the Writerly-Self, and it can be understood that the rest of the entities are put to reference. "In dialogism, the very capacity to have consciousness is based on *otherness*. This otherness is not merely a dialectical alienation on its way to a sublation that will endow it with a unifying identity in higher consciousness. On the contrary: in dialogism consciousness is otherness."[10] Further, the Diarist-Self reflects the underlying dissatisfaction which usually leads one to write a diary and so the dissatisfaction

---

[9] Eco, Umberto: The Limits of Interpretation. Bloomington: Indiana University Press 1990, pp. 23f.

[10] Holquist, Michael: Dialogism: Bakhtin and his World. New York: Routledge 2002, p. 18.

is addressed on paper, whereby the function of Diary is considered as problem solving device or the place to share the sense of dissatisfaction. How these four Selves are dealt in the analysis can now be read as follows.

The Author-Self

17 January. Max read me the first act of *Abschied von der Jugend* (*Parting of the young*). How can I, as I am today, come up to this? I should have to look for a year before I found true emotion in me, and am supposed, in the face of so great a work, some way to have a right to remain seated in my chair in the coffeehouse late in the evening, plagued by the passing flatulence of a digestion which is bad inspite of everything.[11]

The Self here refers to the author because the kind of interaction involved has more to do with the outer world. The Author-Self is more of a public entity and differs vividly from the Writerly-Self. The interaction being focussed here is not of the inner world; Max Brod represents the outer world.

August 11. Nothing, nothing. How much time publishing of the little book takes from me and how much harmful, ridiculous pride comes from reading old things with an eye to publication. Only that keeps me from writing. And yet in reality I have achieved nothing, the disturbance is the best proof of it. In any event, now, after the publication of the book, I will have to stay away from magazines and reviews even more than before, if I do not wish to be content with just sticking the tips of my fingers into the truth. How immovable I have become! Formerly, if I said only one word that opposed the direction of the

---

[11] Kafka, Franz: Diaries (1910–1913). Ed. by Max Brod. Transl. by Joseph Kresh. London: Minerva 1992, p. 36. Original: "17/11 Max hat mir den ersten Akt des *Abschieds von der Jugend* vorgelesen. Wie kann ich so, wie ich heute bin, diesem beikommen; ein Jahr müßte ich suchen, ehe ich ein wahres Gefühl in mir fände und soll im Kaffeehaus spät am Abend von verlaufenen Winden einer trotz allem schlechten Verdauung geplagt einem so großen Werk gegenüber irgendwie berechtigt auf meinem Sessel sitzen bleiben dürfen. In: Kafka, Franz: Tagebücher. Bd. 1: 1909–1912. Frankfurt/Main: Fischer 2008, p. 114.

Interacting Selves in the Diaries of Franz Kafka

moment, I at once few over to the other side, now I simply look at myself and remain as I am.¹²

The above mentioned excerpt begins with the emphasis on 'nothing'. The moment 'nothing' is being uttered, multiple dialogic relations come into being at a semantic level. 'Nothing' means in the *Diaries* more than nothing. It carries meaning beyond apparent possible significance of the lexia. The meaning of 'nothing' can be deduced based on the semiotic analysis as suggested by Umberto Eco in his book *Entwurf einer Theorie des Zeichens*.¹³

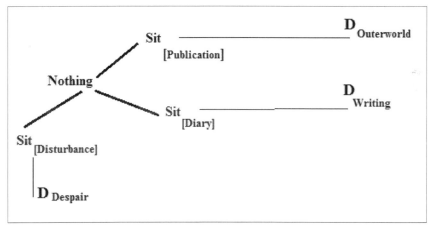

Fig. 1

---

¹² Kafka: Diaries (note 11), p. 205. Original: "11 August 1912. Nichts, nichts. Um wieviel Zeit mich die Herausgabe des kleinen Buches bringt und wieviel schädliches lächerliches Selbstbewußtsein beim Lesen alter Dinge im Hinblick auf das Veröffentlichen entsteht. Nur das hält mich vom Schreiben ab. Und doch habe ich in Wirklichkeit nichts erreicht, die Störung ist der beste Beweis dafür. Jedenfalls werde ich mich jetzt nach Herausgabe des Buches noch viel mehr von Zeitschriften und Kritiken zurückhalten müssen, wenn ich mich nicht damit zufrieden geben will, nur mit den Fingerspitzen im Wahren zu stecken. Wie schwer beweglich ich auch geworden bin! Früher, wenn ich nur ein der augenblicklichen Richtung entgegengesetztes Wort sagte, flog ich auch schon nach der andern Seite, jetzt schaue ich mich bloß an und bleibe wie ich bin." Kafka, Franz: Tagebücher. Bd. 2: 1912–1914. Ed. by Max Brod. Frankfurt/Main: Fischer 2008, p. 76.

¹³ Eco, Umberto: Semiotik: Entwurf einer Theorie der Zeichen. München: Fink 1987.

It can be derived from three possible situations as shown above. Here, the three levels seem to interact in order to locate the state of consciousness of Self in the *Diaries*.

Situation 1: Despair (nothing = inner world)
In the first situation, as the diagram suggests, 'nothing' gets its meaning from disturbance and the meaning of 'nothing' may be deduced to 'despair'. This state of mind is often reflected in the *Diaries* by the Other-Self. Despair arising out of disturbance, produced through inability to write, recurs in the various diary entries. In Bakhtinian terms, these recurrences may be considered as utterances. The frequency of utterance gives rise to the dialogic literary form.

Further, the 'nothing' as a lexia carries its meaning apart from the context and becomes all the more self-explanatory when one reads the *Diaries* of 31st January, 1912: "wrote nothing".[14] The same year, 'nothing' recurs on 1st June as "wrote nothing" and 2nd June as "wrote almost nothing".[15] As it has been seen here, the meaning of 'Nothing' has been deduced on the basis of the other lexia put in the particular frame. Roland Barthes suggests:

> The tutor signifier will be cut up into a series of brief, contiguous fragments, which we shall call lexias, since they are units of reading. This cutting up, admittedly, will be arbitrary in the extreme; it will imply no methodological responsibility, since it will bear on the signifier, whereas the proposed analysis bears solely on the signified. The lexia will include sometimes a few words, sometimes several sentences; it will be a matter of convenience.[16]

The moment 'nothing' is being uttered, the despair, inability to publish and writing as themes begin to assert their significance and thereby also cause a dialogical resonance due to its repetition. 'Nothing' here proves to be more than nothing of dictionary terms and rather carries heavy weightage. It is not something immaterial. This is further emphasised in the literary work *Urban World*,[17] where in a dialogue between father and son (son is

---

[14] Kafka: Diaries (note 11), p. 203
[15] Idem.
[16] Barthes: S/Z (note 1), p. 13.
[17] Kafka: Diaries (note 11), p. 40.

symbolic of the alter ego of the Self), nothing appears with a thrust in the lines "nothing forces me".[18] Here, 'nothing' is not a negative assertion but rather it is the force which drives the Author-Self to write. Despair, writing in the diary and the inability to come to terms with the outer world, produce a force called 'nothing'.

Situation 2: Diary (nothing = inner world)
The situation of 'nothing' arises in the *Diaries* with respect to writing and here it refers to the inner world affairs rather than the outer world. The inability to write is often being shared with the *Diaries* by Franz Kafka. For example, in one of the diary entries, it is written "nothing".[19] "Finally, after five months of my life during which I could write *nothing that would have satisfied me*, and for which no power will compensate me, though all were under obligation to do so, it occurs to me to talk to myself again."[20]

The sheer inability to write makes the Writerly-Self distance from himself. The idea of Self for the Writerly-Self disintegrates here; hence, comes around the role of the Other-Self. The Other-Self is the diarist here now, who takes up this role of writing, when the Writerly-Self fails to assert its existence. This implies the shifting role of the Self.

Situation 3: Publication (Nothing = outer world)
'Nothing' with respect to publication refers to the outer world. The Author-Self is more prevalent in this version of 'nothing'. Here, the need of the I appears to bind with the outer world of society and the publication can be understood as a sign of being accepted in the outer world successfully. But the inner world of writing causes dissonance. Hence, at another level there occurs the dialogic interaction of the inner and the outer world. This interaction results in the diary entry as presented above.

In the sentence "reading old things with an eye to publication. Only that keeps me from writing", there seems to be a conflict between the Author-Self and the Writerly-Self; the Writerly-Self appears to be more significant

---

[18] Idem, p. 42.

[19] Idem.

[20] My emphasis. Idem. Original: "Endlich nach fünf Monaten meines Lebens, in denen ich nichts schreiben konnte womit ich zufrieden gewesen wäre und die mir keine Macht ersetzen wird, trotzdem alle dazu verpflichtet wären, komme ich auf den Einfall wieder einmal mich anzusprechen." Kafka: Tagebücher. Bd. 1: 1909–1912 (note 11), p. 14.

than the Author-Self. The Writerly-Self is being hindered by the outer world to which the Author-Self belongs. Although, 'publication' holds the primary attention here but at the same time, it is being blamed for Writerly-Self's inability to write in the inner world.

The Writerly-Self

13.12.14

Instead of working – I have written only one page (exegesis of the Legend) – looked through the finished chapters and found parts of them good. Always conscious that every feeling of satisfaction and happiness that I have, such, for example, as the 'Legend' in particular inspires me, must be paid for, and must be paid for moreover at some future time, to deny me all possibility of recovery in the present.[21]

In this diary entry, dialogic occurrence is through contradictions. If we take up fragments out of the pragmatic context, one observes, that Barthian lexias co-exist in opposition. A few examples from the above excerpt, like: "Instead of working" / "I have written only one page"; "future"/"present"; "always conscious"/"feeling of satisfaction". These contradictions within the same excerpt reflect the fragmentary state of consciousness. Their co-existence in this diary entry is also dialogic.

Here, striving for writing is quite clear. The dissatisfaction arising out of inability to write can be clearly understood through the line: "I have written only one page" ("Ich habe nur eine Seite geschrieben"). Also, the dichotomy of inner and outer world is clear when the Writerly-Self writes "Instead of working, I have written only one page" ("Statt zu arbeiten – ich habe nur eine Seite geschrieben"). The act of writing and working are being resonated in one single sentence but they are two contradictory aspects as

---

[21] Kafka: Diaries (note 11), p. 321. Original: "13 XII 14 Statt zu arbeiten – ich habe nur eine Seite geschrieben (Exegese der Legende) – in fertigen Kapiteln gelesen und sie zum Teil gut gefunden. Immer im Bewußtsein, daß jedes Zufriedenheits- und Glücksgefühl, wie ich es z. B. besonders der Legende gegenüber habe, bezahlt werden muß und zwar um niemals Erholung zu gönnen im Nachhinein bezahlt werden muß." Kafka, Franz: Tagebücher. Bd. 3: 1914–1923. Frankfurt/Main: Fischer 2008, p. 63.

far as 'working' and 'writing' are concerned because working can be associated with the occupation for earning bread. Also, the tussle can be understood from the following excerpt:

> 19 February. When I wanted to get out of bed this morning I simply folded up. This has a very simple cause, I am completely overworked. Not by the office but my other work. The office has an innocent share in it only to the extent that, if I did not have to go there, I could live calmly for my own work and should not have to waste these six hours a day which have tormented me to a degree that you cannot imagine, especially on Friday and Saturday, because I was full of my own things. In the final analysis, I know, that is just talk, the fault is mine and the office has a right to make the most definite and justified demands on me. But for me in particular it is a horrible double life from which there is probably no escape but insanity. I write this in the good light of the morning and would certainly not write it if it were not so true and if I did not love you like a son.[22]

The Other-Self which engages with occupation is being overpowered by the Writerly-Self. Work belongs to outer world and writing is a private affair. Apart from it, the interaction of present and future is also dialogic which is anticipated from the diary entry of 13th December, 1914. The act of writing puts the present and past also together. Hence, the temporal dialogic relation is also prevalent here.

---

[22] Kafka: Diaries (note 11), p. 37–38. Original: "19/II 11 Wie ich heute aus dem Bett steigen wollte, bin ich einfach zusammengeklappt. Es hat das einen sehr einfachen Grund, ich bin vollkommen überarbeitet. Nicht durch das Bureau aber durch meine sonstige Arbeit. Das Bureau hat nur dadurch eine sonstige Arbeit. Das Bureau hat nur dadurch einen unschuldigen Anteil daran, als ich, wenn ich nicht hinmüßte, ruhig für meine Arbeit leben könnte und nicht diese 6 Stunden dort täglich verbringen müßte, die mich besonders Freitag und Samstag, weil ich voll meiner Sachen war gequält haben daß Sie es sich nicht ausdenken können. Schließlich, das weiß ich ja, ist das nur Geschwätz, schuldig bin ich, und das Bureau hat gegen mich die klarsten und berechtigtesten Forderungen. Nur ist es eben für mich ein schreckliches Doppelleben, aus dem es wahrscheinlich nur den Irrsinn als Ausweg gibt. Ich schreibe das bei gutem Morgenlicht und würde es sicher nicht schreiben, wenn es nicht so wahr wäre und wenn ich sie nicht so liebte wie ein Sohn." Kafka: Tagebücher. Bd. 1: 1909–1912 (note 11), p. 26.

Apart from that, 'Legend' stands as a metaphor for dialogism here, because it suggests juxtaposition of future and present. The moment 'Legend' is being uttered, the future and present resonate together, thereby, opening the possibilities of dialogic interaction across the time and space in the *Diaries*. Further, when 'I' forms a connection with 'Legend', the Self, i. e. the Writerly-Self becomes the epitome of dichotomy. The act of writing about the past is also the process of reconstructing the past on the present paper in the form of diary entry. Hence, the past interacts with the present as soon as it is penned down in *the Diaries*.

The Other-Self

When despair shows itself so definitely, is so tied to its object, so pent up, as in a soldier who covers a retreat and thus lets himself be torn to pieces, then it is not true despair. True despair overreaches its goal immediately and always, (at this comma it became clear that only the first sentence was correct).
Do you despair?
Yes? You despair?
You run away? You want to hide?[23]

Other-Self is a result of inner conflict. Be it against Writerly-Self, Author-Self, or the Self which strives to locate its identity. Writing is the act through which it is strived for. Despair further in this entry results in the dialogue with the Self or the Other-Self. It cannot be clearly stated if this is Other-Self, because the point of reference is in flux all the time. The boundaries of the Self keep shifting and forming numerous dialogic relations.

---

[23] Kafka: Diaries (note 11), p. 10. Original: "Wenn sich die Verzweiflung so bestimmt gibt, so an ihren Gegenstand gebunden ist, so zurückgehalten wie von einem Soldaten, der den Rückzug deckt und sich dafür zerreißen läßt, dann ist es nicht die richtige Verzweiflung. Die richtige Verzweiflung hat ihr Ziel gleich und immer überholt, (bei diesem Beistrich zeigte es sich, daß nur der erste Satz richtig war). Bist Du verzweifelt? Ja? du bist verzweifelt? Läufst weg? Willst Dich verstecken?" Kafka: Tagebücher. Bd. 1: 1909–1912 (note 11), pp. 13–14.

Interacting Selves in the Diaries of Franz Kafka

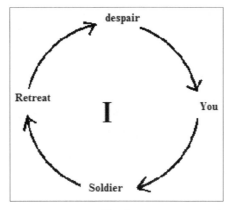

Fig. 2

This 'You-I-relationship', sprouting from despair in Fig. 2, is again seen to be caught in a vicious circle here. As seen previously, meaning of 'nothing' could be deduced to writing and if writing substitutes despair (Fig. 1) then, 'writing', 'soldier', 'you' and 'retreat' prevail in a dialogic circle which may be regarded as vicious because it emerges out of despair of the Writerly-Self and again results in despair due to inability to write. The despaired state of consciousness results in retreating back to the inner world where 'soldier' is a metaphor. The lexia 'soldier' represents writing as a defence mechanism against the Despaired-Self. The Other-Self seeps in when the dialogue in the second person is being emphasised. 'You' represents the Other-Self and the dialogue here is an attempt to overcome this duality resulting from despair. This is ironic that dichotomy is being resolved again through dialogism.

The Diarist-Self

Several diary excerpts deal with the theme of diary writing mainly. Here, the Diarist-Self strives to maintain the diary for not just the personal recordings but also to experiment with literature. A few diary entries suggest the dependence on the diarist. On 16th December, 1910, writes the Diarist-Self: "I won't give up the diary again. I must hold on here, it is the only place I can."[24] Further, on 27th June, 1919, it is written: "A new Diary, only because I have been reading the old ones. A number of reasons and intentions, now, at a quarter to twelve, impossible to ascertain."[25] The dependence on the diary is further emphasised and continues in the diary entry of 16th December 1910:

> I would gladly explain from time to time. It is really something effervescent that fills me completely with a light, pleasant quiver and that persuades me of the existence of abilities of whose non-existence I can convince myself with completely certainly at any moment, even now.[26]

The sense of Self is being achieved only through the diaries here. Unlike other states of consciousness which lead to Writerly-Self, Author-Self and Other-Self, here, the Diarist-Self stands in no conflict, rather it suggests rejoicing Self. But the Other-Self seeps in when the Diarist-Self tries to read his own diaries. Here the Other-Self comes into picture when the Diarist takes up the role of the reader. Reading process distances oneself from one's own diary, and the distancing enables one to develop the otherness. On the other hand, if diary writing may be taken away from the Diarist-Self, that leads to the crises. On 25th February, 1912, Kafka writes: "Hold fast to the diary from today on! Write regularly! Don't surrender! Even if no salvation should come, I want to be worthy of it at every moment."[27] This utterance suggests the necessity to hold on to diary writing.

The Diarist-Self also attempts to resolve the issues by carrying out the dialogue with the Other-Self. On 9th March, 1914, the Diarist-Self displays the refuge in literature by assuming the role of Rense, an unknown figure. Rense is the alter-ego or the Other-Self, which is being deployed in a literary fragment which is quoted below. The dialogue conversation inter-

---

[24] Kafka: Diaries (note 11), p. 29.
[25] Idem, p. 390.
[26] Idem, p. 29. Original: "Gerne möchte ich das Glücksgefühl erklären, das ich von Zeit von Zeit wie eben jetzt in mir habe. Es ist wirklich etwas moussierendes, das mich mit leichtem angenehmen Zucken ganz und gar erfüllt und das mir Fähigkeiten einredet von deren Nichtvorhandensein ich mich jeden Augenblick auch jetzt mit aller Sicherheit überzeugen kann." Kafka: Tagebücher. Bd. 1: 1909–1912 (note 11), p. 103.
[27] Kafka: Diaries (note 11), p. 180.

meshes with the personal issues in the diaries and ends in another literary dialogue. Hence, the dialogism appears in various shades. Beginning with a literary fragment, then shifting to direct issues of the personal life of the Diarist-Self and ultimately coming back to the same literary dialogue between a maid and the student. This manner of interaction of the Selves has been observed on the *Diaries* of 9th March, 1914. The swapping between the Diarist-Self and the literary fragment has been marked by me in the following excerpt.

Literary Fragment:
Rense walked a few steps down the dim passageway, opened the little papered door of the dining-room, and said to the noisy company, almost without regarding them: 'Please be a little more quiet. I have a guest. Have some consideration.
As he was returning to his room and heard the noise continuing unabated, he halted a moment, was on the verge of going back again, but thought better of it and returned to his room [...].

Diarist-Self:
The general argument: I am completely lost in F.

Literary Fragment:
Rense, a student, sat studying in his small back room. The maid came in and announced that a young man wished to speak to him. 'What is his name?' Rense asked. The maid did not know.

Diarist-Self:
I shall never forget F. in this place, therefore shan't marry. Is that definite?
Yes, that much I can judge of: I am almost thirty-one years old, have known F. [...] But you wanted that sort of life for yourself, didn't you? An official's life could benefit me if I were married. [...]
But you could have married, couldn't you?
I couldn't marry then; everything in me revolted against it, much as I always loved F. [...] Moreover, as a result of my dependence, which is at least encouraged by this way of life, I approach everything hesitantly and complete nothing at the first stroke. That was what happened here too.
Why do you give up all hope eventually of having F.?

I have already tried every kind of self-humiliation. In the Tiergarten I once said: "Say 'yes'." [...]
One should really never say that. Didn't your previous behaviour likewise seem hopeless from F.'s point of view? [...]
Then what do you want to do?
Leave Prague. Counter the greatest personal injury that has ever befallen me with the strongest antidote at my disposal. [...]
Then what do you want to do?
I could answer all such questions at once by saying: I have nothing to lose [...]. Aren't you going there because of F.?
No, I choose Berlin only for the above reasons, although I love it and perhaps I love it because of F. [...]
Are you healthy?
No, heart, sleep, digestion.

Literary Fragment:
STUDENT: Come in.
MAID [*a frail girl*]: Good morning.
STUDENT: What do you want? It's still night.[28]

---

[28] Kafka, Franz: The Diaries (1914–1923). Ed. by Max Brod. Transl. by Martin Greenberg / Hannah Arendt. London: Minerva 1992, pp. 261–267. Original: <u>Das literarische Fragment</u>: "9.III 14: Rense gieng paar Schritte durch den halbdunklen Gang, öffnete die kleine Tapetentür des Eßzimmers und sagte zu der überlauten Gesellschaft, fast ohne hinzusehen: Bitte seid ein wenig ruhig. Ich habe einen Gast. Ich bitte um etwas Rücksicht. Als er wieder in sein Zimmer zurückgieng und den unveränderten Lärm hörte, stockte er einen Augenblick, wollte nochmals zurückgehn, besann sich aber anders und kehrte in sein Zimmer zurück." <u>Das Tagebuch-Ich</u>: "Die Argumentation im allgemeinen: Ich bin an F. verloren." <u>Das literarische Fragment</u>: "Rense, ein Student, saß in seinem kleinen Hofzimmer und studierte. Die Magd kam und meldete, ein junger Mann wolle mit Rense sprechen. Wie heißt er denn? fragte Rense. Die Magd wußte es nicht." <u>Das Tagebuch-Ich</u>: "Ich werde hier F. nicht vergessen, daher nicht heiraten. Ist das ganz bestimmt? Ja, das kann ich beurteilen, ich bin fast 31 Jahre alt, kenne F. [...] Du hast doch aber ein solches Leben Dir gewünscht? Das Beamtenleben könnte für mich gut sein, wenn ich verheiratet wäre [...]. Du hättest aber doch heiraten können? Ich konnte damals nicht heiraten, alles in mir hat dagegen revoltiert, so sehr ich F. [...] Übrigens gehe ich bei meiner durch diese Lebensweise zumindest genährten Unselbständigkeit an alles zögernd heran und bringe nichts mit dem ersten Schlag fertig. So war es auch hier. Warum gibst Du alle

And so, the conversation in this literary fragment goes on and the indirect interaction between the two forms of writings lead to the formation of this montage. This montage consists of the story of Rense which is intervened by the dialogic conversation of the Other-Self in order to resolve the personal issues, as mentioned by the Diarist-Self. Hence, the dialogism here occurs at further two levels. Once, at the level of the form, where Rense's story and personal story of the Diarist-Self is being conveyed simultaneously. Further, the story or the issue portrayed by the Diarist-Self is also in the form of a conversation. Although it is monologic the role of listener is being given to the Other-Self in order to attain an objective view of the personal problem with the character F. This kind of switching between two forms of writing also suggests the rapid interaction between the two different spaces and the two spaces manifest different states of consciousness.

From the above discussion, we infer that in the *Diaries* voices interact at infinitely numerous levels. "Dialogue is also the environment for processes in and through which individuals construct their (individual) identities and establish themselves as a responsible social agents."[29] But in the *Diaries* of Franz Kafka, the issues concern not with the individuals but the individual Selves. These Selves do not carry entity but their characteristics define their role in the *Diaries* of Franz Kafka and they establish their entities through inter-dependence. This inter-dependence is important for un-

---

Hoffnung auf, F. doch zu bekommen? Ich habe jede Selbstdemütigung schon versucht. Im Tiergarten sagte ich einmal: "Sag 'ja'." [...] Das sollte man eigentlich niemals sagen dürfen. Schien von F. aus gesehen Dein früheres Verhalten nicht aussichtlos zu sein [...]. Was willst Du also tun? Von Prag weggehn. Gegenüber diesem stärksten menschlichen Schaden, der mich je getroffen hat, mit dem stärksten Reaktionsmittel, über das ich verfüge, vorgehn. [...] Was willst Du also tun? Ich könnte alle derartigen Fragen mit einemmal beantworten, indem ich sage: ich habe nichts zu riskieren [...]. Fährst Du nicht F.'s wegen hin [...]. Bist Du gesund? Nein, Herz, Schlaf, Verdauung." Das literarische Fragment: "Ein kleines Mietzimmer. Morgendämmerung. Unordnung. Der Student liegt im Bett, schläft der Wand zugekehrt [...]. Dienstmädchen (Schwaches Mädchen): Guten Morgen. St.: Was wollen Sie? Es ist ja Nacht. D: Entschuldigung Sie. Ein Herr fragt nach Ihnen [...]." Kafka: Tagebücher. Bd. 3: 1914–1923 (note 21), pp. 133–139.

[29] Linell, Per: Rethinking Language, Mind and World Dialogically. Interactional and Contextual Theories of Human Sense-Making. Charlotte: IAP 2009, p. 186.

derstanding the multitudinous facets of the *Diaries*. Hence, the Self which is often found in despair or fragmentary state and is rescued by dialogism occurring through various Selves. Also, this inter-dependence proves that 'Self' is relative, as suggested by Bakhtin. Further, the non-syntagmatic relations between various signifiers are dialogic at textual as well as formal level. This kind of analysis is a representation of dialogic occurrence and the resultant new formation and recognition of literary write-ups in the *Diaries* of Franz Kafka.

‚Bluhmen-Discurse'
in Johann Rists *Jahreszeitengesprächen*:
Figuren, Texte und epistemische Ordnungen im Dialog

Johanna-Helene Linnemann

In der Vorrede zu seinem ersten *Jahreszeitengespräch* erklärt Johann Rist (1607–1667) der geneigten Leserschaft das Anliegen der Schriftenreihe. Er plant

> nach den zwölf Monahten des Jahres / auch zwölf Gespräche / aufs Papir zu bringen / [...] in welchem [...] jedes mahl etliche Geselschafftere des hochlöblichen Elbischen SchwahnenOrdens [...] als Unterredner / oder Zusammensprächer sollten ingeführt werden / welches den vielen verständigen / sonderlich aber der Kunst- und Tugendlibenden Jugend / nicht nur anmuthig und lustig / sondern auch sehr nützlich würde sein zu lesen und zugebrauchen / zumahlen sie bisweilen solche Sachen in mehrerwähnten Gesprächen werden finden / dergleichen ihnen sonst weinig fürkommen / demnach selbige nicht so viel aus den Bücheren / als aus eigener Erfahrung der rechten und wahren Lehrmeisterinn aller Dinge sind genommen.[1]

Die Monatsunterredungen sind nicht tatsächlich monatsweise erschienen; von den zwölf Jahresgesprächen konnte Rist lediglich sechs fertigstellen, wobei die Juli-Unterredung posthum publiziert wurde. Erasmus Francisci

---

[1] Rist, Johann: Das allerEdelste Nass der gantzen Welt / Vermittelst eines anmuhtigen und erbaulichen Gespräches / Welches ist dieser Ahrt die Erste / und zwahr Eine Jånners-Unterredung / Beschriben und fürgestellet von Dem Rüstigen [Hamburg 1663]. In: Johann Rist: Sämtliche Werke. Hg. v. Eberhard Mannack. Bd. I-VII. Berlin, New York: de Gruyter 1967ff., Bd. IV: Epische Dichtungen, 1972, S. 4–138, hier S. 15f.

besorgte die Komplettierung des Werks. Gegenstand der Untersuchung sollen hier ausschließlich die von Rist angefertigten Texte sein.[2]

Unmittelbar auffallend ist, dass die Disposition der zwischen 1663 und 1668 publizierten *Monatsgespräche* stets gleich gestaltet ist: Zunächst sind da einige Paratexte, die Widmungen, Zuschriften sowie lyrische Elemente umfassen. Es folgen Reflexionen über die göttliche Schöpfung, die der Rüstige (so die binnentextuelle Selbstbezeichnung des Autors) anstellt, während er durch seine Gärten lustwandelt, nicht selten begleitet von seinem Gärtner. Sodann reisen Mitglieder des Elbschwanordens zu ihm, bewundern seine Gärten, um sich anschließend zusammenzusetzen und zu einem zuvor festgelegten Thema ein spielerisches Streitgespräch zu führen. Die Dialoge sind also „ihrer Einkleidung nach als Gastmahlsgespräche zu bezeichnen"[3]. Es zeigt sich weiter, dass jede *Monatsunterhaltung* in einen Rahmen- und einen Binnenteil unterteilt werden kann: Während die Rahmengespräche allesamt ausschließlich botanische Wissensinhalte thematisieren, variiert das Thema der Binnengespräche von Unterredung zu Unterredung. Der Rahmentext umfasst jeweils die Anreise der Gäste, ihre Spaziergänge durch die Gärten des Rüstigen sowie die währenddessen stattfindenden Gespräche, in denen der Gastgeber auf bestimmte Pflanzen hinweist, deren Herkunft bestimmt und ihre Kultivierung erklärt. Es folgt der Binnentext, in dem die Gesprächsteilnehmer in umfangreichen Redeeinheiten versuchen, überzeugende Argumente für ihre Thesen zu präsentieren. Das Jännergespräch dreht sich etwa um die Frage, welches das edelste Nass auf der Welt sei: Wasser, Tinte, Wein oder Milch. Während die Binnengespräche eher die Kennzeichen von diskursiv geprägten Vorträgen mit spielerischem Streitcharakter tragen, muten die Rahmengespräche wie locker geführte Lehrer-Schüler-Dialoge an.

Diese Unterschiede zwischen Rahmung und Binnentext sowie auch die nicht stringente Ausgestaltung der Dialogtypen (Schülergespräch/Streitgespräch)[4] sind dem in der *Jännerunterredung* benannten Vorhabens ge-

---

[2] Zu Francisci siehe genauer: Kramer, Roswitha: Gespräch und Spiel im ‚Lustgarten'. Literatur und Geselligkeit im Werk von Erasmus Francisci. In: Wolfgang Adam (Hg.): Geselligkeit und Gesellschaft im Barockzeitalter. Bd. I. Wiesbaden: Harrassowitz 1997, S. 505–529.

[3] Jericke, Alfred: Johann Rists Monatsgespräche. Berlin, Leipzig: de Gruyter 1928, S. 177.

[4] Ebd.

schuldet, mit den „nützlichen und anmuhtigen Gesprächen" im Horaz'schen Sinne sowohl unterhalten als auch belehren zu wollen.[5] Der in der Forschung nicht selten konstatierte „Mischcharakter"[6] der *Monatsunterredungen* dürfte in nicht unerheblichem Maße darauf zurückzuführen sein, dass *delectare* und *prodesse* gleichermaßen ernstgenommen werden. Wenngleich im 17. Jahrhundert eine kategoriale Unterscheidung zwischen literarischem und wissenschaftlichem Diskurs noch nicht stattgefunden hat, lässt sich doch feststellen, dass es sich bei den *Monatsgesprächen* nicht um fachwissenschaftliche Publikationen (wie etwa diejenigen von Matthioli, Bauhinus oder anderen von Rist genannten Botanikern) handelt, sondern um eine, deren Ziel die Popularisierung von botanischen und anderen Wissensbeständen ist. Die *Monatsunterredungen* sind populärwissenschaftliche Unterhaltungsstücke, die auf Erkenntnis qua Lust am Text abzielen. Rist bezieht seine Wissensbestände sowohl aus eigenen Beobachtungen als auch aus belegten Quellen der (u. a. botanischen) Fachliteratur. Zwar zielt das Erkenntnisstreben in erster Linie auf eigene Erfahrung, diese „rechte[] und wahre[] Lehrmeisterinn aller Dinge"[7], deren epistemologischen Status es im 17. Jahrhundert noch zu festigen galt, doch handelt es sich dennoch mitnichten um einen epistemischen Drang, der von Schriftautoritäten absieht. Vielmehr wird in den verschieden dargestellten Wissenschaftsdiskursen vorhandenes Buchwissen mit empirisch gewonnenem Wissen verknüpft, um das Urteilsvermögen zu fördern. Die umfängliche Akzentuierung des Urteilsvermögens, das bei der Figur des Rüstigen vorbildlich ausgeprägt zu sein scheint und das es bei anderen Figuren und der Leserschaft stärker auszubilden gilt, ist ein charakteristisches Merkmal der *Jahreszeitengespräche*.

Gemeinsam ist den sonst so unterschiedlich gestalteten Rahmen- wie Binnendialogen der stets wiederkehrende Grundzug „der Darstellung einer Gruppe von Menschen, die sich im Gespräche gemeinsam um Erkenntnis bemühen"[8]. Sowohl in den Rahmen- als auch in den Binnentexten sind

---

[5] Vgl. Rist: Das allerEdelste Nass der gantzen Welt (Anm. 1), S. 31f.
[6] Jericke: Johann Rists Monatsgespräche (Anm. 3), S. 192.
[7] Rist: Das allerEdelste Nass der gantzen Welt (Anm. 1), S. 16.
[8] Wildbolz, Rudolf: Dialog. In: Werner Kohlschmidt / Wolfgang Mohr (Hg.): Reallexikon der deutschen Literaturgeschichte. Begr. v. Paul Merker / Wolfgang Stammler. 2. Aufl. Bd. I: A–K. Berlin, New York: de Gruyter 2001, S. 251–255, hier S. 251.

es mehrere unterschiedliche Standpunkte, Denkmöglichkeiten und Fragestellungen, die von den Figuren präsentiert werden. Während das Redeverhältnis in den Binnendialogen allerdings weitgehend ausgewogen ist, dominiert in den Rahmendialogen der Rüstige mit seinen Beiträgen sowohl quantitativ als auch qualitativ. Gleichwohl gehen die Redebeiträge der anderen Figuren über ein glaukon'sches Veranlassen und Bestätigen weit hinaus – vielmehr lenken sie durch ihre Fragen die Gespräche und gewinnen durch die Antworten an Kenntnissen, was wiederum zur Fortsetzung des Erkenntnisstrebens in den Dialogen führt.

Dieses Streben kann sich in „Spielarten des Kämpferischen, des Pädagogischen oder einfach des im höheren Sinne Geselligen"[9] äußern. Der pädagogische Impetus ist vor allem in den Rahmentexten erkennbar: Der Gelehrtenhabitus des Rüstigen wird deutlich hervorgehoben und markiert das freundschaftlich verbundene, durch Ordensmitgliedschaft gesellschaftlich gleichgestellte Verhältnis der Gesprächspartner zueinander deutlich als Lehrer-Schüler-Beziehung, ohne dass sich hieraus jedoch ein Widerspruch oder Spannungsverhältnis ergeben würde. Vielmehr nuanciert das pädagogisch strukturierte Sozialgefüge der Figuren ihre Beziehung zueinander im Sinne einer durchweg positiv konnotierten Anleitung durch den Rüstigen zum geselligen Streben nach Erkenntnis – die Prozesshaftigkeit seiner nicht immer, aber doch häufig ertragreichen Erkenntniswege dient dabei, wie noch zu sehen sein wird, als Exemplum und Movens für die anderen Figuren, wobei der Rüstige zwar als umfassend kenntnisreich, nicht jedoch als Allwissender dargestellt wird. Der polyphon orchestrierte Austausch der Figuren gerät durch die Dominanz des Rüstigen daher auch nicht zu einem fragwürdigen bzw. lediglich vordergründigen Unterfangen. Neben dem Figuren- und Erkenntnisgefüge in den Rahmentexten zeigt sich auch in den im Modus des spielerischen Wettbewerbs vorgetragenen Redeeinheiten in den Binnentexten ein die *Jahreszeitengespräche* als Prinzip durchwirkendes Erkenntnisstreben, dessen Methode und erklärtes binnenfiktionales Ziel der gesellige Austausch zum Zwecke der Erkenntnis ist.

Dieser Austausch und mithin der epistemische Wert basieren in den gesamten *Jahreszeitengesprächen* auch auf einer „dialogische[n] Sprache", die sich durch „die Tendenz zum konkreten Anknüpfen und Formulieren der

---

[9] Ebd.

Gedanken, oft in absichtlicher Ferne von den strengeren Terminologien", um „klare Verständlichkeit, Umgänglichkeit und Gefühlsnähe" bemühe.[10] Dialogische Sprache bildet die Grundlage gemeinsamen Erkennens, insofern die Vermittlung von Informationen wie auch die gemeinsame Anschauung einer Verständigungsbasis bedürfen, mithilfe derer der Austausch, die Urteilsbildung und auch die Kritik von Positionen erst möglich werden. Betrachtet man die intradiegetischen Bemühungen um eine dialogische Sprache, so fallen zunächst die zahlreichen Passagen auf, in denen der Rüstige seinen oftmals lateinunkundigen Gesprächspartnern einerseits kurze Übersetzungen ins Deutsche offeriert, dabei den Mangel an guten Übersetzungen bestimmter Werke kritisiert, andererseits aber auch dazu ermuntert, selbst Latein zu erlernen, um die eigenen Kenntnisse auf wissenschaftlichen Gebieten erweitern zu können.[11] Das Aufgreifen von einzelnen Formulierungen, die Bezugnahmen auf bereits geäußerte Sachverhalte und die Anregungen zum Erzählen bereits bekannter ‚Geschichten' sind ebenso Teil dieser dialogischen Sprache wie neckische Nachfragen, humorvolle Zänkereien, Zustimmung zu und Ablehnung von bestimmten Argumenten, insofern jegliches Bemühen um Anknüpfung an die Rede einer anderen Figur einen Verständigungskosmos generiert, innerhalb dessen ein geselliges Erkenntnisstreben erst möglich wird. Dass die Unterhaltungen keineswegs linear auf ein Erkenntnisziel hinsteuern, sondern in den Rahmendialogen häufig durch emphatische Zwischenrufe von Blumenbegeisterten umgelenkt, durch witterungsbedingte Bedürfnisse abgelenkt oder schlicht durch einsetzenden Hunger oder durch Müdigkeit unterbrochen werden, verdeutlicht den engen Zusammenhang von Erkenntnis und „Affektsphäre und Gestimmtheit"[12].

---

[10] Ebd.
[11] Auch Rists Niederschrift der Monatsunterredungen in der Volkssprache sind in diesem Kontext des (hier wirkungsästhetischen) Bemühens um Dialog und gemeinsame Erkenntnis zu verstehen.
[12] Wildbolz: Dialog (Anm. 8), S. 251. Neben der Orientierung an solchen Bedürfnissen sind es zuweilen aber auch sozialpsychologische Beweggründe, die die Figuren von einer auf stichfesten Kriterien fußenden Argumentation abbringen; mal ist es die Bewunderung für den Rüstigen, mal Höflichkeit gegenüber dem Gastgeber, mal Antipathien gegenüber einer Quelle, mal der selbst auferlegte Zeitmangel aufgrund des noch ausstehenden Argumentationswettbewerbs, der den Binnentext generiert. In den Binnendialogen ist eine affektive Beeinflussung

All dies trägt wesentlich zur Lebendigkeit der Dialoge bei, erhöht somit ihren Unterhaltungswert, plausibilisiert aber durch die Nähe zur menschlichen Bedürfnissphäre auch die Dynamik des Erkenntnisstrebens. Denn ein weiteres Merkmal von Dialogen ist, dass „die Erkenntnis [...] nicht als absolut fertiges Denkergebnis, vielmehr als Prozeß auf[tritt], und dies auch dann noch, wenn das Ergebnis für den Autor von Anfang an feststeht".[13] Der Prozesscharakter der Erkenntnis lässt sich in den Binnentexten schlicht daran festmachen, dass mehrere Positionen vorgetragen werden, letztlich jedoch eine Position den meisten Beifall erhält (zumeist die des Rüstigen), die anderen also überzeugt. Das heißt also, dass eine Entwicklung von Erkenntnis stattfindet. In den Rahmentexten ist die Prozessualität der Aussagen auch innerhalb der einzelnen Beiträge der Figuren sichtbar, insofern alle Figuren ihre aus verschiedenen Quellen stammenden und einander nicht selten widersprechenden Kenntnisse einer kritischen Prüfung unterziehen, indem sie Quellen hinterfragen, Erfahrungswerte miteinander vergleichen, Plausibilitäten abwägen. Der Umstand, dass es sich hier um ästhetisch arrangierte Argumentationswege und Erkenntnisziele handelt, vermag nicht das dialogische Format der Texte in Zweifel zu ziehen, da die ästhetische Gestaltung der Dialoge – sowohl auf intratextueller als auch auf rezeptionsästhetischer Ebene – eine Vielzahl von Stimmen zur Sprache und miteinander ins Gespräch kommen lässt. Die Neugier der Figuren wie auch die der Leserschaft werden dabei stets aufs Neue motiviert.

Warum nun nehmen gerade Pflanzen eine so zentrale Position in Rists *Jahreszeitengesprächen* ein? Dialoge zeichnet aus, dass „die Gestimmtheit des Gedankens oft in der Darstellung des Umgebenden, meist einer Landschaft", eine Entsprechung findet.[14] Für die Binnendialoge lässt sich eine

---

der Erkenntnis wegen der strengen Form des Argumentationsspiels nicht so offensichtlich. Allerdings fällt auf, dass die in den Argumentationswettbewerben dargebrachten Positionen allesamt qualitativ nicht anfechtbar sind, die Figuren jedoch jeweils die Positionen bevorzugen, die in den sehr kurzen abschließend bewertenden Resümees den erklärten Idealen des Gastgebers entsprechen, was einerseits für eine sozial, andererseits für eine ideologisch geprägte und mithin nicht ausschließlich nach intellektuellen Kriterien verfahrende Erkenntnis spricht.

[13] Wildbolz: Dialog (Anm. 8), S. 251.
[14] Ebd.

solche Entsprechung freilich allein in Zusammenschau mit dem in den Rahmentexten ausführlich dargestellten Setting konstatieren, in dem die Binnenunterhaltungen ebenfalls angesiedelt sind.

Die Örtlichkeiten werden bei Rist äußerst konkret beschrieben: Er lässt uns wissen, dass er um seine Pfarrei einen Nord- und einen Südgarten sein Eigen nennt, lokalisiert diese in Wedel bei Hamburg und beschreibt sogar die Bodenbeschaffenheit, die Sonneneinstrahlungsintensität, die klimatischen Verhältnisse und monatsweise den Gartenbewuchs. Dieses konkrete Setting unterstreicht die Glaubwürdigkeit der Gesprächsinhalte, insofern erkennbar faktuale Elemente in den fiktionalen Rahmen integriert werden. So ist es eines der auffälligsten Merkmale der *Jahreszeitengespräche*, dass die Dialoge in großer Abhängigkeit von ihrer Umgebung gestaltet sind: Der Gesprächsfaden der Rahmendialoge verläuft entlang der Anordnung der Pflanzen im Garten bzw. der Gartenpfade. Dabei sind es freilich jeden Monat andere Wege, die die Wissbegierigen beschreiben und auf denen sie saisonal bedingt auf bestimmte Pflanzen treffen, zu denen sie den Rüstigen dann befragen und deren Schönheit, Herkunft, Pflege und Nutzen sie diskutieren. So werden auf unterhaltsame und kurzweilige Weise in den Rahmenfiktionen etwa 30 vegetabile Gesprächsobjekte vorgestellt. Diese von Wesche als „Artendeixis" bezeichnete „floristische lectio" verleiht Figuren wie Lesern „floristische, räumliche, zeitliche, moralische und ästhetische Orientierung".[15] Die ‚Gestimmtheit des Gedankens' findet hier also keine atmosphärische Entsprechung in der umgebenden Gartenlandschaft, sondern die Gartenlandschaft findet ihre atmosphärische Entsprechung in den zur Sprache gebrachten Gedanken der Figuren. Jeglicher Gesprächsinhalt ist in den Rahmenfiktionen der *Monatsunterredungen* Reaktion auf die umgebende Natur mit ihren Blumen, Kräutern, Wetterbedingungen und ihrer Landschaftsbeschaffenheit.

Bei Rist erschöpft sich der Zusammenhang zwischen Landschaft und Dialoginhalten aber nicht in Kommentaren zu Umgebungsvarianten. Vielmehr müssen die Pflanzen auch als Strukturmerkmal der Gespräche ernstgenommen werden. Der besondere Stellenwert der Botanik zeigt sich in

---

[15] Wesche, Jörg: Floriographie bei Rist. In: Johann Anselm Steiger / Bernhard Jahn (Hg.): Johann Rist (1607–1667). Profil und Netzwerke eines Pastors, Dichters und Gelehrten. Berlin, Boston: de Gruyter 2015, S. 655–672, hier S. 660.

den *Jahreszeitengesprächen* nämlich insofern, als in den Binnendialogen zwar auch umfangreiche Ausführungen über andere Wissenschaften (Alchemie und Chemie, Mechanik, Astronomie u. a.) anzutreffen sind, quantitativ und qualitativ jedoch nicht ohne Grund botanische Wissensinhalte die Dialoge dominieren. Denn entlang der Rist'schen Blumenbeete erfolgt eine Verständigung über Wissensordnungen, die es, so das Anliegen des Textes, seitens der Figuren (und des Lesers) stets aufs Neue zu überprüfen und zu aktualisieren gilt – der Text wird dabei „gleichsam zu papierenen Herbar des Pfarrgartens"[16]. Die wörtliche Bedeutung des „Bluhmen-Discurs[es]"[17] offenbart im textstrukturierenden *discurrere* der Figuren durch die Rist'schen Gärten ein für die *Monatsunterredungen* grundlegendes Verfahren:

> Indem sich die florale Schreibweise fortlaufend verzweigt, ineinander verschlingt, Nah- und Fernliegendes vermischt, zugleich nach der botanischen Ordnung wohlgesetzt erscheint und förmlich erblüht, steht die Methode des Blumenentrees im Zeichen einer immanenten Poetik, die ein am Pflanzenideal ausgerichtetes Schreibideal verfolgt.[18]

Botanik ist in den *Jahreszeitengesprächen* mehr als nur ein Wissensgebiet von vielen: Sie bietet vielmehr die Basis für die Gestaltung der Textstruktur. Dabei gewinnt angesichts der Fülle der beiden Gärten des Rüstigen die Einordnung empirischer Kenntnisse in den auf antiken Autoritäten beruhenden Wissenshorizont eine gewisse Dringlichkeit, die „sich in der lebensunmittelbaren Relevanz der behandelten Themen oder auch deren Bedeutung im zeitgenössischen Diskurs"[19] manifestiert. Seine eigenen um-

---

[16] Ebd., S. 664.
[17] Rist, Johann: Die allerEdelste Belustigung Kunst- und Tugendliebender Gemůhter / Vermittelst eines anmuthigen und erbaulichen Gespråches / Welches ist dieser Ahrt / Die Vierte / und zwahr Eine Aprilens-Unterredung / Beschrieben und fůrgestellet von Dem Růstigen [Hamburg 1666]. In: Ders.: Sämtliche Werke. Hrsg. v. Eberhard Mannack. Bd. I-VII. Berlin, New York 1967ff., hier Bd. V = Epische Dichtungen. Berlin, 1974, S. 183–411, S. 252.
[18] Wesche: Floriographie bei Rist (Anm. 15), S. 668.
[19] Heudecker, Sylvia: Modelle literaturkritischen Schreibens. Dialog, Apologie, Satire vom späten 17. Bis zur Mitte des 18. Jahrhunderts. Tübingen: Niemeyer 2005, S. 56.

fangreichen botanischen Kenntnisse ergänzt der Rüstige, indem er Rekurs auf zahlreiche antike wie zeitgenössische Autoritäten aus ganz Europa nimmt.[20] Hierfür werden verschiedene Quellen vor-, nebeneinander- und einander gegenübergestellt, sodass einerseits eine Basis für den Dialog über die Wissensbestände gegeben ist, andererseits sich aber auch das dynamische Streben nach Erkenntnis und ihre Ordnung in der dialogischen Struktur der Quellen widerspiegelt. Die Vielzahl an Referenzen dokumentiert die umfassende Gelehrsamkeit Rists, und der Umstand, dass es mitunter zu Widersprüchlichkeiten und Spannungen zwischen den Aussagen aus verschiedensten Quellen kommt, ist durchaus intendiert. Denn neben der üblichen Berufung auf Autoritäten zwecks Festigung und Beglaubigung der eigenen Position geht es Rist bei der Bemühung um intertextuelle Referenzen auch darum, die Polyphonie der Wissensquellen aufzuzeigen, um allen am Dialog Partizipierenden zu einer profunden Urteilsbildung zu verhelfen.

Der Rüstige arrangiert dabei nicht nur die diversen Quellen, er liefert auch das Vorbild für den Umgang mit diesen: Er referiert ausführlich aus den ihm bekannten Texten etwa dann, wenn er den anderen Figuren Wissen über die Hyazinthe verschaffen möchte:

> Der Jtaliånischer Jesuit Johannes Baptista Ferrarius von Siena, beschreibet in seiner Flora, und zwar in vierten Capittel des andern Buches den Hyacinthum und dessen mancherley Arthen gantz außführlich / in deme er anfänglich einen Unterscheid machet unter den gezeichneten und ungezeichneten / den etliche Hyazinten sind schwartz/etliche roht / etliche purpurfårbig punctiret / und vermeinet

---

[20] Auf Schriften von Avicenna oder Paracelsus nimmt Rist ebenso Bezug wie auf einen der drei sogenannten ‚Väter der Botanik', Leonhard Fuchs. Weitere genannte Autoritäten aus dem botanischen Bereich sind Valerius Cordus, Conrad Gesner, Rembert Dodoens, Carolus Clusius, Joachim Camerarius d. J. und Matthias Lobelius. Caspar Bauhinus wird mit seinem *Pinax theatri botanici* zitiert, Karl Stengel mit seinem *Hortensius et Dea flora, cum pomona, historicè, tropologicè und Anagogicè* und Giovanni Battista Ferrari mit seiner *Flora, overo cultura di fiori*. Sehr häufig rekurriert er auf Texte von Pietro Andrea Mattioli, der nicht nur für seine botanischen Schriften, sondern auch als Kommentator des Dioskurides bekannt ist. Überdies bezieht Rist sich auch oft auf seinen Rostocker Professor Peter Lauremberg, dessen *Apparatus plantarius* ihn in den *Jahreszeitengesprächen* ebenfalls interessiert.

besagter Ferrarius, daß die Hyazinthen mit ihren mancherley Farben / es auch den vielfärbigen Iridibus, Regenbogen- oder Schwertel-Bluhmen zu vor tuhe.²¹

Von seinen eigenen Kenntnissen abweichende Forschungen trägt der Rüstige ebenfalls vor, etwa wenn er verschiedene Bezeichnungen für die Gattung der Seidelbast-Pflanzen vorbringt, auch beispielsweise die von Leonhard Fuchs, jedoch anmerkt, dass dessen Bezeichnung „Daphnoides" seinem „Bedůnken nach / zu disem Gewåchse gantz nicht wil reimen".²² Auch an anderer Stelle nimmt der Rüstige eindeutig Stellung, wenn es um Pflanzenbezeichnungen geht: Der „Fritillaria imperialis" habe sein Lehrer Peter Lauremberg

> den allerfüglichsten namen gegeben / in deme Er sie Archithyrsum / zu Teutsch einen Ertz-Zepter oder Königs-Stab nennet / denn dise Bluhme / welche in meinen Augen die Pråchtigste von allen ist / vergleichet sich treflich wol einem Königlichen Zepter: Mein Freund sehe sie nur recht an / Er wird befinden / das Jhr diser Name mit guhtem Fuge kan gegeben werden.²³

Wieder an anderer Stelle trägt er die Ansichten der „hochberühmten Månner[] [...] Gesnero, Bauhino, Clusio, Hondio" zusammen, um sich ihnen in der Frage, ob es dunkelblaue Tulpen gebe, anzuschließen und schließlich zu der Schlussfolgerung zu gelangen, dass sie, wenn sie überhaupt existieren, „gahr schwehrlich zu finden" seien.²⁴ Häufig liefert er Hinweise auf eingehendere Lektüren, wie etwa angesichts der Fülle an Krokussen: „Wer Lust hat / aller diser Crocus-Bluhmen Namen / Farben / Unterscheid und

---

[21] Rist: Die allerEdelste Belustigung Kunst- und Tugendliebender Gemühter (Anm. 17), S. 258.

[22] Rist, Johann: Das allerEdelste Leben der gantzen Welt / Vermittelst eines anmuhtigen und erbaulichen Gespräches / Welches ist dieser Ahrt Die Ander / und zwhar Eine Hornungs-Unterredung / Beschriben und fürgestellet von Dem Rüstigen [Hamburg 1663]. In: Ders.: Sämtliche Werke, Bd. IV (Anm. 1), S. 121–305, hier S. 188.

[23] Rist, Johann: Die allerEdelste Tohrheit Der gantzen Welt / Vermittelst eines anmuhtigen und erbaulichen Gespräches / Welches ist dieser Ahrt Die Dritte / und zwhar Eine Mårtzens-Unterredung / Beschriben und fürgestellet von Dem Rüstigen [Hamburg 1664]. In: Ders.: Sämtliche Werke, Bd. V (Anm. 17), S. 42.

[24] Rist: Die allerEdelste Belustigung Kunst- und Tugendliebender Gemühter (Anm. 17), S. 247.

Geschlecht zu wissen / der besehe nur in des hochberühmten Caspar Bauhinus Pinax, die dritte Abtheilung / des andern Buches / da wird Er von disem allen ausführlichen Bericht finden."[25] Viele verschiedene Formen intertextueller Bezugnahmen lassen sich deshalb in den *Jahreszeitengesprächen* entdecken, weil die verschiedenartigen Referenzen dazu beitragen, unter den ‚Schülern' einen gemeinsamen und durchaus aspektreichen Wissensstand zu generieren, der zu Urteilsbildungen veranlasst und das Wachstum des dialogisch generierten Wissens garantiert.

Der Vorbildcharakter des Rüstigen beruht eben nicht nur auf seinem immensen (und nicht selten deutlich übersteigert dargestellten) Wissen, sondern vielmehr auf seinem Vermögen, Wissen adäquat aufzubereiten und weiterzuvermitteln. Dass die Ausführungen des Rüstigen pädagogisch wertvoll sind, bestätigen die anderen Figuren beständig in allen Unterredungen – etwa folgendermaßen: Jch bedancke mich höchlich für den guten Unterricht / sagte MICHAEL / man lernet doch noch allemahl etwas".[26] Dafür orientiert Rist sich wiederum an einem Vorbild, nämlich „dem Exempel unseres größesten Lehrers / Jesu Christi", der „in mancherlei Bilderen und Gleichnüssen / seinen liben Jüngern und anderen Zuhörerern hat fürgetragen".[27] Die Gleichnisse, Bilder und Exempel des Wedeler Pastors ahmen die durch die Evangelien vermittelte (pädagogische) Lehrweise und die Weisheitsrede Jesu nach und entstammen dem „Regnum Vegetabile"[28], das „Schattensweise ein Ebenbild für der himlischen Lieblichkeit / Lust und Freude"[29] darzustellen vermag. Die religiöse Grundierung der

---

[25] Rist: Die allerEdelste Tohrheit Der gantzen Welt (Anm. 23), S. 45.
[26] Rist, Johann: Die allerEdelste Zeit-Verkürtzung Der Gantzen Welt / Vermittelst eines anmuthigen und erbaulichen Gespräches / Welches in dieser Art die Sechste / Und zwar eine Brachmonats Unterredungen / Beschrieben und fürgestellet Von Dem Rüstigen. Franckfurt an dem Mayn / Jn Verlegung Johann Georg Schiele. Jm Jahr Christi 1668. In: Ders.: Sämtliche Werke. Hg. v. Eberhard Mannack. Bd. I-VII. Berlin, New York 1967ff., hier Bd. VI = Epische Dichtungen, 1976, S. 241–452, hier S. 281.
[27] Rist: Das allerEdelste Nass der gantzen Welt (Anm. 1), S. 29f.
[28] Rist, Johann: Die allerEdelste Erfindung Der Gantzen Welt / Vermittelst eines anmuthigen und erbaulichen Gespräches / Welches ist dieser Ahrt / Die Fünffte / Und zwar eine Måyens-Vnterredungen / Beschrieben und fürgestellet Von Dem Rüstigen [Hamburg 1667]. In: Ders.: Sämtliche Werke, Bd. VI (Anm. 26), S. 1–240, hier S. 142.
[29] Ebd., S. 64.

wissenschaftlichen Erkenntnis über Pflanzen ist dabei keineswegs als sekundärer Diskurs misszuverstehen. Da, wie oben gezeigt werden konnte, die Gesprächsinhalte stets in Abhängigkeit von der umgebenden Gartenlandschaft und ihren Pflanzen entstehen, besitzt die ‚Lesbarkeit' von Natur in den *Jahreszeitengesprächen* einen immensen Stellenwert.

Besonders die humanistisch gebildeten Theologen und Pastoren des 16. und beginnenden 17. Jahrhunderts, die typischerweise ihren überkonfessionellen Interessenshorizont mit ihrer konfessionellen Identität zu verbinden suchten, scheinen vielfach zu der Überzeugung gelangt zu sein, daß zum wahren Verständnis von Gott und der Welt nicht allein das Lesen in der Bibel, sondern auch das Lesen im ‚Buch der Natur' gehöre.[30]

In den *Jahreszeitengesprächen* stehen „das Naturbuch und die Bibel als Erkenntnisquelle gleichberechtigt nebeneinander", wobei es sich, betrachtet man die Rist'schen Ausführungen zu Beginn der ‚Jännersunterredung', sogar so zu verhalten scheint, „daß ihm erst die Einsicht in die Natur zu einem wahren Verständnis der Schrift verhalf":[31]

Ich laugne es nicht / antwohrtete hierauf DER RÜSTIGE / das unter allen irdischen Dingen nichtes ist zu finden / das mich mehr und hoher konne belustigen / als ein schoner Gahrte. Gleubet mir meine Herren / wen ich eine libliche Bluhme / ein wolgebildetes Kraut / eine anmuhtigriechende Staude / einen zierlich gewachsenen / fruchtbahren Baum mag sehen; so springet gleichsahm mein Hertz für Freuden / und kann ich mir solche guhte Gedanken darüber machen / das ich meine Glukseligkeit / auch mit den allerreichesten nicht begehrete zu vertauschen / den in disen Geschöpfen sehe ich nicht nur die herliche Würkungen der Natur / sondern ich finde auch etwas übernatürliches darinn / ja / ich kann mich in fleissiger Betrachtung allerhand Krauter und Bluhmen / wie diselbe so gahr wunderbarlich aus der Erde herfür

---

[30] Trepp, Anne-Charlott: Im ‚Buch der Natur' lesen: Natur und Religion im Zeitalter der Konfessionalisierung und des Dreißigjährigen Krieges. In: Dies. / Hartmut Lehmann (Hg.): Antike Weisheit und kulturelle Praxis: Hermetismus in der Frühen Neuzeit. Göttingen: Vandenhoeck und Ruprecht 2001, S. 102–143, hier S. 118.

[31] Ebd., S. 136.

kommen / der Aufferstehung der Todten / so festiglich versicheren / das ich mich auch für dem sterben durchaus nicht fürchte / sintemahl ich so wol aus dem Natur- als Schriftbuch nunmehr vollenkommen bin vergewißert / das / so wahr als GOtt unser Schöpfer lebet / der alle Jahr der Welt gleichsahm ein neues Leben wiedergiebet / auch wir / sein Geschöpfe nach dem Tode widrum leben werden.[32]

Es zeigt sich hier, dass Rist „[n]aturwissenschaftlich-gelehrte Neugier und traditionell-geistliches Weltverständnis [...] mühelos miteinander zu verbinden" vermag,[33] denn Gartenpflege heißt bei ihm zugleich Gottesdienst. Angesichts der überirdischen „Pracht und Schönheit" der Gartenpflanzen gilt es dem Rüstigen, diese im Hinblick auf „ihre Kraft und Tugend [zu] erforschen",[34] denn die ‚Lektüre' ihrer Eigenschaften beschränkt sich nicht auf das Erkennen der Nichtigkeit des Weltlichen, sondern sie verschafft vor allem Heilsgewissheit. Das hierbei angewandte Verfahren der Allegorese zielt auf ästhetische Sinnstiftung ab,[35] insofern dabei zwei epistemische Ordnungen, die religiöse und die naturwissenschaftliche, dergestalt miteinander verknüpft werden, dass sich ein „kosmologisch-allegorische[r] Resonanzraum aufspann[t], dessen transzendentale Sinnangebote als übergreifende Verstehensanweisung für die *Monatsgespräche* insgesamt fungieren".[36]

---

[32] Rist: Das allerEdelste Nass der gantzen Welt (Anm. 1), S. 30f.
[33] Mannack, Eberhard: Grimmelshausens Rist-Lektüre und die Folgen. Jupiterepisoden und Friedensspiele. In: Martin Bircher / Jörg-Ulrich Fechner / Gerd Hillen (Hg.): Barocker Lust-Spiegel. Studien zur Literatur des Barock. Amsterdam: Rodopi 1984, S. 279–294, hier S. 282. Zit. nach: Stockhorst: Wissensvermittlung im Dialog. Literarische Pflanzenkunde und christliche Weltdeutung in den Rahmenstücken von Johann Rists ‚Monatsgesprächen' und ihrer Fortsetzung durch Erasmus Francisci. In: Flemming Schock (Hg.): Polyhistorismus und Buntschriftstellerei. Populäre Wissensformen und Wissenskultur in der Frühen Neuzeit. Berlin/Boston: de Gruyter 2012, S. 67–90, hier S. 80.
[34] Rist: Das allerEdelste Leben der gantzen Welt (Anm. 22), S. 183.
[35] Stockhorst: Wissensvermittlung im Dialog (Anm. 33), S. 81.
[36] Ebd., S. 71. Zu Recht konstatiert Stockhorst daher, dass „das Dispositionsschema nach dem Ablauf der Monate eben nicht nur als formale Gliederung der Dialogfolge eintreten soll, sondern regelrecht als ihr semantisches Rückgrat" (Stockhorst: Wissensvermittlung im Dialog (Anm. 33), S. 74.).

Das allegorische Verfahren findet denn auch bei der Gestaltung des Übergangs zwischen Rahmen- und Binnendialogen seinen Einsatz: Wenn die Gesprächsteilnehmer nach ausgiebigem Spaziergang durch die Rist'schen Gärten schließlich zusammenkommen, um dem lustigen und nützlichen Zeitvertreib des spielerisch-kompetitiven Gesprächs nachzugehen, stellt sich, nachdem das Thema der Diskussion ausgegeben worden ist, die Frage, mit wessen Beitrag man beginnen soll. Der Rüstige ersinnt ein Verfahren, das die Reihenfolge der Gesprächsteilnehmer festlegen soll: Jedem der vier Gesprächspartner wird ein Blatt oder Blütenblatt zugeordnet, selbige werden dann in ein Behältnis getan, aus dem ein Knabe, der aus der Nachbarschaft gerufen wird, der Reihe nach die Blätter ziehen soll. Wessen Blütenblatt zuerst gezogen wird, beginnt usw.

Die textuelle Komposition der Binnenerzählung wird also unter Zuhilfenahme der Pflanzen, die durch den Rüstigen zu *res significantes* werden, strukturiert – ein Verfahren, das die Motivierung der Binnendisposition im Kleinen leistet und eine allegorische Lesart im Großen erlaubt. Die Verschränkung der offen gestalteten Lehrdialoge in der Rahmenerzählung und der streng strukturierten und mithin tendenziell in sich abgeschlossenen Binnendialoge liest sich vor diesem Hintergrund als Erweiterung des intradiegetisch thematisierten Kosmologiegedankens und seiner auf Mikro- wie Makroebene verfügbaren Erkenntnishorizonte. Die Transzendierung von Erkenntnis stellt sich somit als eine textinhärente Struktur dar, die die epistemisch motivierte Funktion der *Jahreszeitengespräche* vermittels ihrer Verknüpfung von verschiedenen Ordnungen in allen (religiösen wie wissenschaftlichen) Bereichen, besonders aber im Bereich der Pflanzenwelt, wesentlich erweitert und abrundet.

Die Rahmendialoge in Rists *Jahreszeitengesprächen* können als eine im Bewusstsein um den Wert geselligen Erkennens gestaltete Form von Lehrer-Schüler-Dialog charakterisiert werden. Die Binnendialoge tragen hingegen eher die Kennzeichen von diskursiv geprägten Vorträgen mit spielerischem Wettbewerbscharakter.

Signifikant ist an den Dialogen in Rists *Jahreszeitengesprächen*, das konnte gezeigt werden, ihre auf Erkenntnis ausgerichtete Programmatik: Der hier untersuchte Zusammenhang zwischen Episteme und Dialogizität strukturiert die *Monatsunterredungen* gemäß ihrer intratextuell wie extratextuell auf Erkenntnis abzielenden Funktion, wodurch ein Format generiert wird, das angesichts kaum noch zu bewältigender Wissensbestände eine Lösung anbietet für die damit einhergehende Problematik der Darstellung und v. a. Vermittlung von umfassendem Wissen. Gerade wegen dieses Bildungsanliegens trifft die kritische Beurteilung der *Jahreszeitengespräche* als „enzyklopädisch-aufgeschwelltes Memoirenwerk"[37], trotz aller berechtigten Hinweise auf Rists übersteigerte Selbstdarstellung, nicht den Kern der historischen Funktion der Texte. Denn die aufgezeigten dialogischen Strukturen generieren ein überaus breitgefächertes und auf (wissenschaftlichen wie heilsgeschichtlichen) Fortschritt abzielendes Wissensspektrum, das dem kosmologisch gerahmten Bildungsanliegen der Rist'schen *Jahreszeitengespräche* entspricht.

---

[37] Jericke: Johann Rists ‚Monatsgespräche' (Anm. 3), S. 146.

Hellenization and Romanization
The Dialogue between the Greek and Roman Cultures in the 1st and 2nd Centuries

Valerio Petrucci

It is well known that the Western Culture, as we know it today, pays a big debt to the encounter of two among the biggest civilizations of the antiquity: the Greeks and the Romans. Since the cultural roots of our present European world are to be found in the Greek and Roman cultures, it could be useful to determine to what extent these cultures were related between each other and how they interacted to create the so-called Classical Culture that has proven to be so fundamental for our common cultural development.

The relationship between the Greeks and the Romans began officially with the Battle of Cynoscephalae in 197 BCE, after which the Roman consul Titus Quinctius Flamininus proclaimed the freedom of the Greek cities from the Macedonian dominance, and lasted for other two centuries before the definitive conquest of the Greek mainland by the Romans with the creation of the Province of Achaia in 27 BCE under the rule of the emperor Augustus. During these centuries a continuous contact for the interchange of people and ideas was established that made possible the creation of a fruitful and durable cultural dialogue, the main topic of this paper. We will analyze the meaning of the words Hellenization and Romanization and focus the effects of the reciprocal influences, particularly their literary aspects.

Prior to get into the topic, I would like to recall the famous quote of Horace: "Graecia capta ferum victorem cepit et artes / intulit agresti Latio".[1]

---

[1] Horace, Ep. 2, 1, 156–157. "Greece, the captive, made her savage victor captive, and brought the arts to rustic Latium." Text and translation by: Fairclough, H. Ruston: Horace, Satires, Epistles and Ars Poetica. Loeb Classical Library 194. Cambridge MA: Harvard University Press 1978, pp. 408–409.

The sense of this famous verse is clear, especially if the author is Horace, who owes an enormous debt to the previous Greek lyric poetry.

The Greeks, conquered by the Romans with their army, had in turn conquered the Romans on a cultural level. To what extent is this true?

In order to investigate the Hellenistic influences on the Roman culture in the Imperial age we will take into account three fundamental aspects: 1) the philhellenism in the political and cultural choices of the emperors Augustus, Nero and Hadrian; 2) the influence wielded by the Greek culture on the Roman educational system; 3) the influence wielded by the Greek literature on the Latin one.

First, we must determine what it meant to be Greek and to Hellenize. According to the *Liddell-Scott Jones Greek-English Lexicon*, the verb ἑλληνίζειν (*hellenizein*) had the primary meaning of "speak or write pure or correct Greek".[2] Thus, we could infer that what made a person a Greek was the fact of speaking the most correct possible form of Greek language. Nevertheless, some literary sources shed a light on the real meaning of the word *hellenizein* and on what was the true signal of the Greek identity. The main feature of greekness was to adhere to the cultural, social and moral beliefs shared by the community of the Greeks, a codex of values that overcame the internal differences within the Greek world. Therefore, being Greek meant to embrace the Greek παιδεία (*paideia*), the Greek culture, as pointed out by Isocrates, *Panegyr.* 50:

> τοσοῦτον δ᾽ ἀπολέλοιπεν ἡ πόλις ἡμῶν περὶ τὸ φρονεῖν καὶ λέγειν τοὺς ἄλλους ἀνθρώπους, ὥσθ᾽ οἱ ταύτης μαθηταὶ τῶν ἄλλων διδάσκαλοι γεγόνασι, καὶ τὸ τῶν Ἑλλήνων ὄνομα πεποίηκε μηκέτι τοῦ γένους ἀλλὰ τῆς διανοίας δοκεῖν τεκμήριον εἶναι, καὶ μᾶλλον Ἕλληνας καλεῖσθαι τοὺς τῆς παιδεύσεως τῆς ἡμετέρας ἢ τοὺς τῆς κοινῆς φύσεως μετέχοντας.[3]

> Our city has so far surpassed other men in thought and speech that students of Athens have become the teachers of others, and the city has made the name "Greek" seem to be not that of a people but of a

---

[2] Liddell, Henry George / Robert Scott / Henry Stuart Jones: A Greek-English Lexicon. Oxford: Oxford University Press 1996, Ἑλλενίζω.

[3] Isocrates: Opera Omnia (Bibliotheca Teubneriana), Vol 2. Ed. by Basilius G. Mandilaras. Leipzig: Saur 2003, pp. 77–78.

way of thinking; and people are called Greeks because they share in our education rather than in our birth.[4]

At a thorough analysis of its usage throughout the whole era of the Greek literature, the aforementioned verb *hellenizein* reveals that the Greeks were well aware of their own cultural identity and that they recognized whoever spoke fluent Greek. But, as we have seen before, the fact of just speaking the language fluently was not sufficient to be considered a real Greek.

On the same ideological path shown by Isocrates in that passage of the *Panegyricus*, we can find, several centuries later, in the 2nd century CE, the writings of the sophist Favorinus of Arelate. Favorinus was born as a Gaul, under the Roman dominance, he was part of the *ordo equester*, he was indeed a Roman citizen with all the privileges that this condition carried, and he spoke fluent Greek. We should see now a passage of his speech to the Corinthians which is related to our topic:

> οὐκ ἐχρῆν παρ᾽ ὑμῖν ἑστάναι χαλκοῦν; καὶ κατὰ πόλιν γε: παρ᾽ ὑμῖν μέν, ὅτι Ῥωμαῖος ὢν ἀφηλληνίσθη, ὥσπερ ἡ πατρὶς ἡ ὑμετέρα, παρὰ Ἀθηναίοις δέ, ὅτι ἀττικίζει τῇ φωνῇ, παρὰ Λακεδαιμονίοις δέ, ὅτι φιλογυμναστεῖ, παρὰ πᾶσι δέ, ὅτι φιλοσοφεῖ καὶ πολλοὺς μὲν ἤδη τῶν Ἑλλήνων ἐπῆρε συμφιλοσοφῆσαι αὐτῷ. οὐκ ὀλίγους δὲ καὶ τῶν βαρβάρων ἐπεσπάσατο.[5]

Should he have not a bronze statue set up by you? Yes, and city by city: by you [Corinthians], because though a Roman he has become perfectly Hellenic, just as has your city; by the Athenians, because he speaks Attic dialect; by the Spartans because he is devoted to gymnastics; by all because he philosophizes and he has already inspired many of the Hellenes to philosophize with him, and has in addition pulled in no small number of barbarians.[6]

---

[4] Translation of the passage by: Papillon, Terry L.: The Oratory of Classical Greece. Isocrates II. Austin: University of Texas Press 2004, p. 40.
[5] Favorinos d'Arles: Œuvres. Tome I: Introduction générale – Témoignages – Discours aux Corinthiens – Sur la fortune. Ed. by Eugenio Amato. Paris: Le Belles Lettres 2005, Dio Chrys, Or., 37.26.
[6] Wallace-Hadrill, Andrew: Rome's Cultural Revolution. Cambridge: Cambridge University Press 2008, p. 5.

This passage of the so called *Korinthiakos* speech has been transmitted in the corpus of speeches of Favorinus' teacher, the orator Dio of Prusa and here we can see Favorinus defending himself in front of the whole city of Corinth whose citizens wanted to destroy his bronze statue after his quarrel with the emperor Hadrian. In this context, Favorinus said that he became a perfect greek (*aphelleniste*). This implies that he not only spoke fluent Greek, despite being a Roman Gaul, rather that he lived and thought like a Greek in a perfect manner because of his philosophical activity as a sophist, as he points out in the final part of the reported text.

So, from the two literary passages we have seen, *Hellenize*, in antiquity, meant to embrace the Greek lifestyle and the Greek culture (*paideia*). To what extent is this concept applicable to the Romans? Why and how did they embrace the Greek culture? Certainly, we should not forget that Rome was in a dominant position towards the Greeks. So, we can individuate two main reasons behind the Hellenization of the Roman Culture:

a) A sincere admiration for the ancient Greek tradition, made of culture, philosophy and literature – cultural philhellenism.
b) An attempt to make the Roman ἡγημονία (hegemonia) on Greece more palatable through embracing the Greek παιδεία (paideia) – political philhellenism.

Despite their different premises and purposes, the cultural and the political Philhellenism are not to be considered as opposites. The Romans wanted to legitimate their power on the Greeks and in order to do so, they embraced the Greek culture. The dichotomy *hegemonia/paideia* represents two faces of the same medal. While dominating the Greeks, the Romans used the *humanitas* and the *mediocritas* – that are the virtues considered by the Greeks as inseparable from their own culture. Thus, the cultural Philhellenism of the Romans should legitimate their hegemony, and created the impression that it was palatable and sufferable to the subjected Greeks.[7] Therefore, some emperors, so-called "philhellenes", despite their

---

[7] Ferrary, Jean-Louis: Rome, Athènes et le Philhellénisme dans l'empire Romain, d'Auguste aux Antonins. In: Convegno internazionale Filellenismo e tradizionalismo a Roma nei primi due secoli dell'impero. Atti dei Convegni Lincei 125. Roma: Accademia Nazionale dei Lincei 1996, pp. 183–210, here p. 200.

sincere admiration for the Greek world, nonetheless embraced several aspects of the Greek *paideia* for their own good.

Particularly, I will briefly focus on Augustus, Nero and Hadrian. Augustus (44 BCE-14 CE), amidst his restoration of the *mos maiorum*, the traditional Roman ethos, can be considered as a philhellene emperor. He encouraged bilingualism and created the first library with both a Greek and a Roman section. The monumental altar *Ara Pacis Augustae* that celebrated the Augustan Peace, a great achievement after several years of civil wars, shows the big influence of the Greek art: low-reliefs (recalling the Altar of the Gods in Athens) portray the imperial family parading in Greek fashioned clothes; representations of the city's foundation myths refer to the myth of Aeneas, the Greek hero who escaped from Troy with the very mission of founding the city of Rome. Augustus was also the first emperor to introduce new games in the περίοδον,[8] the *Aktia*, held every four years, which celebrated his victory in the battle of Actium in 32 BCE. During the Augustan age, several Greek authors spent much time in Rome, Diodorus of Sicily, Dionysius of Alicarnassus, Cecilium of Calactes. Rome became in the words of the rhetorician Polemon, reported by Athenaeus of Naucratis, a real ἐπιτομὴ τῆς οἰκουμένης, a privileged place for the encounter of the Greek and Roman cultures.[9] Under Augustus the building of theatres, *odeia*, and gymnasia had a great boost in Rome,[10] in Athens and other cities of Graeco-Roman world.

Nero (54–68 CE) was the first and only emperor who was officially called "Philhellene", in the *Akraiphia* inscription[11] dated at 67–66 CE.[12]

---

[8] περίοδον (*periodon*) was the name given to all of the four major traditional athletic competitions in Greece that took place every two or four years: the *Olympics*, the *Nemeans*, the *Pythians* and the *Isthmian Games*.

[9] Ferrary: Rome, Athènes et le Philhellénisme (note 7), p. 204.

[10] It is well known that the traditional Roman theatres were not permanent. The first permanent theatre in Rome was built in 55 BCE under the second consulship of Pompey the Great. During the Augustan age the building of the Roman theatres reachs its maximum and canonized form with the *Theatrum Marcelli* in 13 BCE. See Paratore, Ettore: Storia del teatro latino. Venosa: Osanna Edizioni 2005.

[11] Holleaux, Maurice: Discours de Néron prononcé à Corinthe pour rendre aux Grecs la liberté. In: Bulletin de correspondance hellénique 12 (1888), pp. 510–528, here p. 526.

[12] Ferrary: Rome, Athènes et le Philhellénisme (note 7), p. 186.

Why, among all of his crazy acts, Nero gained the title of Philhellene? We know that Nero had a sincere admiration for Greek culture and he loved singing and acting like a Greek. His love for the Greek culture led him in 67 CE to pronounce a famous speech, reported in the aforementioned *Akraiphia* inscription, to give the freedom to the Greeks. Nero, after having participated in all the competitions of the περίοδον and having won them all (obviously!) from the city of Corinth, where the Isthmian Games were held, proclaimed the freedom of the Greek people that guaranteed him the title of Philhellene. This kind of declaration was very different from the same kind of declaration made by Flamininus in the 2nd century BCE. This declaration aimed to be a statement of cultural deference, in fact it simply consisted in a tax relief, while the previous one had mainly a political connotation, implying the first real interference of the Romans in the Greek internal affairs.

After the brief parenthesis of Nero (his declaration was repealed immediately after his death by the emperor Vespasian) the main emperor – who can be considered a philhellene – was Hadrian.

Under Hadrian the Romans developed the greatest interest in the Greek culture. The most important thing Hadrian did to underline his love for Greece was the gift of a huge amount of money to Athens, which gained back in the Hadrianic age its supremacy as the leading city of the Greek cultural world. Athens became in this period the object of a series of donations that led to restore its predominant role within the Greek Culture.[13] Another thing that Hadrian did, was the creation of the so-called *Panhellenion*. The *Panhellenion* was primarily a religious institution that tried to recreate the environment of the Classical Greece in the 5th century BCE. Having Athens as its center, this institution, created in 132 CE, had strict admission rules, based primarily on the Greek origin of the cities that required admission.[14] This was the last attempt to relive the big Panhellenic ideal that was so powerful in the classical Greek world. In 137 CE the Panhellenic

---

[13] Spawforth, Anthony J. / Susan Walker: The World of Panhellenion. In: The Journal of Roman Studies 75 (1985), pp. 78–79.

[14] About the criteria of admission of the cities in the Panhellenion see idem, pp. 78–104 and Preston, R.: Roman Questions Greek Answers: Plutarch and the construction of identity. In: Being Greek Under Rome: Cultural Identity, the Second Sophistic and the Development of Empire. Ed. by Simon Goldhill. Cambridge: Cambridge University Press 2001, pp. 86–119.

Games were held in Athens in order to celebrate the restoration of this ancient cultural value.

This project did not last longer than Hadrian's life and the *Panhellenion* disappeared after his death.[15] It is no surprise, given this admiration for the Greek world, that the largest part of Roman education in the imperial age was based on the learning of Greek language and literature.

The main source we possess about the Roman education at this time is Quintilian's *Institutio Oratoria*. The learning of grammar and poetry from the Greek models was a possession of the elites and had its importance in the social life of every Roman noble child. Given also the close relation between culture and power that we have previously noticed, learning the Greek παιδεία was thus considered as an instrument of power. But in the 2nd century CE, learning the basics of the Greek *paideia* was not sufficient anymore. Anyone who wanted to tower above the others had to go deeply in the knowledge of the Greek culture and literary models, in order to enlarge his repertoire of *Exempla* and gain a better eloquence. An example concerning this advanced learning of the Greek models is provided by the famous school of Statius' father. In *Silvae* 5.3, the poet Statius recalls his father and his activity as a teacher. For what we can see, the canon of authors taught by Statius' father was at the very least unusual. In the 1st century CE, the knowledge of Homer and Hesiod only was not sufficient anymore to excel in the Roman imperial world:

> Hinc tibi vota patrum credi generosaque pubes | te monitore regi, mores et facta priorum | discere, quis casus Troiae, quam tardus Ulixes, | quantus equum pugnasque virum decurrere versu | Maeonides quantumque pios ditarit agrestes | Ascraeus Siculusque senex, qua lege recurrat | Pindaricae vox flexa lyrae volucrumque precator | Ibycus et tetricis Alcman cantatus Amyclis | Stesichorusque ferox saltusque ingressa viriles | non formidata temeraria Chalcide Sappho, | quosque alios dignata chelys. tu pandere doctus | carmina Battiadae latebrasque Lycophronis atri | Sophronaque implicitum tenuisque arcana Corinnae.[15]

---

[15] Spawforth/Walker: The World of Panhellenion (note 13), pp. 78–104.

Hence parents' hopes were entrusted to you, and noble youth governed by your guidance, as they learned the manners and deeds of men gone by: the tale of Troy, Ulysses' tardiness; Maeonides' power to pass in verse through heroes' horses and combats; what riches the old man of Ascra and the old man of Sicily gave honest farmers, what law governs the recurring voice of Pindar's winding harp, and Ibycus, who prayed to birds, and Alcman, sung in austere Amyclae, and bold Stesichorus and rash Sappho, who feared not Leucas but took the manly leap, and others by the lyre approved. You were skilled to expound the songs of Battus' son, the lurking places of dark Lycophron, Sophron's mazes, and the secrets of subtle Corinna.[16]

In this brief passage, we are able to recognize some names of the most representative Greek epic and lyric poets but, while some of them, like Homer and Hesiod, were commonly studied in all the schools of the Graeco-Roman world, some others, like Ibycus, Alcman or the poetess Corinna, were not that usual. Their Greek is complex and their literary genre, the choral lyric, due to its typical celebrative function in the Greek society and their polished and subtle language, could appear rather useless to a soon-to-be Roman politician.

Evident in this case is that the knowledge of the Greek poetry, even that which we could consider 'niche literature', was a possession of the elite and if they wanted to maintain this elite status, they had to go deep in Greek literature. The knowledge of the Greek poetry could be useful for a Roman student and provide a wider set of rhetorical means to construct their own speeches – "learning the Greek poets taught by the elder Statius consequently provided access to the language of the élite and led to the possession of a desirable form of cultural capital"[17].

Thus, we witness, in the imperial age, the rise of the Greek culture as a social improvement instrument, through which the Roman elites had the opportunity to legitimate their power both in the Greek provinces and in their hometown.

---

[16] Ed. and transl. by Shackleton Bailey, D. R.: Statius vol. 1. Silvae. Loeb Classical Library 206. Cambridge MA: Harvard University Press 2005, p. 358–361.

[17] McNelis, Charles: Greek Grammarians and Roman Society during the Early Empire: Statius' Father and his Contemporaries. In: Classical Antiquity 21/1 (2002), pp. 67–94, here p. 71.

The last aspect of the so-called Hellenization of the Romans on which I would like to focus, though briefly, is the influence wielded by the Greek literature on the Latin one. Since this topic is boundless and discussing it would deviate us from the main topic of the paper, I decided to recall what two eminent authors, Horace and Ovid, have written about this cultural colonization of the Greeks towards the Latin literature.

As Horace summarized: "Greece, the captive, made her savage victor captive, and brought the arts to rustic Latium" (Ep. 2, 1, 156–157). These two verses, among the most famous ever written by the Apulian author, do not leave room for further interpretations. The Greeks conquered by an army had in turn conquered the Romans on a cultural level. This model implies basically a passive role of the Romans in the process of Hellenization.[18] The Romans, according to this model proposed by Horace, would be the 'willing victims' of the Greek culture, acknowledging their 'rustic' culture as inferior to the sophisticated Greek one.

This model which implies the transformation of the 'loser' – despite, in this case, his willingness in being defeated – reveals itself as unsatisfactory, since it would imply a fusion between the two cultures that never happened, if not a real cultural appropriation of the Greek culture by the fierce Romans. The fusion model proves to be inapplicable to the specific case of the Hellenization because this same process can be seen as a 'defeat' of the Romans (as in the words of Horace) or as a 'victory', as we can read in Ovid`s *Fasti*: "nondum tradiderat victas victoribus artes / Graecia, facundum sed male forte genus".[19] This duplicity of interpretations of the same phenomenon led Andrew Wallace-Hadrill to identify the relationship between the Greeks and the Romans as a "continuous dialogue with no winners and no losers".[20] The dialogic process cannot be better described than Wallace-Hadrill did:

---

[18] Wallace-Hadrill: Rome's Cultural Revolution (note 6), p. 23.

[19] Ovid: Fasti, 3, 101–102. "Conquered Greece, had not yet transmitted her arts to the victors; her people were eloquent but hardly brave." Ed. and transl. by Frazer, James George: Ovid, Vol. 5: Fasti. Loeb Classical Library 253. Cambridge MA: Harvard University Press 1989, pp. 126–127.

[20] Wallace-Hadrill: Rome's Cultural Revolution (note 6), p. 17.

The cultures do not fuse, but enter into a vigorous and continuous process of dialogue with one another. Romans can 'hellenise' (speak Greek, imitate Greek culture) without becoming less Roman: indeed, the mutual awareness may have the effect of defining their Romanness more sharply by contrast. Reciprocally, the Greeks under Roman rule define their own identity more sharply by *paideia* even as they become Romans in other ways.[21]

Thence, given that there are no winners and no losers in this endless dialogue, how should we describe the process of Romanization? In which way we can say that the Greeks were 'romanized'?

Before analyzing the process of Romanization in itself, it could be useful to follow up on the concept of dialogue between cultures and look at the models that have been proposed to describe the relationship between the Greeks and the Romans before attaining the dialogic one. Several models describe the relationship between the Romans and Greeks in the light of the following colonial experiences. Some of them are more convincing than others but none of them reaches the goal of describing accurately this relationship.

I propose here a brief list of the different models proposed in the recent scholarship on the topic:

a) The traditional colonial model (*top-down model*), in which the conqueror takes over the conquered and replaces the original culture and social system with his system cannot be applied in this case, since we have already seen that the Romans did not destroy the Greek traditions.

b) Acculturation (proposed by Martin Millet[22]): this model could not be applied to the present case because it assumes a culturally superior population that replaces certain aspects of the native culture (barbarian) with its own culture (we have seen how Horace brilliantly summarized in just one verse the fact that the Romans considered themselves as barbarians before they came in contact with the Greek culture[23]);

---

[21] Idem, p. 23–24.
[22] Millet, Martin: The Romanization of Britain: An Essay in Archaeological Interpretation. Cambridge: Cambridge University Press 1990.
[23] See the aforementioned passage of Horace's *Epistles* (note 1).

c) Creolization (*bottom-up model* proposed by Jane Webster[24]): from the encounter of colonizer and colonized derives a new culture (fusion) – see e. g. the Creoles of the Caribbean. Certain aspects of the dominant culture blend with the native culture. This is not satisfactory because once again it assumes that the colonizer culture is superior to the new blended culture (which results to be subpar to the 'original').

d) Métissage (proposed by Patrick Le Roux[25]): a sort of cross-breeding. Two *pure* parents generate a brand new blended culture – the Roman Empire becomes a 'middle ground' in which influences came from everywhere and flowed to everywhere.

All these models, despite their intrinsic value, are to be considered fallacious because they do not take into account the plurality of the cultures and propose a fusion *tout-court* between the Greeks and the Romans. However, we must recognize that the Greeks and Romans, even with all the reciprocal influences, always tried to maintain their own cultural identity. Thus, in my opinion, the most fitting model is the *Bilingualism* model proposed by Andrew Wallace-Hadrill, which acknowledges the dialogue between these populations but not the fusion of them.

Taking the use of the Greek and Latin language as a meter to evaluate the interaction between these populations, Wallace-Hadrill recognizes that the Greeks and the Romans were able to sustain simultaneously diverse culture systems in full awareness of their differences and code-switch between them.[26] The code-switching is always an improvisation by players who understand the component language as distinct. The Romans wanted to enable the coexistence of Roman and native (in this case Greek) elements with code-switching as an improvisation. Each speaker of this dialogue remains conscious of his identity and recognizes the other part of the self.

A valid example of this coexistence of multiple but separated cultural identities can be drawn from the bilingual tombstone of the African doctor Boncar Claudius (*CIL* VIII, 15 = *IRT*, 654). Found in Leptis Magna and dated in the late first century CE, this epigraphic text is the witness of the aware-

---

[24] Webster, Jane: Creolizing the Roman Provinces. In: American Journal of Archaeology 105/2 (2001), pp. 209–225.

[25] Le Roux, Patrick: Le Romanisation en question. In: Annales. Histoire, Science Sociale 59/2 (2004), pp. 287–311.

[26] Wallace-Hadrill: Rome's Cultural Revolution (note 6), p. 14.

ness of the coexistence of several cultural identities. The born African, Greek speaking, Roman citizen Boncar felt the urge to display his triple identity in his funerary inscription, inscribed in Greek, Latin and Punic.

Thus, while the Romans, in their dominant position, wanted to hellenize without identifying themselves as Greeks, it could be interesting to hear the voice of the second speaker of this dialogue, the Greeks. The reaction of the Greeks to the Roman dominance can be observed by two different perspectives: the political and the cultural one. On the political side, we need to talk about the Greek elites of the province of Achaia. The Greek elites, during the Roman rule, were extremely powerful, since they had the opportunity to mediate between their oppressors and the oppressed. They were both ruled and rulers. They obtained the Roman citizenship and had the possibility to spend their careers into the Roman administration in spite of their political freedom. They were heirs of the classical culture but highly involved in the imperial system.[27] This not negligible political gain of the elites led, on a cultural level, to a crisis of the Greek cultural identity since the Greeks felt themselves as both Romans and Greeks[28] or, at least, the most Romanized among the imperial local elites.

The so called *pepaideumenoi*, the holders of the Greek *paideia*, the distinctive trait to be identified as a Greek, were now committed to the Roman imperial duties despite being, at the same time, the guardians of the Athenian heritage. Therefore, the Romanization of the Greeks consisted basically of an empowerment of the elites and a progressive weakening of the Greek cultural identity.

How did the Greeks react to this apparent loss of identity? The main concern of the Greeks living under the Roman dominance was to conciliate the glories of the past with the loss of freedom and greatness they were experiencing in the present. Two reactions were possible: flattery or ideological resistance.

After having acknowledged the munificence of the Romans towards their cities and people, since the Caesarian age and then in the Augustan and Imperial age, the Greeks began to be compliant with the Roman dominance and to announce festivals and decrees in honor of the proconsul or the emperor. Even the Greek artists started to celebrate the Roman deeds

---

[27] Preston: Roman Questions Greek Answers (note 14), p. 91.
[28] Idem.

with carving statues of important men and low-reliefs of their victories. Many Greeks started even to use their Roman name, which they received with their Roman citizenship.[29]

The birthday of the emperor Augustus on the 23rd of September began to be celebrated in 9 CE throughout the Greece and in the province of Asia as a national holiday. In 29 BCE, being the emperor Augustus still alive, we witness a deification of his figure following a typical use of the Greeks, and the beginning, in Greece and elsewhere in the empire, of a real cult of Augustus' persona and his family. Many festivals and sportive challenges were held in honor of Augustus and to celebrate the important facts of his reign. The cult of Augustus, Caesar and the following emperors was flanked by the cult of the *dea Roma*, the personification of the city of Rome as a goddess.

An important witness of this cult among the Greek literature is represented by Melinno's *Hymn to Rome*. This hymn, consisting of five stanzas, has been written in the 2nd century CE and presents Rome as the daughter of the god Ares, it celebrates the magnificence and the extraordinary power of the city. Just to give an example of the tone of this poem I report the first stanza as presented by Bowra:

Χαῖρέ μοι Ῥώμα θυγάτηρ Ἄρηος
χρυσεομίτρα δαίφρων ἄνασσα
σεμνόν ἅ ναίεις ἐπὶ γᾶς Ὄλυμπον
αἰὲν ἄθραυστον.[30]

I greet you, Rome, daughter of Ares,
gold crowned, wise queen,
you who dwell the holy and eternally
unbreakable Olympus on earth.[31]

Although the Greek literature seems to have never taken into account the existence of the Latin literature, this poem could hint at the fact that Melinno could have taken Statius as a model. In fact, it was at least unusual

---

[29] On this topic see McMullen, Ramsay: Romanization in the time of Augustus. New Haven, London: Yale University Press 2000, pp. 1–29.

[30] Bowra, C. M.: Melinno's Hymn to Rome. In: The Journal of Roman Studies 47 (1957), pp. 21–28, here p. 21.

[31] Translation by V. Petrucci.

that in a long poem like this each stanza was self-concluded and independent from the other stanzas. The only other witness of this stylistic feature in the 2nd century CE is the Latin poet Statius with his fourteen stanzas poem (*Silvae* 4.7). It is far from certain that Melinno was looking at Statius' poetry when writing her hymn but the analogy between the two pieces in the metrical construction has aroused several suspects of a possible Latin influence in the metric construction of the poem. These suspects could be corroborated by Horace's *Carmen Saeculare*, a hymn similar to Melinno's one, written in the same verse, the Sapphic strophe, and both recited in religious ceremonies.[32] However, despite it might be fascinating to conclude that Melinno could represent a case of influence of the Latin literature on the Greek one, the evidence to draw this conclusion are too scarce to be more than a mere hypothesis. As for Melinno's poetry, the Greek literature acknowledged the importance of Rome in other literary genres, the most important one being the historiography.

A certain school of historiographers took Rome as the center of their narration. They narrated the Universal history from a Roman point of view, because they clearly recognized how the ascent of Rome had changed the course of history. This is the case of Dionysius of Halicarnassus, Appianus and Cassius Dio. These two, one must say, even held prominent positions in the Roman administrative system being the perfect representation of those cultural and social elite that we discussed before.[33] But on the other side, we must acknowledge the existence of voices of resistance among the Greeks. If not resistance, we should talk at least about reluctance in even mentioning Rome.

While some Greek historians of the imperial age recognized the Roman Empire as the acme of the ancient civilization, so that all their histories revolved around Rome and its deeds, some others showed no mercy in ignoring the recent and contemporary events. This applies to the historian Cephalion, who wrote an Universal history from the myth of Ninus to Alexander the Great.

During the early imperial age, we witness a boost even in the writing of local histories and tour guides of the Greek cities, a phenomenon which

---

[32] Bowra: Melinno's Hymn to Rome (note 30), p. 22.
[33] Bowie, Ewen L.: The Greeks and Their Past in the Second Sophistic. In: Past & Present 46 (1970), pp. 3–41, here pp. 10–12.

has been seen as a reaction to the Roman rule which aimed to underline the glory of a single region showing a deep antiquarian interest. The most famous tour-guide written in the 2nd century CE is the *Periegesis of Greece* of Pausanias who memorizes the glorious past by analyzing the monuments and the myths of the classical Greece. It is striking that Pausanias never mentions monuments and dedications later than 150 BCE, neglecting completely the buildings of the Roman epoch.[34] This tendency of looking back at the glorious past of the Greece while ignoring the present is evident in the 2nd century CE with the so called Second Sophistic. The rhetoricians of this school always took their topics from the myth, the classical antiquity and the glorious past of the Athenians. They imitated Pericles and Demosthenes – as unsurpassed models of rhetoric – in language and style. This archaizing fashion in the pure Atticism of Pausanias or in the models adopted by the orators of the Second Sophistic "seem to be an attempt to pretend that the past is still present".[35]

The question is: Why did they lock themselves into the past? We could try to give a psychological interpretation to explain this kind of behavior as it has been proposed by Ewen L. Bowie.[36] They struggled to conciliate the present situation with their glorious past, but since this was impossible, they pretended that the present did not exist. They recognized that they had lost their freedom and their glory so, in order to construct and maintain their own identity, they preferred to lock themselves into their past glories and cultural achievements.

In conclusion, I can infer that the interaction between the Romans and the Greeks can be seen as a dialogue, a profitable and continuous interchange of ideas ad people. The mean of this dialogue is the bilingualism in which each population could sustain diverse cultural systems in full awareness of their difference and code-switch between them.

None the less, it must be recognized that the dialogue was imperfect, since there was an unequal power relation between the speakers. The Romans wanted to take everything they could have from the Greeks, while the Greek elites took advantage of the new rule to give a significant boost to their career into the dominant imperial system. Thus, while the Helleni-

---

[34] Idem, pp. 22–23.
[35] Idem, p. 36.
[36] Idem, p. 37–41.

zation is a cultural process, we can see the Romanization as the political and social outcome of this process. They are interdependent phenomena: everything under Roman control could be taken as 'Roman' whereas within this control 'Greek' remains culturally distinctive.[37]

Certainly, we have seen how the Greeks struggled to maintain their own cultural identity and how, in many cases, they preferred to remember the glorious past instead of dealing with the present. On the other hand, the Romans helped to spread the Greek culture throughout all the empire, so that we can see Hellenization and Romanization as complementary processes: the first cultural and the latter political.

In the very conclusion of the paper I would like to quote here a vivid metaphor by Andrew Wallace-Hadrill:

> It is as if Hellenization and Romanization represented the two phases of the circulation of the blood. If Hellenization is the diastolic phase, by which the blood is drawn in to the center, Romanization is the systolic phase, that pumps the oxygenated blood back to the extremities. It is not enough to have one single, prolonged phase of the one, followed by a similar, single, long phase of the other, because the two need to alternate constantly, to keep the system alive.[38]

---

[37] Wallace-Hadrill: Rome's Cultural Revolution (note 6), p. 27.
[38] Idem.

Der Dialog der Philosophien in Laktanz' *Divinae Institutiones*

Martin Schmidt

Laktanz und der Dialog in der christlichen Apologetik

Der christliche Rhetor und Apologet Laktanz (Lucius Caelius Firmianus Lactantius) machte sich im ersten Jahrzehnt des 4. Jahrhunderts an die Abfassung der *Divinae Institutiones*, einer apologetischen Darstellung des Christentums, worin er, wie schon zahlreiche Christen vor ihm, das Unverständnis der paganen Umwelt gegenüber dem christlichen Glauben zu beseitigen versuchte. Die christliche Apologetik richtete sich an ein gebildetes paganes Publikum mit der Zielsetzung, den neuen Glauben von Vorwürfen der Barbarei, Sinnlosigkeit und Gottlosigkeit reinzuwaschen. Vielmehr sollte der Leser den wirklichen christlichen Glauben kennen lernen und als den einzig wahren, vernünftigen Weg zum Heil erkennen. Dabei konnten sich die Apologeten auf Vernunftgründe sowie auf Meinungen namhafter paganer Philosophen und Dichter berufen, die sie für ihre argumentativen Zwecke passend auswählten.[1]

Durch derartige Argumentation, die zugleich klassische Bildung demonstrierte, stellten die Apologeten sich und ihre Glaubensbrüder als Mitglieder der Gesellschaft vor, die den geistigen Austausch und gütliche Klärung suchten, was sich auch an dialogisch verfassten Apologien[2] ablesen lässt. Laktanz war selbst ein Beispiel für die Wirkung solcher Offenheit gegenüber dem christlichen Glauben: Der um 250 n. Chr. in der Provinz Africa geborene Rhetor war ein Konvertit zum Christentum (die Konversion

---

[1] Vgl. Junod, Eric: Apologien. In: Der Neue Pauly. Bd. 1. Darmstadt: Wissenschaftliche Buchgesellschaft 2015, S. 891–892. Vgl. Skarsaune, Oskar: Apologetik. IV. Kirchengeschichtlich 1. Alte Kirche. In: Religion in Geschichte und Gegenwart. Bd. 1. Tübingen: Mohr Siebeck 1998, S. 616–620, hier S. 616.

[2] Vgl. Görgemanns, Herwig: Dialog. In: Der Neue Pauly. Bd. 3. Darmstadt: Wissenschaftliche Buchgesellschaft 2015, S. 517–521, hier S. 519.

wird Ende des 3. Jahrhunderts erfolgt sein), der anschließend umso entschiedener für die christliche Sache eintrat. Hierbei half ihm seine Meisterschaft in der Rhetorik,[3] die ihm eine Berufung als Rhetorikdozent an die Kaiserresidenz in Nikomedien einbrachte.

Den Austausch von Ideen, die Auseinandersetzung miteinander, kurzum, den Dialog, verstand Laktanz als notwendig für die Erkenntnis von Wahrheit und Irrtum oder wenigstens für die Einsicht, auf dem falschen Weg zur Wahrheitsfindung zu sein. In seinen *Divinae Institutiones* ruft er die Heiden, die an ihren schlechten Göttern hängen und nicht den wahren Gott erkennen, aufgebracht zur Auseinandersetzung mit den Christen auf:

> Wenn sie irgendein Vertrauen in die Philosophie oder die Redekunst haben, sollen sie sich wappnen und unsere Ansichten widerlegen, wenn sie können, sie sollen von Angesicht zu Angesicht mit uns zusammenkommen und jede Sache einzeln diskutieren.[4]

Indessen soll es hier nicht um den Dialog zwischen Christen und Heiden in Laktanz' Werk gehen, sondern um den Stellenwert, den Laktanz der geistigen Auseinandersetzung an sich einräumte, und zu welchem Zweck er in den *Divinae Institutiones* Dialoge inszenierte. Dazu muss zunächst die Arbeit an selbigen und deren Entstehung betrachtet werden: Unter dem römischen Kaiser Diocletian (285–305), der Laktanz an den Hof zu Nikomedien berufen hatte, setzte am 23. Februar 303 eine reichsweite und staatlich gelenkte Christenverfolgung ein. Laktanz begann bald darauf mit der Abfassung seiner Apologie, an deren sieben Büchern er zwischen 303 und 311 arbeitete. Die ersten beiden sollen den polytheistischen Glauben und dessen Kulte als Aberglauben entlarven, das dritte widmet sich der Widerlegung der paganen Philosophie, und die restlichen vier stellen werbend das christliche Leben, den Glauben und dessen Vorzüge vor. Insgesamt

---

[3] Vgl. Lact. inst. 3, 13, 12; 5, 2, 2. (Alle lateinischen Laktanz-Belege in diesem Aufsatz stammen aus: Heck, Eberhard / Antonie Wlosok (Hg.): L. Caelius Firmianus Lactantius. Divinarum Institutionum Libri Septem. Berlin, Boston: de Gruyter 2009–2011).

[4] Lact. inst. (Anm. 3), 5, 19, 8: „quin immo si qua illis fiducia est uel in philosophia uel in eloquentia, arment se ac refellant haec nostra, si possunt, congrediantur comminus et singula quaeque discutiant." Übersetzungen der zitierten Stellen aus den *Divinae Institutiones* von M. Schmidt.

sind die *Institutiones* nicht bloß eine Apologie, sondern auch ein Lehrbuch des christlichen Lebens.[5] Das Werk war im Vorfeld durchgeplant und systematisch angelegt.

Eine konstante, unveränderliche Haltung gegenüber bestimmten Autoren, Themen oder Philosophenschulen findet sich indes nicht. Laktanz zog für seine Argumentation routiniert Autoritäten der Literatur wie auch der Philosophie heran. Dabei dienten sie ihm je nach Bedarf als Argumentationshilfe und Beweise für die göttliche Wahrheit oder als Vertreter der zu bekämpfenden Ansichten, die er besonders gerne mit anderen paganen Autoritäten widerlegte.[6]

Die Philosophie in den *Divinae Institutiones*

Vor Laktanz hatte noch kein lateinsprachiger christlicher Apologet sich in diesem Umfang mit der paganen Philosophie auseinandergesetzt,[7] seine Haltung gegenüber den philosophischen Quellen und deren Inhalten war unterschiedlich motiviert. Sowohl im Falle der Bekräftigung eigener als auch bei der Widerlegung fremder Themen legte er Wert darauf, die Einheit oder Uneinigkeit der Philosophen gelegentlich als Ergebnisse eines Dialogs vorzustellen, der konstruktiv oder destruktiv wirkt.

Im ersten Buch verweist Laktanz mehrfach darauf, dass pagane Dichter und Philosophen in ihren Werken unwissentlich die göttliche Wahrheit als eine *Communis Opinio* verkündet hätten, die so groß sei, dass niemand sie habe völlig übersehen können.[8] Das Zugeständnis, nicht ganz irre gegangen zu sein, erhalten die Philosophen auch im siebten Buch, worin es heißt, dass die Erkenntnis einzelner Wahrheitsaspekte auf die Philosophen und ihre Schulen verteilt gewesen sei und es theoretisch nur eines Mittlers bedurft hätte, um Teile der göttlichen Wahrheit zusammen zu tragen, welche

---

[5] Vgl. Heck, Eberhard: Lactanz und die Klassiker. Zu Theorie und Praxis der Verwendung heidnischer Literatur in christlicher Apologetik bei Lactanz. In: Philologus CXXXII (1988), S. 160–179, hier S. 164: Der Titel „Institutiones" setzt das Werk deutlich von Traktaten, Briefen, Dialogen etc. ab.

[6] Vgl. ebd., S. 173f.

[7] Vgl. Casey, Stephen: Lactantius' reaction to pagan philosophy. In: C & M 32 (1980), S. 203–219, hier S. 204.

[8] Vgl. Lact. inst. (Anm. 3), 1, 5, 2f.

den Christen offenbart worden sei.[9] Hier sollen der Einklang von ‚richtigen' Meinungen, im Sinne Laktanz', und deren potentielle Austauschbarkeit als Beleg dafür dienen, dass die vom Apologeten verteidigte Wahrheit Gottes keine Erfindung ist, sondern allgemein in der Welt waltet.

Viel bitterer klingt Laktanz' Vorhaben in Buch drei, die Falschheit der Philosophie zu zeigen und deren metaphorisches Haupt zu zerschmettern, damit

> die Möglichkeit zur Vernichtung des ganzen Körpers umso leichter offen steht, wenn man das überhaupt einen Körper nennen kann, dessen Teile und Glieder uneins sind und durch überhaupt keinen Zusammenhalt untereinander zusammenhängen, sondern wie zerrissen und zerstreut eher zu zucken als zu leben scheinen.[10]

Die Uneinigkeit und der Unwille zum Austausch scheinen hier die gesamte Philosophie so schwach gemacht zu haben, dass sie dem Angriff des Apologeten erliegen werde. Die Positionen des Autors mögen je nach Bedarf schwanken. Er kann hart und kritisch sein, wenn er einem heidnischen Leser sein altes Weltbild nehmen will. Er kann aber auch entgegenkommend sein, wenn er den Leser nicht vor den Kopf stoßen möchte, sondern das Christentum als den nächsten logischen Schritt in dessen geistiger Entwicklung anbietet. Einheitlich aber kommt in den aus den *Divinae Institutiones* oben zitierten Stellen zum Vorschein, wie Laktanz auch den mangelnden oder feindseligen Dialog zwischen den Philosophenschulen für einen Grund des Scheiterns der Philosophie auf ihrer Suche nach der Wahrheit hält: Einzelwahrheiten seien erkannt, aber nicht geteilt worden, die in verschiedene Richtungen strebenden Philosophenschulen hätten den Gesamtkörper der Philosophie lebensunfähig gemacht.

---

[9] Vgl. ebd., 7, 7, 2; 7, 7, 4.
[10] Ebd., 3, 2, 1f.: „facilior nobis aditus pateat ad excindendum omne corpus, si tamen potest corpus uocari, cuius partes ac membra discordent nec ulla compage inter se cohaereant, sed quasi disiecta et dissipata palpitare potius uideantur quam uiuere."

Laktanz' Inszenierung von Austausch und Auseinandersetzung in der Philosophie

Den Anschein von konstruktiven oder destruktiven Philosophendialogen zu erwecken, gelingt Laktanz in den *Divinae Institutiones* vor allem durch die Makrostruktur seines Werkes, worin die zitierten und zum Teil von Laktanz bewusst missdeuteten Meinungen der verschiedenen Schulen einander gelegentlich wie Reden und Entgegnungen folgen. Ihre Doxographien werden nach Bedarf so angeordnet, dass sie miteinander unvereinbar wirken[11] oder dass ihre von Laktanz eklektisch kombinierten Lehren für ihn brauchbaren Sinn ergeben.[12]

Ebenso findet sich in der Darstellung eine konstruierte Gegenüberstellung philosophischer Meinungen,[13] die in einen destruktiven Dialog mündet, in dem die Teilnehmer vor allem die Meinung ihrer Gegner untergraben. Konstruktive Auseinandersetzungen werden in einigen Beispielen für möglich befunden, doch ist es in Laktanz' Interesse, seine Gegner uneinig und irregeleitet zu zeigen. Hinzu kommt, dass aus seiner Sicht der konstruktive Dialog allein nicht ausgereicht hätte, um die pagane Gesellschaft und ihre Philosophen zum Wahren oder höchsten Gut zu führen, denn dazu gelange man nur durch Gotteserkenntnis.[14] Jedoch weist eine der vielen Stellen, an denen diese Meinung formuliert wird, darauf hin, dass durch generelle Offenheit und die Bereitschaft zum Dialog die Heiden vom Austausch mit den Christen hätten profitieren können.[15] Die unwissenden Philosophen haben das höchste Gut nicht finden können, weil sie nicht um dessen Ursprung und Wirkung wussten, was allein den Christen bekannt sei, die dieses Wissen

---

[11] Vgl. Goulon, Alain: Lactance et les philosophes: réfutation ou dialogue? In: Jean-Michel Poinsotte (Hg.): Les chrétiens face à leurs adversaires dans l'Occident latin du IVe siècle: actes des journées d'études du GRAC, Rouen, 25 avril 1997 et 28 avril 2000. Mont-Saint-Aignan: Publications de l'Université de Rouen 2001, S. 13–22, hier S. 19.

[12] Vgl. Perrin, Michel: Lactance (250–325) et les mouvements philosophiques et religieux de son temps. In: Kentron 9 (1993), S. 149–168, hier S. 150.

[13] Vgl. Goulon: Lactance et les philosophes (Anm. 11), S. 17.

[14] Vgl. Lact. inst. (Anm. 3), 5, 15, 1. Vgl. Freund, Stefan: Laktanz, Divinae Institutiones, Buch 7: De vita beata. Einleitung, Text, Übersetzung und Kommentar. Berlin, New York: de Gruyter 2009, S. 314–316.

[15] Vgl. Lact. inst. (Anm. 3), 5, 15, 1.

vermitteln können. Bedenkt man den Missionseifer der Christen, lässt diese Stelle die Deutung zu, dass der Unwille zum Dialog den paganen Philosophen bei der Wahrheitserkenntnis im Wege gestanden habe.[16]

Nun inszeniert Laktanz einen Dialog ohne christliche Dialogpartner, um die Falschheit des paganen Denkens aufzuzeigen. Seine eigene Meinung hält er oft sogar zurück, um den Fokus nur auf die von ihm entworfene Auseinandersetzung zu lenken.[17] Eine Abbildung der Realität zeigen diese inszenierten Begegnungen zwischen Vertretern verschiedener Philosophien jedoch nicht. Laktanz stellt vor allem die berühmten Philosophenschulen vergangener Jahrhunderte einander gegenüber.[18] Die Wirkung einiger Stellen als Streitgespräch wird dadurch unterstützt, dass der Apologet eine überschaubare Menge an Gewährsmännern stellvertretend für ihre Schulen und Lehren nennt.[19] Die Auseinandersetzung mit verschiedenen Anschauungen und Lehren wird durch die Konfrontation berühmter Größen der Philosophie, die einander im Gespräch hätten begegnen können, sofern nicht unterschiedliche Lebensdaten dagegen gestanden hätten, zu einem Dialog: Sokrates (469–399 v. Chr.) steht für die philosophische Skepsis und seine Erben Platon (428/7–348/7 v. Chr.), Aristoteles (384–322 v. Chr.) sowie Cicero (106–43 v. Chr.) für die Akademie.[20] Zenon (334–262/

---

[16] Minucius Felix, dessen christliche Apologie in Dialogform Laktanz bekannt war (vgl. Lact. inst. (Anm. 3), 5, 1, 22), konstruierte ein literarisches Beispiel der Bekehrung eines starrköpfigen Heiden, nachdem dieser sich die Argumente eines Christen angehört hat (vgl. Heck, Eberhard: Minucius [II 1] M. Felix. In: Der Neue Pauly. Bd. 8. Darmstadt: Wissenschaftliche Buchgesellschaft 2015, S. 241–242).

[17] Vgl. Casey: Lactantius' reaction to pagan philosophy (Anm. 7), S. 206.

[18] Vgl. Fàbrega, Valentin: Lactantius. In: Reallexikon für Antike und Christentum. Bd. XXII. Stuttgart: Hiersemann 2008, S. 795–825, hier S. 805: „[D]er von ihm selbst angekündigten, angeblich vernichtenden Auseinandersetzung [ist Laktanz] in Wahrheit ausgewichen, indem er seine philosophischen Kontrahenten nicht unter den Zeitgenossen, sondern in den philosophischen Schriften Ciceros gesucht hat." Laktanz gibt als Motivation und Zweck der *Institutiones* den Widerspruch gegen philosophische Positionen an, die er selbst zu seiner Zeit am Hofe zu Nikomedien gehört habe (Lact. inst. (Anm. 3), 5, 4, 1f.).

[19] Vgl. Lact. inst. (Anm. 3), 5, 3, 1.

[20] Vgl. Perrin, Michel: Le Platon de Lactance. In: J. Fontaine / M. Perrin (Hg.): Lactance et son temps. Recherches actuelles. Actes du IVe Colloque d'Études historiques et patristiques, Chantilly, 21–23 septembre 1976. Paris: Beauchesne 1978, S. 203–234, hier S. 208. Vgl. Lact. inst. (Anm. 3), 1, 5, 24; 3, 3, 7; 3, 14, 14; 3, 25, 1.

1 v. Chr.) und Seneca (rd. 5 v. Chr.-65 n. Chr.) vertreten häufig die Stoa,[21] Epikur (342/1–271/0 v. Chr.) und Lukrez (96/94–55/54 v. Chr.) sind die Sprecher des Epikureismus.[22] Indem Laktanz sich vor allem mit philosophischen Klassikern aufhält (nur im fünften Buch der *Institutiones* setzt er sich mit zeitgenössischer Philosophie auseinander),[23] gewinnt der von ihm inszenierte Dialog zwischen den hochkarätigen Diskussionsteilnehmern an Glanz.

Dass beim Philosophieren, laut Laktanz ein Austausch von Vermutungen,[24] zwangsläufig Auseinandersetzungen um Meinungen entstehen, zeigt er beiläufig in einem Beispiel, worin er die Sinnlosigkeit des Philosophierens über die Natur als ebenso fruchtlos darstellt wie das Spekulieren über die Beschaffenheit einer vollkommen unbekannten Stadt.[25] Wenn man nun über diese Stadt rede, werde es ganz verschiedene Meinungen und Widersprüche unter den Diskutierenden geben: „Aber wenn wir das [über die Stadt] gesagt haben, wird jemand anders das Gegenteil erörtern, und weil er sich auch geirrt hat, wird sich ein dritter erheben und danach andere und sie werden so verschiedenes vermuten wie wir vermutet haben."[26] Dabei könne niemand wissen, was richtig und was falsch sei. Ebenso sei es bei den Philosophen, die sich ohne Furcht vor Widerlegung in ihrer Diskussion sicher wägten.

Diese Stelle ist eigentlich nicht zur Illustrierung des philosophischen Vorgehens gedacht, da Laktanz mit besagtem Beispiel die Dreistigkeit der Philosophen anklagt, mit der sie vage Vermutungen als Wahrheit aufstellen, welche allein bei Gott liege. Dennoch gibt das Beispiel der Stadt, in dem Behauptungen sofort Widerspruch und neue Meinungen hervorrufen, einen Vorgeschmack darauf, wie Laktanz das Philosophieren und die Interaktion der Philosophen untereinander sieht beziehungsweise konstruiert.[27]

---

[21] Vgl. Lact. inst. (Anm. 3), 3, 4, 1; 3, 6, 7; 3, 23, 14.

[22] Vgl. Perrin: Le Platon de Lactance (Anm. 20), S. 208. Vgl. Lact. inst. (Anm. 3), 3, 16.17 passim.

[23] Vgl. Goulon: Lactance et les philosophes (Anm. 11), S. 14.

[24] Vgl. Lact. inst. (Anm. 3), 3, 3, 8.

[25] Vgl. ebd., 3, 3, 4f.

[26] Ebd., 3, 3, 10: „sed cum haec dixerimus, alius contraria disputabit et cum hic quoque perorauerit, surget tertius et alii deinceps et opinabuntur multo disparia quam nos opinati sumus."

[27] Vgl. ebd., 3, 3, 9–16.

Gleiches gilt für die fingierte Reaktion der Philosophenschulen, die Laktanz aus der Erkenntniskritik des Arkesilaos aus Pitane (316/5–241/0 v. Chr.) zieht,[28] der sich, zweifelnd an den menschlichen Erkenntnismöglichkeiten, gegen philosophische Lehren aussprach und sie widerlegte.[29] Andere könnten darauf antworten (*respondere*), dass Arkesilaos entsprechend seiner Lehre auch nichts wissen könne.[30] Die Antwort, die der Apologet stellvertretend für alle Philosophen formuliert, lässt vor den Augen des Lesers das Bild von Streitenden entstehen, die auf jede Meinung Andersdenkender stets reagieren, als begegneten sie sich in einem Raum. Dargestellt wird das ‚Hin und Her' einer dialogartigen Auseinandersetzung zwischen Philosophen, von denen der erste eine Ansicht oder Behauptung äußert, der zweite diese widerlegt, woraufhin der erste dem Skeptiker den Vorwurf macht, dass er – gemäß seines Widerspruchs – selbst nichts wissen könne.

Konstruierte Philosophendialoge in den *Divinae Institutiones*

Den vermeintlichen Streit der Philosophen inszeniert Laktanz besonders im dritten Buch der *Divinae Institutiones*, das sich dem fehlerhaften Denken der Philosophen widmet, um ihnen aufgrund dessen Autorität und Wahrheitsanspruch abzusprechen. Deren angeblich so destruktive Haltung gegenüber dem Anderen verbildlicht er effektvoll und mit sprachlicher Wucht in der oben zitierten Metapher vom zerstückelten Körper, dessen Haupt den Namen sowie Anspruch der Philosophie darstellt und dessen verdrehte Körperteile die verschiedenen Lehren und Schulen symbolisieren.[31] Diese als inkompatibel angeprangerten philosophischen Richtungen treibt er in seinem Werk in einen Streit, indem er die eine Lehre der anderen gegenüberstellt:

---

[28] Vgl. ebd., 3, 4, 11–14.
[29] Vgl. Görler, Woldemar: Älterer Pyrrhonismus, Jüngere Akademie. Antiochos aus Askalon. In: Hellmut Flashar (Hg.): Grundriß der Geschichte der Philosophie [Abt. 1]: Die Philosophie der Antike. Bd. 4/2. Völlig neubearb. Ausg. Basel: Schwabe & Co. AG 1994, S. 717–989, hier S. 796–798: Eine eigene Lehrmeinung formuliert er nicht, sondern widerlegt fremde Ansichten durch Gegenargumente.
[30] Vgl. Lact. inst. (Anm. 3), 3, 5, 6f.
[31] Vgl. ebd., 3, 2, 2.

> Die Philosophie ist in viele Schulen unterteilt und alle haben verschiedene Ansichten. In welcher verorten wir die Wahrheit? In allen kann man das sicherlich nicht. Wir wollen mal eine beliebige angeben! Dann wird in allen anderen sicher nicht die Weisheit sein. Gehen wir zu den einzelnen über! Wir werden auf die selbe Weise alles, was wir einer zugestehen, den übrigen absprechen. Eine jede einzelne Schule stürzt nämlich alle anderen um, um sich und ihre Lehre zu bekräftigen, und gesteht keiner einzigen anderen zu, Weisheit zu besitzen, um nicht zuzugeben, dass sie selbst sie nicht besitzt. Aber so wie sie die anderen beseitigt, wird sie selbst auch von allen anderen beseitigt.[32]

So wie Lactanz die Problematik beschreibt, die Sachlage darlegt und auf die Schwierigkeiten hinweist, einer Seite recht zu geben, bringt er sich selbst beinahe als Advokat in die Szene ein – der er zwar nie war, aber durch seine Ausbildung hätte sein können[33] – und stellt beide Parteien einander gegenüber. Das Bild der sich gegenseitig anklagenden Philosophievertreter, die gewissermaßen vor einem Richter in einem Dialog stehen, um sich gegenseitig zu diskreditieren, wird in der Auseinandersetzung um das höchste Gut noch präziser ausgeführt:

> Was bleibt also anderes übrig als dass wir, nachdem wir die rasenden und starrsinnigen Streithähne beiseitegelassen haben, zu einem Richter kommen, natürlich zu diesem Geber einer einfachen und ruhigen Weisheit, die uns nicht nur formen und auf den Weg führen, sondern auch über die Streitfälle dieser Männer ein Urteil abgeben kann.[34]

Es finden sich mehrere Begriffe aus dem Wortfeld ‚Streit' bzw. ‚Gerichtsstreit'. Auch das für die Gegner gewählte Wort *litigator* wird nicht nur im

---

[32] Ebd., 3, 4, 3f.: „In multas sectas philosophia divisa est et omnes varia sentiunt. in qua ponimus ueritatem? in omnibus certe non potest. designemus quamlibet; nempe in ceteris omnibus sapientia non erit. transeamus ad singulas; eodem modo quidquid uni dabimus, ceteris auferemus. una quaeque enim secta omnes alias euertit, ut se suaque confirmet, nec ulli alteri sapere concedit, ne se desipere fateatur. sed sicut alias tollit, sic ipsa quoque ab aliis omnibus tollitur."

[33] Vgl. ebd., 3, 13, 12.

[34] Ebd., 3,8,1: „Quid ergo superest nisi ut omissis litigatoribus furiosis ac pertinacibus ueniamus ad iudicem, illum scilicet datorem simplicis et quietae sapientiae, quae non tantum formare nos et inducere in uiam possit, uerum etiam de controuersiis istorum ferre sententiam?"

Allgemeinen für streitende Personen benutzt, es kommt auch in der Terminologie der Gerichtssprache vor, zur Bezeichnung des Prozessführenden oder der prozessführenden Partei.[35] Auch das Wort *controversia* gibt sowohl den wahren Rechtsfall vor Gericht wie auch einen fiktiven Gerichtsstreit an, der zu Übungszwecken in der Rhetorenschule durchgenommen wurde.[36]

Die Unfähigkeit zur Einigung der von Laktanz vor den Richter gestellten Streitenden zeigt sich ebenfalls in der oben besprochenen Stelle über Arkesilaos: Die kritisierten Philosophen finden keine richtigen Argumente für ihre nicht zu beweisenden Meinungen, sondern verweisen lediglich darauf, dass Arkesilaos auch nichts wissen könne, also keine Grundlage zur Argumentation habe.[37] In Laktanz' Darstellungen scheint es den Philosophen gar nicht um die Bewahrung ihrer eigenen Meinungen zu gehen, sondern nur um die Ablehnung der gegnerischen Ansichten. So klassifiziert Laktanz die Philosophen lediglich nach zwei Oberkategorien, von denen die eine Wissen beansprucht und die andere bestreitet, dass dieses erlangt werden könne.[38] Die Vertreter der zweiten Kategorie sind nach seiner Ansicht in der Mehrheit.

Eine Gegenüberstellung der Philosophenschulen erfolgt auch indirekt. Am Ende des Kapitels über die Epikureer tadelt Laktanz deren Lehre über die Seele, die sich angeblich auflöse und vergehe.[39] Im folgenden Kapitel schickt er Epikur in einen Streit mit den Pythagoreern und Stoikern, die lehren, dass die Seele Bestand habe.[40] Nicht nur durch die textuelle Positi-

---

[35] Vgl. Thesaurus Linguae Latinae 7.2, 1505, 57f. und 1505, 64–66.
[36] Vgl. ebd., 4.0, 782, 82ff.
[37] Vgl. Lact. inst. (Anm. 3), 3, 5, 6f.
[38] Vgl. Gigon, Olof: Lactantius und die Philosophie. In: Adolf Martin Ritter (Hg.): Kerygma und Logos. Beiträge zu den geistesgeschichtlichen Beziehungen zwischen Antike und Christentum. Festschrift für Carl Andresen zum 70. Geburtstag. Göttingen: Vandenhoeck & Ruprecht 1979, S. 196–213, hier S. 202.
[39] Vgl. Lact. inst. (Anm. 3), 3, 17, 42.
[40] Vgl. ebd., 3, 18, 1. In der stoischen Lehre war die rationale sowie körperliche Seele Teil des Körpers, durchdrang ihn, war aber nie fest an ihn gebunden (vgl. Inwood, Brad: Stoizismus. In: Der Neue Pauly. Bd. 11. Darmstadt: Wissenschaftliche Buchgesellschaft 2015, S. 1013–1018, hier S. 1016). Pythagoras lehrte die Seelenwanderung (vgl. Riedweg, Christoph: Pythagoras [2]. In: Der Neue Pauly. Bd. 10. Darmstadt: Wissenschaftliche Buchgesellschaft 2012, S. 649–653, hier S. 651).

onierung der philosophischen Richtungen wird eine Auseinandersetzung konstruiert, sondern auch durch die folgende Kapitelüberleitung: „Andere aber führen Gedanken aus, die diesen gegensätzlich sind."[41] Hier liest sich die Zusammenfassung der stoischen und pythagoreischen Seelenlehre wie eine kritische Antwort auf die Epikureer.

Durch eine ähnliche Technik macht der Apologet die Philosophie selbst, die sich seiner Ansicht nach nur aus Wissen und Vermutung zusammensetzt,[42] schon zu Beginn des dritten Buches zunichte, indem er die Positionen von Sokrates und der ihm nachfolgenden Akademie konträr setzt zu Zenon und der Stoa, welche in Laktanz' Augen die zwei großen Rivalen der Philosophie sind:[43] Wenn man nichts wissen könne (so Sokrates) und keine Vermutungen anstellen solle (so Zenon), habe sich die Philosophie selbst zur Strecke gebracht.[44] Diese fiktive Begegnung von Philosophen unterschiedlicher Lebenszeiten führt zu keinem Ergebnis, sondern zu einem (eigens konstruierten) Patt, den Laktanz mit dem Scheitern der Philosophie gleichsetzt.[45]

Der inszenierte Dialog findet auch statt, ohne dass die Sentenzen oder Köpfe verschiedener Philosophenschulen einander gegenübergestellt werden. Durch Satzformen und Stilfiguren kann die Rede und Gegenrede eines philosophischen Dialoges erzeugt werden, indem bloß kurze Zusammenfassungen unterschiedlicher Lehren aufeinander folgen. Wenn es heißt, dass die Philosophen der Akademie gegen die Naturphilosophen argumentieren, dass die Existenz von unerklärlichen Dingen es verbiete, über irgendetwas sicheres Wissen zu beanspruchen, so steht dieser Satz antithetisch zu der vermeintlichen Entgegnung der Naturphilosophen – den Bezug der Argumente aufeinander kann dadurch niemand übersehen:

> Die Akademiker haben gegen die Naturphilosophen aufgrund verborgener Dinge argumentiert, dass es kein Wissen gibt und haben, zufrieden mit den Beispielen weniger, unbegreiflicher Dinge, die Unwissenheit angenommen, als ob sie alles Wissen beseitigt hätten, weil sie es teilweise beseitigt hatten.

---

[41] Lact. inst. (Anm. 3), 3, 18, 1: „Alii autem contraria his disserunt."
[42] Vgl. ebd., 3, 3, 1.
[43] Vgl. Perrin: Le Platon de Lactance (Anm. 20), S. 207.
[44] Vgl. Lact. inst. (Anm. 3), 3, 4, 2.
[45] Gigon: Lactantius und die Philosophie (Anm. 38), S. 202.

Die Naturphilosophen hingegen zogen aus diesen Dingen, die offenkundig sind, das Argument, dass man etwas wissen kann und, zufrieden mit offenkundigen Dingen, hielten sie am Wissen fest, als ob sie es ganz verteidigt hätten, weil sie es teilweise verteidigt hatten.[46]

In den beiden Sätzen stehen sich die Urheber der Meinung, die Argumentationsweise und deren vermeintliche Schlussfolgerung parallel gegenüber. Der Präpositionalausdruck *contra physicos* beziehungsweise das Adverb *contra*[47] suggerieren eine verbale Auseinandersetzung. Als „wahnsinnig vor Widerspruchseifer"[48] bezeichnet Laktanz jene „Akademiker, deren Ziel es ist, allem zu widersprechen, was mehr destruktives Kritisieren und Verspotten ist"; das Problem beim Zusammentragen ihrer Entdeckungen sei das Fehlen eines Mittlers gewesen, der die göttliche Wahrheit kenne,[49] doch als den außerordentlichen Fehler (*incredibilis error*) der Philosophen benennt Laktanz die Haltung, fremde Meinungen rundheraus zu verdammen und die eigenen unreflektiert zu verteidigen.[50] Einmal mehr behauptet er somit, dass sich Teile der paganen Gesellschaft aufgrund ihrer mangelnden Offenheit die Möglichkeit zur geistigen Weiterentwicklung verbaut hätten.

Laktanz' Schlussfolgerung lautet, dass aus der Unstimmigkeit und Inkompatibilität der Philosophenschulen ihre Fehlerhaftigkeit und Entfernung von der Wahrheit resultieren.[51] Auch seine Leser sollten angesichts so vieler inszenierter Streitigkeiten den Eindruck gewinnen, dass von den angeblich weisen Philosophen keine Einigung oder Wahrheit zu erwarten sei.

Doch es spricht vielleicht auch eine Spur von Bedauern aus obigem Zitat. Denn nur das Scheitern der Philosophie anzuprangern, wäre für Lak-

---

[46] Lact. inst. (Anm. 3), 3, 6, 5f.: „Academici contra physicos ex rebus obscuris argumentati sunt nullam esse scientiam et exemplis paucarum rerum inconprehensibilium contenti amplexi sunt ignorantiam, tamquam scientiam totam sustulissent, quia in parte sustulerant. Physici contra ex iis quae aperta sunt argumentum trahebant <omnia> sciri posse contenti que perspicuis retinebant scientiam, tamquam totam defendissent, quia ex parte defenderant."
[47] Ebd., 3, 6, 5f.
[48] Ebd., 7, 7, 3: „contradicendi studio insaniunt."
[49] Vgl. ebd., 7, 7, 4f.
[50] Vgl. ebd., 7, 7, 6.
[51] Vgl. ebd., 5, 3, 1.

tanz auch nicht zweckmäßig gewesen, da er selbst ausgewählte Argumente für seine Sache aus philosophischen Lehren schöpfte, um sein paganes Publikum zu erreichen.[52] Will er im dritten Buch noch das Haupt der Philosophie zerstören und ihren Körper auslöschen, so beteuert er im letzten Buch der *Institutiones*, er wolle nicht die Philosophie so vernichten, wie das die Akademiker gewöhnlich tun.[53] Er gesteht den Philosophen zu, einige Teile der Wahrheit erfasst zu haben, doch durch die destruktive Skepsis der Akademie, die zerstrittenen Schulen und aus Unkenntnis nicht zur ganzen Wahrheit gelangt zu sein.[54]

Mehr als ein Zugeständnis spricht aus diesen Worten. Sie sind ein Plädoyer für einen konstruktiven Dialog, der Laktanz zumindest immer dann freut, wenn die einhellige – gegebenenfalls auch zufällig übereinstimmende – Meinung von Philosophen zur christlichen Lehre passt,[55] selbst wenn sie nicht das Ergebnis eines Laktanz'schen Dialoges ist.[56]

Zusammenfassung und Ergebnisse

Das Scheitern aller paganen Philosophien stellt Laktanz einerseits durch die Konstruktion und Inszenierung destruktiver Dialoge dar, worin die verschiedenen Schulen scheinbar nur um des Widerspruchs Willen einander Erkenntnisse absprechen; andererseits zeigt er dies vielleicht noch eindringlicher, indem er hypothetische, konstruktive Dialoge unter den Philosophenschulen durchspielt, die näher zur Wahrheitserkenntnis hätten führen können.

---

[52] Vgl. Walter, Jochen: Pagane Texte und Wertvorstellungen bei Lactanz. Göttingen: Vandenhoeck & Ruprecht 2006, S. 150f., 237f.
[53] Vgl. Lact. inst. (Anm. 3), 7, 7, 2.
[54] Vgl. ebd., 7, 7, 1–4; vgl. Freund: Laktanz, Divinae Institutiones, Buch 7 (Anm. 14), S. 314–316.
[55] Vgl. Heck: Lactanz und die Klassiker (Anm. 5), S. 173f.
[56] Vgl. Lact. inst. (Anm. 3), 1, 5, 15ff. (alle Philosophen und Dichter erahnen „die Existenz einer einzigen Vorsehung"); ebd., 4, 27, 15 (Dichter und Philosophen waren sich einig, den Jupiter zu den Dämonen zu zählen); ebd., 6, 12, 5–10 (Einigkeit der alten Philosophen und besonders Ciceros darüber, dass die Menschen von Geburt an nach Gerechtigkeit streben); ebd., 7, 23, 5 (einhellige Meinung von Philosophen, Dichtern, Propheten und Sehern über die Auferstehung der Toten).

Die Konstruktion von streiterfüllten Dialogsituationen zwischen Philosophenschulen – vielmehr zwischen deren prominenten Vertretern als Aushängeschilder und Protagonisten – erscheint in der Werkstruktur als Gegenüberstellung oder Aufeinanderfolge von Meinungen. Ebenso verweist das häufig benutzte Vokabular der Gerichtssprache und der verbale Austausch in den *Divinae Institutiones* auf eine bühnenreife Gegenüberstellung der Philosophen als Dialogpartner.

Dass diese Darstellungen vielleicht auch ein Plädoyer für eine gelingende Kommunikation sein mögen, sollte in Erwägung gezogen werden. Denn Laktanz blickte auf drei Jahrhunderte zurück, in denen die Koexistenz von Christen und ihren paganen Mitmenschen wiederholt durch Repressionen und Verfolgungen gestört wurde, und erlebte, wie seine Glaubensgemeinschaft im Römischen Reich aus Unverständnis zum Sündenbock für aktuelle Übel in der Welt gemacht wurde.[57] Erst die Beendigung der Verfolgung durch Kaiser Galerius im Jahre 311 und die verstärkte Einbindung der Kirche ins Reich unter Kaiser Konstantin (324–337) beförderte die endgültige Einbindung des Christentums in die Reichskultur. Das wäre dann der Beginn eines neuen Dialoges.

---

[57] Vgl. Lepelley, Claude: Die Christen und das Römische Reich. In: Luce Pietri (Hg.): Die Geschichte des Christentums. Religion, Politik, Kultur. Bd. 1: Die Zeit des Anfangs (bis 250). Freiburg, Basel, Wien: Herder 2003, S. 229–268, hier S. 245–251.

An early Modern Conception of Dialogism: Giovanni Pontano and the Neapolitan Academy (1476–1503)

Georges Tilly

It is always useful to be told the truth about ourselves – even if truth sometimes involves the most embarrassing details. Count Richard, once leaving the house of the bishop of Verona, where he had been hosted for a few days, and being courteously escorted by one of his host's relative, a very witty old man, received an unexpected farewell gift from the bishop. The old man told the count that his host had been so delighted by the company of such a well-mannered man that he had decided to observe every details of his behavior and hadn't found any grain of unpleasantness in it – except a very disgraceful grimace he does with his lips and mouth while masticating, and the resultant chewing sound that is unbearable to hear. This very practical warning was considered as a wise farewell gift by the bishop of Verona and by his witty relative, whose name, Galateo, would be reported as the title of the treatise in which this famous anecdote was drawn: the *Galateo, ovvero de' costumi* of the Tuscan Giovanni Della Casa, published posthumously in Venice in 1558.[1] The fictive count Richard was so witty and so well-mannered himself that he only experienced an imperceptible moment of indignation, and almost immediately asked Galateo to thank the bishop for one of the most precious gifts he had ever been granted.

In the beginning of the twentieth century, this anecdote would epitomize Norbert Elias' theory on behavioral changes during Renaissance. In *Über den Prozeß der Zivilisation*, the sociologist argued that new 16th century standards of behavior were made more binding and efficient than any for-

---

[1] The *Galateo* was published in 1558, posthumously (Della Casa, Giovanni: Rime et prose. Venice: Nicolo Bevilacqua 1558, pp. 83–170; see pp. 91–92 for the anecdote). For a recent English translation of the anecdote see Della Casa, Giovanni: Galateo. The Rules of Polite Behavior. Ed. and trans. by M. F. Rusnak. Chicago: University of Chicago Press 2013, pp. 9–10.

mer boundaries of social conduct by the fact that they were now grounded in habits of mutual monitoring. Commenting Galateo's observation on count Richard's flaw, Elias argues:

> It is immediately apparent that this polite, extremely gentle and comparatively considerate way of correcting was, particularly when exercised by a social superior, much more compelling as a mean of social control, much more effective in inculcating lasting habits, than insults, mockery or any threat of outward physical violence.[2]

These new standards would have been given (by Galateo and count Richard himself) the name of "civilitas".[3]

Though the *Galateo* has become the symbol for Renaissance thought on standards of behavior in Elias' theory, it is now seen by many as carrying the symptoms of an exhaustion of the moral values brought by humanism.[4] If one now recalls the great season of humanist diplomacy, when the rise of ciceronian eloquence was supposed to improve relations between entire states and to be the cornerstone of universal peace, Della Casa's version of *civilitas* is indeed anticlimactic. Della Casa's converting the diplomatic ideal of *civilitas* into a mere advice to avoid someone being mocked

---

[2] Elias, Norbert: On the Process of Civilization. Sociogenetic and Psychogenetic Investigation. Transl. by Edmund Jephcott. Dublin: University College Dublin Press [revised one-volume edition, volume 3 of the collected works 2012], p. 88. Original: Elias, Norbert: Über den Prozess der Zivilisation. Soziogenetische und psychogenetische Untersuchungen. Band 3.1. Frankfurt/Main: Suhrkamp 1997.

[3] For a good synthesis on 'civilitas' during the Renaissance see Margolin, Jean-Claude: La civilité nouvelle. De la notion de civilité à sa pratique et aux traités de civilité. In: Alain Montadon (Ed.): Pour une histoire des traités de savoir vivre en Europe. Clermont-Ferrand: Association des Publications de la Faculté de Lettres et Sciences humaines de Clermont-Ferrand 1994, pp. 151–177.

[4] See for instance: Picquet, Théa: Un manuel de savoir-vivre Giovanni della casa: Galateo, ovvero de' costumi. In: http://italies.revues.org/841 (12.09.2016). Picquet's conclusions are partly based on the judgement that was carried out by Ruggero Romano: Tra due crisi: l'Italia del Rinascimento. Torino: Einaudi 1971, pp. 179–180. The same fade-out of humanistic values was noticed by Philippe Guérin in Stefano Guazzo's 'civil conversazione'. See: Guérin, Philippe: La civil conversazione de Stefano Guazzo: du dialogue à la conversation. In: Id.: Le dialogue: Ou les enjeux d'un choix d'écriture [pays de langues romanes]. Rennes: Presses universitaires de Rennes 2006, pp. 235–296.

on the way he chews, is maybe as unsettling as Machiavel's turning into precepts of cynical and individual behavior the virtues, which were commonly seen as the boundaries of the ruler's conduct in the genre of the mirrors for princes. Before being dazed by the many wars subsequent to the French descent into Italy in year 1494, before the Sack of Rome (1527), humanism had had a different face.

Recently, Richard Sennett tried to put Nobert Elias' point of view into perspective, claiming that, instead of being obsessed by the severe observation of their fellows, the authors of the Renaissance placed emphasis on pleasure in social relations. Renaissance's change in terms of moral and social conduct had been, hence, partly misinterpreted by the German sociologist, and some of the original aspects of the idea of *civilitas* had been ignored by him. In this assertion, Sennett was mostly considering Della Casa's treatise and Castiglione's *Cortegiano*[5], but his remark can easily be extended to other authors and treatises or dialogues.

During the fifteenth and the sixteenth century, dialogues devoted an important part to what might as well be called "civilitas", namely the pleasure of interacting, of cooperating in order to solve a problem or, basically, the pleasure of being in good company. Sennett, while trying to define sociologically this type of pleasure and its role in building up the social bounds, carves out a central role for the concept of dialogism:

> Perhaps you, like me, dislike the phrase 'social skills', which suggests people good at cocktail party talk or adept at selling you things you don't need. Still, there are social skills of a more serious sort. These run the gamut of listening well, behaving tactfully, finding points of agreement and managing disagreement, or avoiding frustration in a difficult discussion. All these activities have a technical name: they are called "dialogic skills".[6]

---

[5] ‚Il libro del Cortegiano' was first published in Venice by Aldo Manuzio in 1528.

[6] Sennett, Richard: Together. The Rituals, Pleasures, and Politics of Cooperation. New Haven CT/London: Yale University Press 2012, p. 6. These two different types of skills overlap with differences between the late 'socially skilled' conception of Della Casa and the early 'dialogically skilled' intentions of some authors like Giovanni Pontano. We are aiming to show these differences.

It would be worthy to show that Renaissance evolution regarding behavior is far more rooted in a genuine conception of that type of dialogic skills than in any other things. We would like to put forward brand new conceptions of social relations that appear during the Renaissance. Therefore, we will analyse how Renaissance authors thought to improve their dialogic skills.

We will focus on the treatise and the dialogues of Giovanni Pontano (1429–1503), which were all written between 1476 and 1503 and published shortly after – so they are representative of Quattrocento literature and influential for Cinquecento Italian dialogic production.[7]

Being one of the most prolific authors of Quattrocento, Pontano's prosaic and poetical works offer a heuristic field of study, enabling us to understand what humanism actually was. But our method will be scarcely different from philosophical attempts[8], since we will dwell on philological

---

[7] Giovanni Pontano (1429–1503) was a prominent humanist and political figure of late Quattrocento Naples. For a short biographical insight see Monti Sabia, Liliana: Un profilo moderno e due Vitae antiche di Giovanni Pontano. Naples: Accademia pontaniana 1998; his English biography offers interesting insights on his political career: Kidwell, Carol: Pontano. Poet and Prime Minister. London: Duckworth 1991; the classical reference for Pontano's life is Percopo, Erasmo: Vita di Giovanni Pontano. Napoli: ITEA Industrie Tipografiche 1936. Pontano's dialogues (*Charon, Antonius, Actius, Aegidius, Asinus*) have been edited altogether in a few modern editions: Pontano, Giovanni: Dialoghi. Ed. by Carmelo Previtera. Firenze 1943 [Latin text]; Pontano, Giovanni: Dialoge. Ed. by Hermann Kiefer. München: Fink 1984 [Latin text with German translation]; they are currently being published with an English translation, the only issue already available is Pontano, Giovanni: Dialogues: Charon and Antonius. Ed. and transl. by Julia H. Gaisser. Cambridge/London: Harvard University Press 2012 [Latin text with English translation]. Here we will refer to the dialogues in Kiefer's edition while giving our own English translation – although for *Charon* and *Antonius* we will quote the translation of Julia H. Gaisser and add the reference in her edition. For a stylistic overview of Pontano's dialogues and their place in the evolution of the genre see Marsh, David: The Quattrocento Dialogue. Classical Tradition and Humanist Innovation. Cambridge/London: Harvard University Press 1980, pp. 100–116.

[8] Mostly Ernesto Grassi's works, of which his preface of Kiefer's edition of Pontano's Dialogues gives an excellent idea (see Pontano: Dialoge (note 7), pp. 7–24). See also Grassi, Ernesto: Humanistic Rhetorical Philosophizing. Giovanni Pontano's Theory of the Unity of Poetry, Rhetoric, and History. In: Philosophy &

facts, like composition, invention, sources and influences. We will focus on Pontano's use of the dialogue genre showing the way he built those philological facts up to reveal his (philosophical, ideological or political) concern for representing a space of idealized social relations.[9]

In Pontano's dialogues, parts of argumentation, harsh disputation and polemics are never caused by the members of the academy who constitute the main core of interlocutors. This occurs in two different ways.

Firstly, in a satirical way, which is present in Pontano's works, since his first experiment with the dialogue genre, the *Charon*, inspired by Lucian's *Dialogues of the Dead* (Νεκρικοί Διάλογοι), which features the shadows of two dead *grammatici* – i.e. masters of grammar, in a stichomythia on the proper use of words and tenses:

> *Mercury.* But who is laughing at you so hard behind your back? Turn around and look at him.
> *Theanus.* I am Theanus, the grammatist.
> *Pedanus.* Wrong. You ought to have said, "grammarian", not "grammatist". So you need to learn this in addition.
> *Thean.* You've misspoken, for no one has said "learn" yet. And so you need to have said "learn", not "learn in addition".
> *Ped.* You have misspoken right back, for "to say", not "to have said" was needing to be said.
> *Thean.* You also have misspoken right back. For not "was needing", but "needed" was to be said.

Rhetoric 17/3 (1984), pp. 135–155; Weiss, Rainer / Yvonne Mundy: The Humanist Rediscovery of Rhetoric as Philosophy. Giovanni Giovano Pontano's 'Aegidius'. In: Philosophy & Rhetoric 13/1 (Winter 1980), pp. 25–42; Grassi, Ernesto / Kiaran O'Malley: Why Rhetoric Is Philosophy. In: Philosophy & Rhetoric 20/2 (1987), pp. 68–78; Nauta, Lodi: Philology as Philosophy. Giovanni Pontano on Language, Meaning, and Grammar. In: Journal of the History of Ideas 72/4 (2011), pp. 481–502.

[9] Our method will be quite similar to the method of Goddard, Charlotte: Pontano's Use of the Didactic Genre: Rhetoric, Irony and the Manipulation of Lucretius in 'Urania'. In: Renaissance Studies 5/3 (1991), pp. 250–262. Goddard has shown how Pontano was able to use mythological representation and imitation of Lucretius for polemical use against Pico's ideas on incompatibility between astrology and free will.

Ped. You have broken the skull of Priscian. For you had had to say not "was" but "had".

Thean. You have broken Priscian's feet: "you had", not "you had had."

Ped. On the contrary, "you had had", not "you had."

Thean. On the contrary, "you had", not "you had had."

Ped. On the contrary, the latter.

Thean. No, the former.

Ped. No, I.

Thean. No, you.

Ped. No, well.

Thean. No, badly.

Ped. Woe is me!

Thean. Woe is you![10]

Pontano uses this type of petty disputes in many contexts but always in order to satirize what is for him an improper use of language or science. In his dialogue *Antonius*, Enrico Puderico refers to a struggle between grammarians that ends by swordplay:

> *Enrico.* I can scarcely express how much that discourse of yours delighted me, especially when I recall how a dispute between two grammarians was once settled by swordplay. One of them charged the other with a fault for constructing impleo ["fill"] with the genitive case [...]. In fact, the ancients joined this word with the genitive and the ablative case indiscriminately, and since those learned and keen-

---

[10] Translated by Julia H. Gaisser. See Gaisser: Dialogues (note 7), pp. 90–3, § 50–1; Kiefer: Dialoge (note 7), pp. 108–111: "MERCVRIVS: [...] Sed quis est qui tam te irridet a tergo? illum respice. / THEANVS: Ego sum theanus grammatista. / PEDANVS: Errasti, "grammticum" te, non "grammatistam" debuisti dicere. Addisce igitur. / THEAN.: Peccasti, "addisce" enim nondum quisquam dixit. Itaque "disce" non "addisce" dixisse oportuit. / PED.: Rursum peccasti "dicere" enim, non "dixisse" oportebat dici. / THEAN.: Et tu rursum item peccasti, nam non "oportebat" sed "oportuit" dicendum erat. / PED.: Prisciano caput fregisti, neque enim "erat", sed "fuit" dicere debueras. / THEAN.: Prisciano pedes fregisti; "debuisti" enim, non "debueras". / PED.: Immo "debueras", non "debuisti". / THEAN.: Immo "debuisti", non "debueras". / PED.: Immo hoc. / THEAN.: Immo illud. / PED.: Immo ego. / THEAN.: Immo tu / PED.: Immo bene. / THEAN.: Immo male. / PED.: Hei mihi! / THEAN.: Hei tibi!"

witted grammarians were ignorant of the fact, when one spat in the lap and the face of the other, the matter came to swords, and finally passed from grammar to surgeons.[11]

In this very context, the members of the academy are clearly opposed to that type of dispute and they reject it.

Secondly, members of the academy sometimes don't fear to take a stand in some polemical topics. But if they become virulent, it is never towards each other but always towards these external categories of the grammarians who seem to perform a confiscation of language – i. e. Latin language – through their philological activity. In *Actius*, for example, Compater complains about some grammarians who have corrected the word "Aegocerontis" in "Aegocerotis" in a very ancient manuscript on the ground of modern learning without knowing that this special pronunciation was also very ancient and came from the Greek people of Sicily and Calabria.[12] Shortly after (p. 158), Actius laughs on Servius' comment of the verse 224 in the second book of the *Georgics* – "Talem diues arat Capua et uicina Veseuo / Ora iugo"[13] –, in which Virgil is said to have erased the name of the town "Nola" replacing it by "Ora" because the people of Nola would have denied him water.[14] But, according to Actius, Virgil was a man of science and he did know that Nola's territory was unfertile, so it would have been nonsense to list it in the fertile territory of Campania. In short, Pontano represents his companions condemning other literates for having restrained the natural variety of language or for having based their decrees on opinions instead of observation. But polemics in Pontano's dialogues can also turn

---

[11] Translated by Julia H. Gaisser. See Gaisser: Dialogues (note 7), pp. 162–3, § 29; Kiefer: Dialoge (note 7), pp. 166–169: "Dici vix potest quam me serme iste delectet, praesertim cum in memoriam ueniat inter duos olim grammaticos gladiis actam rem esse, dum alter alteri uitio daret quod uerbo impleo generandi casum adiunxisset [...]. Adeo promiscue ueteres uerbum hoc et secondo et sexton casui iunxere, quo docti illi et acuti grammatici dum ignorant, dum alter alterius sinum atque os despuit, res ad gladius uenit tandemque a grammaticis ad chirurgos."

[12] See Kiefer: Dialoge (note 7), pp. 316–319.

[13] "Such is the soil rich Capua ploughs, and the coast near the Vesuvian ridge." Translated by H. Rushton Fairclough in: Virgil: Eclogues, Georgics, Aeneid I-VI. Revised by G. P. Goold. London: Harvard University Press 1999, p. 153.

[14] See Kiefer: Dialoge (note 7), pp. 354–357.

An early Modern Conception of Dialogism

to insults. Against Macrobius for instance: "In fact, to begin with the last point, grammarian, you didn't know how to make verses, I think"[15] – "So stop barking, whelp, and learn what *fama* is".[16]

This polemic against grammarians is rooted in different language conceptions or methods of comments: for Pontano, only poets can judge poetry. But it features as well a different conception of conversation since it satirizes harsh debates, which was sent outward from the little group of members of the *Accademia pontaniana*. Indeed, the relationships between members of the Pontanian academy are stripped of any controversial exchange. At the beginning of their talk or when they let another speaker talk, speakers of the academy sometimes betray the use of conversation rules as the written dialogues illustrate. These rules regulate the changes of speaker by underlining mutual consideration or the interests of each one in what has just been said. No speaker is supposed to start his speech abruptly. The following passage is highly representative:

> *Paulus.* That oracle, in the totally faithful account you gave of it, is filled with sanctity, and your speech itself was worthy of such an oracle [...]. Indeed we are all Christians and we follow the same faith – but, Pardo, I see that you have been considering for a while what is to be said on that point. So, let us rather listen to you.
> *Pardus.* [...] The things you have just said, Paulus, they are true and I hear them with pleasure [...].[17]

There is an obvious discrepancy between the attitude of Theanus – making fun of Pedanus behind his back and breaking into conversation – and Pau-

---

[15] Translated by Julia H. Gaisser. See Gaisser: Dialogues (note 7), pp. 203–204, § 58; Kiefer: Dialoge (note 7), pp. 196–197: "Atque, ut ab ultimo incipiamus, nesciebas, puto, grammatice, uersus facere".

[16] Translated by Julia H. Gaisser. See Gaisser: Dialogues (note 7), p. 207, § 60; Kiefer: Dialoge (note 7), pp. 198–199: "Desine igitur oblatrare, catelle, et fama quid sit [...] disce."

[17] My translation. Kiefer: Dialoge (note 7), pp. 310–314: "Pavl. Et oraculum ipsum summa a te cum fide recitatum plenum est diuinitatis et oratio haec ipsa tua teque atque oraculo tali digna [...]. Christiani enim cuncti sumus solamque pietatem sequimur, teque, Parde, uideo iam pridem pensitare quid ad haec dicturus sis; itaque te ipsum potius audiamus. / Pard. [...] Paule Prassici, quae a te dicta non minus sunt recte quam a nobis grate accepta".

lus, who is so attentive to his fellow companions while speaking himself that he feels Pardus was ready to talk back. This is nearly systematic both in *Actius* and *Aegidius*. Though Antonius is not deprived of such politeness when conversation turns to serious topics:

> *Enrico*. Do this, dear Elisio; I beseech and entreat you by the spirit of our Antonio, since I can compel you with no greater appeal.
> *Elisio*. Andrea could also take on this responsibility on behalf of his Vergil.[18]

In contrast to the stichomythia seen before, in which interlocutors nearly interrupt each other, most of the interlocutors' replicas here begin by thanking their predecessors; some of them also finish by designating their successor and giving the next one the right to talk. But the preceding quotation is representative of some features of the Renaissance dialogue in Pontano's style. Firstly, there is no *princeps sermonis*: no one is *a priori* the master of the conversation, even Pontano, the master of the academy, is just an interlocutor among others in the dialogue *Aegidius*. Though, someone can become *princeps sermonis* on one topic, since he is nominated by the others as the expert on that topic. The right to talk does not come from the speaker himself, like, for instance, in Cicero's dialogues; it emerges from the assembly's consensus respecting one's expertise. In *Actius*, the conversation sometimes seems to rely on implicit rules occasionally recalled to barely transgressive speakers:

> *Puderico*. Personally, Compater, I easily put up with the fact that you were a bit long dwelling on the grammarians' unfortunate scruple, which you bear with difficulty. However, every entertaining discourse has to avoid tediousness and primarily the lassitude of his listeners.[19]

---

[18] Translated by Julia H. Gaisser. Gaisser: Dialogues (note 7), pp. 172–173, § 37–8; Kiefer: Dialoge (note 7), pp. 174–175: "HERR. Quod te, Elisi suauissime, per Antonii nostri Manes, quando qua te maiore obtestatione cogam non habeo, oro atque obtestor. / ELIS. Et poterat Andreas et sponte etiam debeat provintiam hanc pro Virgilio suo suscipere."

[19] My translation. See Kiefer: Dialoge (note 7), pp. 326–327: "PUD. Ego vero, Petre Compater, facile sum passus aegre ferentem te grammaticorum importunam diligentiam euagatum longiuscule; omnis tamen dicendi oblectatio vacare debet taedio cum primis audientium defatigatione."

The dialogue *Antonius* sometimes betrays the same concern to avoid any tediousness during the conversation: "But I don't want to bore any of you, especially this visitor."[20] Similarly, speakers are urged to restrain from popular speech:

> *Visitor.* The highest, by Priapus!
> *Compater.* No obscenities, visitor! I obsecrate you.
> *Visitor.* But I thought I was allowed to use obscenities in Oscan territory, since I hear that in common parlance people swear by the bellies of the saints and their livers and by the part that made even the Cynics blush.
> *Compater.* Don't you know that the masses are the worst authority on behavior? For what attribute do they have that you might not most justly condemn?[21]

The members of the academy gather around a special conception of conversation that seems to exclude any argumentative debate, any crosstalk, any interruptions during the speeches and any form of tediousness. This type of dialogue deliberately excludes the *disputatio in utramque partem*, which was a common feature in Cicero's dialogues and got more prominent in Renaissance dialogues, enforced by the medieval *disputatio*. Instead, it features a perfect agreement on conversation rules and a very ritualized context of speech which was built on purpose by Pontano. It shows no parallel in ancient exempla[22] and does not seem to be rooted in any rhetorical precept. But on what purpose was it built in such a way?

---

[20] Translated by Julia H. Gaisser. Gaisser: Dialogues (note 7), pp. 160–161, § 27; Kiefer: Dialoge (note 7), pp. 166–167: "Sed nolo uobis, hospiti praesertim huic, esse molestior."

[21] Translated by Julia H. Gaisser. Gaisser: Dialogues (note 7), pp. 128–9, § 6; Kiefer: Dialoge (note 7), pp. 144–5: "HOSPES. Per Priapum, summa! / COMPATER. Parce, hospes, oscenis, obsecro. / HOSP. Atqui putabam mihi in Osca regione uti oscenis licere, cum populariter audiam iurari per deorum uentres perque iecinora atque per eam partem cuius ipsos etiam Cynicos perpuderet. / COMP. An ignores pessimum morum auctorem populum esse? Quid enim habet quod maximo etiam iure non improbes?"

[22] However, one could compare it to the rules established by Plato in some of his dialogues like *Phaedra* or *Symposion*. The rules of Pontano's dialogues might be quite similar but they are implicit and aim to seem spontaneous.

The literary criticism of the Pontanian school – at least in its beginnings[23] – is mostly inventive in defending Vergil (among others) from the judgments put forward by ancient critics like Gellius or Macrobius, but above all by Pontano's senior colleague Lorenzo Valla.[24] This posture has been pointed out by Giacomo Ferraù who evidenced the polemics against grammarians as a hallmark of Pontano's school – other hallmarks, like the rejection of popular talk and the aristocratic conception of poetry have been evidenced by Marc Deramaix, as we have just seen.[25] Though Pontano rejected Valla's method and temper, he was himself greatly indebted to his senior's works: for instance, after accusing Macrobe of not knowing the meaning of the word "fama" (fame) in *Antonius*, Pontano undertakes to give its significance by considering how ancient authors use it. This way of defining a word by referring to the context of their use is the method used by Valla in his *Elegantiae*. There are other compelling evidences Pontano had studied in his works. Indeed, in our particular case, some of Pontano's dialogues echo some of Valla's works. Ferraù has pinpointed the fact, that there are quotations of Valla's dialogue against Poggio Bracciolini (*Antidotum in Poggium liber I*)

---

[23] The starting point of Ferraù's classic analysis of Pontano's criticism was the dialogue *Antonius* written by Pontano during the 1470's. Ferraù, Giacomo: Pontano critico. Messina: Centro di Studi umanistici 1983; on Antonius, see the chapter 'Le strutture o del decorum'. Idem, pp. 16–43. Today, some perspectives on his earlier conceptions can be brought by reading Germano, Guiseppe: Il 'De aspiratione' di Giovanni Pontano e la cultura del suo tempo. Napoli: Loffredo 2005 and Iacono, Antonietta: Uno studente alla scuola del Pontano a Napoli: le Recollecte del ms. 1368 (T. 5.5) della Biblioteca angelica di Roma. Napoli: Loffredo 2005.

[24] Lorenzo Valla (1407–1457) has changed the face of humanism with the *Elegantiae*, the *Repastinatio*, the *De falso credita et ementita constantini donatione*. They were all deeply influential works thanks to their new methods and accurate insights on lexicology, grammar, and philosophy. Valla was hired by Alfonso the Magnanimous before he became king of Naples and he accompanied him in his conquest of the Realm. He also wrote dialogues such as *De vero falsoque bono* and *De libero arbitrio*. The latter was considered a masterpiece by Calvin and turned out to be of no little importance in his thoughts.

[25] See Deramaix, Marc: Excellentia et admiratio dans l'Actius de Giovanni Pontano: Une poétique et une esthétique de la perfection. In: Mélanges de l'École française de Rome [Moyen Âge – Temps modernes] 99/1 (1987), pp. 171–212.

in the stichomythia cited before. We would say in addition that the forged anecdote of the swordplay (which seems to have been a topic in the Neapolitan circle[26]) is a burlesque way to take literally the frequent metaphors of struggle in Valla's dialogues such as this one:

> *Antonius*: Do not expect me to give in to you so easily or to flee without sweat and blood.
> *Laurentius*: Good luck to you; let us contend closely in hand-to-hand and foot-to-foot conflict. Let the decision be by the sword, not spear.[27]

In the mid-fifteenth century, Lorenzo Valla, being himself in the service of Alfonso the Magnanimous, king of Naples, was involved in numerous polemics against important humanists of the Neapolitan circle, like Bartolomeo Facio and Antonio Beccadelli (who was Pontano's master). Valla wrote a harsh attack against Facio[28] in which he criticized some of his works, in particular his dialogue on happiness: *De humanae vitae felicitate*.[29] His main criticism against Facio's dialogue pertains the weakness of argumentation, especially in the first part of the dialogue devoted to refute common ideas on man's happiness. Facio defends himself by arguing that he was forced by the decorum, the verisimilitude, to represent an unequal debate, since the character he had chosen to

---

[26] See Giacomo Ferraù: Pontano critico (note 22), pp. 14–15, n. 1.
[27] Translated by Charles Trinkaus. See Trinkaus, Charles: Lorenzo Valla. On Free Will to Garsia, Bishop of Lerida. In: Ernst Cassirer / Paul Oskar Kristeller / John Herman Randall (Ed.): The Renaissance Philosophy of Man. Chicago, London: The University of Chicago Press 1948, pp. 155–184, here p. 162: "ANT. Noli expectare ut tibi tam facile dem manus aut terga uertam sine sudore et sanguine. / LAU. Macte uirtute esto, congredere propius, et comminus collato pede non telo decerne, sed gladio."
[28] For Valla's polemic against Facio and the different conceptions of dialogue revealed by it, see Pignatti, Franco: Dialogisme, dialogicité, dialogue. Le dialogue en Italie entre Quattrocento et Cinquecento. In: Emmanuel Buron / Philippe Guérin / Claire Lesage (Ed.): Les états du dialogue à l'âge de l'humanisme. Tours, Rennes: Presses Universitaire de Tours & de Rennes 2015, pp. 27–37.
[29] On Facio's dialogue, see Tufano, Vera: Il 'De humanae vitae felicitate' di Bartolomeo Facio tra modelli classici e fonti patristiche. In: http://mefrm.revues.org/2928 (03.01.2017).

feature, a certain Lamola, was particularly good natured: "I wanted to feature this man as he is and as he behaves in conversation."[30] Answering to that argument, Valla simply blames Facio to have chosen the wrong interlocutor. Instead of dwelling on principles of imitation or verisimilitude, Valla's innovative conception of dialogue relies on disagreement and discussion. Dialogue's very nature implies a heuristic confrontation.

Valla's dialogic works have been highly influential in the 16th century, both regarding their philosophical contents and their constructions of a strong opposition between the interlocutors. The first theorizations of dialogue as a genre, which occurs in the late sixteenth century, show how important the conception of dialogue as a heuristic structure became, especially when rooted in dialectics.[31] This is, for example, the opinion of Sigonio's treatise *De dialogo* (1561). Sigonio is responsible for anchoring dialogue in its mimetic role on the basis of Aristotle's *Poetics*. On the other hand, he also uses his sound knowledge of Aristotle's *Topics* to redefine the genre by its dialectic structure. Sigonio's treatise mostly confirms dialogue as a major heuristic genre for humanism. This is also the case of Tasso's brief discourse on dialogue. For Tasso, in the 1580's, dialogue is characterized by argumentation, by series of questions and answers.[32] Dialogue as a genre is the forged depiction of a plausible argument between several people. This conception is still indebted to Valla's conception of the mid fifteenth century.

But getting back to Pontano's works, it is certain that his conception of the dialogue genre implies a completely different role for conversation, being accurately thought and composed as a response to Valla's conception

---

[30] My translation. "Volui hominem secundum naturam et consuetudinem eius disputantem facere", quoted by Pignatti: Dialogisme (note 26), p. 29.

[31] On dialogue and dialectic see Spranzi Zuber, Marta: The Art of Dialectic between Dialogue and Rhetoric. The Aristotelian tradition. Amsterdam: John Benjamin Publishing 2011, especially pp. 133–160 (chapter 6). The same topic had been previously developed in Spanzi Zuber, Marta: Le traité du dialogue de Carlo Sigonio et la dialectique d'Aristote. In: Guérin (Ed.): Le dialogue ou les enjeux d'un choix d'écriture (note 29), pp. 203–217.

[32] See Tasso, Torquato: Tasso's Dialogues. A Selection, with the 'Discourse on the Art of Dialogue'. Ed. and transl. by Carnes Lord and Dain A. Trafton. Berkeley, Los Angeles, London: University of California Press 1982, pp. 24–25.

of the genre as a heuristic contest. But this does not mean that it is not philosophically relevant.[33]

In his treatise on conversation (*De sermone*, 1509), written about fifty years after Valla's death, Pontano remembers him as an unbridled polemicist. He discredits the efficiency of Valla's eristic method – both in conversation and in treatises. Pontano pretends to consider that Valla's goal was neither to seek the truth in a given subject nor to teach anything, but simply to speak ill of one another and even to attack the authors of Antiquity on their use of Latin. In *De sermone*, Valla is part of the portrait gallery in which are listed some ill-tempered characters. These characters' main flaw lies in their immoderation (either in flattery or in blame). They are likely to threaten the harmony between different individuals and the pleasure they can get by being together. These remarks put forward the fact, that Pontano had probably kept some memories of the time when the young academy of Naples was torn by the polemics initiated by Valla. Once being himself in charge of the academy, Pontano would like to prevent that this will happen again.

The dialogue genre is rather for Pontano a way to feature how people can exchange information with one another without getting into controversy, animosity and frustration. This idealized representation shows how sophisticated a conversation can and must be between literates, how cheerful the cooperation in sharing knowledge. This pleasure of being together, as Sennett could have said, is not without a certain aristocratic pride that forbids popular language and trivial subjects. In the meantime, Pontano, faithful to the Aristotelian concept of virtue as a medium-term between two flaws, points out the ideal behavior of the pleasant man (*uir facetus*) who is neither a flatterer nor a naysayer, neither a smuggler nor a boring man. In that perspective, Valla plainly assumes the role of the troublemaker.

If Valla's dialogue was dedicated to the search of the truth, Pontano's main pictured behavior in his dialogues deserves to be called truth as well. Indeed, in *De sermone* Pontano opposes two conceptions of truth:

> Here, we are not speaking about that one type of truth searched by physicians or mathematicians, which concerns the basis of syllogism

---

[33] Pontano's thought has sometimes suffered from the comparison with Valla's. See the remarks, otherwise pertinent, of Caserta, Ernesto: Il problema religioso nel *De voluptate* del Valla e nell' *Aegidius* del Pontano. In: Italica 43/3 (Sept. 1966), pp. 240–263, here p. 253.

in this type of disputes that deals with nature. We are speaking of that one type of truth that shows nothing faint, false or forged in conversation or in discourses, nothing of such type in behaviors neither.[34]

The first conception is Valla's one, it demonstrates logic and syllogism. The second one is related to social behavior. For Pontano, there is a special type of behavior that can be called *veritas*, in which great virtue is to maintain the social bonds. It is a special requirement of conversation that consents to exchange information in the appropriate way and to cooperate. Valla's use of sharp dialectic controversy in dialogues jeopardizes, for Pontano, the goodwill and friendship of conversation, and hence, the bond to keep people together (*uinculum retinendae societatis*). That's why one can't witness any controversy in Pontano's dialogues.

Though, it is shaped by a certain conception of truth in behavior that enhances the quality of social relations. Instead of featuring first a reason, like Tasso suggested, Pontano's dialogue features how to keep a network of friends or relatives alive and efficient by improving its dialogic skills. This particular concern of the humanist was probably born out of his own experience as the leader of the academy, and it was also shaped by his refusal of the academy's convention to tear each other apart as he has seen it during Valla's employment at the court of Naples. This conception of social relation was nevertheless as influential as Valla's conception of dialogue since the academy of Pontano has been one of the main prototypes for European sodalities.[35]

---

[34] My translation. Pontano, Giovanni: De sermone. Transl. by Alessandra Mantovani. Roma: Carocci editore 2002, p. 108: "Loquimur autem de ueritate hoc in loco, non illa quidem a physiciis quaeritur aut mathematicis quaeue uersetur circa certitudinem syllogismorum in ipsisque disputationibus, quae sunt de rerum natura […], uerum de ueritate ea, quae nihil in sermonibus atque in oratione, nihil etiam in moribus inesse fictum, fallax, fucatum indicet […]."

[35] Our study is too short to consider the important question of the humanistic network and the role played by conversation or even dialogism in the shaping of Quattrocento humanism. I hope to be able to dwell on that problem soon. On that point, it will undoubtedly be of some interest to read the recent study of Furstenberg-Levi, Shulamit: The Accademia Pontaniana. A Model of a Humanist Network. Leiden, Boston: Brill 2016. See the introduction for methodological aspects and the bibliography.

Pontano's use of the dialogue genre denotes a clear conscience of what Richard Sennett has called "dialogic skills", that is every behavioral norm both in manners and in conversation that enables people in a group to give their best in a collaboration. We would consequently be prone to follow Sennett's point of view by putting into perspective some of Norbert Elias's assertions on the behavioral change in the Renaissance. Although one can argue that the members of the academy ensure one towards another the respect of some common rules – mostly in relation with their aristocratic pride –, their motivation in monitoring oneself is the pleasure of being together and sharing ideas of common interest. Another important fact is that, paradoxically enough, those norms in conversation have been theorized by Pontano only in *De sermone*, years after he wrote his first dialogues.[36] So it is likely that, instead of composing his dialogues according to an abstract idea of conversation, the humanist has used the dialogue genre to *experiment* what conversation should be. Hence, it almost seems that the written dialogue shares some of the heuristic interests philosophers have found in the thought experiment.

It is certain that we are far from Facio's conception of dialogue in both Valla's and Pontano's conception of the genre. As we have seen, Facio's *De hominum felicitate* suffers from a lack of innovative views on his topic and betrays a conception of the written dialogue as an 'imitation of reality'. Both Valla and Pontano, for their part, see the genre of dialogue as the best mean to express their ideas on conversation. However, it would be nonsense to make Pontano the unique forerunner of any modern theory on social relations – like a 'protos euretes' of some kind. We shall go beyond our case study and see that – even if this contrast between Valla and Pontano was easy to stress and to substantiate, thanks to some theoretical sources on dialogue, like Valla's polemics against Facio or Pontano's *De sermone* – many humanists have used this genre to express – or more accurately to experiment – a special point of view on conversation and social relation.

---

[36] On Pontano's conception of conversation and on the groundbreaking – though invisible – role played by *De sermone* in the European tradition, see Quondam, Amedeo: La conversazione. Un modello italiano. Roma: Donzelli editore 2007, pp. 35–132. Quondam had seen before Sennett how the model of the 'civile conversazione' could put into perspective some aspects of Norbert Elias' theory on the 'civilitas'. See idem, p. 73.

Furthermore, it is likely that, at a certain point in the mid Quattrocento, the dialogue genre became itself the center of a dialogic process between literates from all Europe, being almost always in relation one to another, just like Pontano's dialogues are a response to Valla's dialogues.[37] The genre of dialogue became a specific cluster in which problems of aesthetics and social relations were discussed, involved in a negotiation on new behavioral norms and standards of artistic judgment. In short, this genre became, for a bit less than two hundred years, the place for a dialogue on dialogue.

As such, it consented to invent collectively the paradigm of European sodalities that would embody in the informal then institutional humanist academies, then in *salons*, in learned societies, in artists' societies, inner circles or cenacles of all kinds. From the very beginning, this use of conversation – instead of abstract individual reasoning – was the best way to establish new norms – may they be political, like in the *Orti oricellari*, or esthetical, like in Madame de Scudéry's salon.

---

[37] On what we may call the dialogic character of the dialogue genre in the Renaissance see Burke, Peter: The Renaissance dialogue. In: Renaissance Studies 3/1 (1989), pp. 1–12, especially pp. 11–12: "There is in fact a veritable chain of dialogues from the mid 1520s to the mid 1530s which are concerned with overlapping themes, especially language, and often make references one to another." I think we can discover many more connections of that type (or of the type we have just stressed in this article) between dialogues of different authors in the Renaissance.

Pope Leo IX: Three Letters containing Dialogues and Decisions in 1049 and 1050

Andrew Smith

The letters of Pope Leo IX (1049–1054) are a little used and under-recognised resource for coming to a new historiographical understanding of Leo's pontificate. This paper takes a small step towards rectifying this situation. It does so by putting forward a new analysis of three of Leo's papal letters and by concluding with a number of areas for debate. This approach is underpinned by an apposite quote: "only daring speculation can lead us further and not accumulation of facts."[1] This sets the overall theme for the paper and in particular provides the backdrop for the concluding remarks. The paper delivers a new analysis of three letters of Pope Leo IX. These letters contain dialogues which took place in three Synods held by Leo in 1049 and 1050. The dialogues also led to decisions and this paper will analyse, in as much detail as the parameters for this paper allow, what these letters can tell us about the nature of the dialogue itself, who was involved and how this led to decisions. The concluding part of the paper focusses on a number of issues raised by these letters. These relate to Pope Leo and his pontificate together with a number of questions concerning the wider implications for the history of the papacy in mid 11th century Europe.

The first letter[2] was written in April 1049 after Leo's first Synod in Rome. It is an account of a dispute between two bishops, John of Porto (situated

---

[1] Einstein, Albert: Letter to Michele Besso, 8th October 1952. In: Oxford Dictionary of Quotations, 8th Edition. Ed. by Elizabeth Knowles. Oxford: Oxford University Press 2014, p. 293.

[2] Jasper, Detlev (Ed.): Die Konzilien Deutschlands und Reichsitaliens (1023–1059). Monumentia Germaniae Historica (MGH): Concilia 8. Hannover: Hahnsche Buchhandlung 2010, Nr. 25, pp. 218–220. Compare: Reg. Imp. III/5/2 Nr. 550. See also in: http://acta.chadwyck.co.uk/: Patrologia Latina Full Text Database. Vol. 143, Sancti Leonis IX, Romani Pontificis Epistolae et Decreta Pontificia. Hereafter referred to as Migne PL with Letter number and Column reference. All translations by Dr. David Butterfield.

near the mouth of the River Tiber) and Crescenzo, bishop of the church of Santa Rufina (Silva Candida), both of whom claimed a particular church to be within their "bishopric"[3]. Both bishops were located geographically near to Rome and thus this was a quarrel between two close neighbours engaged in a dispute over the rights to a church. It is clear, at least in the beginning of the dialogue, that both disputants were set to conduct their argument in the Synod itself. However, events did not turn out quite as planned as one of them, Crescenzo decided for reasons which remain obscure, that he was not going to turn up to argue his case in person. The letter recorded "on the advice of the judges"[4] that "our" Archdeacon Hugh was sent to fetch him but he [Crescenzo] merely "sent some letters offering pardon"[5]. Thus, at this point the Synod agreed to make a decree without this disputant being there and the letter went on to contain a long account of the discussion which took place in arriving at the decree. The details of this discussion are, within the parameters of this paper, too long and complex to set out in detail, but there are a number of crucial points in the letter which form the basis of the analysis below.

Firstly, the Synod's decree was actually in favour of Bishop John of Porto and written in legalistic language. The letter recorded: "When this sentence had been passed by us and approved by all, it was confirmed."[6] This formulation confirms that Leo and the Synod saw themselves as operating in a legal as well as an administrative capacity.[7] Secondly, it is not clear whether or not the two disputants were invited to the Synod or whether they attended, essentially uninvited, in the hope that their case could be heard. It is acknowledged that the role of a Synod as a dispute resolution mechanism was regarded as an appropriate forum for making decisions.[8] There is, therefore, at the very least, a case for agreeing that they simply

---

[3] "Episcopatui". In: Migne PL VII, Col. 0601D.
[4] "Ex concilio judicum". In: Migne PL VII, Col. 0602A.
[5] "Scilicet epistolas quasdam veniam praeferentes misit". In: Migne PL VII, Col. 0602B.
[6] "Qua prolata sententia a nobis, et ab omnibus laudata, confirmata fuit". In: Migne PL VII, Col. 0602B.
[7] McKitterick, Rosamond: The Church. In: Timothy Reuter (Ed.): The New Cambridge Medieval History, Vol 3, c. 900–1024. Cambridge: Cambridge University Press 1999, pp. 130–162, here p. 155.
[8] Idem, p. 154.

turned up with the background knowledge that there was a probability, based on previous experience, that they would be heard.[9] The letter itself simply stated that "both parties were standing before my presence and that of the whole Synod".[10] Thirdly, it is an open question whether the two disputants were, in fact, both willing participants. In other words, was this a mutual agreement to go before a third party, i. e. the Pope in a Synod, and to agree to a form of arbitration to resolve the dispute? It seems that one of the disputants was less than a willing participant. Finally, the Synod had some distinct characteristics of a legal tribunal or court – both disputants were asked to submit written evidence to support their claims, as the letter noted, so that it could be brought forth "into the open to be seen and read"[11], thus conforming with the common practice of the time.[12] The letter talks about "all the judges"[13] – the term 'judge' could be taken to mean dignitary rather than in the sense of the judiciaries.[14] The letter declares that no one should transgress this decision "under the entreaty of law",[15] likewise it describes Archbishop Halinard of Lyon as having "passed the canonical and definitive sentence".[16]

The second letter[17] is dated six months later, in October 1049, and was sent after Leo's third Synod which was held in Mainz. The dialogue recorded in the letter is an account of another dispute, this time between Bertald and Hugo, regarding the question who was the rightful archbishop of Besancon. The dialogue starts with Bertald, who "presented himself"[18]

---

[9] Idem, pp. 153–154.
[10] "Cum vero ambae partes ante praesentiam nostrum et totius synodi staretis". In: Migne PL VII, Col. 0601D.
[11] "Placuit ut si scripturam exinde haberes, in medium videndam legendamque proferres". In: Migne PL VII, Col. 0601D.
[12] Melve, Leidulf: Assembly Politics and the Rules of the Game (CA. 650–1150). In: Viator 41, No. 2 (2010), pp. 72–73.
[13] "Omnibus judicibus". In: Migne PL VII, Col. 0602A.
[14] Idem; Blumenthal, Uta-Renata: The Papacy, 1024–1122. In: David Luscombe / Jonathan Riley-Smith (Ed.): The New Cambridge Medieval History, Vol 4, Part 1, c. 1024 – c. 1198. Cambridge: Cambridge University Press 2004, pp. 8–37, here p. 17.
[15] "Sub divini judicii obtestatione". In: Migne PL VII, Col. 0603D.
[16] "Canonicam et diffinitivam protulit sententiam". In: Migne PL VII, Col. 0602B
[17] Migne PL XXII, Col. 0622A.
[18] "Ecce quidam Bertaldus nominee coram se protulit." Migne PL XXII, Col. 0622B.

in the Synod, to which he had not been invited but had simply arrived in the hope that his case would be heard. However, the phrase "presented himself" is slightly ambiguous in terms of deciding whether Bertald (and Hugo) had been invited or not. On the one hand, to be practical, it would have been a long journey from Besancon to Mainz and Bertald and Hugo, if uninvited, must have been informed, in some manner, about the forthcoming Synod well in advance and thought it worthwhile to travel. On the other hand, they could both have been invited to attend, with no specific purpose in mind, and then taken the opportunity, once at the Synod, to ask to have their case and arguments heard. In coming to a tentative decision on this matter it is worth bearing in mind that many of Leo's letters throughout 1049–1050 specifically acknowledge when a request has been made to the papacy/papal office.

This particular letter makes no such reference, on this basis the phrase "presented himself" would rather suggest that, on the balance of probability, both Bertald and Hugo attended uninvited and took the opportunity to ask the Synods permission to present their respective arguments and evidence. The two disputants were both given the chance to present their cases and also given the opportunity to have someone speak on their behalf "secretly obtained for himself [Bertald] our brother as a *lawyer*"[19]. Therefore, it is clear that this Synod was to be seen and used as part of a legal dialogue and decision making process. The parameters of this paper prevent the putting forward of all the details of the arguments used by Bertald and Hugo, but once again one or two crucial points will be highlighted:

The legal nature of the process was emphasised when Bertald was asked "by the Synod" if he "could prove with clear testimonies what he had proposed".[20] The letter implies furthermore that he "sought counsel"[21] but "could not prove what he had proposed"[22]. At this moment, it would have been very clear to Bertald, as well as to all those in the Synod, that he was in deep trouble and that the dialogue and arguments had finally swung

---

[19] My emphasis. "Sibi clam causidicum fratrem nostrum." Migne PL XXII, Col. 0622B.

[20] "Requisitus est autem a synodo ipse Bertaldus si quid proposuisset evidentibus testimoniis probare potuisset." Migne PL XXII, Col. 0623A.

[21] "Consilium petiit." Migne PL XXII, Col. 0623A.

[22] "Quae proposuit cum probare non posset." Migne PL XXII, Col. 0623A.

against him. At this juncture, Leo acted in true collegiate fashion and "asked the holy Synod what should be decided"[23]. The dialogue was now leading by the proviso to bring about a decision "with equal consent and common advice, having set forth the opinions of the holy canons"[24]. It was abundantly clear that Leo was not content with merely having this dialogue and through such dialogue reaching a decision, but he showed himself collegiate. The letter recorded that Leo had "fortified this page" with his own signature "so that everything that is read may be regarded as more certain"[25]. This is a revealing insight into how Leo thought the papacy was perceived in the wider world, i. e. the legitimacy of the decision was reinforced by it being written down. This analysis also throws an interesting light on Leo's need to ensure that his decisions and those of the Synods were actually put into effect by writing everything down – this increased the likelihood of realization. The letter goes on to say that the decision would also be "confirmed by the august hands of our fellow bishops"[26] of which forty were present at this Synod. In other words, this collegiate decision making was a method of saying, in the clearest possible manner, that we are in this together, in collective responsibility, and that no one present at the Synod can, at a later date, back down and deny their part in the dialogue.

We now come to the third letter[27] which is dated May 1050. The dialogue recorded here was about the nomination Gerard as a saint, which approached, perhaps, rather the intentions of the church than the two disputes outlined above. This man, Gerard, was a former bishop of Toul (962–994) in north east France, where Leo himself was bishop from 1026 until 1051; at the time of this letter it needs to be emphasised that he still was the bishop of Toul. The letter begins with a long description of why Gerard should be made a saint, praising his "angelic life"[28], his

---

[23] "Interrogavimus a sancta synodo quid super hoc decerni debuisset." Migne PL XXII, Col. 0623A.
[24] "Pari consensu et communi consulto, prolatis sanctorum canonum sententiis." Migne PL XXII, Col. 0623B.
[25] "Vero paginam, ut omne quod legitur certius habeatur propriae manus subscriptione et ipsi corroboravimus." Migne PL XXII, Col. 0623D.
[26] "Et augusta manu coepiscoporumque nostrorum." Migne PL XXII, Col. 0623D.
[27] Migne PL XXXVIII Col. 0645A.
[28] "Angelicam vitam". Migne PL XXXVIII, Col. 0645D.

"pious deeds"[29], his "many prodigious miracles"[30] and his "day bringing Christ to table amidst the poor"[31].

This eulogy was followed by Leo who saw it as his responsibility – "once we reached the Apostolic Summit"[32] – to confirm Gerard in the "catalogue of saints"[33]. But, and this is an important analytical point, before he did this, he also made it plain that the confirmation of Gerard would only be done on a collegiate basis and thus Leo "asked the holy Synod if it would be right for him [Gerard] to be venerated […] and named as a saint"[34]. At this point the brief dialogue becomes crucial: "The archbishops and bishops, abbots, clergy and laymen of which a great crowd was present, shouted as if with one mouth that Gerard should be numbered among the saints and venerated by man for that reason."[35] It is acknowledged that this event exhibits elements of an acclamation as opposed to a dialogue. However, it is crucial to note that Leo specifically asked the Holy Synod for its approval and without this interplay there was a possibility that Gerard might not have been canonized – an outcome, we can confidently argue, that Leo was definitely not seeking. It is also accepted that such dialogue was a common feature of medieval assemblies[36] and therefore, such an approach to decision making would have been anticipated and expected by those present.

After this, the letter noted that it was "decreed with the holy Synods approval and praise"[37] that Gerard should be "regarded as a saint"[38]. Thus

---

[29] "Piis actibus". Migne PL XXXVIII, Col. 0645D.

[30] "Multis miraculorum prodigiis". Migne PL XXXVIII, Col. 0645D.

[31] "Quotidie Christum in pauperibus ad mensam suscipiens." Mign PL XXXVIII, Col. 0645D.

[32] "Ubi ad culmen conscendimus Apostolicum." Migne PL XXXVIII, Col. 0646A.

[33] "In catalogo sanctorum". Migne PL XXXVIII, Col. 0646A.

[34] "Et sequenter sanctam synodum interrogavimus si deberet ut sanctus venerari et sanctus deinceps nominari." Migne PL XXXVIII, Col. 0646B.

[35] "Ad quod, tam archiepiscopi quam episcopi, tam abbatis quam clerici ac laici, quorum utrorumque magna intererat multitudo, quasi uno ore clamaverunt ipsum domnum Gerardum a Deo inter sanctos numeratum et ab homnibus inter sanctos numerandum et venerandum." Migne PL XXXVIII, Col. 0646C.

[36] Melve: Assembly Politics and the Rules of the Game (note 12), p. 79.

[37] "Decrevimus sic sancta annuente ac laudante synodo." Migne PL XXXVIII, Col. 0646C.

[38] "Ut ex hoc sanctus habeatur." Migne PL XXXVIII, Col. 0646C.

the dialogue, although brief, was a vital part of the canonisation and decision making process, without which Leo was unwilling to proceed. The letter was signed by, amongst others, eight archbishops, forty three bishops, thirty four abbots but, interestingly, by not one of the unnamed laymen present at the Synod. Although, this latter point should not obscure or in any way diminish the fact that the laity played an important role in the early 11th century.[39]

In this letter and dialogue it is evident that Leo was exercising his papal power and authority, in a similar fashion to the two Synods set out above, with collegiate approval. It is also important to note that few Popes previously played a role in creating saints. The first Pope to do so was John XV in 993[40], the latest previous example was Pope Benedict VIII in 1032[41]. Therefore, the canonisation of Gerard can be seen, if not as an entirely unknown act for a Pope, as quite an unusual step by Leo.[42] However, to counterbalance this, we must turn to the statement by Leo's biographer (writing around 1058–1061), which explicitly mentions that Gerard was very important to Leo when, as a young man called Bruno, the biographer wrote that "with Gods approval it was Gerard whom he [Bruno] imitated before the others"[43]. The biographer also wrote that once he had become Pope Leo's decision to canonise Gerard, it was "urged by a revelation from heaven"[44],

---

[39] Hamilton, Sarah: Church and People in the Medieval West 900–1200. Harlow: Pearson 2013, p. 358.

[40] Bartlett, Robert: Why can the Dead do such Great Things? Saints and Worshippers from the Martyrs to the Reformation. Princeton, Oxford: Princeton University Press 2013, p. 57; Blumenthal: The Papacy (note 14), p. 13; Kemp, Eric Waldram: Canonisation and Authority in the Western Church. London: Oxford University Press 1948, p. 57.

[41] Smith, Julia M. H.: Saints and their Cults. In: Thomas F. X. Noble / Julia M. H. Smith (Ed.): The Cambridge History of Christianity, Vol 3: Early Medieval Christianities c. 600 – c. 1100. Cambridge: Cambridge University Press 2008, pp. 581–605, here p. 594.

[42] Howard, Paul Anthony: Translation Narratives in Post-Conquest Hagiography and English Resistance to the Norman Conquest. In: Christopher Harper Bill (Ed.): Anglo-Norman Studies, Vol 21: Proceedings of the Battle Conference 1998. Woodbridge: Boydell Press 1999, pp. 67–93, here p. 76.

[43] Robinson, Ian: The Papal Reform of the Eleventh Century. Lives of Pope Leo IX and Pope Gregory VII. Manchester: Manchester University Press 2004, p. 103.

[44] Idem, p. 141.

i. e. there were no base motives being suggested here. However, in spite of these seemingly pious and altruistic grounds we cannot escape the fact that Leo was still the bishop of Toul, when this canonisation took place and it can, therefore, also be seen as a specific means by which Leo reinforced his own power and prestige in his bishopric. In other words, this canonisation was an exercise of realpolitik as well as one of papal and ecclesiastical power.

This paper has outlined three letters, three dialogues and three decisions and – as set out in the introduction to this paper – we can now focus on a number of issues, which arise from these letters. Why do these three letters and their accounts of dialogues and decisions matter to the history of 11th century Europe? A number of perhaps preliminary answers can be put forward. Firstly, the letters show that, contrary to most historiographies written in the last 150 years, Leo was not simply using his Synods to pursue his so called reform agenda. He was using them partly as a means of reinforcing his and the papacy's power and authority, partly as an exercise in realpolitik and partly as a means of resolving disputes. Secondly, the letters show that Leo adopted a collegiate approach to the decision making, using and allowing dialogue to present the cases and to influence them. This illustrates that Leo was not a Pope simply focused on implementing his own so called reform policy to the exclusion of almost everything else but more of a leader keen to tie in his own ecclesiastical elite to the decisions being made. Leo was also conducting his Synods in a relatively open manner and therefore, these were not decisions taken behind closed doors, even laymen were involved and present thereby conferring a broader and not simply an ecclesiastical legitimacy to the decisions.[45] Thirdly, they show that in the case of the two disputes Leo's papal office was primarily a reactive one, in other words, the disputants were approaching him and his office (whether invited or not is a more open question), and he was not taking the initiative in policy or dispute resolution terms. Leo was not behaving as a reforming or initiating Pope taking Europe by 'the scruff of its neck' but as a new and untested papal leader working within the framework and the grain of power and authority.

---

[45] Koziol, Geoffrey: Begging Pardon and Favour. Ritual and Political Order in Early Medieval France. Ithaca: Cornell University Press 1992, p. 57.

In conclusion, as it was set out at the beginning of this paper, there are a number of issues raised by this paper, which open up topics for a degree of debate. In the first instance, why did the disputants regard or look upon Leo as the arbiter and 'the man to go to' when you needed an argument to be resolved? Was this seen as a legitimate or even a new role for the papacy and an initial part of a general rise in papal power from 1049 onwards?[46] Secondly, why were these particular dialogues and decisions recorded in such detail? Were they the only ones which are extant or the only ones per se, or, for some unknown reason, the only ones thought worth recording? Thirdly, can the Synods still continue to be seen primarily as instruments of Leo's so called reform agenda or had they more to do with the exercise of traditional ecclesiastical and papal power? And finally, can these dialogues and decisions be seen as the papacy beginning to act in a more forceful and direct manner in terms of making decisions and taking upon itself? Is this perhaps a previously under-recognised pre-cursor for the so called Gregorian Reform Movement?

---

[46] Jones, Anna Trumbore: The Power of an Absent Pope. Privileges, Forgery and Papal Authority in Aquitaine, 877–1050. In: Uta-Renate Blumenthal / Anders Winroth / Peter Landau (Ed.): Canon Law, Religion, and Politics: Liber Amicorum Robert Somerville. Washington, D. C.: Catholic University of America Press 2012, pp. 118–135, here p. 122.

Die päpstlichen Subdiakone als Mittel der Kommunikation zwischen Rom und der Lombardei (1198–1216)

Caterina Cappuccio

Rom und die Provinzen bedienten sich seit der Zeit der Reformpäpste nicht mehr nur des Briefwechsels oder anderer traditioneller Mittel der Kommunikation (Konzilien, Synoden, Predigten),[1] sondern setzten verstärkt auch Personen ein, welche die Beziehungen zwischen dem Papst und den Regionen festigen sollten. Die Päpste benutzten zunehmend unterschiedliche Methoden, um ihre Präsenz innerhalb der Ortskirchen zu stärken. Den Dialog in einer größeren Institution zu thematisieren bedeutet auch, Formen non-verbaler Kommunikation einzubeziehen. Die Form des Dialoges, die hier untersucht wird, beinhaltet ein Phänomen, das in unterschiedlichen Entwicklungen und Ausformungen in der gesamten *Christianitas* zu beobachten ist. Hierbei handelt es sich um die Präsenz von Mitgliedern der päpstlichen Kapelle in den lokalen Domkapiteln. Im Folgenden konzentriere ich mich auf den besonderen Fall der Kirchenprovinz Mailand, die in dieser Zeit die Lombardei, Piemont und Ligurien umfasste,[2] auf eine bestimmte Zeit, das Pontifikat Innozenz' III.

---

[1] Vgl. dazu die Beobachtungen von Johrendt, Jochen / Harald Müller: Zentrum und Peripherie. Prozesse des Austausches, der Durchdringung und der Zentralisierung der lateinischen Kirche im Hochmittelalter. In: Dies. (Hg.): Römisches Zentrum und kirchliche Peripherie: Das universale Papsttum als Bezugspunkt der Kirchen von den Reformpäpsten bis zu Innozenz III. Berlin: de Gruyter 2008, S. 1–16; Johrendt, Jochen / Harald Müller: Rom und die Regionen. Zum vorläufigen Abschluss eines Forschungsprojektes. In: Dies. (Hg.): Rom und die Regionen: Studien zur Homogenisierung der lateinischen Kirche im Hochmittelalter. Berlin, Boston: de Gruyter 2012, S. 1–9.

[2] Zur Entstehung und Entwicklung der Kirchenprovinz Mailand vgl. Violante, Cinzio: Le istituzioni ecclesiastiche nell'Italia centrosettentrionale durante il Medioevo: province, diocesi, sedi vescovili. In: Gabriella Rossetti (Hg.): Forme di potere e struttura sociale in Italia nel Medioevo. Bologna: Il Mulino 1977, S. 83–111.

(1198–1216),³ und auf eine besondere Institution, die päpstliche Kapelle. Die Forschung hat bereits mehrere Formen von Kommunikation identifiziert: die päpstlichen Gesandten (die Legaten *in primis*), die päpstliche Delegationsgerichtsbarkeit und nicht zuletzt die Mitglieder der päpstlichen Kapelle. Letztere waren in den lokalen Domkapiteln als Kanoniker tätig, trotz – oder gerade auf Grund – ihrer engen Beziehung zur Person des Papstes.⁴

Das Papsttum war auf die Anbindung der lokalen Kapitel angewiesen. Da die Mitglieder der päpstlichen Kapelle zugleich Kanoniker waren, vermochten sie die Kirche von Innen heraus zu gestalten und neue Beziehungen mit den Regionen zu knüpfen. Die Besonderheit der päpstlichen Kapelle als herausragendes Mittel der Kommunikation ist damit zu begründen: Zum einen stellte die päpstliche Kapelle befähigte Gesandte, um die Entscheidungen des Papstes den lokalen Kirchen zu übermitteln. Zum anderen gehörte es zu den alltäglichen Handlungen der päpstlichen Subdiakone, in den lokalen Domkapiteln als Sprachrohr des Papstes zu fungieren. Diese Tatsache erlaubt es, von einer realen Form des Dialoges zu sprechen, da die päpstlichen Kapläne und Subdiakone ein Beispiel der Integration zwischen Kurie und Kirche bildeten. Dies wird aus den lokalen Handlungen der Mitglieder der päpstlichen Kapelle und aus der generellen Zustimmung der Kapitel zu den Subdiakonen ersichtlich.⁵

Wie fand dieser Dialog praktisch statt? Es handelt sich hier um eine Form von nonverbaler Kommunikation, die in den einzelnen Fällen und Handlungen zwischen der römischen Kurie und dem Domkapitel stattfand. Es ist also weder möglich, diese Kommunikation auf einen Briefwechsel zurückzuführen noch zu reduzieren, vielmehr ereignete sich der Dialog zwischen den einzelnen Personen.⁶

Die folgenden Ausführungen gliedern sich in zwei Teile. Ein erster Teil ist der Institution der päpstlichen Kapelle und den damit verbundenen Fragestellungen gewidmet: Was war die päpstliche Kapelle? Wer gehörte dazu? Welche Funktion hatten ihre Mitglieder in der Kommunikation zwi-

---

³ Vgl. Maleczek, Werner: Innocenzo III. In: Enciclopedia dei papi. Bd. II. Roma: Treccani 2000, S. 326–350.
⁴ Johrendt/Müller: Zentrum und Peripherie (Anm. 1), S. 14.
⁵ Johrendt/Müller: Rom und die Regionen (Anm. 1), S. 2–4.
⁶ Johrendt/Müller: Zentrum und Peripherie (Anm. 1), S. 3.

schen Rom und den Provinzen? Der zweite Teil nimmt die Laufbahnen der beiden päpstlichen Subdiakone Aliprand Visconti und Wilhelm Balbo (zwischen 1197 und 1213) in den Blick. Sie waren während des Pontifikats Innozenz' III. im Domkapitel von Mailand tätig und dienen uns als Fallbeispiele für die Kommunikation zwischen Rom und der Lombardei.

Betrachtet man die päpstliche Kapelle, so wird offenkundig, dass es sich dabei um eine wirkungsvolle Institution der römischen Kirche handelte.[7] Ihre Funktion war es, den Dialog zwischen Rom und den Kirchenprovinzen der *Christianitas* aufzubauen; ihre Mitglieder waren nicht nur in Rom tätig, sondern auch mit Pfründen in verschiedenen Domkapiteln der einzelnen Kirchenprovinzen ausgestattet.[8] Höchstwahrscheinlich wurde die päpstliche Kapelle nach dem Muster der Hofkapelle errichtet, die zumindest im 10. und 11. Jahrhundert die gleiche Bündnis-Funktion zwischen Hof und Ortskirchen versah.[9]

---

[7] Die maßgeblichen Studien zur päpstlichen Kapelle sind: Elze, Reinhard: Die päpstliche Kapelle im 12. und 13. Jahrhundert. In: Ders.: Päpste – Kaiser – Könige und die mittelalterliche Herrschaftssymbolik. Ausgewählte Aufsätze. 2 Bde. Hg. von Bernhard Schimmelpfenning / Ludwig Schmugge. London: Ashgate Publishing 1982, hier Bd. 2, S. 145–202; Johrendt, Jochen: Die päpstliche Kapelle als Bindeglied zwischen Kurie und Kirche. In: Maria Pia Alberzoni / Claudia Zey (Hg.): Legati e delegati papali. Profili, ambiti d'azione e tipologie di intervento nei secoli XII-XIII. Milano: Vita e Pensiero 2012, S. 261–282; Johrendt, Jochen: Der vierte Kreuzzug, das lateinische Kaiserreich und die päpstliche Kapelle unter Innozenz III. In: Maria Pia Alberzoni / Pascal Mountabin (Hg.): Legati, delegati e l'impresa d'Oltremare. Turnhout: Brepols 2014, S. 53–114. Zu den italienischen Regionen vgl. Alberzoni, Maria Pia: Gli interventi della Chiesa di Roma nella provincia ecclesiastica milanese. In: Klaus Herbers / Jochen Johrendt (Hg.): Das Papsttum und das vielgestaltige Italien. Hundert Jahre Italia Pontificia. Berlin, New York: de Gruyter 2009, S. 135–182.

[8] Elze: Die päpstliche Kapelle (Anm. 7), S. 145. Die Brückenfunktion der Kapelle wird auch betont bei Johrendt: Die päpstliche Kapelle (Anm. 7), S. 261–164.

[9] Vgl. die Studien zur Hofkapelle von Fleckenstein, Josef: Die Hofkapelle der deutschen Könige. 2 Bde. Stuttgart: Hiersemann 1959–66. Zur Stauferzeit vgl. Schaller, Hans Martin: Stauferzeit. Ausgewählte Aufsätze. Hannover: Hansche Buchhandlung 1993, S. 479–523; Haider, Sigfried: Zu den Anfängen der päpstlichen Kapelle. In: Mitteilungen des Instituts für Österreichische Geschichtsforschung 83 (1979), S. 38–70.

Reinhard Elze verortet die Entstehung der päpstlichen Kapelle in die Mitte des 11. Jahrhunderts, in die Zeit der Reformpäpste. Es ist kein Zufall, dass die Einrichtung der Kapelle eben im Zeitraum der so genannten *papstgeschichtlichen Wende* stattfand.[10] Es war der Beginn einer Umgestaltung der Universalkirche von einer kollegial organisierten Bischofskirche hin zu einer hierarchisch gegliederten Papstkirche. Für die Umsetzung dieses von Rom aus betriebenen Prozesses waren die Päpste auf verschiedene Instrumente angewiesen. Als eines dieser Instrumente kann die päpstliche Kapelle betrachtet werden. Ihre größte Ausformung erhielt die Kapelle aber höchstwahrscheinlich erst während des XII. und XIII. Jahrhunderts, da für diese Zeit eine bemerkenswerte Menge an Subdiakonen und Kaplänen in der urkundlichen Überlieferung nachweisbar ist.[11]

Was war die päpstliche Kapelle und wer wurde päpstlicher Kaplan? Aus den oben genannten Studien von Elze und Johrendt gewinnt man einen genaueren – aber noch nicht vollständigen – Überblick über die Institution ‚päpstliche Kapelle': Sie war eine kirchliche Institution, an der Kapläne und Subdiakone teilhatten, und sie war von einer starken Beziehung zur Person des Papstes geprägt. Sowohl Kapläne als auch Subdiakone waren mit dem Papst verbunden, da sie mit liturgischen Aufgaben an seinem täglichen Gottesdienst teilnahmen. Die Subdiakone waren mit dem Inhaber der *Cathedra Petri* eng verbunden, weil sie vom Papst selbst das Subdiakonat empfangen hatten. Deshalb konnten sie nur von ihm oder von einer von ihm beauftragten Person die nächste Weihestufe (also die Diakon- und die Priesterweihe) verliehen bekommen.[12]

Diese Kleriker kamen ursprünglich aus allen Orten der *christianitas* und wurden unter verschiedenen Umständen Mitglieder der Kapelle, wobei die aus Italien stammenden Mitglieder zahlenmäßig dominierten. Tatsächlich besaß der Papst das Recht, wie schon von Gregor VII. in seinem *Dicta-*

---

[10] Schieffer, Rudolph: *Motu proprio*: Über die papstgeschichtliche Wende im 11. Jahrhundert. In: Historisches Jahrbuch 122 (2002), S. 27–41.

[11] Elze: Die päpstliche Kapelle (Anm. 7), S. 151. Jüngst hat Johrendt eine präzise Darstellung des Umfangs der päpstlichen Kapelle unter Innozenz III. geboten, vgl. Johrendt: Der vierte Kreuzzug (Anm. 7), S. 56f.

[12] Der Forschung zufolge, ist die Weihe durch den Papst ein besonderes Merkmal der Mitglieder der Kapelle. Vgl. dazu Elze: Die päpstliche Kapelle (Anm. 7), S. 153–154; Alberzoni: Gli interventi (Anm. 7), S. 160–161; Johrendt: Die päpstliche Kapelle (Anm. 7), S. 268.

tus Papae formuliert worden war, Kleriker aus allen Diözesen zu weihen.¹³ Daher ist es nicht erstaunlich, päpstliche Kapläne und Subdiakone außerhalb Roms zu finden, da sie fast immer ein Kanonikat in einer anderen Diözese besaßen.

Wenn wir uns auf die Subdiakone in der Kirchenprovinz Mailand während des Pontifikats von Innozenz III. konzentrieren, wird aus den Quellen ersichtlich, dass es sich um mindestens sechzehn Personen handelte, die dort tätig waren.¹⁴ War die Präsenz der päpstlichen Subdiakone von Vorteil für die lokalen Domkapitel? Welche Rolle spielten die Subdiakone im Dialog zwischen Rom und den Kirchenprovinzen?

Es wäre einseitig, den Blick nur auf die päpstliche Sicht zu beschränken. Den gesamten Prozess der Kommunikation auch aus einer lokalen Perspektive zu beobachten, entspricht neuen Tendenzen der Forschung, die einen neuen Blick nicht nur auf die Kommunikation Roms mit den Kirchenprovinzen ermöglicht, sondern auch auf die Position der lokalen Kleriker gegenüber dem Papst.¹⁵ Man sollte ihre gesamte Laufbahn und ihre Aufgaben in den lokalen Kapiteln untersuchen, um herauszufinden, ob die Subdiakone tatsächlich das von Johrendt als solches charakterisierte Verbindungsglied zwischen Kurie und Kirche waren.¹⁶

Um zu klären, ob diese Hypothese bezüglich der Funktion der Subdiakone plausibel ist, muss man einzelne Fälle untersuchen, was am Beispiel der Biographien von Aliprand Visconti und Guglielmo Balbo erfolgen soll.

---

[13] „Quod de omni ecclesia quocumque voluerit clericum valeat ordinare. Quod ab illo ordinatus alii ecclesiae praeesse potest, sed non militare; et quod ab aliquo episcopo superiorem non debet gradum accipere". Caspar, Erich (Hg.): Gregorii VII Registrum. Monumenta Germaniae Historica, epistolae selectae II, 1, 2. Berolini: apud Weidmannos 1920–1923, S. 200.

[14] Es handelt sich hier um Aicardo da Burolo, Alberto Amicone, Alberto Marcellino, Alcherio da Terzago, Aliprand Visconti, B. Bongiovanni, Guglielmo Balbo, Enrico da Settala, Giacomo Tornielli, Giovanni Tornielli, Oldeberto Tornielli, Nicola da Cremona, Obizo de Castello, Raynerio und Uberto da Pirovano.

[15] Vgl. die beiden in Anm. 1 erwähnten Sammelbände, welche die Beziehung zwischen dem Papsttum und den Ortskirchen perspektivieren; vgl. auch die abschließenden Bemerkungen von Herbers, Klaus: Im Dienste der Universalität oder der Zentralisierung? Das Papsttum und die Peripherien im hohen Mittelalter – Schlussbemerkungen und Perspektiven. In: Johrendt/Müller (Hg.): Römisches Zentrum und kirchliche Peripherie (Anm. 1), S. 323–344.

[16] Johrendt: Die päpstliche Kapelle (Anm. 7), S. 269.

Der päpstliche Subdiakon Aliprand gehörte einer der wichtigsten adeligen Familien Mailands an, die mit Guiscardo Visconti seit der Mitte des 12. Jahrhunderts im *ordo maior* des mailändischen Klerus erscheint. Davor war die Familie Visconti zumeist in der Politik der Kommune tätig.[17]

Schon im Oktober 1197 ist Aliprand Visconti als Subdiakon und Kanoniker des Domkapitels von Mailand bezeugt, da er eine Urkunde des Erzbischofs von Mailand, Filippo da Lampugnano, unterschrieben hat.[18] Dank eines späteren Papstbriefes, der in der *Compilatio III* überliefert wurde, ist es möglich, mehr über die Stellung des Subdiakons Aliprand im Kapitel von Mailand in Erfahrung zu bringen. In diesem von Maria Pia Alberzoni auf die Zeit zwischen 1199 und 1201 datierten Brief wendet sich Papst Innozenz III. an das Domkapitel von Mailand, weil sich ein Streit zwischen Aliprand und einem anderen Kanoniker um den Besitz einer Pfründe entwickelt hatte. Daraus wird ersichtlich, dass Aliprand, obwohl er schon seit einigen Jahren im Kapitel tätig war, noch keine Pfründe besaß und so noch kein *canonicus*, sondern nur *intitulatus* war.[19] Im Falle Pfründe

---

[17] Aliprand Visconti fand in der jüngsten Forschung mehrfach Erwähnung: Johrendt: Der vierte Kreuzzug (Anm. 7), S. 78; Pellegrini, Michele: L'„ordo maior" della Chiesa di Milano (1166–1230). Milano: Biblioteca Francescana 2009, S. 136–137; Alberzoni, Maria Pia: Città, vescovi e papato nella Lombardia dei Comuni. Novara: Interlinea 2001, S. 189–190; Behrmann, Thomas: Domkapitel und Schriftlichkeit in Novara (11.–13. Jahrhundert). Sozial- und Wirtschaftsgeschichte von S. Maria und S. Gaudenzio im Spiegel der urkundlichen Überlieferung. Tübingen: Niemeyer 1994, S. 267; zur Familie Visconti vgl. Occhipinti, Elisa: I Visconti di Milano nel XIII secolo. In: Archivio Storico Lombardo 136 (2010), S. 11–24; vgl. auch Grillo, Paolo: Milano in età comunale (1183–1276). Istituzioni, società, economia. Spoleto: CISAM 2001, S. 291–296.

[18] Baroni, Maria Franca: Le pergamene del secolo XII della Chiesa maggiore di Milano (Capitolo Maggiore – Capitolo minore – Decumani) conservate presso l'Archivio di Stato di Milano. Milano: Università degli Studi 2003, n. 38, S. 163–164.

[19] Alberzoni: Città, vescovi e papato (Anm. 17), S. 189. Die *Compilatio III* ist eine Sammlung von Dekretalen, die das *Decretum Gratiani* ergänzen sollten. Die *Compilatio III* wurde von Petro Collevacino im Auftrage Innozenz' III. erstellt und enthält Dekretalen der ersten Jahre (1198–1210) seines Pontifikats. Sie wurde ediert: Friedberg, Emil (Hg.): Quinque compilationes antiquae nec non Collectio canonum Lipsiensis. Graz: Akademische Druck- u. Verlagsanstalt 1956. Vgl. dazu auch Ferme, Brian Edwin: Quinque compilationes antiquae: a turning point in the history of canon law. In: James J. Conn / Luigi Sabbarese (Hg.): Ius-

für einige Jahre vakant waren, hatte der Papst das Recht, den letztlichen Nutznießer dieser Pfründe zu bestimmen.[20] So löste Papst Innozenz – der 1198 Papst geworden war – den Streit zwischen den beiden Kanonikern folgendermaßen: „Unde ipse, qui fuerat similiter intitulatus, ad obtinendam ipsam prebendam erat aliis merito preferendus, qui a nobis meruerat in subdiaconum ordinari" (Der, der den gleichen Titel hat, sollte bevorzugt die Pfründe bekommen, da er von uns die Subdiakonsweihe verliehen bekommen hat).[21] Aus diesem kurzen Satz lassen sich zwei wichtige Informationen entnehmen: Zunächst hatte Innozenz III. Aliprand als päpstlichen Subdiakon privilegiert; sodass er seinen Subdiakon gerade wegen der Verbindung mit ihm selbst unterstützten konnte. Diese Unterstützung der Mitglieder der päpstlichen Kapelle durch den Papst, besonders bei der Verleihung von Pfründen oder wichtigen Ämtern in den lokalen Kapiteln, erscheint in den Biographien der Subdiakone häufig. In einem ganz ähnlichen Vorgang wurde Aliprand auch 1203 privilegiert: Innozenz schrieb dem Domkapitel von Novara und übertrug ihm die Aufgabe, die nächste frei werdende Pfründe seinem Subdiakon Aliprand zu verleihen.[22] Auch in diesem Fall stellte gleichsam der Papst, wie es schon bei der Pfründe in

---

titia in caritate (Rom): miscellanea di studi in onore di Velasio de Paolis. Città del Vaticano: Urbaniana University Press 2005, S. 41–55.

[20] Über das Kollationsrecht des Papstes vgl. Willich, Thomas: Wege zur Pfründe. Die Besetzung der Magdeburger Domkanonikate zwischen ordentlicher Kollatur und päpstlicher Provision 1295–1464. Tübingen: Niemeyer 2005, S. 181–206.

[21] Dieser Brief befindet sich in der sogenannten *Compilatio tertia* 3.5.10 (in: Friedberg (Hg.): Quinque compilationes antiquae (Anm. 19), S. 120) und wurde von Maria Pia Alberzoni zuerst erwähnt, vgl. Alberzoni: Città, vescovi e papato (Anm. 17), S. 189, Anm. 77.

[22] „[…] Dilecto filio Aliprando Vicecomiti, subdiacono nostro, Mediolanensi ordinario, quem virum esse novimus providum et discretum et tam scientia quam moribus adornatum". Die Registerbände Innozenz III. werden – sofern sie bereits in der kritischen Edition vorliegen – nach diesen unter der Siegle Reg. Inn. III. und daran anschließend das Pontifikatsjahr und die Briefnummer der Edition zitiert. Hageneder, Othmar u. a: Die Register Innocenz' III., Bd. 1–11 (Publikationen der Abteilung für historische Studien des Österreichischen Kulturinstituts in Rom. 2. Abt., Quellen. 1. Reihe). Graz, Köln, Wien: Böhlau 1964 [im Folg. Reg. Inn. III.], V., n. 143, S. 283f. Der Hinweis auf die *scientia* des päpstlichen Subdiakons erscheint hier als besonders wichtig, denn eines der Merkmale der Subdiakone konnte der Bezug zur Universität und höheren Schule sein.

Mailand geschehen war, seinen Subdiakon dem Kapitel vor: ein weiser Mensch, begabt mit *bona scientia* und *boni mores*. Außerdem wurde der Subdiakon so eingeführt, als wäre er dem Papst bekannt. Auch diese Andeutung, die fast als eine Feinheit interpretiert werden könnte, gibt einige wichtige Informationen: Der Papst kannte seine Subdiakone und war über ihre Ausbildung unterrichtet. Ende September des gleichen Jahres erscheint Aliprand namentlich unter den Kanonikern von Novara; die Anfrage des Papstes war auch in diesem Fall erfolgreich.[23]

Neben seinen alltäglichen Geschäften als Kanoniker in Novara und Mailand amtierte Aliprand in mehreren Angelegenheiten als delegierter Richter im päpstlichen Auftrag.[24] Das erste Mal war er für die Diözese Mailand, im Rahmen eines Verfahrens innerhalb des mailändischen Klerus, als Schiedsrichter tätig. Hier wurde Aliprand als *sindicus* von den *Ordinarii* (also dem *Klerus maior*, der die adligen Familien repräsentierte) ernannt, damit er diesen Klerus vor den päpstlich delegierten Richtern verteidigen konnte. Höchstwahrscheinlich wurde Aliprand von den anderen *Ordinarii Mediolanenses* dazu erwählt, weil er als Subdiakon schon Beziehungen zur römischen Kurie hatte.[25] Dieser Umstand kann als sehr bedeutend inter-

---

[23] Aliprand war tatsächlich in Novara tätig. Für die Jahre bis 1206 hat Behrmann drei Erwähnungen des päpstlichen Subdiakons in der Urkundenüberlieferung des Kapitels gefunden (Behrmann: Domkapitel (Anm. 17), S. 267). Ab 1206 erscheint Aliprand nicht mehr im Domkapitel von Novara, was bedeuten könnte, dass er kontinuierlich in Mailand residierte. Seine Besitztümer in Novara sind in einem Handlungsakt des Kapitels überliefert: „Ariprandus vicecomes habet in manso quem tenet Iacobinus de palioto starios. XII. sicalis. Et in terra quam tenet triphonia. Starios. II frumenti. Et comune debet ei starium I. milii et starium I. panici." Scarzello, Oreste / Giovanni Battista Morandi / Andrea Leone (Hg.): Le carte dell'archivio capitolare di S. Maria di Novara (1172–1205), 3 Bde. Torino: Stabilimento tipografico Cattaneo 1924, hier Bd. 3, S. 332–336.

[24] Über die päpstliche Delegationsgerichtsbarkeit vgl. Müller, Harald: Päpstliche Delegationsgerichtsbarkeit in der Normandie (12. und frühes 13. Jahrhundert). Bonn: Bouvier 1997.

[25] Zur Auseinandersetzung innerhalb des mailändischen Klerus vgl. Pogliani, Marco: Il dissidio fra nobili e popolari a Milano. La controversia del 1203 tra l'arcidiacono e il primicerio maggiore. In: Ricerche storiche sulla Chiesa ambrosiana 10 (1981), S. 5–89. Zum Eingriff von Aliprand Visconti in den Streit als *sindicus* der ordinarii vgl. ebd., S. 84–85: „dominus Ariprandus Vicecomes ordinarius Ecclesie Mediolanensi, in eadem causa a suis fratribus sindicus constitutus".

pretiert werden: Das Kapitel war sich durchaus bewusst, dass ein Mitglied der päpstlichen Kapelle in einem Verfahren der *prima sedes* von Vorteil sein konnte. Dieses Bewusstsein der Ortskirchen findet sich auch bei anderen Gelegenheiten wieder, wenn Mitglieder der päpstlichen Kapelle als *procuratores* des Kapitels in Rom beim Papst vorsprachen.[26] Der Papst selbst betonte bei verschiedenen Gelegenheiten, dass es für die Regionen von Vorteil sein könnte, wenn sie einen päpstlichen Subdiakon aufnähmen. Es ist kein Zufall, wenn sich in einem päpstlichen, an ein Domkapitel gerichteten Brief, Sätze wie „qui multum potuerit esse fructuosus" oder auch „qui pro te apud sedem apostolicam laboraverit" finden lassen.[27]

Erst nach zwei Jahren wurde Aliprand als päpstlicher delegierter Richter tätig: 1205 wurde er von Innozenz III. bei der Wiedervereinigung der Diözesen Acqui und Alessandria als Richter eingesetzt. Dieser Vereinigungsprozess ist von großer Bedeutung, da er bereits unter Papst Alexander III. eingeleitet worden war, mit der Einsetzung des päpstlichen Subdiakons Arduin als Bischof der neu gegründeten Diözese von Alessandria (1175).[28] In den folgenden Jahren betrieb der Bischof von Alessandria die Vereinigung mit der Diözese Acqui. Im ersten Teil des langwierigen Verfahrens wurde der Erzpriester von Monza, Oberto da Terzago, seinerseits ein päpstlicher Subdiakon, involviert. Die definitive Lösung brauchte aber noch einige Jahre bis zum Pontifikat Innozenz III. Die Regelung dieser Angelegenheit wurde größtenteils von päpstlichen Subdiakonen beaufsich-

---

[26] Ein Fallbeispiel bietet die Biographie von Guglielmo Balbo. Ähnliche Umstände finden sich in den Biographien anderer Subdiakone, die hier nicht behandelt werden können. Zur Anwesenheit mailändischer Kleriker bei der römischen Kurie vgl. auch Ambrosioni, Annamaria: Ecclesiastici milanesi presso la curia romana fino all'età del cardinale Pietro Peregrosso. In: Dies.: Milano, papato e impero in età medievale. Raccolta di studi. Hg. von Maria Pia Alberzoni / Alfredo Lucioni. Milano: Vita e Pensiero 2003, S. 499–510.

[27] Reg. Inn. III., I, n. 120, S. 183f. Diese Wendungen finden sich in einem Brief, in dem Papst Innozenz III. das Domkapitel von Mailand darum bittet, seinem Subdiakon Enrico da Settala das Amt des Kanzlers zu verleihen. Ähnliche Ausdrücke wurden von Innozenz in Bezug auf den Subdiakon Bongiovanni benutzt, vgl. Reg Inn. III., I., n. 339, S. 508f.

[28] Kehr, Paul Friedolin: Regesta pontificum Romanorum. Italia Pontificia, 6 Bde. Berolini: Apud Weidmannos 1911–1923, hier Bd. 6/2, S. 202. Die Rekonstruktion des ganzen Verfahrens findet sich bei Alberzoni: Città, vescovi e papato (Anm. 17), S. 173–211.

tigt und durchgeführt; außer Visconti wurden hier auch Johannes Tornielli, Bongiovanni und Wilhelm Balbo – jeder in einer anderen Angelegenheit – einbezogen. Wie bereits erwähnt, war Aliprand 1205 hier als Richter tätig. Gemeinsam mit Wilhelm Balbo wurde Aliprand vom Papst in die Stadt Alessandria geschickt, um als Subdiakon der Stadt Alessandria den Treueid abzunehmen.[29] Wiederum mit Wilhelm Balbo war Aliprand 1208 erneut als päpstlich delegierter Richter tätig, um sich um die Ansprüche, u. a. um eine Pieve der Diözese, des Bischofs von Acqui und Alessandria, Ugo Tornielli, zu kümmern.[30]

Im gleichen Jahr erlangte Aliprand das Bischofamt von Vercelli.[31] Während seines Episkopats war er auch als päpstlicher Legat in der Lombardei tätig. 1213, als das Erzbistum Mailand vakant war, galt Aliprand als einer der Kandidaten für den Bischofsstuhl. Offensichtlich wollte der Papst ihn wählen lassen, als der Subdiakon plötzlich im September verstarb. So ernannte Innozenz III. schließlich Enrico da Settala, der ebenfalls ein päpstlicher Subdiakon war.[32]

---

[29] Reg. Inn. III., IX, n. 93, S. 174–176: „Placuit beatitudine vestre, pater sanctissime, nobis servulis vestris dare in mandatis, ut ad civitatem Alexandrie personaliter accedentes clerum et populum ad pacem et concordiam cum Acquensibus faciendam necnon ad unionem acceptandam prudenter admonere et diligenter inducere studeremus." Die Stadt Alessandria war der „sedes apostolica" seit ihrer Gründung im Jahre 1175 zu Gehorsam verpflichtet; die Stadt sollte ihren Treueid (zusammen mit einem Almosen) auch den Nachfolgern Alexander III. leisten. Vgl. Fiaschini, Giulio: La fondazione della diocesi di Alessandria ed i contrasti con i vescovi acquesi. In: Popolo e Stato in Italia nell'età di Federico Barbarossa. Alessandria e la Lega Lombarda. Relazioni e comunicazioni al XXXIII Congresso storico subalpino per la celebrazione dell'VIII centenario della fondazione di Alessandria. Torino: Deputazione subalpina di storia patria 1970, S. 496–519.

[30] Über die von Bischof Ugo Tornielli geführte Auseinandersetzung zwischen Acqui und Alessandria um den Besitz der Pieve in Fubine vgl. Alberzoni: Città, vescovi e papato (Anm. 17), S. 186–190; Gasparolo, Francesco: Cartario alessandrino fino al 1300, Bd. II. Torino: Casale Monferrato, stabilimento tipografico Miglietta 1930, S. 154.

[31] Die wichtigen Ereignisse seines Episkopats sind verzeichnet bei Savio, Fedele: Gli antichi vescovi d'Italia. Piemonte. Bologna: Forni Editore 1971 [Nachdruck der Ausg. Torino 1899], S. 488.

[32] Zur Wahl von Enrico da Settala zum Erzbischof von Mailand vgl. Alberzoni, Maria Pia: Nel conflitto tra papato e impero: da Galdino della Sala a Guglielmo

Die zweite Laufbahn, mit der ich mich beschäftigen möchte, ist die von Wilhelm Balbo, der in einigen Angelegenheiten gemeinsam mit Aliprand agierte.[33] 1203, im Rahmen eines Prozesses innerhalb der mailändischen Kurie, behauptete Balbo, dass er schon 1197 als Subdiakon am Domkapitel tätig gewesen sei.[34] Dies ist das erste Zeugnis seiner Tätigkeit in Mailand als Kanoniker: Balbo war, häufiger noch als Aliprand Visconti, als delegierter Richter im päpstlichen oder bischöflichen Auftrag tätig; er erscheint in einigen Quellen mit dem Magistertitel und war in mehrere juristische Angelegenheiten involviert. Er tat sich mit seinen juristischen Kompetenzen hervor und wurde in der offiziellen Biographie Innozenz' III. erwähnt, weil er ein schwieriges Verfahren zu einer Lösung brachte. Daher könnte man vermuten, dass er eine juristische Ausbildung absolviert hatte.[35]

1198 erteilte Innozenz III. ihm und dem päpstlichen Subdiakon Oldeberto Tornielli, Propst von S. Gaudenzio in Novara, ein Exekutionsmandat zugunsten des päpstlichen Subdiakons Bongiovanni, der Propst

---

da Rizolio (1166–1241). In: Adriano Caprioli / Antonio Rimoldi / Luciano Vaccaro (Hg.): Storia religiosa della Lombardia, Bd. 9: Diocesi di Milano. Milano: Editrice la Scuola 1990, S. 227–257.

[33] Zu Guglielmo Balbo gibt es bisher keine belastbare Biographie; immerhin berichten einige Historiker über ihn und seine Tätigkeit innerhalb des Kapitels von Mailand und der päpstlichen Kapelle: Johrendt: Der vierte Kreuzzug (Anm. 7), S. 113; Pellegrini: L'"ordo maior" (Anm. 17), S. 193 (auch wenn dort die Zugehörigkeit von Wilhelm Balbo zur päpstlichen Kapelle nicht erwähnt wird); Alberzoni: Città, vescovi e papato (Anm. 17), S. 187f.

[34] „[I]nterrogatus quotiens vidit vesperas pulsari cum licentia archiepiscopi, respondit multotiens. Interrogatus quotiens vidit illam licentiam dari, respondit multotiens. Interrogatus cui, respondit sibi fuit data quando erat subdiaconus, quia subdiaconus cum custode petit eam, et Lanterio de Lampugnano, et preposito de Setala et multiis aliis." Pogliani: Il dissidio (Anm. 25), Appendice I, S. 68, Z. 997–999.

[35] Zum Magistertitel vgl. Herkenrath, Rainer Maria: Studien zum Magistertitel in der frühen Stauferzeit. In: Mitteilungen des Instituts für Österreichische Geschichtsforschung 88 (1980), S. 3–35; vgl. auch die interessanten Beobachtungen von: Schwarz, Brigide: Die Organisation kurialer Schreiberkollegien von ihrer Entstehung bis zur Mitte des 15. Jahrhunderts. Tübingen: Niemeyer 1972, S. 75–78 und Johrendt, Jochen: Die Diener des Apostelfürsten: das Kapitel von St. Peter im Vatikan (11.–13. Jahrhundert). Berlin, New York: de Gruyter 2011, S. 254.

des Domkapitels von Ivrea werden sollte.[36] Da aber schon jemand anderes das vakante Amt bekommen hatte, blieb Wilhelms Intervention erfolglos.

Im gleichen Jahr, September 1198, wurde Wilhelm in eine prekäre Konstellation verwickelt: Innozenz hatte den Erzbischof von Mailand, Filippo da Lampugnano, aufgefordert, das seit einem Jahr vakante Verwaltungsamt der Kirche Mailand dem päpstlichen Subdiakon Enrico da Settala zu verleihen.[37] Gegen den ausdrücklichen Willen des Papstes bevorzugte Filippo da Lampugnano seinen Verwandten Enrico da Lampugnano, dem der Erzbischof das Amt des Kanzlers heimlich verliehen hatte. Daher leitete Innozenz III. ein Verfahren ein. Im Zuge dessen sollte der Erzbischof von Mailand sich dem Papst gegenüber verteidigen, da er den ausdrücklichen päpstlichen Wunsch bewusst nicht erfüllt hatte. Als *procurator* des Erzbischofs wurde Wilhelm Balbo ausgewählt.[38] Man könnte vermuten, wie es sich schon bei Aliprand abgezeichnet hatte, dass gerade er ausgewählt wurde, weil er als päpstlicher Subdiakon bereits in Verbindung mit dem Papst stand. In diesem Fall war das Wirken Balbos erfolgreich: Enrico da Lampugnano durfte sein Amt behalten, während dem Erzbischof Filippo da Lampugnano sein Kollationsrecht entzogen wurde. Dieses war

---

[36] „Noveritis etiam nos dilectis filiis, preposito sancti Gaudentii Novariensis et magistro Wilelmo Balbo, canonico Mediolanensi, subdiaconis nostris, precipiendo mandasse, ut si vos, quod scribimus, nolueritis vel distuleritis adimplere, ipsi id auctoritate apostolica exequantur." Reg. Inn. III., I, n. 339, S. 509.

[37] „[I]nde est quod, cum sicut audivimus, cancellarie dignitas per annum et ultra iam in ecclesia Mediolanensi vacaverit – licet iurisditio conferendi eam ad nos iuxta lateranensi statuta concili [...] Dilectus filius Henricus, subdiaconus noster, pro te tam apud sedem apostolicam quam alias fideliter laboraverit et devote [...] nos tamen devotionem tuam rogamus affectuosius et monemus, per apostolica script precipiendo mandantes, quatenus eidem subdiacono, qui tam per se quam per consaguineos suos tibi et ecclesie tue plurimum esse poterit fructuosus et ad ipsius executionem officii probatur idoneus, quem nos etiam quadam speciali prerogativa diligimus, dictam cancellariam sine cuiuslibet difficultatis obstaculo tam nostrarum precum intuitu quam ipsius meritorum et probitatis obtentu non differas assignare" Reg. Inn. III. I., n. 120, S. 183f.

[38] „[T]ibi dedimus in mandatis, ut ad presentiam nostram procuratorem idoneum destinares, qui tuo nomine legitime nobis ostenderet, quod dictam cancellariam persone idonee modo canonico tempore tibi competente donasses" Reg. Inn. III. I., n. 368, S. 556.

nur das erste Anzeichen einer schwierigen Beziehung zwischen Innozenz III. und Filippo da Lampugnano, der 1206 sein Amt aufgab.[39]

Gleichfalls als Procurator von Filippo da Lampugnano verhandelte Wilhelm 1199 in einem langen Verfahren zwischen Gerardo, dem Abt des Benediktinerklosters von Scozola, in der Nähe des Lago Maggiore gelegen, und dem Erzbischof von Mailand über das Jurisdiktionsrecht in einigen Gebieten. Im Grunde hatte diese Auseinandersetzung ihre Wurzel schon im Pontifikat Coelestins III.[40] Auch für diese Zeit ist die Tätigkeit eines gewissen G. als nuntius des Erzbischofes im Prozess bezeugt. Wilhelm Balbo wurde aller Wahrscheinlichkeit nach in dem zweiten und wichtigeren Teil des Verfahrens als *procurator* von Filippo da Lampugnano hinzugezogen und beeindruckte die Beteiligten offenbar so sehr, dass sein Wirken auch in der Biographie Papst Innozenz' III., der *Gesta*, überliefert ist.[41] Durch eine diplomatische und paläographische Untersuchung konnte der Subdiakon nachweisen, dass unter den vom Abt vorgelegten Nachweisen einige Fälschungen waren. So wurden das Verfahren und die damit verbundenen Rechte über die Gebiete am Lago Maggiore von Erzbischof Filippo da Lampugnano gewonnen.[42]

---

[39] Alberzoni, Maria Pia: Filippo da Lampugnano. In: Dizionario Biografico degli Italiani, Bd. 63. Roma: Enciclopedia Treccani 2004, S. 285–287.

[40] „Cumque dilectus filius G(erardus) tunc prior nunc vero abbas eiusdem monaterii, et G., nuntius adverse partis, super hoc ad sedem apostolicam accessissent cone memorie C(elestinus) papa, predecessir noster [...] per bone memorie Al(binum) Albanensem episcopum, sic suum interpretatus fuit rescriptum, quod tam causa possessionis quam proprietatis fuerat iudici delegato commissa." Reg. Inn. III., I, n. 37, S. 52. Falls es sich hier um den päpstlichen Subdiakon Wilhelm handelt, könnte man seine Tätigkeit im Domkapitel von Mailand schon während des Pontifikats von Coelestin III. datieren.

[41] Gress-Wright, David: The Gesta Innocentii III: Text, introduction and commentary. PhD thesis. Bryn: Mawr College 1981, S. 63.

[42] Der Nachweis, dass es sich bei den von Abt Gerard vorgelegten Urkunden um Fälschungen handelt, nimmt viel Raum ein in einem Brief von Innozenz, der, wie üblich, eine wichtige Quelle des Verfahrens wurde: „Cum autem super hiis, que premisimus, in nostra et fratrum nostrorum presentia fuisset diutius litigatum, quia legittime probatum non fuerat ea, que petebantur, ad monasterium pertinere, de communi fratrum nostrorum consilio ab impetitione ipsius prefatum procuratorum tuum nomine tuo et mediolanensis ecclesie sententialiter duximus absolvendum: quoniam, cum obscura sunt iura partium, consuevit contra eum, qui petitor est, iudicari." Reg. Inn. III. II., n. 37, S. 62–65, hier S. 65.

1202 wurde Balbo erneut als delegierter Richter in einem Prozess zwischen der Äbtissin des Klosters Meda und dem Kaplan von Barlassina Gerard über das Recht der Zinsauszahlung in Barlassina tätig.[43] Wilhelm Balbo unterschrieb eine spätere Urkunde als Erzpriester des Domkapitels von Mailand, eines der wichtigsten Ämter innerhalb des Kapitels.[44] Aufgrund dieses Umstands hat Maria Franca Baroni jüngst die Datierung des Anfangs seiner Tätigkeit als *archipresbiter* ins Jahr 1202 verlegt.[45]

Im Rahmen der oben genannten Verfahren zur mailändischen Kurie wurde auch Wilhelm Balbo 1203 als Zeuge ernannt. Da er schon Erzpriester des Domkapitels war und eine wichtige Stellung innerhalb des *clerus maior* innehatte, wurde Balbo zwei Tage lang über das Wesen des mailändischen Klerus und über die Existenz von zwei ordines, die *Ordinarii* und die *decumani*, befragt.[46]

Außer in dem oben erwähnten Vereinigungsprozess der Diözesen Acqui und Alessandria agierte Wilhelm Balbo auch als delegierter Richter in dem Verfahren zwischen dem päpstlichen Subdiakon Aicard von Burolo, Kanoniker und Propst im Domkapitel von Ivrea, und der Kommune Vercelli. Dieses ganze Verfahren über einige umstrittene Besitztümer in Burolo dauerte einige Jahre und wurde 1205, auf Anregung der Stadt Vercelli, wieder eröffnet. Es war sicher kein Zufall, dass Balbo von der Stadt Vercelli – die ein Verbündeter von Mailand war – als Richter ernannt wurde. Der bekannte Richter Balbo war auch Erzpriester von Mailand und besaß als päpstlicher Subdiakon eine verlässliche Verbindung zu Papst Innozenz

---

[43] Baroni, Maria Franca: Gli atti dell'Arcivescovo e della curia arcivescovile di Milano (1196–1241). Milano: Università degli Studi 2007, S. 35f., Nr. 39: „Sententiam protulit dominus Guilielmus Balbus, sancte mediolanensis ecclesie ordinarius, assessor domini Phylippi Die Gratia sancte Mediolanensis ecclesie archiepiscopi. [...] Predictus dominus Guilielmus de mandato eiusdem domini archiepiscopi predictum Iacobum seu predictam abbatissam nomine predicti monasteri a petitione suprascripti Gilberti quam faciebat nomine ecclesie de Barnaxina contra dictam abbatissam absolvit. Et sic ita finita est causa."

[44] Ebd., S. 37, Nr. 40.

[45] Traditionell setzt die Forschung den Anfang der Tätigkeit Balbos als Erzpriester in das Jahr 1201. Vgl. Pellegrini: L'"ordo maior" (Anm. 17), S. 193.

[46] Vgl. Pogliani: Il dissidio fra nobili e popolari (Anm. 25), S. 28, Anm. 86. Balbos Zeugnis wird überliefert ebd., Appendice I, S. 63–71, Z. 775–1099.

III.[47] An dem Verfahren sollte Balbo als delegierter Richter bis 1207 arbeiten, ohne dass sich eine definitive Lösung ergab. 1208 beschäftigte sich Balbo noch mit einem weiteren Prozess, und zwar mit dem schon erwähnten Anspruch des Bischofs von Acqui und Alessandria auf die Pieve in Fubine, bei dem Balbo im Verein mit Aliprand Visconti agierte.[48]

Zum Schluss sei noch eine der letzten Aufgaben des päpstlichen Subdiakons Wilhelm Balbo erwähnt. Da 1211 Gerardo da Sesso, Erzbischof von Mailand, verstarb und die Diözese wegen der Streitigkeiten innerhalb des Kapitels zwei Jahre ohne Erzbischof blieb, sandte der mailändische Klerus Wilhelm Balbo, Stephan Balbo und den päpstlichen Subdiakon Alcherius 1213 nach Rom, um den Papst zu bitten, einen Erzbischof für die Stadt zu ernennen.[49] Wahrscheinlich war Wilhelm Balbo selbst einer der Kandidaten für den Vorsitz des Erzbistums, aber am Ende wurde der Subdiakon Heinrich von Settala vom Papst ernannt.

Da Wilhelm Balbo nicht mehr in den Quellen erscheint und im gleichen Jahr Alberto Amicone, ein weiterer päpstlicher Subdiakon, Erzpriester von Mailand wurde, könnte dies Balbos letzter Auftrag gewesen sein.

Anhand der Untersuchung der Laufbahnen der päpstlichen Subdiakone Aliprand Visconti (1197–1213) und Wilhelm Balbo (1197–1213) zeigt sich deutlich, dass der Papst seine Subdiakone bevorzugte. Er gab ihnen wich-

---

[47] Verschiedene Urkunden nehmen Bezug auf das Verfahren: Colombo, Giuseppe (Hg.): Documenti dell'archivio comunale di Vercelli relativi ad Ivrea 1141–1309. Pinerolo: Chiantore-Mascarelli 1901; Gabotto, Ferdinando (Hg.): Le carte dello archivio vescovile di Ivrea fino al 1313 I. Pinerolo: Chiantore-Mascarelli 1900. Die Darstellung des ganzen Prozesses ist zu finden bei Alberzoni: Città, vescovi e papato (Anm. 17), S. 230–250.

[48] Vgl. Alberzoni: Città, vescovi e papato (Anm. 17), S. 186–190; Gasparolo: Cartario alessandrino (Anm. 30), S. 154.

[49] „[A]lioquin ex tunc procuratores idoneos ad nostram curaretis praesentiam destinare, pastorem quem Domino inspirante vobis et eidem providerimus Ecclesiae recepturos, nuper dilectos filios *Alkerium subdiaconum nostrum, Stephanum Balbum, et Willelmum canonicos vestros* ad sedem apostolicam cum vestris litteris destinatis, cum multimoda gratiarum actione, mandatum nostrum humiliter admissuros, suppliciter postulantes ut quem mallemus de graemius ecclesie vestrae vobis dignaremur concedere in pastorem." In: Migne, Jean Paul (Hg.): Patrologiae latinae cursus completus. 221 Bde. Paris: Excudebat Migne 1879–1974, hier Bd. 216, col. 932. Der vollständige Prozess wurde schon thematisiert von Alberzoni: Nel conflitto tra papato e impero (Anm. 32), S. 227–257.

tige Aufgaben wie die Vertretung in bedeutenden juristischen Verfahren. Er versuchte zudem, sie mit neuen Pfründen zu versorgen. Zu diesem Zweck stellte der Papst dem lokalen Domkapitel seinen Subdiakon als ihm persönlich bekannt vor und beeinflusste damit die Wahl. Höchstwahrscheinlich kannte der Papst tatsächlich die Mitglieder der päpstlichen Kapelle persönlich, auch wenn sie ihre Tätigkeit entfernt von Rom ausübten. Gleichzeitig lässt sich beobachten, dass der Aufbau einer persönlichen Bindung zum Papst durch einen der Kanoniker auch ein Privileg für das lokale Domkapitel bedeutete, das auf diese Art und Weise eine direkte Verbindung mit der römischen Kurie erlangte und damit bei verschiedenen Gelegenheiten die Möglichkeit hatte, aus dieser Bindung Nutzen zu ziehen und so in der Lage war, den Dialog mit der Hauptkirche in besonderer Weise weiterzuführen.

Das kamerunische Grasland und der ‚Afroatlantische Dialog'

Ricardo Márquez García

Ein spezifischer Aspekt in der Historiographie des kameruner Graslands (geographisch-kulturelle Bezeichnung für eine Hochlandregion im Westen des Landes) wird aufgrund der schwierigen Rekonstruktionsmöglichkeiten im wissenschaftlichen Diskurs oft vernachlässigt: die Verflechtungen des Graslandes mit dem transatlantischen Sklavenhandel und die damit einhergehenden kulturellen Transformationen in den Herkunfts- und Ankunftsorten sowie entlang der Transportwege zum Atlantik. Die folgenden Überlegungen bezwecken eine Neuinterpretation dieses Kapitels in der Geschichte des Graslands, die Licht wirft auf die involvierten Akteure. Versklavte, Versklaver, Sklavenhalter und Sklavenhändler werden als Teilnehmer eines breit angelegten ‚Afroatlantischen Dialogs'[1] betrachtet, in ihrer aktiven Rolle als Nehmer, Geber, Schöpfer und Übersetzer von Kulturen.[2] Ethnographisch-historische Studien des letzten Jahrhunderts widmeten sich vor allem der Ethnographie einzelner dezentralisierter Königreiche oder ‚ethnischer' Gruppen des Gras-

---

[1] Zur Theoriebildung des Begriffs siehe Matory, James Lorand: The „New World" Surrounds an Ocean. Theorizing the Live Dialogue between African and African American Cultures. In: Kevin A. Yelvington (Hg.): Afro-Atlantic Dialogues. Anthropology in the Diaspora. Santa Fe, New Mexico: School of American Research Press 2006, S. 151–192. Zur Begriffsentwicklung vgl. Matory, James Lorand: From „Survival" to „Dialogue": Analytic Tropes in the Study of African-Diaspora Cultural History. In: Ingrid Kummels / Claudia Rauhut / Stefan Rinke / Birte Timm (Hg.): Transatlantic Caribbean. Dialogues of People, Practices, Ideas. Bielefeld: transcript 2014, S. 33–55.

[2] Kultur wird hier verstanden im Sinne von Geertz als ein Bedeutungsgewebe, in das der Mensch verstrickt ist. Siehe Geertz, Clifford: Dichte Beschreibung. Bemerkungen zu einer deutenden Theorie von Kultur. In: Stephan Kammer / Roger Lüdeke (Hg.): Texte zur Theorie des Textes. Stuttgart: Reclam 2005, S. 274–292.

landes,[3] weniger translokalen und -regionalen Aspekten. Erst in den letzten Jahrzehnten ist ein größeres akademisches Interesse an transregionalen Verflechtungen im (vor)kolonialen Zeitalter festzustellen.[4] In diesem Sinne bauen die folgenden Überlegungen auf ausgewählte aktuelle interdisziplinäre Forschungen zum Grasland und zu benachbarten Regionen auf, wobei das Konzept des ‚Afroatlantischen Dialogs' nach Matory als Interpretationswerkzeug verwendet wird, um nach der Rolle der Bewohner des Graslandes im transatlantischen Sklavenhandel zu fragen. Matorys Konzept wird im Folgenden auf Bereiche der Politik, Religion und Kunst innerhalb des Graslands angewendet.

Matorys ‚Afroatlantischer Dialog'

Lorand Matory studierte lange Zeit die Verflechtungen und gegenseitigen Wechselwirkungen afrikanischer und afroamerikanischer Religionen.[5] In seinen ethnohistorischen multilokalen Analysen gelang es ihm zu beweisen, dass religiöse Akteure in der atlantischen Welt zu (vor)kolonialen Zei-

---

[3] Vgl. Tardits, Claude: Contribution à l'étude des populations Bamiléké de l'ouest Cameroun. Paris: Berger-Levrault 1960; Millicent Chilver, Elizabeth / Phyllis Kaberry: Traditional Bamenda. The Pre-colonial History and Ethnography of the Bamenda Grassfields. Buea: Ministry of Primary Education and Social Welfare, West Cameroon Antiquities Commission 1968; Geary, Christraud: We. Die Genese eines Häuptlingtums im Grasland von Kamerun. Wiesbaden: Steiner ¹1976; Hamadjoda Abdoullaye, Alhadji / Eldridge Mohammadou: Ray ou Rey-Bouba. Traditions historiques des Fulbés de l'Adamâwa. Paris: Centre National de la Recherche Scientifique 1979.

[4] Vgl. z. B. Seige, Christine: Die Vute in Kamerun. Veränderungen in der Gesellschaft der Vute (Zentralkamerun) unter dem Einfluss der Fulbe-Herrschaft in Südadamaua in der zweiten Hälfte des 19. Jahrhunderts. Münster: LIT 2003; Röschenthaler, Ute: Purchasing Culture. The Dissemination of Associations in the Cross River Region of Cameroon and Nigeria. Trenton NJ: Africa World Press 2011.

[5] Siehe dazu Matory, James Lorand: Sex and the empire that is no more. Gender and the politics of metaphor in Oyo Yoruba religion. Minneapolis Minn.: Univ. of Minnesota 1994; Matory, James Lorand: Black Atlantic Religion. Tradition, Transnationalism, and Matriarchy in the Afro-Brazilian Candomble. Princeton, N. J.: Princeton University Press 2005.

ten einen hohen Mobilitätsgrad erreichten und ihre religiösen Praktiken im Dialog zwischen dem afrikanischen Herkunftsort und der amerikanischen Diaspora ständig neu aushandelten. Das Neuartige daran ist, Afrika und die Amerikas als Orte der sich gleichzeitig entwickelnden Kulturen zu betrachten, anstatt das heutige Afrika als die Vergangenheit der ‚schwarzen Amerikas' zu verstehen.[6] Seine Befunde nutzte Matory als Grundlage für seinen innovativen theoretischen Rahmen, der hier im Mittelpunkt steht: der ‚Afroatlantische Dialog'.

Matory bedient sich dabei der Überlegungen Michail Bachtins zur Funktion des Dialogs im Roman. Für Bachtin leben Texte nur dann, wenn sie in Berührung mit anderen Texten kommen. Denn dadurch nehmen sie am Dialog teil.[7] Damit dieses Konzept in der Geschichtsschreibung angewendet werden kann, muss der Text in seinem breiten Spektrum verstanden werden. Kulturen kann man auch als Texte bzw. Bedeutungsgewebe verstehen und sie leben auch nur, wenn sie in Dialog mit anderen Kulturen stehen. Diese Feststellung mag zunächst banal klingen, doch im Hinblick auf die Entwicklung der Historiographie Afrikas, Afroamerikas und des Sklavenhandels trägt sie eine große Bedeutung, da afrikanische Gesellschaften oft als abgeschottet, unverändert und sogar geschichtslos gedacht wurden.[8] Die Anwendung von Bachtins Dialog-Konzept in Bezug auf afrikanische und afroamerikanische Kulturen erklärt Matory wie folgt: Bachtin benutzt die analytische Metapher des Dialogs, um den Roman als Verkörperung der Interaktion der zahlreichen darin involvierten Stimmen zu definieren. Im Roman sprechen so viele Stimmen, dass man sogar die Autorität des Autors anzweifeln kann. Übertragen auf die Analyse von Kulturen heißt das Folgendes: In der Produktion jeder Kultur sind zahlreiche Akteure involviert und sie ‚zitieren' immer mehrere weitere Kulturen

---

[6] Matory: The „New World" (Anm. 1), S. 183.

[7] Polubojarinowa, Larissa N.: Intertextualität und Dialogizität: Michail Bachtins Theorien zwischen Sprachwissenschaft und Literaturwissenschaft. In: TRANS 3 (1998), S. 1–5, hier S. 1.

[8] Zur Entwicklung der Geschichtsschreibung Afrikas siehe exemplarisch: Feierman, Steven: Afrika in der Geschichte: Das Ende der universalen Erzählungen. In: Sebastian Conrad / Shalini Randeria / Regina Römhild (Hg.): Jenseits des Eurozentrismus. Postkoloniale Perspektiven in den Geschichts- und Kulturwissenschaften. 2. erw. Aufl. Frankfurt/Main: Campus 2013, S. 405–437.

bei der Produktion ihrer eigenen.⁹ Bei Bachtin lebt also der Text nur im Dialog mit anderen Texten. Und bei Matory leben Kulturen auch nur, wenn sie in Dialog mit anderen Kulturen stehen.

Um weiter mit Matory zu sprechen, muss das Dialog-Konzept Bachtins allerdings um einen wichtigen Aspekt bei der Analyse von Kulturen ergänzt werden: die Macht. Bei der Reproduktion und Produktion von Kultur sind die Akteure und ‚zitierten Kulturen' eben nicht gleich stark, sondern von den führenden Machtverhältnissen geleitet.¹⁰ Die Dialog-Metapher ist also nützlich, um Akteure als ‚Sprecher' zu verstehen, die nicht isoliert ihre eigenen lokalen Kulturen produzieren. Stattdessen stehen sie in einem ständigen systematischen Dialog mit weit entfernten Kulturen, wobei Machtverhältnisse die unterschiedlichen Stimmen verstärken, verändern oder verstummen lassen können.¹¹ Mit der Dialog-Metapher können also kulturelle Praktiken und Diskurse in einem breiteren Kontext betrachtet werden, jenseits der üblichen Kategorien von Nation und Region.¹²

Dieser ‚Afroatlantische Dialog' ist, Matory zufolge, nicht nur religiös transnational, sondern auch wirtschaftlich, politisch, literarisch und musikalisch transnational.¹³ Er wird außerdem in mindestens sechs europäischen, zwölf kreolischen und Hunderten von afrikanischen Sprachen geführt, was auf seine ausgeprägte Polyphonie hindeutet.¹⁴

Dynamiken des Sklavenhaltens und -handels im Grasland

Die Bezeichnung ‚Grasland' wurde beim Eindringen ins kamerunische Hinterland von deutschen Kolonialbeamten, -forschern und Missionaren eingeführt und bezieht sich in erster Linie auf eine sehr dicht besiedelte Savannenregion im Westen Kameruns, die sich auf Hochplateaus zwischen ca. 1.000 und 1.800 Metern befindet. Mit der englischen Machtübernahme erhielt der größte Teil dieser Region das englische Pendant ‚Grass-

---

⁹ Matory: Black Atlantic Religion (Anm. 5), S. 285.
¹⁰ Ebd., S. 286.
¹¹ Ebd.
¹² Ebd., S. 285.
¹³ Ebd., S. 288.
¹⁴ Ebd., S. 287.

fields'.¹⁵ Die Bezeichnung ist nicht nur topographisch, sondern erhebt auch den Anspruch, einen weiten Kulturraum zu definieren.¹⁶ Bereits die Tatsache, dass die Bezeichnung ‚Grasland' in einem kolonialen Kontext mit sehr ungleichen Machtverhältnissen aus einer etischen Perspektive vergeben wurde, lädt zum Nachdenken über seine Verwendung ein. ‚Grasland' wird hier deswegen nicht als eine geschlossene räumliche Einheit betrachtet, sondern vielmehr als ein Sammelbegriff, der sich auf zahlreiche dezentralisierte Königreiche bezieht. Es werden hierfür keine festen geographischen Grenzen gedacht, sondern vielmehr diverse ‚Kontaktzonen'¹⁷. Sie werden verstanden als soziale Räume der Begegnung diverser Kulturen unter ungleichen Machtverhältnissen und sind daher durch einen hohen Grad an Transkulturation geprägt. Bezogen auf den Sklavenhandel lässt sich für das Grasland das Konzept einer ‚slaving zone' anwenden, d. h. ein weites geographisches Gebiet, das von der Nachfrage an Sklaven bestimmter Gesellschaften betroffen war.¹⁸

Das Grasland kann als Wohnraum zahlreicher dezentralisierter Gesellschaften verstanden werden.¹⁹ Politisch betrachtet, funktionierte das Grasland zu vorkolonialen Zeiten nämlich anders als große zentralisierte Reiche wie beispielsweise Dahomey im heutigen Benin oder Ashanti im heutigen Ghana. Dezentralisierte Gesellschaften konnten sich besser vor sogenannten

---

[15] Argenti, Nicolas / Ute Röschenthaler: Introduction: Between Cameroon and Cuba: Youth, slave trades and translocal memoryscapes. In: Social Anthropology 14 (2006), S. 33–47, hier S. 36. Im vorliegenden Text wird die deutsche Bezeichnung ‚Grasland' nur aufgrund der sprachlichen Einheitlichkeit bevorzugt.

[16] Jean-Pierre Warnier hat mit seinen Publikationen womöglich am meisten im akademischen Diskurs zu einer Etablierung des Begriffs ‚Grassfields' beigetragen. Vgl. Nkwi, Paul Nchoji / Jean-Pierre Warnier: Elements for a History of the Western Grassfields. Yaoundé: Department of Sociology, University of Yaoundé 1982; Warnier, Jean-Pierre (Hg.): Cameroon Grassfields Civilization. Mankon, Cameroon: Langaa Research & Pub. CIG 2012.

[17] Pratt, Mary L.: Imperial eyes. Travel writing and transculturation. New York: Routledge ²2008, S. 7.

[18] Der Begriff ‚slaving zone' wird bei Julia Martínez in Anlehnung an Jeff Fynn-Paul verwendet. Martínez, Julia: Mapping the Trafficking of Women across Colonial Southeast Asia, 1600s–1930s. In: Journal of Global Slavery 1 (2016), S. 224–247, hier S. 227.

[19] Warnier, Jean-Pierre: The linguistic situation and the history of the Grassfields. In: Warnier (Hg.): Cameroon Grassfields (note 16), S. 41–48, hier S. 41f.

Sklavenjägern schützen.[20] Der Sklavenhandel konnte daher nur durchdringen, indem persönliche Verbindungen mit den Bewohnern dieser Gesellschaften geknüpft wurden, und zwar auf wirtschaftlicher, sozialer und politischer Ebene.[21] Dezentralisierte Gesellschaften, wie die des Graslands, sollten daher nicht als Opfer, sondern als aktive Teilnehmer eines globalen wirtschaftlichen Systems betrachtet werden, in dem Machtpositionen eine grundlegende Rolle spielten. Der Handel mit Menschen ergab sich hier weniger auf eine gewaltsame Art und Weise, vielmehr durch Intrigen und Verrat von Bekannten und Verwandten.[22] Warnier spricht den Menschen im Grasland einen ausgeprägten Handels-Habitus zu, wodurch der Zugang zum profitablen Geschäft mit Menschen möglich wurde.[23]

Es ist nun wichtig zu schauen, welche strapaziösen Wege den versklavten Menschen nach ihrer Entführung aus dem Grasland bevorstanden, um die möglichen Verbreitungswege kultureller Praktiken aus und zu dieser Region zu identifizieren. Die möglichen Schicksale, die eine versklavte Person erleben musste, reichten vom Verkauf an ein benachbartes Königreich, um dort zu arbeiten, über die Zwangsehe einer Frau in einer ihr fremden Gegend bis hin zum Verkauf an weiter entfernte Sklavengesellschaften in Afrika oder in den Amerikas.[24] Die Transportwege für versklavte Menschen wurden selbstverständlich nicht jedes Mal neu erfunden, sondern entsprachen in der Regel den bereits existierenden Handelswegen, die auch dem Transport ‚anderer Waren' dienten. Diese wurden aus Sicherheits- und praktischen Gründen nicht selten in Karawanen benutzt. Ein Großteil der versklavten Menschen aus dem Grasland, der dem transatlantischen Sklavenhandel übergeben wurde, verließ den afrikanischen Kontinent nicht über die heutige Hafenstadt Douala, sondern über Old Calabar im heutigen Nigeria oder diente dort der Elite.[25] Aus dem Grasland heraus wurden Sklaven, Elfenbein und Nahrungsmittel, zurück

---

[20] Klein, Martin A.: The Slave Trade and Decentralized Societies. In: The Journal of African History 42 (2001), S. 49–65, hier S. 50.
[21] Ebd.
[22] Ebd., S. 59.
[23] Warnier, Jean-Pierre: Slave-Trading without Slave-Raiding in Cameroon. In: Paideuma. Mitteilungen zur Kulturkunde 41 (1995), S. 251–272, hier S. 263.
[24] Ebd., S. 270.
[25] Nwokeji, Ugo: Caracteristics of Captives Leaving the Cameroons for the Americas, 1822–37. In: The Journal of African History 43 (2002), S. 191–210, hier S. 204.

ins Grasland Waffen, Perlen, industrielle Produkte, Schnaps, Rechte für Geheimgesellschaften[26] u. a. transportiert. Der Cross River fungierte als effektiver Transportweg zwischen Old Calabar und dem Grasland, während die langen Fußmärsche bis nach Douala das Volumen des Handels dorthin geringer ausfallen ließen.[27]

Politisch-religiöse Verflechtungen

Der Handel mit Menschen aus dem Grasland kann nicht als eine bloße wirtschaftliche Transaktion betrachtet werden, bei der ein Mensch, wider seinen Willen, gegen einen kommodifizierten Gegenstand ausgetauscht wurde. Denn durch diese Art der Betrachtung entsteht der Eindruck, die Gesellschaften des Graslandes seien ausschließlich Geber unmündiger, ‚kulturloser' unterdrückter Menschen und Empfänger von Konsumwaren gewesen. Dies wäre höchst problematisch, weil dann die kulturellen Transformationen, die an verschiedenen Orten damit einhergingen, und vor allem die Agency[28] der Versklavten komplett ausgeblendet würden. Vielmehr sollte ein Verständnis der Transportrouten im Sinne von Heintze einbezogen werden. Ihr zufolge fungierten die Wege vom Hinterland zum Meer in West- und Zentralafrika häufig als Adern eines Austauschs von Menschen und Waren, aber vor allem auch von Fähigkeiten und Wissen.[29]

---

[26] Röschenthaler, Ute: Translocal cultures: The slave trade and cultural transfer in the Cross River region. In: Social Anthropology 14 (2006), S. 71–91, hier S. 72.

[27] Austen, Ralph A.: Douala: Slave Trade and Memory on the Periphery of the Nigerian Hinterland. In: Robin Law / Silke Strickrodt (Hg.): Ports of the Slave Trade (Bights of Benin and Biafra). Papers from a conference of the Centre of Commonwealth Studies, University of Stirling June 1998. Stirling: Astron Group 1999, S. 71–83, hier S. 73f.

[28] Hier verstanden als die Handlungsfähigkeit eines Individuums. Siehe dazu: Helfferich, Cornelia: Einleitung. In: Stefanie Bethmann / Cornelia Helfferich / Heiko Hoffmann / Debora Nierman (Hg.): Agency. Die Analyse von Handlungsfähigkeit und Handlungsmacht in qualitativer Sozialforschung und Gesellschaftstheorie. Weinheim, Basel: Beltz Juventa 2012, S. 9–39, hier S. 9f.

[29] Heintze, Beatrix: Long-distance Caravans and Communication beyond the Kwango (c. 1850–1890). International symposium Angola on the Move:

Die Bewohner des Graslands – um mit Matory zu sprechen – produzierten und reproduzierten also ihre lokalen Kulturen in einem ständigen Dialog mit sehr weit entfernten afrikanischen, amerikanischen und europäischen Kulturen. Daher verlangt die historische Erforschung dieser Kulturen einen interdisziplinären Zugang, der zunächst mit einem Beispiel aus dem politisch-religiösen Bereich erläutert wird. In dem Fall geht es um die Verbreitung des Bundes Ekpe (– Ekpe bedeutet Leopard in der Efik-Sprache und ist der Titel mehrerer Männergesellschaften), dessen Einflussbereich sich von Old Calabar im Südwesten bis zum Grasland im Nordosten erstreckte.[30]

Dieser Bund aus dem sogenannten Ejagham-Gebiet im heutigen Grenzgebiet Nigeria/Kamerun wurde zu einer regulierenden Institution des Sklavenhandels für Afrikaner und in Old Calabar auch für Europäer. Zunächst hatte dieser Bund eine politisch-religiöse Funktion im Ejagham-Gebiet, doch mit der Zeit wurden seine ‚Geheimnisse' (Informationen zur Funktion und Ausführung von Ritualen und Tänzen) von anderen Gruppen gekauft, um Zugang zu den Handelsnetzwerken zu bekommen. Auch von versklavten Menschen wurden die Geheimnisse des Bundes teilweise weitergegeben. Röschenthaler studierte die Verbreitungswege und -formen von Bünden im Cross River-Gebiet und liefert wertvolle Einblicke in dieses Forschungsfeld.[31] Aus ihren Studien werden zudem die Verflechtungen zwischen der Verbreitung dieser Bünde und dem Sklavenhandel ersichtlich.[32] Regional betrachtet, fokussiert Röschenthaler hauptsächlich die Waldregion des Cross Rivers an der heutigen Grenze Nigeria/Kamerun. Sie konstatiert, dass diese Region als Durchlaufstation für versklavte Menschen aus dem Grasland, Richtung Old Calabar, oft auch als Endstation diente.

Beide Phänomene, der Durchlauf wie auch die Ankunft fremder versklavter Menschen, brachten bedeutende Veränderungen auf gesellschaftlicher, politischer und kultureller Ebene mit sich. Der Handel mit Menschen fand hier etappenweise statt, d. h. in einem System aus Zwischen-

---

Transport Routes, Communication, and History. 24.–26.09.2003, Berlin. In: https://www.zmo.de/angola/Papers/Heintze_(29-03-04).pdf, S. 1 (08.03.2017).
[30] Röschenthaler: Purchasing Culture (Anm. 4), S. 139.
[31] Ausführlicher dazu ebd.
[32] Vgl. Röschenthaler: Translocal cultures (Anm. 26).

händlern, die den Verkauf von Dorf zu Dorf organisierten.[33] Für die versklavten Menschen, die in dieser Waldregion bleiben mussten, entstanden oft neue Siedlungen, da sie als eine potenzielle Gefahr für die Gemeinschaft galten und daher räumlich abgetrennt wurden.[34] Aus demselben Grund wurde die Verbreitung von Ekpe gefördert. Denn durch die Neuankömmlinge in den Dorfgemeinschaften stellte sich oft die Frage nach den Verwaltungsmöglichkeiten, und Ekpe lieferte Lösungsansätze, zum Beispiel eine Vorlage für das Regieren von Gemeinschaften oder das Eintreiben von Schulden.[35] Dies erklärt zum Teil, warum der Sklavenhandel mit der Verbreitung von Ekpe einherging.

Dessen Rechte, entsprechende Rituale und Tänze auszuführen, wurden sogar in Bali im Nordwesten des Graslands erworben. Hierbei wird erkennbar, dass der Sklavenhandel und die Verbreitung von Geheimgesellschaften in beide Richtungen verliefen. Während aus dem Hinterland (Grasland und Cross River-Gebiet) versklavte Menschen, Elfenbein u. a. Richtung Küste exportiert wurden, nahmen nicht nur europäische Konsumgüter, sondern eben auch immaterielles Kulturgut in Form von Bünden den Weg von der Küste ins Hinterland. Die Kontaktzonen verschiedener Kulturen wurden somit zu besonderen Räumen kultureller Transformationen. Röschenthaler erklärt, dass die meisten versklavten Menschen aus dem Grasland Jugendliche waren, die aufgrund ihres Alters noch nicht alle Funktionsweisen von Bünden aus ihren Herkunftsregionen kennen konnten. Diese besonderen Geheimnisse waren vielmehr den älteren Mitgliedern der Gemeinschaft vorbehalten, die in den seltensten Fällen selbst Opfer von Menschenhandel wurden und eher den Handel dominierten.[36] Dadurch, dass die jungen Versklavten geringe Kenntnisse von Bünden mit sich trugen, gaben sie oft nur Teile dessen weiter. Von ihren ‚Besitzern' wurden sie oft nach solchen Geheimnissen befragt und in manchen Fällen für deren Enthüllung sogar belohnt.[37]

Da die Macht von Ekpe (aber auch ähnlicher Bünde) durch Tänze, Rituale und bestimmte Kleidung artikuliert wurde, können bis heute visuelle

---

[33] Ebd., S. 72.
[34] Ebd.
[35] Ebd., S. 76.
[36] Ebd., S. 87ff.
[37] Ebd., S. 88.

Indizien für ihre Verbreitung zwischen dem Grasland und Old Calabar gefunden werden. Diese Elemente lassen sich nicht nur auf afrikanischem Boden wiederfinden, sondern auch auf der anderen Seite des Atlantiks, vor allem auf Cuba, wo viele Menschen aus Old Calabar und Umgebung hingeschleppt wurden.[38] Dabei werden verschiedene Richtungen der kulturellen Einflüsse deutlich. Einerseits fungierten versklavte Menschen als Träger kultureller Praktiken, wenn auch mit ‚unvollständigen' Kenntnissen. Andererseits wurden Rechte von Geheimgesellschaften in größerem Stil in der Waldregion des Cross River erworben, um in den profitablen Handel mit Sklaven einzutreten und die wachsende versklavte Population besser unter Kontrolle zu halten. Doch nicht nur auf politisch-religiöser Ebene fanden Transformationen im Grasland und in der Umgebung statt, sondern auch auf ästhetisch-künstlerischer Ebene.

Ästhetisch-künstlerische Verflechtungen

Der Begriff der ‚Kunst' wird hier als relativ verstanden, da die Empfindung von Objekten als Kunstwerke von jedem Individuum und den jeweiligen gesellschaftlichen Normen abhängt.[39] Keinesfalls soll aber dadurch angedeutet werden, dass gegenseitige ästhetische Einflüsse keine politische oder religiöse Wirkung hätten. Die zwei wichtigsten Studien, auf die hier Bezug genommen wird – die Studien von Wilcox und Thompson zu den Verflechtungen des Graslands mit Douala und Old Calabar[40] – kommen aus dem kunsthistorischen Bereich und gebrauchen das entsprechende Vokabular.

Wilcox analysiert die Kunst der Region Douala in diachronischer und transregionaler Perspektive und liefert durch diesen Ansatz wertvolle Einblicke in deren Komplexität. Sie charakterisiert künstlerische Traditionen als ein Produkt komplexer lokaler, regionaler und externer Beziehungen

---

[38] Argenti/Röschenthaler: Introduction (Anm. 15), S. 37.
[39] Vgl. Hahn, Hans Peter: Materielle Kultur. Eine Einführung. Berlin: Reimer 2005, S. 20.
[40] Wilcox, Rosalinde G.: Commercial Transactions and Cultural Interactions from the Delta to Douala and beyond. In: African Arts 35 (2002), S. 42–55; Thompson, Robert Farris: Tres flechas desde el monte: La influencia ejagham en el arte mundial. In: Anales del Museo de América 6 (1998), S. 71–83.

zwischen den Bevölkerungen Doualas und des Graslands, des Cross Rivers, des Nigerdeltas und Europas. Diese künstlerische Vielfalt, so Wilcox, verlor sich allerdings, als Kolonialbeamte, Forscher und Missionare Ende des 19. Jahrhunderts in der Gegend um Douala Objekte sammelten, sie nach Europa brachten und mit dem Titel ‚Douala' versahen. Dadurch gingen genaue Informationen über die Herkunft der Objekte und deren Schöpfer – die Gruppen, die sich als Duala[41] verstanden oder die Region, in der die Objekte gesammelt wurden[42] – verloren. Die multikulturelle Zusammensetzung der Doualas zu (vor)kolonialen Zeiten versucht Wilcox anhand der Analyse von Objekten und ästhetischen Einflüssen zu rekonstruieren. Sie versucht zu beweisen, dass entlang der Guineaküste nicht nur ähnliche Glaubensvorstellungen von Meeresgeistern die Verbreitung und Aneignung ritueller Objekte förderten, sondern auch der Handel sowie kurz- und langzeitige Migrationsbewegungen.[43]

Bezüglich der Handelsbeziehungen der Doualas betont Wilcox die wichtige Rolle der Insel Bioko, heute ein Teil von Äquatorialguinea. Hier wurden ab dem 19. Jahrhundert unter britischer, danach unter spanischer Führung zahlreiche Plantagen angebaut. Als Arbeitskräfte wurden nicht nur die lokale Bevölkerung der Insel ausgebeutet, sondern auch die Kru aus den heutigen Sierra Leone und Liberia sowie Menschen aus der Region um Douala[44] und viele Ijo aus dem Nigerdelta[45]. Dabei muss betont werden, dass die Duala als Mittelsmänner[46] zwischen ihrem Hinterland und den Händlern am Atlantik fungierten. Daher waren viele der nach Bioko

---

[41] Diese Schreibweise wird in der Fachliteratur verwendet, wenn von der entsprechenden Bevölkerungsgruppe und nicht vom Douala-Gebiet die Rede ist.
[42] Wilcox: Commercial Transactions (Anm. 40), S. 44.
[43] Ebd. S. 50.
[44] Sundiata, Ibrahim K.: From Slaving to Neoslavery. The Bight of Biafra and Fernando Po in the Era of Abolition, 1827–1930. Madison: Univ. of Wisconsin Press 1996, S. 122ff.
[45] Wilcox: Commercial Transactions (Anm. 40), S. 55.
[46] Austen und Derrick benutzen diesen Begriff in ihrer Studie: Austen, Ralph A. / Jonathan Derrick: Middlemen of the Cameroons Rivers. The Duala and their Hinterland, c. 1600 – c. 1960. Cambridge: Cambridge University Press 1999. Eine Problematisierung des Begriffs erfolgt bei Michels, da ihrer Meinung nach diese Bezeichnung als Legitimation für die Kolonisierung des Hinterlands diente. Michels, Stefanie: Schutzherrschaft revisited – Kolonialismus aus afrikanischer Perspektive. In: Andreas Fahrmeir / Annette Imhausen (Hg.): Die Vielfalt norma-

verschleppten Menschen nicht ursprüngliche Bewohner Doualas, sondern kamen aus dem Grasland.[47] So entstand in der Bucht von Biafra, im Dreieck Douala – Old Calabar – Bioko, ein Netzwerk kultureller Einflüsse, das bis heute noch erkennbar ist, so Wilcox.[48]

Wilcox' Erkenntnisse über die Verflechtungen ästhetisch-künstlerischer Einflüsse zwischen den Gebieten des heutigen Nigeria und Kamerun werden durch die Fallstudie von Thompson[49] komplettiert. Thompson analysiert die Kunst der Ejagham in ihrer internationalen Dimension und identifiziert drei Gründe für ihre globale Verbreitung: In erster Linie ist sie in der heutigen südlichen Grenzregion Kamerun/Nigeria zu finden, doch aufgrund von größeren Bantu-Migrationsbewegungen (ca. 200 n. Chr.) hinterließ sie sogar bei den Kongo-Kulturen ihre Spuren. Des Weiteren fand die Kunst in der genannten Grenzregion starke Verbreitung, da sie in enger Verbindung mit dem mächtigen Bund Ngbe stand (Ngbe und Ekpe bedeuten in den Ejagham- und Efik-Sprachen ‚Leopard'[50]). Dieser Bund ist im Grasland, im Ejagham-Gebiet und in Old Calabar zu finden, wo er eine wichtige Rolle im transatlantischen Sklavenhandel spielte. Der Zusammenhang mit dem Ngbe/Ekpe-Bund führte dazu, dass die Ejagham-Kunst auch in der weiten atlantischen Welt Einfluss ausübte, beispielsweise auf Cuba, vor allem in La Habana, Matanzas und Cárdenas.[51] Dieser letzte Aspekt wird von Thompson auch erklärt. Er behauptet, dass die in Old Calabar verkauften Sklaven in Richtung Amerika, vor allem in die Karibik verschleppt wurden und oft Kenntnisse von Ngbe/Ekpe mit sich trugen. Die Kenntnisse über das Funktionieren dieses Bundes hätten dann oft der Bildung neuer sozialer Gruppen in der amerikanischen Diaspora gedient.[52]

Wilcox und Thompson verweisen auf die Verflechtungen zwischen dem Grasland, Old Calabar, Douala und sogar Bioko zu (vor)kolonialen Zeiten. Es wird dabei erkennbar, dass kulturelle Einflüsse multidirektional waren

---

tiver Ordnungen. Konflikte und Dynamik in historischer und ethnologischer Perspektive. Frankfurt/Main: Campus 2013, S. 243–274, hier S. 253f.

[47] Sundiata: From Slaving (Anm. 44), S. 124f.
[48] Wilcox: Commercial Transactions (Anm. 40), S. 55.
[49] Thompson: Tres flechas (Anm. 40).
[50] Röschenthaler: Translocal cultures (Anm. 26), S. 76.
[51] Thompson: Tres flechas (Anm. 40), S. 71f.
[52] Ebd., S. 74.

und dadurch kaum als einzelne zu erfassen sind. Vielmehr ist es erstrebenswert, weiterhin die Gründe und Folgen solcher Verflechtungen zu studieren, um der Komplexität von Kulturen gerecht zu werden.

Das Grasland im Dialog mit dem Afroatlantik

Die hier präsentierten Überlegungen basieren hauptsächlich auf aktuellen Forschungen unterschiedlicher Regionen, die zu vorkolonialen Zeiten mit dem Grasland in Verbindung standen. Durch das Zusammenbringen dieser Arbeiten war es möglich, eine transregionale Perspektive auf kulturelle Transformationen im Grasland einzunehmen. Anhand der erbrachten Beispiele konnte bewiesen werden, dass das Grasland eine ausschlaggebende Rolle in der frühen Prägung der afroatlantischen Welt spielte. Nicht nur diente diese dichtbesiedelte Region als ‚slaving zone' für Menschenhändler aus den strategischen Küstengebieten von Old Calabar und Douala, sie wurde auch durch die Anbindung an den transatlantischen Handel geprägt und beeinflusste gleichzeitig den Afroatlantik.

In Anlehnung an die führende Arbeit von Röschenthaler konnte gezeigt werden, dass der Handel mit Menschen im Cross River-Gebiet und im Grasland zu steigendem Wohlstand führte, sodass im Gegenzug Rechte für neue Bünde erworben werden konnten. Von der Küste ins Hinterland fand der mächtige Bund Ekpe seinen Weg bis zum Grasland. Seine Geheimnisse wurden dort erlernt und erneut Richtung Atlantik und Amerikas durch die versklavten Menschen transportiert, wenn auch nur bruchstückhaft.[53] Hierbei wird erkennbar, dass die Menschen aus dem Grasland, die in verschiedene Richtungen verschleppt und sowohl auf afrikanischem wie auf amerikanischem Boden versklavt wurden, nicht als bloße Arbeitskräfte ohne kulturelle Identitäten betrachtet werden können. Vielmehr prägten sie ihre Ankunftsgesellschaften in unterschiedlichem Maße, gleichzeitig wurden ihre Herkunftsgesellschaften durch die Dynamiken des Handels kulturell transformiert. So diente die Migration als Katalysator für den künstlerischen Austausch in mehreren Regionen. Ästhetische Muster zirkulierten mit den Menschen, die – freiwillig oder gezwungenermaßen – eine Reise antraten.

---

[53] Röschenthaler: Translocal cultures (Anm. 26), S. 88.

Die dargestellten Dynamiken des afrikanischen Sklavenhandels werfen weitere Fragen auf, besonders im Hinblick auf die Möglichkeiten und Grenzen der jeweiligen Akteure.[54] Es geht darum, die historischen Akteure in ihren jeweiligen lokalen Kontexten zu verorten und gleichzeitig den Einfluss ihrer Handlungen auf globaler Ebene zu interpretieren.[55] Dieser globalgeschichtliche Ansatz in der Erforschung des Graslands ist bislang ein Desiderat. Forschungen in diese Richtung könnten mehr Klarheit über kulturelle Transformationen im Zeitalter des Sklavenhandels schaffen.

---

[54] Zeuske, Michael: Handbuch Geschichte der Sklaverei. Eine Globalgeschichte von den Anfängen bis zur Gegenwart. Berlin: de Gruyter 2013, S. VIII.
[55] Feierman: Afrika in der Geschichte (Anm. 8), S. 423.

The Risk of Homogenization in the Dialogue between the Disciplines: the Case of Foucault's Reuse of Ancient Philosophy

Martina Di Stefano

Introduction

Over the past few decades, contemporary philosophy has renewed the philosophical debate, recovering ancient notions, such as "virtue" and "care of self". On the one hand, such reuse often neglects the historical frame and has made scholars of Antiquity suspicious of it. On the other hand, a certain philology, haunted by concerns about authenticity, denies all manners of theoretical applications of such notions.[1] This case could be indicative of a tension between the history of the disciplines and other kinds of approach.[2] In this paper, I will focus on a particular risk inherent to the dialogue between the disciplines, homogenization, as a case-study. I will address Foucault's notion of "pastoral power" and his reading of Greek texts.

Firstly, I will focus on Foucault's growing interest in ancient thought and I will mention the importance of his contacts with scholars of Classics, for instance with Pierre Hadot. I will report some objections addressed to Foucault's treatment of Antiquity, focusing on criticism of his projection of a homogeneous representation. Secondly, I will tackle the notion of "pastoral power", reconstructing how Foucault coins it and for what purpose. I will then briefly examine Foucault's treatment of Greek texts and suggest a possible different account. My main hypothesis is that Foucault, as other philosophers do, sometimes neglects to put ancient concepts or images into

---

[1] For an excellent discussion of the topic see Cambiano, Giuseppe: Perché leggere i classici? Bologna: Il Mulino 2010.

[2] Marchand, Suzanne: Has the History of the Disciplines Had its Day? In: Darrin M. McMahon / Samuel Moyn (Eds.) Rethinking Modern European Intellectual History. Oxford: Oxford University Press 2014.

their historical context, underestimating their links with and oppositions to other phenomena and shrinking the synchronic plurality of practices and forms of knowledge (*synchronic homogenization*). At the same time, he teleologically projects modern or contemporary notions on ancient concepts (*diachronic homogenization*). Finally, I will briefly discuss the meaning of "historical thinking" for Foucault's project.

1. Foucault and Antiquity

The second and the third volumes of the *History of Sexuality* were published in June 1984, some days before Foucault's death, and dealt with the problematization of a domain – sexuality – normally taken for granted.[3] But, differently to what he had announced during the first time, Foucault tackles with this issue while going back to Antiquity, and upon their publication much criticism was addressed to his work. To some of his readers this "classical turn" is indeed a withdrawal, which has been disappointing particulary the Classics specialists. It was not even possible to start a debate with the French philosopher because of Foucault's immediate death. Although these texts got a cold reception in Europe, yet they have influenced Ancient Studies in the United States: A 2014 collection has gathered comments of that period and, if they witness a general suspicion, one might note the attention of American scholars.[4] Moreover, as he states in the "Introduction" of *The Use of Pleasure*, his reading of Antiquity is indebted to Classical scholars, such as Peter Brown, Pierre Hadot, and Paul Veyne.[5]

Since the latter was an enthusiastic supporter of his friend Foucault, one may note some criticism from Pierre Hadot. Hadot and Foucault had

---

[3] Between the publication of the first (1976) and the two other volumes have passed eight years.

[4] Artières, Philippe / Jean-François Bert / Sandra Boehringer / Philippe Chevallier / Frédéric Gros / Luca Paltrinieri / Judith Revel: Introduction. In: Luca Paltrinieri (éd.): L'usage des plaisirs et Le Souci de soi de Michel Foucault. Regards critiques 1984–1987. Caen: Presses universitaires de Caen 2014, p. 33.

[5] Foucault, Michel: The History of Sexuality. Vol. 2: The Use of Pleasure (1984). Transl. from the French by Robert Hurley. New York: Vintage Books Edition 1990, p. 8.

never met until the autumn of 1980, when Foucault, who was at that time professor at Collège de France, encouraged him to candidate for a chair at the same institution. He was in fact acquainted with Hadot's texts since the late 1970s and he was especially interested in the notion of "philosophy as a way of life"[6]. Concerning the second and the third volume of the *History of Sexuality*, Hadot recognized Foucault's ability as historian of social phenomena and ideas, but blamed him for not having practiced philology.[7] He also criticized Foucault's dismissal of some aspects of the ancient notion of the "care of the self". However, in Foucault's courses at Collège de France one may notice a new attention to texts and his attempt to mould concepts starting from ancient terms. He read Louis Gernet, Gustave Glotz et Édouard Will's texts, as well as the works of Moulinier and Detienne[8]; moreover, one should not forget how much he was influenced by Dover's *Greek Homosexuality*, even though their works are dramatically different in methodology.[9] In addition, one might say that Foucault worked on Antiquity in a very traditional way, focusing his interest on normative texts and taking for granted what they promote. As Henri Joly, the French historian of ancient Philosophy, has pointed out, he excluded poets and iconography as cultural sources.[10]

Even some Italian classical scholars, deeply indebted to Foucault's lessons, criticized his works and were disappointed by his treatment of Antiquity. In particular, Mario Vegetti and Giuseppe Cambiano have pointed out that his representation of Antiquity was essentially homogeneous and that Greece appears free from conflict and apolitical, not passed through

---

[6] This was also the title of Hadot's course at Collège de France (1984–85).

[7] Hadot, Pierre: Philosophy as a way of life. Oxford-Cambridge: Blackwell 1995, pp. 206–212; Daraki, Maria: Le voyage en Grèce de Michel Foucault. In: Esprit 100, No. 4 (1985), pp. 55–83, both quoted in Fruchaud, Henri-Paul / Jean-François Bert: Un inédit de Michel Foucault: La Parrêsia. Note de présentation. In: Anabases 16 (2012), pp. 149–156, here p. 153, n. 13.

[8] Fruchaud/Bert: Un inédit de Michel Foucault (note 7), p. 154.

[9] Dover's analysis of sexual practices was mostly based on iconography and not philosophical or normative texts. See Dover, Kenneth J.: Greek Homosexuality. London, Oxford, New York: Bloomsbury Academic 2016.

[10] Joly, Henry: Retour aux Grecs: réflexions sur les "pratiques de soi" dans L'usage des plaisirs. In: Le Débat 41/4 (1986), pp. 100–120.

differences.[11] To these scholars, his writings on Antiquity appeared methodologically regressive. Foucault treats Greek thought as origin of the present, adopting the traditional continuity approach to history. His later texts, moreover, fundamentally pass over the connection between the systems of power and ideas and reinvent a kind of "authorial" history of ideas, based on normative works of canonized authors.[12]

We do not have time to deal in detail with Foucault's reading of Antiquity, thus I will take into account a significant case-study, the notion of "pastoral power". I will just sum up the main features, which Foucault associates with the pastorate, but I do not discuss it in its theoretical implications. Although, I could not provide here a complete textual and historical analysis, I will shortly grapple with the image, paving the way to a possible positive critical use of historical notions.

2. The "Pastoral Power"

Foucault first mentions the notion of "pastoral power" in his course at Collège de France in 1977/78 (*Security, territory and population*). At the end of his lecture on the 1st of February, he outlines the project of a history of governmentality. Under this label, he explains this term at three levels:

1) The ensemble formed by institutions, procedures, analyses and reflections, calculations, and tactics that allow the exercise of this very specific, albeit very complex, power that has the population as its target, political economy as its major form of knowledge, and apparatuses of security as its essential technical instrument.[13]

---

[11] See Vegetti, Mario: Foucault e gli antichi. In: Pier Aldo Rovatti (a cura di): Effetto Foucault. Milano: Feltrinelli 1986, pp. 39–45; Cambiano, Giuseppe: Il ritorno degli antichi. Bari: Laterza 1988; Vegetti, Mario: L'ermeneutica del soggetto. Foucault, gli antichi e noi. In: Mario Galzigna (a cura di): Foucault, oggi. Milano: Feltrinelli 2008, pp. 150–161. They also blame Foucault for having practiced the history of ancient philosophy in a very traditional way.

[12] Vegetti: L'ermeneutica del soggetto (note 11), pp. 152–153.

[13] Foucault, Michel: Security, Territory and Population. Lectures at the Collège de France 1977–78 (2004). Transl. by Graham Burchell. London: Palgrave Macmillan 2009, p. 108.

2) The tendency, the line of force, that for a long time, and throughout the West, has constantly led towards the pre-eminence over all other types of power — sovereignty, discipline, and so on — of the type of power that we can call 'government' and which has led to the development of a series of specific governmental apparatuses (*appareils*) on the one hand, [and, on the other] to the development of a series of knowledges (*savoirs*).[14]
3) The process, or rather, the result of the process by which the state of justice of the Middle Ages became the administrative state in the fifteenth and sixteenth centuries and was gradually 'governmentalized'.[15]

In this analysis, he suggests that the governmentality would have been appeared from the archaic pastoral model together with the use of a diplomatic-military technique and the institution of the police. However, in his lecture on 8th February he defines this more precisely: it consists in a power of care exercised over population (and not over a territory); it is a beneficent power, whose aim is firstly "the salvation of the flock", that is its livelihood; it is an individualizing power, which takes care of the flock *omnes et singulatim*, namely, of the flock globally and of every member singly.[16] According to Foucault, this power has nothing to do with Greek thought and it would be rather typical of the East, from which it would have been spread, because of the dissemination of Christianity.[17] In short:

1) The Greek tradition rejects the idea of pastorate.
2) There is no political reflection on it.
3) It is not one of the greatest forms of organization which may witness an interest in this kind of power, but rather it is exhibited in the small communities, be it philosophical or religious, that is, all those communities in which different forms of spiritual direction were possible.

---

[14] Idem.
[15] Idem, pp. 108–109.
[16] Idem, p. 128.
[17] Idem, p. 147.

In conclusion, he states that pastoral power would have been imposed by itself through Christianity and its daily government of men and their lives.[18] As we will see further, while resuming some features of pastoral power, Foucault devotes a considerable part to analyzing Greek texts in the lecture which he delivered on 15th February.

Foucault returns to this notion during three conferences and all of them took place in 1978 or later: This fact confirms the pivotal role of that year.[19] The most famous formulation of "pastoral power" is to be found in *Omnes et Singulatim: Towards a Criticism of Political Reason*, a text which gathers two lectures delivered at the University of Stanford.[20] During these lectures, he resumed the analysis of the course of the previous year, but proposed a strong schematization between the "Greco-Roman moment" and the Christian one.[21] In April 1978, he delivered two lectures (*La philosophie analytique de la politique* and *Sexualité et pouvoir*) in Japan.[22] During these conferences, he insisted on the role of Christianity in the development of this kind of power. In the first of the two, *Sexualité et pouvoir*, Foucault aimed to present to his public the state of his research and his focus during that time: the history of sexuality. He explained his concern to the topic as the interest towards what he called a form of "sur-savoir", that is an excessive knowledge. He defines this knowledge as a special attention to the topic not limited to a particular individual, but culturally and socially widespread. According to Foucault, the outbreak of this interest and the consequent development of the psychoanalysis was dependant on the tension between this

---

[18] Idem, pp. 148ff.
[19] Fruchaud/Bert: Un inédit de Michel Foucault (note 7), p. 154.
[20] Foucault, Michel: Omnes et singulatim: Towards a Criticism of Political Reason. In: Sterling M. McMurrin (Ed.): The Tanner Lectures on Human Values. Vol. 2. Salt Lake City: University of Utah Press 1981, pp. 223–254.
[21] We do not have time to deal with the issue, but this reading seems particularly in debt with Nietzsche's view on Antiquity. Foucault declares his "nietzschéisme fondamental" and claims the reading of Nietzsche's works as one of his most important philosophical experiences. It should also be clarified how Heidegger influences his view on Antiquity. See Foucault, Michel: Le retour de la morale. In: Daniel Defert / François Ewald (Eds.): Michel Foucault, Dits et écrits II, 1976–1988. Paris: Gallimard 2001, pp. 1515–1526.
[22] Foucault, Michel: La philosophie analytique de la politique. In: Defert/Ewald (Eds.): Michel Foucault (note 21), pp. 534–551; Foucault, Michel: Sexualité et pouvoir. In: Idem, pp. 552–570.

hyperproduction of the discourse about sexuality and people's unfamiliarity to their own desires.[23] According to the traditional account, the history of Western sexuality is divided in three phases (Antiquity, Christianity, Bourgeoisie age), and Christianity would have played the interdictory role.[24]

On the basis of Paul Veyne's works on Roman sexuality, Foucault rejected this tripartite scheme.[25] His research clearly showed that sexual interdiction norms were present also before Christianity: In fact, Stoicism, circulating throughout the Roman world and strengthened by social and ideological structures of the Empire, had already spread a different code of sexual morality.[26] So what has changed? According to Foucault, Christianity would not have introduced new ideas about morality; rather, it would have promoted new techniques, that is, new mechanisms of *power*, in order to impose this morality, which in fact was not new.[27] The old and the new "regimes of morality" differ mainly in that Christianity is characterized by pastoral power, a kind of power represented by individuals, who take the role of a shepherd and exercise a spiritual direction on other people.[28] To him, Greek and Roman texts did not witness this pastoral image to define the ruler. On the contrary, the pastorate was to be found in the Eastern Mediterranean, in particular in Jewish culture;[29] the shepherd rules over a multitude and not a territory and Foucault stressed the idea of a "wandering God" in the Oriental tradition.[30] At the end of the lecture, after tackling the same features of pastoral power which has already been mentioned,[31] Foucault connected the spread of pastorate and the new morality to the practical organization of Christianity (churches, status and offices of the

---

[23] Foucault: Sexualité et pouvoir (note 22), p. 554.
[24] Idem, p. 558.
[25] Idem, p. 559. Due to their friendship, Foucault could read and discuss Veyne's works before their publication.
[26] Idem, pp. 558f.
[27] Idem, p. 560.
[28] See Carrette, Jeremie: Rupture and Transformation: Foucault's Concept of Spirituality Reconsidered. In: Foucault Studies 15 (2013), pp. 52–71 on the translation of "direction de la conscience" with "spiritual direction".
[29] Idem, p. 561.
[30] Foucault: Omnes et Singulatim (note 20), pp. 125–126.
[31] See above the discussion of his course *Security, Territory and Population*.

priests).[32] Although, passing over the concrete dynamics of its success, he affirms that Christianity succeeded in discrediting body and sexual pleasure; sexuality became therefore a means of control and power over individuals.[33] At the same time, the pastorate based this kind of control on a number of techniques, such as internalization, confession, awareness of your own faults, which contributed to develop conscience and subjectivity.[34] Christian pastorate, thus, connects the domain of power and control with that of knowledge and subjectification. This change in perspective — from an analysis of repression and interdictions to an interest in scientific discourses and subjectification through moral conducts — was observed and underlined by Shigehiko Hasumi, a film critic and academic scholar, during the debate following this lecture: Hasumi added that the same change occurred between the first course at Collège de France and the *History of Sexuality*.[35] As in *Sexualité et pouvoir*, in the authorized volumes, Foucault contrasts the Graeco-Roman world to Christianity and likewise he argues that an ethics of austerity was already endorsed and at work in the "not Christian" epoch.[36] In the second conference, *La philosophie analytique de la politique*, Foucault advocates the new task for philosophy. After having observed the example of analytical philosophy and its effect on language, the political philosophy should analyse the ordinary power relationships which are carried out in the society everyday.[37] In particular, one of the goals of this new kind of philosophy should be to assess the importance of apparently marginal political actions: These fights did not aim to revolutionize or reform the society, but rather to destabilize it.[38] Foucault maintained that the hidden target of these struggles was the pastorate, a kind of power which claims to direct the people throughout their lives and steer moral behavior.[39]

---

[32] Foucault: Sexualité et pouvoir (note 22), p. 562.
[33] Idem.
[34] Idem, p. 564.
[35] Idem, p. 567.
[36] Foucault: The History of Sexuality (note 5), pp. 14–15.
[37] Foucault: La philosophie analytique (note 22), p. 541.
[38] Idem, pp. 542–546.
[39] Idem, p. 548.

3. Pastoral power and Foucault's Greek sources

We have seen that Foucault's texts which concern pastoral power were elaborated by reflecting upon Antiquity. I will now illustrate Foucault's analysis of Greek sources and then point out some limits of his reading.

Foucault did not examine Greek texts in all the contributions in which he mentioned the pastoral power. He treated extensively Greek sources only during his course *Security, territory and population* and returned to some issues in *Omnes et singulatim;* the two other conferences, instead, were more concerned with defining the features of pastoral power and the task of philosophy.

The lecture, which Foucault delivered on 15th February from his 1977/78 course, deals with those sources which help to prove the importance of pastoral image of the Greeks. First of all, he identifies three groups of texts: Homeric poems, Pythagorean writings, and political literature. Foucault admits that in the first group one may find a great number of occurrences of the "shepherd", namely the expression ποιμὴν λαῶν (poimēn laōn), with regard to the king and in particular Agamemnon; he suggests, however, that this case is consistent with the rest of Indo-European literature and might be understood as a ritual title.[40] The Pythagorean tradition was interested in the image for two reasons: Firstly, they made derive νόμος (nomos), "the law", from νομεύς (nomeus), "the shepherd". Secondly, because in Pythagorean thought the magistrate is benevolent. Yet, he observes that Pythagoreanism was a marginal tradition and cannot be considered as largely influential.[41] As for the last group, Foucault points out that two interpretations exist: The first asserts that the image of the shepherd was rare and coming from the East, while the other maintains that this metaphor was a commonplace.[42] He acknowledges nevertheless that Platonic writings are an exception and he commits himself to a close analysis of these texts.[43]

---

[40] Foucault: Security, territory, population (note 13), p. 136.
[41] Idem, p. 137.
[42] Idem, pp. 137–138. For our purpose it is important to notice that even Delatte, who does not deny the existence of this image, refers to "political literature" of 4th century B.C. See: Delatte, Armand: Essai sur la politique pythagoricienne. Geneva: Slaktine 1979, p. 121.
[43] Idem, p. 138.

Putting aside the *Statesman*, Foucault identifies three uses of the image. The shepherd could firstly recur in relation to gods, who nurtured and watched over humanity at the moment of their birth: The *Critias* and the *Statesman* witness this association.[44] Secondly, it is in reference to the magistrate of the present that one may find the metaphor in the *Laws*; in Book X the magistrate is presented as a shepherd, but, according to Foucault, this officer should not be considered as the essence of power in this city. According to Foucault, this magistrate does not represent other than a subordinate and his condition is intermediate between that of a "policeman" and that of the major magistrates in the city. Moreover, this "shepherd" is neither the founder of the city nor the legislator and he is different from those figures: he is only a functionary.[45] Finally, in the *Republic* Thrasymachus recalls the image of the shepherd, in order to challenge the idea of a beneficent power and, on the contrary, conceives the ruler as someone who serves his own ends. This thesis is in line with his idea about justice: this is the interest of the stronger.[46] In this case, Foucault acknowledges that the image of the shepherd probably represents a commonplace, if not in collective imagination of the Greeks, at least in Socratic circles. In his opinion, this metaphor witnesses the interest of these circles to the Pythagorean idea of politics as shepherding.[47] According to Foucault, the *Statesman* is specially committed to this theme and he analyzes in detail how the argument against this idea is built up. The French philosopher identifies the method of division as the first instrument to rebut the politician-shepherd. The divisions allow to point out two implications of the image, which turns

---

[44] Delatte: Essai sur la politique pythagoricienne (note 42), p. 139; Plato: Critias. In: Id.: Timaeus, Critias, Cleitophon, Menexenus, Epistles. Transl. by R. G. Bury. Cambridge, MA: Harvard University Press 1942, 109 b-c.

[45] Delatte: Essai sur la politique pythagoricienne (note 42), p. 139. Plato: Nomoi. In: Id.: Laws. Vol. 2. Transl. by R. G. Bury. Cambridge, MA: Harvard University Press 1926, Book X, 906 b-c.

[46] Plato: Politeia. In: Id.: Republic. Books 1–5. Ed. and transl. by Chris Emlyn-Jones / William Preddy. Cambridge, MA: Harvard University Press 2014, Book I, 343 a-345 e; 416 a-b, 440 d. One might state that he has in mind the tyrant; at the end of 5th century the crisis of democratic institutions in Athens brought some groups to revalue this figure. See: Giorgini, Giovanni: La città e il tiranno. Il concetto di tirannide nella Grecia del VII-IV secolo a. C. Milano: Giuffrè editore 1991.

[47] Foucault: Security, territory, population (note 13), p. 140.

to be useless to define the politician. Indeed, the analogy between animals and men, as well as the plurality of functions which this metaphor implies, pose problems and do not exactly correspond — according to Foucault's reading — to Plato's idea of politics. The third step is, therefore, to determine the nature of politics; Foucault considers that the answer is to be found in the myth.[48] The myth indeed tells us that politics began when the gods retreated: Before this moment, humanity did not need political constitution, precisely because they had the gods-shepherds who provided everything.[49] However, it remains to establish a positive image for the politicians. Hence, Plato proposed the weaver as an effective model, since politics would be the *techne* able to weave together all the individuals in the *polis*. At the end of this detailed analysis, Foucault underlines Plato's strong criticism towards this image. According to the French philosopher, the platonic refusal, together with the absence of the shepherd in classical Greek political vocabulary, clearly indicate the exclusion of such representation in Greek thought.[50]

While in *Sexualité et pouvoir* Foucault just states that Plato's *Statesman* confirms the refusal of this notion,[51] in *Omnes et singulatim* he proposes again a brief discussion of platonic texts. The analysis is fundamentally the same of *Security, territory and population*. In the Stanford lectures, however, Foucault insists on *Statesman's* myth and his importance to understand the image of the shepherd. One could notice that Foucault contradicts himself or rather seems uncertain about the diffusion of this image.[52]

In short, if the figure of the "shepherd of the people" as commander appears in Homer's texts, in Foucault's opinion it rarely occurs after, and

---

[48] Idem, p. 144; Plato: Politikos. In: Id.: The Statesman, Philebus, Ion. Transl. by Harold N. Fowler. Cambridge, MA: Harvard University Press 1975, 267 c-277 d; Plato: Ion. Transl. by W. R. M. Lamb. Cambridge, MA: Harvard University Press 2014. The myth narrates that before the present age, the age of Zeus, there was the age of Chronos. In this past time, humanity lived in peace with the animals, should not work to feed themselves and was ruled by the gods, who were their shepherds.

[49] Foucault: Security, territory, population (note 13), p. 144–145.

[50] Idem, p. 146.

[51] Foucault: Sexualité et pouvoir (note 22), p. 560. Foucault does not mention any Greek text.

[52] Compare for instance: Foucault: Security, Territory, Population (note 13), pp. 138, 140 and Foucault: Omnes et singulatim (note 20), p. 233.

Plato mentions it to turn its positive meaning upside down. Foucault interprets the platonic rebuttal of the image *consistent* (i. e. *homogeneous*) with its absence from other "political texts". But then, if the image of the shepherd was not common, why should Plato have shown so much concern to dismantle and disprove it? I will just take a quick look at the occurrences of the shepherd in Greek texts previous and contemporary to Plato's dialogues.

4. Ancient Philosophy in its Context

As we have seen, Foucault's remarks on Plato's texts were generally quite accurate. In *Security, territory and population* he analyzed platonic occurrences and put them into their contexts. However, Foucault excluded some other texts and thus tracked the occurrences only partially; this choice prevented him to have a global understanding of the pastoral image.[53] In fact, he explicitly declared his decision to confine himself to political writings.[54] As we will see, this reading was biased by a certain interpretation of ancient philosophy, particularly, Platonic writings and their goals.

Even though we cannot analyse the texts in detail, one may briefly list the occurrences of different terms, which mean "shepherd" and make a few general comments. Purposely I have omitted the verb νέμω (nemō), whose occurrences should be examined accurately case by case, in order to distinguish its different meanings. Due to the lack of space I also leave out the different terms which mean "flock" and the different kinds of cattle (sheep, goats, etc.), which in fact contribute towards creating this imagery network. Ποιμήν (poimēn) is a general and vague word, which means "herdsman", both of sheep and oxen,[55] and equally

---

[53] We have carried out the research through: Thesaurus Linguae Graecae® (TLG). A Digital Library of Greek Literature. Ed. by Maria C. Pantelia. University of California, Irvine. http://www.tlg.uci.edu/ (10.10.2016).

[54] Foucault: Security, Territory, Population (note 13), p. 137 and Foucault: Omnes et Singulatim (note 20), p. 232.

[55] Occurrences of ποιμήν: Homer (68), in particular ποιμήν λαῶν (poimēn laōn), "the shepherd of the people"; Hesiod (12); lyric poetry (4); Aesop (67); Pindar (2), Aeschylus (10); Sophocles (7); Euripides (11); Cratinus (2); Plato (24); Xenophon (3).

indistinct is the word νομεύς.⁵⁶ There are then specific terms for "specialized" shepherds: βουκόλος (boukolos)⁵⁷ – "the cowherd", συβώτης (sybōtēs)⁵⁸ – "the swineherd", αἰπόλος (aipolos)⁵⁹ – "the goatherd", οἰοπόλος (oiopolos)⁶⁰ – "who takes care of the sheep". Special attention must be paid to the formulaic expression ποιμὴν λαῶν (poimēn laōn).⁶¹ This homeric formula occurs in military contexts and, according to Brock, it refers to "directing and marshalling an unruly crowd".⁶² Haubold maintains that in Homeric texts the shepherd appears as a paradoxical figure: important and valued, yet often ineffective.⁶³ Moreover, Haubold notices that, at least in Homer, the shepherd is not the owner of the flock; Thrasymacus in the *Republic* is the first who associates the two.⁶⁴ To the same lexical domain belong the generic verbs ποιμαίνω (poimainō)⁶⁵ "to herd" and βόσκω (boskō)⁶⁶ "to tend", as well as the more concrete βουκολέω

---

[56] Occurrences of νομεύς: Homer (13); Hesiod (1); Sophocles (1); Plato (22); Xenophon (11).

[57] Occurrences of βουκόλος: Homer (15); Hesiod (2); Lyric poetry: 2 (Archilocus and Anacreon); Aesop (7); Aeschylus (2); Euripides (14); Sophocles (4); Cratinus (9); Xenophon (3); Plato (10).

[58] Occurrences of συβώτης: Homer (70); Plato (2).

[59] Occurrences of αἰπόλος: Homer (11); Hesiod (1); Aesop (5); Sophocles (1); Cratinus (1); Eupolis (2); Plato (2).

[60] Occurrences of οἰοπόλος: Homer (5); Pindar (2).

[61] As observes Benveniste, λαός expresses the personal relationship between a group of men and their chef by mutual agreement. See: Benveniste, Émile: Le vocabulaire des institutions indo-européennes. Pouvoir, droit, religion. Vol. 2. Paris: Les Éditions de Minuit 1969, pp. 90, 95.

[62] Brock, Roger: Greek Political Imagery. From Homer to Aristotle. London, New York: Bloomsbury Academic 2013, p. 43.

[63] Haubold, James: Homer's People. Epic Poetry and Social Formation. Cambridge: Cambridge University Press 2000, pp. 17–20.

[64] Idem, p. 23.

[65] Occurrences of ποιμαίνω: Homer (4); Hesiod (1); Lyric poetry (3); tragedy (7); Crates (1); Plato (3).

[66] Occurrences of βόσκω: Homer (22); Aesop (1); lyric poetry (2); tragedy (21); comedy (20) Aeschylus (2); Plato (3). After Homer, the verb refers to slaves, soldiers and women. See Chantraine, Pierre: Dictionnaire étymologique de la langue grecque. Paris: Éditions Klincksieck 1990, pp. 185–186.

(boukoleō)[67], συβωτέω (sybōteō)[68], αἰπολέω (aipoleō)[69], οἰοπολέω (oiopoleō)[70].

From this general overview, it results in the idea that the majority of the occurrences are to be found in Homer and also Plato's writings show a great number of examples,[71] as Foucault has rightly remarked. But one may frequently find words belonging to this semantic domain in other texts, such as Aesop's fables and tragedies; these genres were not of little significance for collective imagination.[72] As Brock has argued, notably absent are also the occurrences within Xenophon's corpus.[73] Although they are fewer, they referred to the ruler, and thus appear of crucial importance for 4th century's political thought, both in connection with and in opposition to Plato's texts.[74] In Plato's texts, the image has a negative value or qualifies a divine ruler, which does not belong to this time – and this

---

[67] Occurrences of βουκολέω Homer (5); Aesop (1); tragedy (3); comedy (4); Plato (1). I follow here Benveniste, who argues that the verb is specific for "herding cows". In fact, one might remark that the verb is used also for horses (Ilias 20.221), goats (Eupolis, fr. 18) and with the direct objet βοῦς (cows) expressed (Ilias 21.448). This last case shows that the meaning of "tending cows" is not necessarily implicit, as argued by Benveniste. Benveniste: Le vocabulaire des institutions indo-européennes (note 61). Vol. 1, p. 41. I have excluded two occurrences, both in Menander's *Samia*, because in these cases βουκολέω means "to cheat". It would be however interesting to understand how the word has changed meaning.

[68] Occurrences of συβωτέω: Plato (1).

[69] Occurrences of αἰπολέω: tragedy (1); comedy (1).

[70] Occurrences of οἰοπολέω: Euripides (1), but in this case, according to the scholion, it means "roam alone".

[71] Total occurrences: Homer (208); Plato (56)

[72] Total occurrences: Aesop (83), tragedy (81).

[73] Brock: Greek Political Imagery (note 62), n. 1, p. 49. It seems to me, however, that Brock makes the same error of Foucault: He excludes comic texts from consideration.

[74] See Noël, Marie-Pierre: Cyrus, bon roi et bon pasteur selon Xénophon (Cyropédie, VIII, 2, 13–25). In: Troïka. Parcours antiques 2 (2012), pp. 191–201. See also Nicolaïdou-Kyrianidou, Vana: Autorité et obéissance: le maître idéal de Xénophon face à son idéal de prince. In: Michel Narcy / Alonso Tordesillas (Éds.): Xénophon et Socrate. Actes du colloque d'Aix-en-Provence (6–9 novembre 2003). Paris: Vrin 2008, pp. 205–234.

world.⁷⁵ It is Xenophon who employs the image in its positive connotations: To him the shepherd symbolizes a mutual relationship, in which the sovereign makes his subordinates happy, while he 'uses' and profits from them.⁷⁶ This means, as Brock has remarked, that probably this image was a commonplace within Socratic circles, where references to concrete images were common.⁷⁷

One further observation could however be made. In the overall calculation, we find 18 occurrences in comedy, often in fragments.⁷⁸ In these cases it is hard to reconstruct the precise context, but comic occurrences should draw our attention, because comic representations extensively deal with politics and collective imagination.⁷⁹ One comic occurrence has been analysed in a recent article by Olimpia Imperio, where she shows that Aristophanes' *Ecclesiazusae* contains an allusion to the image of the Demagogue as shepherd.⁸⁰ But in fact, we have other comic texts, where this metaphor is employed. One fragment of Cratinus, not attributed to any comedy, says:

---

[75] See Brock: Greek Political Imagey (note 62), pp. 45–48. In addition to Plato's standard occurrences (see notes 42, 43, 44 and 46), I suggest that it should be also considered ὄνων [...] ἐπιμελητὴς καὶ ἵππων καὶ βοῶν ("a herdsman in charge of asses or horses or oxen"), in: Plato: Gorgias. In: Id.: Lysis, Symposium, Gorgias. Transl. by Walter R. M. Lamb. Cambridge, MA: Harvard University Press 1925, 516 a5.

[76] The Greek word is χρῆσθαι (chrēsthai), which means "use" and it often occurs with an instrumental dative.

[77] Brock: Greek Political Imagery (note 62), p. 45.

[78] I have considered only those occurrences which are or could be relevant to the shepherd or shepherding as metaphors for the politician and ruling. I have excluded titles and occurrences which evidently could not have to do with this use, such as some of βόσκω and βουκολέω.

[79] Interestingly, in the *Statesman* and in the *Critias* the image of the shepherd occurs together with the motif of the Golden Age. Many scholars have rightly observed that the Golden Age motif dates back to Hesiod, but one should not forget that the theme was popular also in the comedy. For the relationship between Golden Age and politics in comedy: Ceccarelli, Paola: L'Athènes de Périclès: Un "Pays de cocagne"? L'idéologie démocratique et l'αὐτόματος βίος dans la comédie ancienne". In: Quaderni Urbinati di Cultura Classica 54 (1996), pp. 109–159.

[80] Imperio, Olimpia: Utopie antiche (e moderne) tra commedia e filosofia: a proposito di Aristofane, Ecclesiazuse, vv. 76–81. In: Dionysus ex machina 5 (2014), pp. 77–92.

"My post is herder; goats and kine I tend."[81] This fragment is quoted by Dio Chrysostom in the discourse on kingship, with reference to the rulers (archontes).[82]

> Are there certain persons who are rulers of men, just as there are some who are rulers of goats, others of swine, others of horses, others of cattle, these one and all having in common the title herders; or have you not read this verse of Cratinus? *My post is herder; goats and kine I tend. Int.* I could not tell you whether it is better to call all who tend animals herders or not. *Dio.* Not merely those who tend brute beasts, my good fellow, but human beings too, if one should put any faith in Homer regarding these matters.

Moreover, various comedies bear pastoral names: We know Cratinus's *Boukoloi*, Sophocles' satirical drama *Poimenes*, Alexis' *Aipoloi*. These are all clues that the image was a widespread commonplace. One might suppose that, after the great crisis of democratic institutions, authority and the rulers' qualities had probably become an important issue of debate.

To sum up, every author and corpus could have stressed upon different aspects of the image of the shepherd, though within a defined network of possible meanings; nevertheless, one may suppose that Plato adopted this metaphor because it was generally linked to rulers and was quite widespread.

After having quantitatively reconstructed the network of occurrences and having placed them within their broader context, I will deal with the second risk: the "teleological" reading[83]. Teleological readings are interpretations which fail to find a discontinuity and project features of modern or contemporary phenomena to ancient ones.

Foucault characterizes the Greek and the Christian image of the shepherd in the same way. According to him, in both tradition the shepherd is the one who watches over and takes care of his flock. However, as Haubold

---

[81] ποιμὴν καθέστηκ᾽· αἰπολῶ καὶ βουκολῶ. Cratinus. In: Poetae Comici Graeci. Vol. 4: Aristophon – Crobylus. Ed. by Rudolf Kassel / Colin Austin. Berlin: de Gruyter 1983, fr. K.-A. 313.

[82] Dio Chrysostome: Vol. IV: Discourses 37–60. Transl. by H. Lamar Crosby. Cambridge, MA: Harvard University Press / Loeb Classical Library 1946, 56.2.

[83] Cambiano: Perché leggere i classici (note 1), p. 162.

has underlined, one must be cautious to equalize the two[84] and only recontextualization could avoid undifferentiated readings.[85] Certainly, Plato could not accept the idea of quasi-divine and all-powerful men and should have considered such image as an improper tool to conceive the ruler; it was likely the main reason for which he refused the metaphor.[86] In the political debate of 4th century, what mattered was less the subordinate's features than the ruler's ones.[87] One might suppose that within Christian pastorate such dissymmetry was accepted because of special link between God and the "Christian shepherd". Anyway, also in this case it would be better to reconstruct the more general context and, as far as possible, use different kinds of sources, as Foucault has done for Modern Age.

From this brief and general outline, one may draw some provisory conclusions. One may affirm that in this case, Foucault fails to apply to Antiquity the method which he advocates in the introduction of *The Use of Pleasure*.[88] The limits of his analysis concern homogenization in two respects. On the one hand, Foucault provides a homogeneous account of pastorate over the centuries (*diachronic homogenization*). Especially in *Omnes and sin-*

---

[84] Haubold: Homer's people (note 63), p. 20: "The shepherd of biblical narrative is a far more positive figure than the one we find in Homer, and it is he, rather his hapless counterpart, who came to dominate the imagination of Europe and its cultural descendants."

[85] Alain Brossat, specialist of Foucault's thought, has recently addressed criticism on this point, arguing that the pastorate establishes a huge dissymmetry between the ruler and the ruled. According to Foucault's categories, this means that within the pastorate the equal and active nature of the subjects is not acknowledged and the human condition, shepherd metaphors aside, is exclusively reserved to the ruler. See Brossat, Alain: Pouvoir pastoral et "vie bête". In: https://appareil.revues.org/898 (10.09.2016).

[86] We do not have time to deal with this topic, but one may incidentally remark that *Gorgias* is also devoted to make clear that no man, not even the tyrant, could have such a divine power.

[87] On the importance of the debate about "the best (rulers)" see: De Luise, Fulvia: La scienza del potere ovvero il potere dei tecnici: la questione dei "migliori" tra Repubblica e Politico. In: Fulvia de Luise (a cura di): Legittimazione del potere, autorità della legge: un dibattito antico. Trento: Edizioni del Dipartimento di Lettere e Filosofia 2016, pp. 75–105. On Plato's *Statesman* see: El Murr, Dimitri: Savoir et gouverner. Essai sur la science politique platonicienne. Paris: Vrin 2014.

[88] Foucault: The History of Sexuality (note 5), pp. 3–13.

gulatim, he attributes to the metaphor of the shepherd the same features throughout the ages and retroactively looks for characteristics of Christian pastorate into the Greek texts.[89] On the other hand, restricting his analysis to political literature, Foucault conceives Plato's texts as the mirror of 5th and 4th century Athens, or atleast gives the impression to do so (*synchronic homogenization*). In fact, as we have seen, it may be useful to extend the analysis in Greek texts of genres other than "political literature". The number of occurrences in epics and fables alone should warn us to exclude the presence of the image of the shepherd from the collective imagination of the Greeks of 5th and 4th century B. C. In addition, the history of textual transmission should also be considered: Comic occurrences, indeed, are sporadic, but one should not forget the narrow amount and the fragmentary state of these texts. In addition, although the almost complete loss of comedies, one may notice how the comic occurrences seem to be associated with political leaders.[90] One should also consider the remarks about shepherding and medical profession which we have already mentioned. On the basis of these remarks, one might suppose that the association shepherd-leader was relatively common and that Plato devoted much attention to this metaphor precisely because it was present over the 5th and the 6th Century B. C.[91]

The notion of "pastoral power" bridges Foucault's interest in power to his attention to the subject: Its discussion witnesses the shifting from the so called political to the ethical Foucault, and the issue of subject involves an increasing interest for Antiquity. Besides the ethical concerns, however, in

---

[89] Foucault: Omnes et singulatim (note 20), p. 234–235.
[90] I think that a quantitative and a quality approach should be combined as far as possible.
[91] I believe that this limit in Foucault's analysis depends on a "philosophical bias". Socratic literature and Plato's dialogues in particular are linked only to "serious philosophy". In my opinion, this bias prevents to understand that Plato's dialogues deal with all forms of knowledge. Through dialogues Plato claimed to deeply revise both knowledge and believe in the πόλις. Therefore his writings deal at the same time with the most "intellectual" theorizations (Pythagoreanism, for instance) and the most common and widespread images (the kind of culture whose comedy could be representative). Although on a different scale, I think that a similar bias generally recurs in the study of ancient philosophy.

Foucault's questioning on Antiquity, one may see the rise of an epistemological issue about cultural representation: How change has to be conceived, avoiding the trick of the invariant, the traditional concept of continuity and the idea of sudden and inexplicable ruptures? Indeed, if we consider the cultures as coherent and homogeneous agglomerates, as we do when we refer to "the Greeks" or "the Greek culture", this last option is unavoidable.

5. Conclusion

In my paper I have tried to examine Foucault's approach to Antiquity through a case-study, the notion of "pastoral power". I have shown how some philosophical bias are present in Foucault's analysis of Greek texts and I have sketched a different interpretation of the image of the shepherd, including genres he had excluded. In particular, what I wanted to underline is the importance of "less serious" texts for the understanding of ancient societies.

Foucault's approach to Antiquity has, thus, some limits in historical reconstruction and conceals a certain resistance to make Greek texts undergo the same treatment he previously reserved for Modern age.[92] Despite these limits, it seems that Foucault's work on Antiquity leads to the emergence of a different gaze in this field of interest. Through the *History of Sexuality*, Foucault aims to question the everyday-life and recent notion of "sexuality", to put it into perspective, to skirt its familiar obviousness, to examine the theoretical and practical context to which it is related, as he declares in the "Introduction" of *The Use of Pleasure*.[93] But why is this concern to Antiquity and history in general so important for Foucault? To him, historical thinking turns out to be the most effective instrument for critical thinking[94] and the past could offer a view from afar, from which one may look criti-

---

[92] See Vegetti: L'ermeneutica del soggetto (note 11).
[93] Foucault: The History of Sexuality (note 5), p. 3.
[94] At the beginning of *The Use of Pleasure* (in: *The Historiy of Sexuality*), Foucault maintains the importance of "the effort to think one's own history", because it "can free thought from what it silently thinks, and so enable it to think differently". Idem, p. 9. See Cremonesi, Laura: Michel Foucault e il mondo antico. Spunti per una critica dell'attualità. Pisa: Edizioni ETS 2008.

cally towards Western world.[95] For a specialist of Classics, this attitude sounds very similar to historical anthropology, an approach to Antiquity, which was spreading during those years, mostly in France: Antiquity could now be examined as "a foreign country" and it does not work as the unquestioned origin of Western values.[96] As it has been remarked, Foucault fails to apply the contextual approach he advocates in *The History of Sexuality* to ancient practices and problematizations – his treatment of ancient philosophy and the image of thinkers, such as Plato, persists fundamentally traditional.

Nevertheless, Foucault had a strong influence on the following course of historical disciplines, providing theoretical references to Classics scholars. But above all, his works on Antiquity involuntarily succeeded to show that power behind the mask of authoritative knowledge is hard to unveil, to such an extent that, even for posterity, it is so hard to get rid of it.[97]

---

[95] Foucault explicitly endorses "an ethnological gaze on Western world from Greece" in: Foucault: La philosophie analytique (note 22), p. 537.

[96] For historical anthropology's critical approach, see for example Vernant, Jean-Pierre: Introduction. In Marc Augé / Cornélius Castoriadis / Maria Daraki / Philippe Descola / Claude Mosse / André Motte / Gilbert Romeyer-Dherbey / Marie-Henriette Quet (Éds.): La Grèce pour penser l'avenir. Paris: L'Harmattan 2000, pp. 13–23. Although according to Joly, Foucault did not read much Vernant and Detienne's works, their projects sound extraordinarily similar. Joly underlines Foucault's combination of this view from afar together with a close vision speaks about a transformation of the view through distance and modification of the landscape through study, enough to think differently. See Joly: Retour aux Grecs (note 10).

[97] I think that Foucault's case is instructive for two reasons: On the one hand, because it clearly appears the (often) prejudicial mistrust of specialists towards new approaches; on the other, because Foucault was mislead by ancient discursive practices, which still exert their "power" as the "noble" origins of Western culture. This is especially the case for philosophy.

Der ununterbrochene Dialog
zwischen Jorge Luis Borges und Michel Foucault

Valeria Fernandez Blanco

In seinem Text *Der ununterbrochene Dialog: zwischen zwei Unendlichkeiten, das Gedicht*[1] legt Derrida die Eigenart seines Gesprächs mit Hans-Georg Gadamer dar, ein gewissermaßen paradoxes Gespräch, das trotz Unterbrechungen, zuletzt infolge von Gadamers Tod, ununterbrochen anhält. Am Anfang des Textes spricht Derrida von einer gewissen Melancholie, die seiner Bewunderung für Hans-Georg Gadamer anhaftet, unmittelbar danach erklärt der französische Philosoph den genauen Modus zweier Erscheinungsformen dieser Melancholie:

> Der Tod hat diese Melancholie sicherlich verändert, durch ihn lastet sie unendlich schwerer. Der Tod hat sie besiegelt. Für immer. Es fällt mir aber dennoch schwer zu unterscheiden, unter diesem starr gewordenen, versteinerten Siegel, in dieser schwer zu lesenden, aber auch irgendwie gesegneten Unterschrift, inwiefern sie auf den Tod des Freundes zurückgeht oder ihm schon lange vorangegangen ist. Schon bei unserer ersten Begegnung in Paris 1981 muß mich diese Melancholie, eine andere damals und doch dieselbe, befallen haben. Unsere Diskussion konnte wohl nur mit einer merkwürdigen Unterbrechung beginnen, die nicht etwa ein Missverständnis war, sondern eine Art Sprachlosigkeit, eine Hemmung des noch unentschiedenen […]. Da stand ich, mit offenem Mund, sprachlos. Ich sprach kaum mit ihm. Und was ich damals sagte, richtete sich nur indirekt an ihn. Und doch war ich mir sicher, dass wir von nun an auf eine merkwürdige, aber innige Weise etwas teilen würden. Vielleicht eine Teilhaberschaft. Damals schon hatte ich eine Vorahnung. Was Gadamer wahr-

---

[1] Jacques, Derrida: Der ununterbrochene Dialog zwischen zwei Unendlichkeiten, das Gedicht. In: Ders. / Hans-Georg Gadamer: Der ununterbrochene Dialog. Frankfurt/Main: Suhrkamp 2004, S. 8.

scheinlich einen „inneren Dialog" genannt hätte, sollte in jedem von uns weitergeführt werden, manchmal wortlos, unmittelbar in uns oder indirekt.[2]

Was schon den Anfang dieses Textes so interessant macht, ist die Erwähnung der Sprachlosigkeit und die Tatsache, dass der Dialog mit Gadamer mit dieser Sprachlosigkeit beginnt. Mit Teilhaberschaft meint Derrida ein – im ersten Moment überraschend klingendes – Ereignis, das zwischen zwei Individuen stattfindet: Es handelt sich um eine bestimmte Form von Anwesenheit und Energie, die auch die Abwesenheit des Dialogpartners oder sogar den Tod überdauern kann.

Diese Abwesenheit beider Gesprächspartner, an der nicht nur der Tod Schuld trägt, ist zentral für meine These: Trotz des nicht zustande kommenden Zusammentreffens beider Gesprächspartner findet im Text ein Dialog statt. Wie dies genau passiert, wird zu erklären versucht.

Der Text von Derrida übertrifft gewissermaßen sich selbst: Es handelt sich eher um die Suche Derridas nach seinem Gesprächspartner Gadamer als um eine tatsächliche Begegnung zwischen beiden. Was Derrida in dem oben erwähnten Zitat beschreibt, klingt auf den ersten Blick wie das Scheitern eines Dialogs: Derrida erwähnt, dass er „kaum" mit Gadamer spricht und sich nur indirekt an ihn richtet.

Aus Derridas Beschreibung dieser ersten Begegnung mit Gadamer kann man folgern, dass er sich ehrlich mit diesem Gefühl der Melancholie auseinandersetzt, ohne sich ganz darüber bewusst zu sein, was sie verursacht. Es gibt ihm zufolge eine Melancholie, die ihren Grund im Tod des Freundes hat und eine andere Melancholie, die aus dem unterbrochenen Anfang des Dialogs resultiert, aus dem der innere Dialog entsteht. Das ist wiederum ein Paradox, denn der sogenannte Dialog wird von jedem der Gesprächspartner allein weitergeführt, „manchmal wortlos, unmittelbar in uns, oder indirekt".[3] Das Indirekte kennzeichnet also diesen Dialog zwischen Derrida und Gadamer, und man könnte sich fragen, ob es eigentlich ein Dialog ist, der tatsächlich stattfindet. Und gerade wenn Derrida wiederum den „inneren Dialog" als Beweis für die Teilhaberschaft zwischen ihm

---

[2] Ebd.
[3] Ebd.

und Gadamer zu erklären versucht, besagt dies im Grunde, dass er keinen Wert auf die Anwesenheit des Anderen legt:

> Wenn es darum geht, genau zu sagen, was „innerer Dialog" heißt, bin ich froh, dass ich Gadamer schon in mir habe sprechen lassen. Ich übernehme von ihm und zwar wörtlich, was er kurz nach unserer ersten Begegnung 1985 gesagt hat, zum Schluß seines Textes *Destruktion und Dekonstruktion*: „Vollends das Gespräch, das wir *in unserem eigenen Denken* weiterführen und das sich vielleicht in unseren Tagen um neue große Partner aus einem sich planetarisch erweiternden Menschheitserbe bereichert, sollte überall seinen Partner suchen – und insbesondere wenn er ein ganz anderer ist. Wer mir Dekonstruktion ans Herz legt und auf Differenz besteht, steht *am Anfang eines Gesprächs*, nicht an seinem Ziele."[4]

Diese Aussage Gadamers, die Derrida so optimistisch wiederholt, um die Geltung des Terminus' „innerer Dialog" zu bestätigen, ist in Wirklichkeit eine scharfe, wesentlich metonymische Operation, die den Fokus von der Person Derridas auf dessen Gedanken und Philosophie verschiebt: Das Relativpronomen „Wer" – in dem Satz „Wer mir Dekonstruktion ans Herz legt und auf Differenz besteht, steht *am Anfang eines Gesprächs*, nicht an seinem Ziele" – ist doppeldeutig: „Wer" bezieht sich zum einen auf jenen Derrida, der als Anlass für ein Gespräch dient, der sich Gadamers Begriffen der Dekonstruktion und Differenz annähert. In der Annäherung an die Begriffe und Gedankenverläufe Gadamers führt Derrida ein Gespräch im eigenen Denken ohne den Anderen, also einen „inneren Dialog" weiter fort. Dieser imaginierte Andere steht am Anfang eines Gesprächs, die anwesende Person, auf die das „wer" ebenfalls rekurriert, ist eigentlich nicht *das Ziel* des Gesprächs. Die anwesende Person Derrida ist für Gadamer nebensächlich.

So erwähnt Derrida die Freude am Gespräch mit Gadamer, um den wahrhaftigen Dialog zwischen ihm und dem deutschen Philosophen zu bestätigen, versteht aber selber nicht den Grund für diese Melancholie, die er verspürt und die der Text doch durchschauen lässt. In diesem Sinn befreit sich der Text von den unbeantworteten Fragen Derridas in Bezug auf die Melancholie und gibt doch eine Antwort: Die beiden Gesprächspartner sind immer nur teilweise anwesend; zu Beginn des Textes ist

---

[4] Ebd., S. 9.

Gadamer nicht anwesend, wenn Derrida sagt, dass er sich nur indirekt an Gadamer wendet. Dann wiederum, im Augenblick des gesprochenen Wortes, das Derrida zitiert, ist dieser nicht anwesend. An dieser Stelle im Text Derridas vereinen sich beide erwähnten Melancholien, die Melancholie der Unterbrechung (also die vom Scheitern des eigentlichen Dialogs) und die Melancholie, die der Tod Gadamers auslöst. Der Text erweist sich dennoch als eine Suche, ein Verlangen Derridas nach der Anwesenheit seines Freundes. Dies wird sichtbar durch verschiedene diskursive Verfahren im Text, z. B. in der Deutung des Verses „Die Welt ist fort, ich muß dich tragen" aus Paul Celans *Atemwende*. Wiederum versucht Derrida, anknüpfend an die Vorliebe Gadamers für Paul Celan, einen Dialog mit Gadamer herzustellen, indem er Paul Celan zum Sprechen bringt:

> Wenn ich hier seine Stimme zu Gehör bringe, wenn ich sie jetzt in mir höre, so zunächst deshalb, weil ich Gadamers Bewunderung für diesen anderen Freund teile, der Paul Celan uns war. Wie Gadamer habe auch ich oft versucht, Paul Celan zu lesen, nachts, und mit ihm zu denken. Wenn es mir jetzt noch einmal darum geht, mich dem Gedicht zu nähern, geschieht dies im Versuch, mich an Gadamer zu wenden, an ihn selbst, in mir, außer mir, oder zumindest zu simulieren, um mit ihm zu sprechen.[5]

Lesen wird hier mit Sprechen und Denken gleichgesetzt und ermöglicht zugleich einen unendlichen Dialog (mit Gadamer). Derrida findet durch die Lektüre eine Form des ununterbrochenen Gespräches mit seinem Freund (und damit die Möglichkeit, den Tod zu bannen).

Ein anderer Philosoph, Michel Foucault, versteht sich ebenfalls als ein Leser im Sinne Derridas. Man könnte die These aufstellen, dass Foucault Borges in der oben beschriebenen Weise liest. Wenn dies so wäre, könnte man auch von einem Dialog zwischen beiden Autoren sprechen. Auf diesen Dialog zwischen Borges und Foucault deuten zwei Texte Foucaults hin, das „Vorwort" in *Die Ordnung der Dinge*[6] und *Die Sprache*,

---

[5] Derrida: Der ununterbrochene Dialog zwischen zwei Unendlichkeiten, das Gedicht (Anm. 1), S. 16.
[6] Foucault, Michel: Vorwort. In: Ders.: Die Ordnung der Dinge. Frankfurt/Main: Suhrkamp 1971 (1966), S. 17–30.

unendlich.[7] Foucaults *Archäologie des Wissens* beruft sich auf die erste Borges-Lektüre, der zweiten Lektüre folgt der Entwurf einer literarischen Ontologie.[8]

Das Vorwort in *Die Ordnung der Dinge* (*Les Mots et les Choses*) beginnt allerdings mit der Beschreibung einer literarischen Erfahrung:

> Dieses Buch hat seine Entstehung einem Text von Borges zu verdanken. Dem Lachen, das bei seiner Lektüre alle Vertrautheiten unseres Denken aufrüttelt, des Denkens unserer Zeit und unseres Raumes, das alle geordneten Oberflächen und alle Pläne erschüttert, die für uns die zahlenmäßige Zunahme der Lebewesen klug erscheinen lassen und unsere tausendjährige Handhabung des *Gleichen* und des *Anderen* schwanken lässt und in Unruhe versetzt.[9]

Foucault zitiert hier aus Borges *Die analytische Sprache von John Wilkins*. Dieser Text geht zurück auf „eine gewisse chinesische Enzyklopädie", in der es heißt, dass die Tiere sich wie folgt gruppieren: „a) Tiere, die dem Kaiser gehören, b) einbalsamierte Tiere, c) gezähmte, d) Milchschweine, e) Sirenen, f) Fabeltiere, g) herrenlose Hunde, h) in diese Gruppierung gehörige, i) die sich wie Tolle gebärden, j) zahllose, k) die mit einem ganz feinen Pinsel aus Kamelhaar gezeichnet sind, l) und so weiter, m) die den Wasserkrug zerbrochen haben, n) die von Weitem wie Fliegen aussehen".[10]

In alphabetischer Aufzählung finden sich Kategorien aneinandergereiht, die auf existierende und imaginäre Tiere verweisen. Der Brennpunkt besteht aber gerade in der Existenz einer Meta-Kategorie: „in diese Gruppierung gehörige", die in der spanischsprachigen Klassifikation Borges bedeutsam unter dem stummen Buchstaben „h" [hache] aufgezählt wird:

---

[7] Foucault, Michel: Die Sprache, unendlich. In: Ders.: Schriften in vier Bänden. Dits et Ecrits. Bd. 1: 1954–1969. Hg. von François Ewald / Daniel Defert. Aus dem Französischen von Michael Bischoff / Hans-Dieter Gondek / Hermann Kocyba. Frankfurt/Main: Suhrkamp 1963, S. 342–356.
[8] Ebd.
[9] Foucault: Vorwort. In: Ders.: Die Ordnung der Dinge (Anm. 6), S. 17.
[10] Ebd.

Die Zentrale Kategorie der „in diese Gruppierung gehörigen" Tiere bezeichnet durch den expliziten Bezug auf bekannte Paradoxe, dass man nie zur Definition eines stabilen Verhältnisses von Inhalt und Beinhaltendem zwischen jeder dieser Mengen (ensambles) und derjenigen kommt, die sie alle vereint.[11]

Damit stoßen wir auf die Grenze des Denkens, von der Foucault am Anfang des Textes sprach. Diese stumme Kategorie „h) in diese Gruppe gehörige" nimmt verschwiegen alle Tiere der Enzyklopädie in sich auf, absorbiert sie von Innen und sprengt von dort aus den Modus Operandi jeder Klassifikation.

Es ist erstaunlich, dass Foucault beim Lesen von Borges Text mit einem Lachen reagiert und damit zu erkennen gibt, worauf Borges zweifellos mit Humor die Aufmerksamkeit lenken möchte, nämlich auf „die nackte Erfahrung der Ordnung und ihrer Seinsweisen",[12] die im Falle Foucaults eine Perspektivierung der *Epistemen* in ihren archäologischen Schichten ermöglicht und im Falle Borges die Kraft des Heterotopischen erkennen lässt, indem die paradoxen Verfahren die Sprache unterminieren. Dies bestätigt der argentinische Kritiker Jaime Rest:

> Was bis hier über die Haltung Borges' gesagt worden ist, in Bezug auf die Versuche, eine systematische Erkenntnis der Wirklichkeit zu entwickeln, erlaubt eine offensichtliche Wiederholung aus der spezifischen Perspektive der Theorie der Sprache. Der untersuchte Autor [...] legt die Grenzen des Wissens – mindestens jene, die kumulativ und übertragbar sind – in dem kombinatorischen Rahmen der verbalen Materie fest, so dass die menschlichen Fähigkeiten des Wissens und Denkens im Bereich der Aussagen beschränkt bleiben und sich vielleicht sogar mit ihm identifizieren [...]. Im Laufe seiner Interviews mit Milleret verweigert Borges systematisch seinen Status als „Philosoph" oder „Denker", darüber nachdenkend, dass jedes systematische Denken, da es uns ein geordnetes Bild der Wirklichkeit vorschlägt, immer dazu neigt uns zu täuschen.[13]

---

[11] Ebd., S. 19.
[12] Ebd., S. 24.
[13] Übersetzt von V. F. Blanco. In: Rest, Jaime: El laberinto del universo. Buenos Aires: Eterna Cadencia 2009, S. 83.

Meiner Meinung nach ist es Foucault, der am deutlichsten erkennt, welche Funktion das Paradoxe in Borges Werk hat.[14] Interessant ist diese Perspektivierung der *Episteme* im ‚Außen' der einzelnen Diskurse, wodurch die Wirkung und Macht der Anschauungen der *Episteme* in Frage gestellt werden. Die Logik dieses Gedankenverlaufs ist folgende: Jede epistemische Schicht bestimmt die zu ihr gehörigen Denkformen, das gilt auch für die Urteilsformen jeder Epoche. Wenn man sich, wie es Foucault darlegt, außerhalb dieser *Episteme* befindet, ist man in einer Position, in der das Urteilen sozusagen aufgehoben ist – in einer reinen Beobachtung. Es ist deshalb ein neutraler Platz, der ein Lachen und einen wirklichen Dialog ermöglicht, weil er die Beharrlichkeit jeder inneren epistemischen Gedankenform mindert.

Es ist nicht nebensächlich, wie Foucault das Paradoxe in Borges Werk versteht; nämlich nicht als eine philosophische Spekulation, die er verachtet, sondern als eine vollständige Stellungnahme, die sogar als ethisch bezeichnet werden kann. Hier entsteht der Dialog zwischen den beiden Autoren, als ein Zusammenfließen von Gedanken. Borges schreibt in *Avatares de la tortuga* (*Sinnfiguren der Schildkröte*), dass er die Schrift einer Biographie des Unendlichen vorhabe, weil das Unendliche ein Begriff sei, der die Fähigkeit habe, die ganzen anderen Begriffe zu korrumpieren.[15] Das ist genau das, was die Archäologie Foucaults mit dem Begriff *Episteme* und der Perspektivierung von *Epistemen* beabsichtigt. So bewirkt die Lektüre Borges bei Foucault ein Lachen (auch wenn es eines voller Schauder ist), während Derridas Text Empfindungen von Melancholie hervorbringt.

---

[14] Die Tiere, die zu „dieser Gruppierung gehören", sind alle Tiere der chinesischen Enzyklopädie. Es handelt sich also nicht nur um ein Verschwinden, sondern auch um eine Verdoppelung: Die chinesische Enzyklopädie in der chinesischen Enzyklopädie, eine mise in abyme. Und dies ist eine Erscheinungsform des Paradoxen.

[15] Borges, Jorge Luis: Avatares de la tortuga. In: Ders.: Discusión, Obras Completas. Buenos Aires: Emecé 2007, S. 268. „Zu dieser illusorischen Biographie des Unendlichen sind auch diese Seiten irgendwie ein Beitrag. Es ist mit ihnen beabsichtigt, gewisse Sinnfiguren des zweiten Paradoxes von Zenon aufzuzeichnen." Borges, Jorge Luis: Sinnfiguren der Schildkröte. In: Ders.: Gesammelte Werke. Bd. 5/I: Essays 1932–1936. Übersetzt von Karl August Horst / Curt Meyer-Clason / Melanie Walz. München: Hanser 1981, S. 122–129, hier S. 122.

Die melancholische Gewissheit, von der ich hier rede, beginnt also wie immer bereits zu Lebzeiten der Freunde. Nicht nur durch eine Unterbrechung, sondern durch ein Wort der Unterbrechung. Ein *cogito* des Adieu, dieses endgültigen Grußes, zeichnet den Atem selbst des Dialoges, eines Dialoges in der Welt oder eines innersten Dialoges. Die Trauer wartet nicht mehr. Seit dieser ersten Begegnung kommt diese Unterbrechung dem Tod zuvor, sie geht ihm voran und hüllt einen jeden in die Trauer einer unerbittlichen zukünftigen Vergangenheit.[16]

So bedient sich Derrida des paradoxen Gedankens: Diese Unterbrechung wird unendlich wiederholt, der ununterbrochene Dialog ist eigentlich ein unendlich unterbrochener. Dies bezieht sich direkt auf einen anderen Text Foucaults, den ich hier nur kurz einleite, *Die Sprache, unendlich*. Aber zuvor noch eine Bemerkung: Das Lachen Foucaults ist sicherlich ein privates, ein innerliches und entspricht damit auch den Merkmalen des von Derrida beschriebenen inneren Dialogs. Wenn wir an den Text von Derrida denken und an die Empfehlung Gadamers, sich einen Partner auszusuchen, mit dem man einen inneren Dialog führen kann, so trifft dies auch auf Foucault und Borges zu. Denn Foucault versteht vielleicht wie kein anderer, welche die dichterischen Absichten Borges sind, in denen Foucault zugleich ethische und ontologische Aspekte zu erkennen vermag.[17] Die ontologischen Aspekte in Borges Werk arbeitet Foucault in *Die Sprache, unendlich* heraus. In seiner Deutung von Borges Erzählung *Das Geheime Wunder* erklärt Foucault, was er als Phänomene der Selbstrepräsentation bezeichnet:

Borges erzählt die Geschichte eines verurteilten Schriftstellers, dem Gott in genau dem Augenblick, da er erschossen wird, eine Frist von einem Jahr gewährt, um das begonnene Werk zu vollenden; dieses im Aufschub des Todes in der Schwebe bleibende Werk ist ein Drama, in dem sich alles wiederholt und das (noch zu schreibende) Ende Wort

---

[16] Derrida: Der ununterbrochene Dialog zwischen zwei Unendlichkeiten, das Gedicht (Anm. 1), S. 14.
[17] Ein Missverständnis, wie es sich zwischen Derrida und Gadamer ergab, wäre bei Borges und Foucault eigentlich nicht möglich. Foucault hat Borges nie getroffen und Borges hat Foucault auch nie erwähnt. Sie sind aber Zeitgenossen gewesen. Zwar ist es schwierig zu beweisen, dass eine Annäherung an Borges Foucaults Absicht gewesen ist, doch hat niemand wie er Borges so gut gelesen.

> für Wort den (bereits geschriebenen) Anfang wiederaufnimmt, jedoch so, dass gezeigt wird, dass die Figur, die man kennt und die seit den ersten Szenen spricht, nicht dieselbe ist, sondern eine, die sich dafür hält. Im unmittelbaren Bevorstehen des Todes, während des einen Jahres, das so lange dauert, wie ein Regentropfen seine Wange hinunterrollt und der Rauch einer letzten Zigarette verweht, schreibt Hladik, doch mit Worten, die niemand je wird lesen können, nicht einmal Gott, das große, unsichtbare Labyrinth der Wiederholung, der Sprache, die sich zweiteilt und zum Spiegel ihrer selbst wird. Und wenn das letzte Epitheton gefunden ist (zweifellos dürfte es auch das erste sein, da das Drama aufs Neue beginnt), hämmern ihm die weniger als eine Sekunde zuvor abgefeuerten Kugeln ihr Schweigen in die Brust. Ich frage mich, ob man nicht, ausgehend von diesen Phänomenen der Selbstrepräsentation der Sprache, eine Ontologie der Literatur schreiben oder zumindest von ferne umreißen könnte; ausgehend von solchen Figuren [...], die den Bezug, den die Sprache zum Tod unterhält, verbergen, das heißt verraten – Bezug der Sprache zu jener Grenze, an die sie sich richtet und gegen die sie errichtet wird.[18]

Foucault geht in diesem Text davon aus, dass die Nähe des Todes ein Anlass ist, um zu sprechen, zu erzählen und damit den Tod zu bannen:

> Schreiben um nicht zu sterben, wie Blanchot sagte, oder vielleicht sogar sprechen, um nicht zu sterben, ist eine Aufgabe, die gewiss so alt ist wie das Sprechen selbst. Für die Zeit noch einer Erzählung bleiben Entscheidungen mit tödlichen Konsequenzen unvermeidlich in der Schwebe.[19]

Foucault untersucht in zwei verschiedenen Texten paradoxe Verfahren in Borges Werk. Was Foucault als Reduplikationsphänomene bezeichnet, kann auch als eine Erscheinungsform eines unendlichen Regresses verstanden werden. Sofern es sich um Reduplikationsphänomene handelt, wie in der literarischen Ontologie oder Archäologie, trifft der französische Philosoph genau den Punkt in der Beschreibung dieser Phänomene, die Borges zweifellos in seinem Werk, im Laufe seiner ganzen dichterischen

---

[18] Foucault: Die Sprache, unendlich (Anm. 7), S. 342f.
[19] Ebd., S. 342.

Aktivität, stets wiederholt hat. Foucault ist mit seiner Lektüre Borges Gedanken so nah, dass ich mich frage, ob man nicht von einem Dialog (einen „inneren Dialog") zwischen Foucault und Borges sprechen kann. Aber der Zirkel schließt sich erst, wenn man bedenkt, dass das, was Foucault in Bezug auf Borges untersucht, sich eigentlich auch im Text von Derrida ereignet. Denn ich frage mich, ob Derrida durch das Lesen und das Sprechen nicht so etwas wie einen Aufschub des Todes mit seinem Text versucht und eine literarisch-ontologische Funktion im Sinne Foucaults ausübt. Die Wiederholung der Trauer infolge des Todes des Freundes und die Unterbrechung als paradoxes unaufhörliches Merkmal deuten dies an.

Topic Drop and Coherence in Dialogue

Janina Beutler

Considered from a linguistic perspective, a dialogue is a structure – construed by at least two participants – which is built through the sequence of grammatically well-formed sentences of a natural language. There are various mechanisms which constitute a successful dialogue. Apart from the fundamental maxims, which Paul Grice declares to be compelling to adhere to, speakers have to silently agree on what they think to be true or false and, thus, assuring that the contents that are included in a discourse are mutually and consciously shared by the participants of a dialogue. This shared knowledge existing between two speakers is called the common ground. In order to establish an efficient common ground, certain communicational rules have to be abided by; this means amongst others, that a constituent can only be a topic throughout a dialogue, if it is already known to the hearer. Moreover, only the (aboutness) topic can be omitted in a sentence without endangering the grammaticality of a sentence. Finally, topic drop is restricted to a specific syntactic position in a sentence that shows features of coherence referring to the preceding dialogue.

1. Introduction

The first section will deal with the notion of dialogue and which conditions embody the base of a functioning dialogue. Section 2 will be concerned with the definition of topics and the sentences they appear in. Furthermore, it will be discussed what the participants of a dialogue have to know about each other in order to fulfil the conditions of a functioning dialogue. This will be followed by explanations concerning the preferred positions of topics in a sentence, which will already be shedding light on the dialogical anchor of coherence. Having established a basis for understanding topics and topic positions, section 3 is concerned with the phenomenon of topic drop and the kinds of sentences which are able to host topic drop. In contrast to that, it will be analysed which sentences cannot contain topic drop and what the reasons for this missing ability are. The results of that passage will lead to a closer examination of the prefinite position and its function as a link of coherence in dialogue.

2. Dialogue

Before one asks, what topics are and what do they do in a dialogue, one should stop and think about asking, what a dialogue actually means and whether there are different sorts to be separated. Although, at first glance, it might seem like that there is only one notion of dialogue, but there are at least two fundamental divisions that have to be made:

i. ideal dialogue
ii. empirical dialogue

The problem that emerges with respect to some theories about the dialogical processing between at least two discourse participants has to do with a too idealistic view on how dialogues work. Those theories are based on dialogues that are built up on equal parts of speech, showing no emotional or social interference, asymmetry concerning people's relationships, or any other kind of negative influence on the outcome of a discourse. This perfect picture of human interaction can be categorised as an ideal dialogue, as it does not contain any problems that stand in the way of a completely positive structure of coherence.[1]

To receive a more realistic kind of dialogue we should take the mentioned aspects of interference into account. There is barely a conversation, oral or written, that is conducted ideally, because dialogue participants always share a certain kind of relationship with each other, converging from neutral to less neutral. The distribution of parts of speech can differ greatly, since one person may get to talk more than the other. This in turn may be caused by the circumstance that the person representing the dominant speaker holds a higher social status than his counterpart. Or in another

---

[1] Linell, Per: Rethinking Language, Mind, And World Dialogically – Interactional And Contextual Theories Of Human Sense-Making. Schweden: Information Age Publishing 2012.

case the imbalance of conversational turns arises from an intense emotional involvement of the discourse participants, which might again provoke an irrational line of reasoning that does not promote a positive, healthy outcome of the conversation.[2]

Yet, no matter what the preference of the dialogue is – whether it rather reflects the ideal or the empirical dialogical concept – Paul Grice amongst others believes that speakers of a natural language communicating with each other in most cases try to work towards an ideal dialogue. Their shared would therefore be a dialogue at least close to possessing the features that are listed under what we defined to be an ideal dialogue. In order to achieve this aim, however, they have – as far as the theory goes – to adhere to specific principles that constitute an ideal dialogue:

> COOPERATIVE PRINCIPLE: Make your conversational contribution such as required, at the stage at which it occurs, by the accepted purpose or direction of the talk exchange in which you are engaged.
> MAXIM OF QUANTITY: 1. Make your contribution as informative as is required (for the current purposes of the exchange). 2. Do not make your contribution more informative than is required.
> MAXIM OF QUALITY: 1. Do not say what you believe to be false. 2. Do not say that for which you lack adequate evidence.
> MAXIM OF RELATION: Be relevant.
> MAXIM OF MANNER: 1. Avoid obscurity of expression. 2. Avoid ambiguity. 3. Be brief (avoid unnecessary prolixity). 4. Be orderly.[3]

Indicators of a coherent dialogue can be found when considering structures of omission in language that are carried out without violating principles of grammar. The specific kind of omission that I will be concerned with in this article is topic drop. What topic drop is and under which circumstances it works will be illustrated in section 4. Before one can understand what topic drop is, however, one has to be able to identify a topic in a sentence. Thus, the next section deals with the question of what a topic is and where exactly in a sentence it can be found.

---

[2] Idem.
[3] Grice, Paul: Logic and Conversation. In: Peter Cole i. a. (Eds.): Syntax and Semantics. New York: Academic Press 1975, pp. 41–58, here p. 46.

3. What are we talking about?

3.1. What are you talking about?

about is actually the apt expression to start this section with. A topic[4] namely is a part of a sentence that the speaker transmits information about to the hearer. The information that is shared about the topic is called the comment. To get a better understanding about what a topic looks like in a sentence, please, consider the examples below:

(1) *categorical sentences*
/**PEter** \SCHLÄFT.
[Peter TOPIC][schläft COMMENT]

(2) *Linksversetzung*
/**PEter**, der kommt \MORgen.
[Peter TOPIC][schläft COMMENT]

(3) *hanging topic with Linksversetzung*
PEter, ich habe ihn heute nicht ge\TROFfen.
[Peter TOPIC][ich habe ihn heute nicht getroffen COMMENT]

(4) *free topic*
Was **Peters Ge/BURTStag** betrifft, so habe ich noch keine Idee für ein Ge-SCHENK.
[Was Peters Geburtstag betrifft TOPIC][so habe ich noch keine Idee für ein Geschenk COMMENT]

(5) *I-topicalisation*
√**JEden Freund Peters** kenne ich \NICHT.
[Jeden Freund Peters TOPIC][kenne ich nicht COMMENT][5]

The examples above are prototypical topic-comment structures of the German language.[6] Accordingly, they all contain a topic. The definition of a topic as the constituent in a sentence that is being talked about is too rough and diffuse to use as a proper description. This is due to the problem that

---

[4] Topics are highlighted via bold type.
[5] Jacobs, Joachim: The Dimensions of Topic-Comment. In: Linguistics 39 (2001), pp. 641–681. Find here further informations about typical topic-comment structures. Slashes represent rising intonation, radical signs firstly falling then rising, and backslashes falling intonation.
[6] There are sentences in German that do not contain any topic at all. Those sentences are called thetic sentences. Due to the restricted length of this paper, I will not go into this matter any deeper, but the reader can find examples of thetic sentences below: (1) Es regnet. (2) Die Poli\ZEI kommt.

one could assume that, if a sentence contains more than one constituent, theoretically each one of these constituents could be talked about and thus qualify for a topic.[7][8] Yet, there are syntactic and context sensitive indicators with reference to which expression can be a sentence topic. Before we look at those indicators, it has to be said that the relationship between topic and comment cannot be compared to the semantic relationship between a subject and its predicate. Despite the occasional assumption that subjects always signify the topic of a sentence,[9] it can easily be shown that there are constituents representing other syntactic functions which qualify for the role of the topic. However, this aspect will be explained more closely after the features of an adequate topic will have been deduced. For this purpose, let us consider sentence (1):

(1) *categorical sentences*
    /**PEter** \ SCHLÄFT.
    [Peter $_{TOPIC}$][schläft $_{COMMENT}$]

When a person utters this sentence, we can expect him[10] to do so while being cooperative towards the hearer he is speaking to. In the case of (1), the speaker behaves cooperatively if he uses the constituent *Peter* only if *Peter* represents the name of an individual the hearer has sufficient knowledge about. Otherwise, the speaker would violate at least two maxims, namely the Maxim of Quantity and the Maxim of Manner. If the hearer did not know Peter or the person the speaker refers to, through uttering the expression *Peter*, he would not be able to associate any meaning with the same, which would make the rest of the sentence *schläft* useless. In more general terms, one can say that a topic has to reflect given information.[11]

---

[7] Though there are certain constituents that can never be topics, as e. g. expletives ('es').

[8] Reinhart, Tanya: Pragmatics and linguistics. An analysis of sentence topics. In: Philosophica 27 (1981), pp. 53–94.

[9] Strawson, Peter Frederick: Identifying reference and truth values. In: Theoria 30 (1964), pp. 96–118.

[10] I will not use gender distinctions throughout my article, as I expect the reader to understand that both female and male individuals are being referred to through the use of personal pronouns.

[11] Chafe, Wallace: Givenness, Contrastiveness, Definiteness, Subjects and Topics. In: Charles N. Li (Ed.): Subject and Topic. New York u. a.: Academic Press 1975, pp. 25–56.

Now, one might stop to think about how a speaker of a dialogue actually knows that the hearer knows what *Peter* signifies. A possible answer to this will be given in the next section.

3.2. I figure you agree on this, right?

A fundamental piece that makes the Cooperative Principle work is the circumstance that the participants of a dialogue take into account – concerning the communication with each other – what they already know and what is new to them. In linguistic terms, they share a base of propositions[12] about which they, additionally, consciously know that it is mutually shared among them. This propositional base is called the common ground.[13] The common ground therefore contains given information which has either been used in some former discourse or which is part of the higher set of propositions that covers the cultural knowledge or world knowledge an individual has adopted in the course of his life and that is neutral w.r.t. specific contexts and shared among members of a culture or even all individuals in the world:

(6) Ein Hund liebt eine Katze.

Uttering (6), the context under which the sentence is embedded does not need to be as specific as in (1) since a native speaker of German can be expected to know what the DPs *ein Hund* and *eine Katze* stand for, as well as, the predicate of $lieben(x, y)$.

In order to act cooperatively in a dialogue, the participants construct their parts of speech in accordance with the common ground. In case they introduce new propositions to it, they mark the new information contained in the proposition via prosodic means like a focus-background structure that differs from the one marking already given information. Apart from this, the speaker has syntactic means, in order to manage the information in the common ground wrt. emphasising that this information is given (7):

---

[12] *Proposition* is the modern term for the thought as it was defined by Gottlob Frege.
[13] Krifka, Manfred / Renate Musan: Information structure: Overview and linguistic issues. In: Id. (Eds.): The expression of information structure. Berlin: de Gruyter 2012, pp. 1–43; Farkas, Donka / Kim Bruce: On Reacting to Assertions and Polar Questions. In: Journal of Semantics 27 (2009), pp. 81–118; Stalnaker, Robert: Assertion. In: Peter Cole (Ed.): Syntax and Semantics 9. New York: Academic Press 1978, pp. 315–32.

(7) A: Erzähl mir mal was über Fritz.
     B: **Fritz** hat den Hund gefüttert
     A: Was ist mit dem Hund?
     B: **Den Hund** hat Fritz gefüttert.

(7) is an example of common ground management, since the information that is salient and given (and thus highlighted) varies, despite the consistency of the proposition. As one can see immediately, the propositions in speaker B's reaction (7a) and (7b) are one and the same; only the syntactic structure changes. In (7a) the old information that the speaker talks about is represented by the expression *Fritz*, whereas in (7b) it is represented by *den Hund*. In the former, the topic coincides with the syntactic function of the subject, in the latter, it is the direct object; i. e. that the relationship between the topic and comment is not equivocal to the one between the subject and predicate, as the first is context dependent and thus pragmatic, the second, however, is purely grammatical and stays stable and independent of the context.[14]

3.3. Topics and their one and only place

Coming back to common ground management, we have seen that it corresponds to transformation – constituent movement or move α[15] – in a sentence. Considering yet another example, one may also see that there is a specific position which is a predestined place for a topic (8):

(8) A: Erzähl mir mal was über Fritz.
     B: Fritz hat den Hund gefüttert.

As German is an SOV language, the finite verb and the constituent in front of the same have to undergo certain operations in order to generate a topic-comment structure:

i. movement of the finiteness[16] to the C^0-position
ii. movement of a constituent from the middle field to the CP-position

---

[14] Reinhart: Pragmatics and linguistics (note 8).
[15] This is the generative term for the transformation.
[16] Bayer, Josef: How much verb moves to second position? – Theoretical and experimental evidence. Talk given at the 2nd International V2-Workshop, 29.–31.07.2016, Bergische Universität Wuppertal. In: http://www.linguistik.uni-wuppertal.de/v2-workshop-2016/handouts/Bayer-Freitag.pdf (18.03.2017).

According to Werner Frey[17] and Ewa Trutkowski[18], topics can also be found in the environment of the middle field (9):

(9) a. Ich erzähle dir etwas über Maria.
    b. Nächstes Jahr wird Maria wahrscheinlich nach London gehen.

However, we will see later that topics in the middle field do not behave as topics in the prefield do. In the following, we will focus on topics in the prefield.

4. And suddenly it's gone – or not?

4.1. Topic Drop

In the last section, we saw that topics usually appear in the left periphery of a sentence, more exactly in the prefield or the position in front of the prefield. Thus, one could assume that, if a speaker wants to share information about a certain entity, he would always have to fill the prefield of a sentence. With the help of the upcoming examples, we will see that this is only half the truth:

(10) A: Was war mit Sofia?
    B: Ich hab' sie seit zwei Wochen nicht geseh'n.
    B: (Sofia) Hab' ich seit zwei Wochen nicht geseh'n.
    B: *Ich hab' (Sofia) seit zwei Wochen nicht geseh'n.[19]

An individual already included in the common ground *Sofia* is picked up within the current discourse and simultaneously the current context. Speaker A asks B to tell him something about this individual, mutually known to them. Now, it is possible to use the introduced topic in one's answer as in the first B sentence, via an anaphora. Yet one can also omit the topic completely as it is done in the second sentence uttered by B. The only thing that does not work in (15) is the omission of the constituent being categorised as the topic in the middle field. In order to drop a topic the said constituent has to be moved to the prefield. For this transformation to take

---

[17] Frey, Werner: Über die syntaktische Position der Satztopiks im Deutschen. In: ZAS Papers in Linguistics 20 (2000), pp. 137–172.
[18] Trutkowski, Ewa: Topic Drop and Null Subjects in German. Potsdam. Berlin: de Gruyter 2016.
[19] Fries, Norbert: Über das Nulltopik im Deutschen. In: Sprache & Pragmatik 3 (1988), pp. 19–49.

place, however, the finiteness has to be fronted first of all. As soon as the finiteness and the selected constituent have been fronted, the chosen topic can be deleted, leaving a trace of its existence in SpecCP[20].

What we can deduct from this is that the position in front of the finite verb possesses features that allow the topic to directly adhere to and be included into the preceding discourse; a quality that the middle field position does not have and in which the topic may, thus, not only exist as a silent trace but has to be phonetically realised.[21]

Apart from the question concerning if and where a topic can be dropped, we have not talked about the possibility that sentences do not contain a clear division of topic and comment. This shall be our point of discussion in the next section.

4.2. Where they've never found a place

The German language contains sentences which are not equally comparable to the sentences we have seen so far when it comes to topic-comment structures. The reader will see what is meant by that, considering the examples below:

Comparison of v2-declaratives and other sentences wrt. Topics

v2-ds[22] vs. v1-ds	(11)	A:	Wer hat den Hund gefüttert?
		B:	*Hat Fritz den Hund gefüttert.
		B:	Den Hund hat Fritz gefüttert.
v2-ds vs. exclamatives	(12)	A:	Wer hat den Hund gefüttert?
		B:	*Hat den Hund doch Fritz gefüttert!
		B:	Den Hund hat Fritz gefüttert.
v2-ds vs. imperatives	(13)	A:	Wer hat den Hund gefüttert?
		B:	*Füttere den Hund, Fritz!
		B:	Den Hund hat Fritz gefüttert.
v2-ds vs. interrogatives	(14)	A:	Wer hat den Hund gefüttert?
		B:	*Wer hat den Hund gefüttert?
		B:	*Hat den Hund Fritz gefüttert?
		B:	Den Hund hat Fritz gefüttert.

---

[20] SpecCP is the generative term for prefield; I will be using them interchangeably.
[21] Assuming topics can be surfaced in the middle field.
[22] ds = declarative sentence.

The sentences used to answer questions showing a clear topic-comment structure have so far been grammatically adequate when it comes to answering questions. According to that, it seems that the sentences provided above do not have the same division of topic and comment as the sentences have that are apt to answer a question.[23] Thus, a syntactic structure is needed that can form a grammatically proper response to a question. But what kind of sentence is this?

Firstly, it is a declarative sentence. In order to construct a declarative sentence, Frege said that three steps are necessary:

Declarative Sentence
i. Thinking   – grasping a thought
                   ➢ selecting a proposition
ii. Judgement – accepting that the thought is true
                   ➢ assigning a truth value to the proposition
iii. Assertion – proclaiming the judgement
                   ➢ establishing the judgement of the proposition w.r.t. the context[24]

It is stated that declarative sentences show a division of topic and comment. A problem that arises with respect to this thesis is, that German is considered to have more than one kind of declarative sentence: the one with the finite verb or finiteness respectively in the second position (in C^0 + a topicalized constituent in SpecCP) and one in which the finite verb occupies the first position (no constituent in front of the finite verb). But, as we have already seen, v1-ds cannot answer questions. Why is that? The reason is that v1-ds do not carry assertion, whereas v2-ds do.[25] Only v2-declaratives have the ability of reducing the n-partitioned room of answers left open by a wh-question and the bipartitioned room left open by a y-/n-interrogative to the true proposition, satisfactorily fulfilling the speaker's

---

[23] Önnerfors, Olaf: Verb-erst-Deklarativsätze: Grammatik und Pragmatik. Stockholm: Almqvist & Wiksell International 1997.
[24] Frege, Gottlob: Über Sinn und Bedeutung (1892). In: Günther Patzig (Ed.): Funktion, Begriff, Bedeutung. Göttingen: Vandenhoeck & Ruprecht 2008; Lohnstein, Horst: Satzmodus – kompositionell. Zur Parametrisierung der Modusphrase im Deutschen. Berlin, New York: Akademie Verlag (= studia grammatica 49) 2000.
[25] Önnerfors: Verb-erst-Deklarativsätze (note 23).

need for information.[26] Though the sentences showing v1-positioning of the finite verb are generally called v1-<u>declarative</u> sentences, while not representing y-/n-interrogatives, they differ greatly from their v2-counterparts, as they do not carry assertion and do not show a topic-comment-division. The topic is not moved to the prefield and therefore is not only inadequate when it comes to answering questions, but it also cannot be the basis to a topic drop construction. Yet in the following section, I will argue that a (formerly) filled prefield is a crucial anchor for a coherent dialogue.

5. The place of the thread

The important thing about the distinction of topic drop sentences and v1-ds is that there once was a prefield that was occupied by a constituent. This has to be said, because at first glance, topic drop sentences and v1-ds appear to be syntactically and semantically identical.

(15) A: Was war mit Sofia?
      B: (Sofia) Hab' ich seit zwei Wochen nicht geseh'n.[27]
(16) Kommt ein Mann in die Bar.

In contrast to the v2-ds containing topic drop, the v1-ds still possesses all the constituents in the middle field; this means, that none of them have been moved to be deleted in the prefield, which, however, is not the case in v2-ds with topic drop. In the latter, a constituent destined to be the sentence topic has been moved to the prefinite position and deleted afterwards. Consequently, even though the topic is not phonetically realised in a topic drop sentence, it is still there – though invisible – as it can be restored, because the hearer knows from the preceding discourse which constituent is dropped. Despite of topic drop, this is the reason why the prefield is invisibly filled and thus, shows a v2-structure. Furthermore, if a

---

[26] Lohnstein: Satzmodus – kompositionell (note 24); Lohnstein, Horst / Nathalie Staratschek: V2, Finiteit und die Satztypen. 2nd International V2-Workshop, 29.–31.07.2016, Bergische Universität Wuppertal. In: http://www.linguistik.uni-wuppertal.de/v2-workshop-2016/handouts/Lohnstein-Staratschek.pdf (01.04.2017).

[27] Fries: Über das Nulltopik im Deutschen (note 19).

topic is dropped, it is always bound to some referent in the discourse or adherent to the common ground.[28]

What are the effects of those contrasting structures and what kind of role does the prefield play in a discourse? From the previous observations, one can derive that it is the left periphery of a German sentence that determines its sentence mood.[29]

(17) | **Left periphery** | | | |
| --- | --- | --- | --- |
| SpecCP | C⁰ | FinP | Fin⁰ |
| Ø | dass | du heute den Förster umgebracht | ~~hast~~ |
| Heute | hast | du den Förster umgebracht | ~~hast~~ |
| Ø | Hast | du heute den Förster umgebracht? | ~~hast~~ |
| Wen | hast | du heute umgebracht? | ~~hast~~ |
| Ø | Bring | (du) heute den Förster um! | ~~bring~~ |
| Ø | Hast | du doch heute den Förster gestern umgebracht! | ~~hast~~ |
| Ø | Brächtest | du doch heute den Förster um! | ~~brächtest~~ |

The distinction between the sentences is drawn within the left periphery and consists in whether the finite verb is fronted and if and how the prefield gets filled. The only two sentence moods in which the prefield actually contains an element are the wh-interrogative and the v2-declarative sentence.[30] It was stated before that – when it comes to topic drop – only declarative sentences carrying assertion are adequate candidates considering the selection of a topic; this implies a v2-structure. The wh-interrogative sentence shows a v2-strucure, too. Thus, one might assume that it likewise is a host for topics and the phenomenon of topic drop. Yet, this is not possible for three reasons:

1. wh-interrogatives lack assertion.
2. wh-interrogatives are not informative but inquisitive.
3. The expression that occupies the prefield in wh-interrogatives can only be a wh-expression.

---

[28] Trutkowski: Topic Drop and Null Subjects in German (note 17).
[29] Lohnstein, Horst: Verb second, inflectional morphology, and sentential force – the case of German. (To be published) 2017.
[30] I do not want to discuss the question whether embedded sentences have sentence mood.

For once, wh-interrogatives cannot be assertive, because they do not reduce the possible space of answers to the one true proposition as declarative sentences carrying assertions do, they rather bring about the direct opposite: They leave the room of answers n-fold, which cannot induce assertion. This actually leads to the second circumstance, namely that wh-interrogatives are inquisitive objects, which means that the room they denote is made up of n-fold partitions: "An inquisitive object leads to a partition of the possible states of affairs into classes which are disjoint in pairs, and which yield the whole set under set union [...]."[31]

Inquisitiveness is contrasted with informativeness:

> A typical property of inquisitive objects is that they are not informative. They just split up the available possibilities into classes of equivalent elements, but they do not add any information with the effect that the number of available alternatives becomes reduced.[32]

Inquisitive objects of the German language are wh-questions and y-/n-interrogatives, whereas, informative objects are v2-ds. As already noted, the wh-interrogatives show an occupied prefield and the y-/n-interrogatives only show fronting of finiteness. Although Declarative sentences have both, yet they are not inquisitive but informative. The difference arises from the fact that the prefield of a wh-interrogative is filled with a wh-expression and the one of a v2-ds is not filled with a wh-expression but instead contains constituents of the sort [-wh].

We subsumed beforehand that for a constituent to qualify as a topic, the chosen constituent has to be given, hence, introduced in the previous dialogue. Now, I suggest another feature to be added to the feature of givenness: A topic has to lead to informativeness which excludes the usage of [+wh]-expressions as possible topics. The kinds of expressions which can be taken as topics are, therefore, specified as follows: They are given [-wh]-expressions positioned in the prefield. Topics can stand in the prefield and, as assumed by Ewa Trutkowski and Werner Frey, in the middle field. The objection here is: They can only be left out in the former. The SpecCP, thus, is a restricted position. It is a position in which the speaker and the listener are bound by a constituent, whose knowledge they want so share and

---

[31] Lohnstein: Verb second (note 29).
[32] Ebd.

thereby, it links them to the discourse and their dialogue. The freedom of omission connected with the prefinite position, therefore, signifies the location where the hitherto discourse is updated through new information, whereas the link builds the interface between previous discourse and the updated one. Topic drop can thus be described as a coherent link in dialogical structures.

6. Conclusion

Though certainly every example of a dialogue shared by speakers of a natural language is empirical, the idealized perspective of theorizing about it states that the aim of two people conversing – a coherent dialogue – can be achieved via abiding by the maxims established by Paul Grice. By using a constituent representing unknown information or through using an appropriate constituent but dropping it in a position not licensed for omission, those maxims are violated. The deletion of given information is, therefore, restricted to the SpecCP position/prefield of a v2-delarative sentence containing assertion. This sentence mood is the only possible access to the topic drop, as it does not merely possess the apt semantic properties, but it also shows the necessary syntax and morphology: fronting of finiteness and a [-wh]-expression in the prefinite position.

Accordingly, fronting of finiteness has to be processed before a constituent can even enter the current discourse in order to be omitted leaving a phonetically silent trace of itself behind. As topic drop is, additionally, only possible in the prefield, the prefinite position is the only place in which information can form a coherent link to the preceding discourse, because information in the shape of a topic can only be bound to the discourse in SpecCP in the first place. The significance of topic drop as a marker of coherence becomes even more transparent if the dialogue participants' behaviour wrt. the common ground, is taken into account: In processing topic drop, a speaker accepts that the omitted information is already part of the common ground. Hereby, he confirms the other dialogue participant's premise that the information contained by the topic is shared by the conversational partners. In summary, this means that as soon as topic drop is possible on the grounds of grammar and pragmatics, a dialogue is coherent, whereas the prefinite position is the anchoring position for a coherence interface.

Die dialogische Funktion des Höflichkeitskonjunktivs

Benjamin Richarz

Abstract

This article is intended to shed light on the question whether the phenomenon of the German politeness subjunctive (polite Konjunktiv: PolK) is just conversational and therefore should only be dealt with through pragmatic means or if arguments can be found in favour of the subjunctive being able to fulfil polite functionalities through its inherent semantic properties. Politeness is a category mostly dealt with in social science, but can be and often is realized through language.

While a (declarative) sentence uttered in indicative mood is mostly understood as: „*p is true*", a polite subjunctive declarative could have an interpretation such as „*I suggest p is true, but p's evaluation in the conversational background is transferred to the listener*".[1]

1. Funktionsbereiche des deutschen Konjunktivs

In den von Fabricius-Hansen[2] festgehaltenen Funktionsbereichen des Konjunktivs im Deutschen wird der Konjunktiv der Höflichkeit nur als Subklasse des irrealen Konjunktivs geführt:

---

[1] Ich danke Horst Lohnstein und Janina Beutler für wertvolle Kommentare und Anregungen im Entstehungsprozess dieses Papiers. Maurice Lorenz danke ich für das gründliche Lektorat. Alle noch verbliebenen Fehler sind mir anzurechnen.

[2] Fabricius-Hansen, Cathrine: Das Wort: Die flektierbaren Wortarten: 4. Das Verb. In: DUDEN. Die Grammatik. Mannheim: Bibliographisches Institut & F. A. Brockhaus AG 2006.

a. Funktionsbereich 1: Irrealität/Potenzialität: Konjunktiv II[3];
b. Funktionsbereich 2: Referat, besonders indirekte Rede: Konjunktiv I und II[4];
c. Funktionsbereich 3: Wunsch/Aufforderung: Konjunktiv I[5].

Die Autorin sortiert die höflichen Verwendungen des Konjunktivs in ihrer Auflistung in der Duden-Grammatik dem Funktionsbereich I zu. Eine modifizierte Gliederung findet sich bei Sode[6]:

a. Konjunktiv der Indirektheit (= KdI)
b. imperativischer Konjunktiv (= ImpK)
c. konditionaler Konjunktiv (= KondK)

Sie unterscheidet sich dahingehend, dass ‚Irrealität/Potentialität' auf einen gemeinsamen Ursprung, nämlich die konditionale Semantik, die Sodes (u. a.) Ansicht nach stets zugrunde liegt, zurückgeführt werden. Den bisher unter ‚Wunsch/Aufforderung' gefassten Funktionsbereich hebt Sode an und weist ihm ähnliche Funktionen wie dem Imperativ zu.

Beide Autoren behandeln den höflichen Konjunktiv als Randfunktion. Er wird als Konjunktiv II-Form dem Funktionsbereich 1 bzw. dem KondK zugerechnet.

2. Gegenstand der Betrachtung und Kritik der Zuordnung zu den Funktionsbereichen

Potenzial[7] zu interpretierende Konstruktionen, zu denen der höfliche Konjunktiv bei Fabricius-Hansen gehört, fallen verschiedenartig aus. Konstruktionen wie (1a) weisen vollkommen andere Bezüge auf, als solche wie (1b).

(1) a. Wären wir nur schon da!
     b. Da wären wir!

---

[3] Ebd. S. 523ff.
[4] Ebd. S. 529ff.
[5] Ebd. S. 543ff.
[6] Sode, Frank: Zur Semantik und Pragmatik des Konjunktivs der Indirektheit im Deutschen. Berlin 2014 (Diss., Humboldt Universität), S. 9f.
[7] Oft auch: real bzw. *realis*.

Während (1a) geäußert werden kann, wenn das beschriebene Ereignis noch nicht eingetreten ist, aber im erwartbaren weiteren Verlauf der Ereignisse wahrscheinlich (oder sogar auch dann, wenn nicht) eintreten wird – bspw. weil man sich gerade auf der Autofahrt zu einem Urlaubsziel befindet –, kann der Satz in (1b) nicht als eigentlich gemeinter, deklarativer Sprechakt geäußert werden, solange nicht das beschriebene Ereignis eingetreten ist, etwa das Erreichen des Urlaubsziels.

(2) a. Wären wir nur schon da! (Wir sind noch nicht da./*Wir sind da.)
    b. Da wären wir! (*Wir sind noch nicht da./Wir sind da.)

Der höfliche Konjunktiv tritt als Konjunktiv II auf und hat ähnliche Formen und Vorkommen wie der potenziale/irreale Konjunktiv, jedoch gibt es entscheidende Unterschiede: Dem irrealen Konjunktiv kann keine indikativische Entsprechung zur Seite gestellt werden, oder der Indikativ ist sogar für einige Satztypen blockiert (bzw. auf Spezialfälle beschränkt), vgl.:

(3) a. Peter äße Kuchen(, wenn er jetzt hier wäre.)
    b. Peter isst Kuchen*(, wenn er jetzt hier wäre.)
(4) a. Wenn ich doch nur fliegen könnte!
    b. ?Wenn ich doch nur fliegen kann![8]

In Verwendungen mit realem Bezug jedoch sind Indikativ und Konjunktiv gleichermaßen akzeptabel.

(5) a. Ich bräuchte ein Zimmer.
    b. Ich brauche ein Zimmer.
(6) a. Ich würde sagen[9], wir verkaufen.
    b. Ich sage, wir verkaufen.

---

[8] Nur möglich, kurz bevor der Sprecher es herausfindet. Vgl. Grosz, Patrick G.: Optativsätze. In: Jörg Meibauer / Markus Steinbach / Hans Altmann (Hgg.): Satztypen des Deutschen. Berlin/New York: de Gruyter 2000, S. 146–170, hier S. 148.

[9] Mit Fabricius-Hansen (2000, 1999) werden an dieser Stelle die würde-Konstruktionen ohne futurischen Bezug als äquivalente Formen zu den synthetischen Bildungen angenommen: Fabricius-Hansen, Cathrine: Die Geheimnisse der deutschen würde-Konstruktion. In: Thieroff, Rolf et al. (Hgg.): Deutsche Grammatik in Theorie und Praxis. Tübingen: Niemeyer 2000, S. 83–96; Fabricius-Hansen, Cathrine: „Moody Time": Indikativ und Konjunktiv im deutschen Tempussystem. In: Zeitschrift für Literaturwissenschaft und Linguistik 29/113 (1999), S. 119–146.

In der Bedeutung von (3) und (4) ist jeweils die Negation der Proposition enthalten. Diese Negation ist beim höflichen Konjunktiv ausgeschlossen: (5) kann nicht gelesen werden als *Es ist nicht der Fall, dass ich ein Zimmer brauche*, und (6) nicht als *Ich sage nicht, dass wir verkaufen*.

(3a') Peter äße Kuchen(, wenn er jetzt hier wäre).
→ Es ist gerade nicht der Fall, dass Peter Kuchen isst.
(4a') Wenn ich doch nur fliegen könnte!
→ Ich kann nicht fliegen.

Gleichermaßen kann ein Dialog geführt werden. Obwohl beide Sprecher in (7a) wissen, dass ein Zimmer benötigt wird und es auch ein freies gibt, kann vollständig der Konjunktiv verwendet werden.

(7) a. A: Ich bräuchte ein Zimmer.
B: Wir hätten nur noch die Hochzeitssuite.
A: In Ordnung, auch die würde ich nehmen.
b. A: Ich brauche ein Zimmer.
B: Wir haben nur noch die Hochzeitssuite.
A: In Ordnung, auch die nehme ich.

Die Lesarten *Ich brauche kein Zimmer, Wir haben kein Zimmer (oder ein ähnliches Objekt)* und *Dieses Objekt nehme ich nicht* bleiben ausgeschlossen. Auf dieser Grundlage glückt der Dialog.

Sode nimmt an, dass alle Konjunktive, die klassisch unter *realis/ irrealis* gefasst werden, konditionale Konjunktive sind und auf elliptischen Konstruktionen basieren.[10] Damit hätte (7a) die folgende Repräsentation:

(7a') A: Ich bräuchte ein Zimmer, (wenn ich hier schlafen möchte).
B: Wir hätten nur noch die Hochzeitssuite(, wenn Sie ein Zimmer wollen).
A: In Ordnung, auch die würde ich nehmen(, wenn es das einzige freie zimmerartige Objekt ist).

---

[10] Sode: Zur Semantik und Pragmatik des Konjunktivs der Indirektheit im Deutschen (Anm. 6), S. 213ff.

3. Der Konjunktiv als Verschiebeinstanz

Der Konjunktiv verschiebt eine Instanz der Weltverortung weg vom Sprecher. Eine solche ‚Syntax der Perspektive' findet sich bereits angelegt bspw. bei Fabricius-Hansen[11], Lohnstein[12] oder Bredel/Lohnstein[13].

Ausgearbeitet wurde sie bei Sode[14] und Truckenbrodt/Sode[15]. Als Grundlage dient der ‚Origo'-Begriff Bühlers[16]:

(8) **Origo**[17] (im Sinne von Bühler)
    i. < Person$_S$, Zeit$_S$, Modalität$_S$,   Ort$_S$, ... >
    ii. < Ich$_S$,   Jetzt$_S$, aktuelle Welt $w_{0,S}$, Hier$_S$, ... >

Sode und aufbauend Truckenbrodt/Sode nehmen eine Origoinstanz an, von der aus eine Verschiebung stattfinden muss, damit der Konjunktiv möglich ist. Bleibt der Sprechakt an den Sprecher zur Äußerungszeit gebunden, kann kein Konjunktiv gesetzt werden.

---

[11] Fabricius-Hansen: „Moody Time" (Anm. 9), S. 135.
[12] Lohnstein, Horst: Satzmodus – kompositionell. Zur Parametrisierung der Modusphrase im Deutschen (studia grammatica 49). Berlin: Akademie-Verlag 2000.
[13] Bredel, Ursula / Horst Lohnstein: Zur Analyse und Verwendung der Tempus- und Modusformen im Deutschen. In: Oddleif Leirbukt (Hg.): Tempus/Temporalität – Modus/Modalität. Tübingen: Stauffenburg 2002, S. 87–117; Bredel, Ursula / Horst Lohnstein: Zur Ableitung von Tempus und Modus in der deutschen Verbflexion. In: Zeitschrift für Sprachwissenschaft 20/2 (2001), S. 218–250.
[14] Sode: Zur Semantik und Pragmatik des Konjunktivs der Indirektheit im Deutschen (Anm. 6).
[15] Truckenbrodt, Hubert / Frank Sode: Parenthesen und V-nach-C-Bewegung. 2nd International V2-Workshop. 29.–31.07.2016. http://www.linguistik.uni-wuppertal.de/v2-workshop-2016/handouts/Truckenbrodt-Sode.pdf (01.11.2016); Truckenbrodt, Hubert / Frank Sode: Wurzelphänomene und die Syntax der Perspektive. 1st international V2-Workshop. 24.–26.06.2015. Bergische Universität Wuppertal. http:// http://www.linguistik.uni-wuppertal.de/v2-workshop-2015/handouts/truckenbrodt.pdf (01.11.2016).
[16] Bühler, Karl: Sprachtheorie. Die Darstellungsfunktion der Sprache. Stuttgart: Lucius & Lucius 1982 (ungekürzter Neudruck der Ausgabe Jena: Fischer 1934), S. 102f.; Rauh, Gisa: Temporale Deixis. In: Veronika Ehrich / Heinz Vater: Temporalsemantik. Beiträge zur Linguistik der Zeitreferenz. Tübingen: Niemeyer 1988, S. 26–51.
[17] Nach Bredel / Lohnstein: Zur Ableitung von Tempus und Modus (Anm. 13), S. 13.

(9) [Maria erzählte von ihrem Urlaub.][18]
  a. Die Sonne[Maria][+origo]   hat die ganze Zeit geschienen.
  (Maria als Sprecherin)
  b. Die Sonne[Maria][-origo]   habe die ganze Zeit geschienen.
  (Maria als Figur)

Die Origo bildet das Zentrum (den Nullpunkt) des Koordinatensystems, in dem sich Individuen hinsichtlich verschiedener Dimensionen (Person, Zeit, Raum, ...) orientieren. Jedes Individuum setzt sich dabei als Origo eines je eigenen Koordinatensystems. Der Index [Maria][+origo] markiert entsprechend, dass aus Marias Perspektive erzählt wird, während der Index [Maria][-origo] ausdrückt, dass dies aus einer anderen Perspektive geschieht.

Der KdI stellt eine grammatische Form dar, deren Bedeutung darin besteht, auf eine andere Origo-Instanz und damit auf eine andere (tatsächliche oder vorgestellte) Sprechsituation zu verweisen bzw. zu verschieben. Die grammatische Form des KondK dient hingegen dem Verweis auf eine von der aktuellen Welt verschiedene, alternative Welt, sei sie nun zugänglich oder auch nicht.

3.1. Der KdI als logophorischer Modus

‚Logophorizität', mit der Bedeutung ‚Diskurs tragend', ist der etablierte Begriff für die sprachliche Markierung von ‚Verschiebung der Perspektive':

> Logophoricity refers to the phenomenon whereby the ‚perspective' of an internal protagonist of a sentence or discourse, as opposed to that of the current, external speaker, is being reported by some morphological and/or syntactic means. The term ‚perspective' is used here in a technical sense and is intended to encompass words, thoughts, knowledge, emotion, perception, and space-location.[19]

---

[18] Truckenbrodt/Sode: Wurzelphänomene und die Syntax der Perspektive (Anm. 15), S. 2. Neue Zusammenstellung durch BR.
[19] Huang, Yan: Anaphora: A Cross-linguistic Approach. Oxford Studies in Typology and Linguistic Theory. Oxford: Oxford University Press 2010, S. 172f.

Festgemacht wurde der Begriff in der jüngeren Literatur nach Schlenker[20] am Konjunktiv der Indirektheit, der wie ein sog. ‚logophorisches Pronomen' funktioniert, wie es bspw. in der Kwa-Sprache Ewe aus der Sprachgruppe der Niger-Kongo-Sprachen existiert:

(10) a. Kófí   bè   yé-dzó.
        Kofi   say   LOG-leave
        'Kofi said that he (= Kofi) left'
   b. Kófí   bè   é-dzó.
        Kofi   say   3SG-leave
        'Kofi said that he (≠ Kofi) left'[21]

Schlenker trägt in seinen Arbeiten seit 1999 Argumente dafür zusammen, dass der KdI des Deutschen sich verhält wie ein logophorisches Pronomen:

(11) a. *Ich glaube, dass Maria krank sei.
   b. Ich dachte, dass Maria krank sei.
   c. Peter denkt, dass Maria krank sei.
   d. Peter dachte, dass Maria krank sei.[22]

Die Beispiele zeigen, dass es eine vom Sprecher verschiedene Sprecherinstanz geben muss, die für den ausgedrückten propositionalen Gehalt verantwortlich zeichnet. Diese kann auch der Sprecher selbst, aber zu einem anderen (vergangenen) Zeitpunkt sein.[23]

Schlenker postuliert: „The Konjunktiv I cannot be used in the 1st person present singular of ‚believe'."[24] Dies hängt mit einem Widerspruch zusammen, der sich schon in den älteren Paradoxien der *notorious yacht*-Beispiele bei Russel[25] findet. Schlenker konstruiert zu diesem Zweck ein ähnliches Beispiel:

---

[20] Schlenker, Philippe: Propositional Attitudes and Indexicality: A Cross-Categorial Approach. Cambridge: Massachusetts Institute of Technology 1999.
[21] Glossen nach Huang: Anaphora, S. 174. Beispiel aus: Clements, George N.: The logophoric pronoun in Ewe: its role in discourse. In: Journal of West African Languages 10 (1975), S. 141–177, hier S. 142.
[22] Schlenker, Philippe: A Plea for Monsters. In: Linguistics and Philosophy 26/1 (2003), S. 29–120, hier S. 36.
[23] Dies findet sich auch so bei Lohnstein: Satzmodus – kompositionell (Anm. 12), S. 103.
[24] Schlenker: A Plea for Monsters (Anm. 22), S. 87.
[25] Russell, Bertrand: On denoting. In: Mind, New Series 14/56 (1905), S. 479–493.

(12) Der Peter meint,
   a. es sei später, als es tatsächlich ist.
   b. es ist später, als es tatsächlich ist.
   c. *es sei später, als es tatsächlich sei.
   d. *es ist später, als es tatsächlich sei.[26]

Der Widerspruch besteht nun darin, dass Peters eingeschätzt reale Welt nicht mittels des KdI markiert werden kann, da dieser durch das Einstellungsverb gebunden ist: Der Indikativ kann inner- oder außerhalb des Skopus eines Einstellungsverbs interpretiert werden, für den Konjunktiv ist die außerhalb-Lesart ausgeschlossen.[27] Deshalb kann der Indikativ mit Bezug auf die aktuelle Welt interpretiert werden, der Konjunkiv I nicht – so entsteht die widersprüchliche Lesart.

Sode gibt die folgenden Formalisierungen des Beispiels von Schlenker[28]:

(13) a. wλ1 t1 der Peter meint λ2 w2 t spät [ER w1 tatsächlich spät]
   b. *wλ1 t1 der Peter meint λ2 w2 t spät [ER w2 tatsächlich spät]

3.2. Der KondK als Verschiebung auf mögliche Welten

Der KondK (ausschließlich repräsentiert durch den Konjunktiv II) verschiebt entlang einer anderen Achse: Während im KdI auf eine andere Sprecherinstanz bzw. eine solche zu einem vergangenen oder vorgestellten Zeitpunkt verwiesen werden muss, kann diese Perspektive im KondK unverschoben bleiben. Diese Erkenntnis fand verschiedene Ausbuchstabierungen bspw. in Fabricius-Hansen (1999), Lohnstein (2000), Bredel/Lohnstein (2001, 2002) und zuletzt wieder in Lohnstein/Staratschek[29].

An dieser Stelle soll exemplarisch die Arbeit von Bredel/Lohnstein (2001) – über die grundsätzliche Verschiebeeigenschaft des Konjunktivs,

---

[26] Schlenker: A Plea for Monsters (Anm. 22), S. 29.
[27] Ebd.
[28] Sode: Zur Semantik und Pragmatik des Konjunktivs der Indirektheit im Deutschen (Anm. 6), S. 99.
Sode entwickelt in seiner Arbeit diesen Ansatz weiter, was an dieser Stelle nicht vertieft werden soll.
[29] Lohnstein, Horst / Nathalie Staratschek: V2, Finitheit und die Satztypen. 2nd International V2-Workshop, 29.–31.07.2016, Bergische Universität Wuppertal http://www.linguistik.uni-wuppertal.de/v2-workshop-2016/handouts/Lohnstein-Staratschek.pdf (01.11.2016).

repräsentiert durch seine Flexionsmorpheme – knapp erläutert werden. Das Flexionsinventar des Deutschen sieht aus wie folgt:[30]

(14)

Ind.1 (schwach)	Ind.1 (stark)	Konj.1 (schwach)	Konj.1 (stark)
lach – e	geb – e	lach – e	geb – e
lach – s – t	gib – s – t	lach – e – s – t	geb – e – s – t
lach – t	gib – t	lach – e	geb – e
lach – e – n	geb – e – n	lach – e – n	geb – e – n
lach – t	geb – t	lach – e – t	geb – e – t
lach – e – n	geb – e – n	lach – e – n	geb – e – n

Ind.2 (schwach)	Ind.2 (stark)	Konj.2 (schwach)	Konj.2 (stark)
lach – t – e	Gab	lach – t – e	gäb – e
lach – t – e – s – t	gab – s – t	lach – t – e – s – t	gäb – e – s – t
lach – t – e	Gab	lach – t – e	gäb – e
lach – t – e – n	gab – e – n	lach – t – e – n	gäb – e – n
lach – t – e – t	gab – t	lach – t – e – t	gäb – e – t
lach – t – e –n	gab – e – n	lach – t – e – n	gäb – e – n

In dieser Arbeit wird den Tempora-Modi-Formen des Deutschen und konkreter den Markierungen (Morphem M) -t und -ə jeweils eine verschiebende Funktion (temporal oder modal) zugeordnet; je nachdem, ob sie ‚basiskonfigurierend' oder ‚wortform-konfigurierend' gebunden sind:

(15) i. Basiskonfiguration: [Stammform + M]$_{Basis}$
 ii. Wortformkonfiguration: [Stammform]$_{Basis}$ + M[31]

-ə und -t strukturieren das verbale Paradigma in Hinsicht auf indikativische und konjunktivische sowie präsentische und präteritale Verbformen in der folgenden Weise:[32]

(16)

Indikativ 1 -t_w – $ə_w$	Konjunktiv 1 *-t, -$ə_b$
Indikativ 2 -b_b, *-ə	Konjunktiv 2 -t_b -$ə_b$

---

[30] Bredel/Lohnstein: Zur Ableitung von Tempus und Modus (Anm. 13), S. 221.
[31] Ebd., S. 226.
[32] Ebd., S. 229.

Zusammengenommen ergeben sich somit in der kompositionellen Analyse dieses Ansatzes die folgenden Funktionen für die Markierungen durch die Flexionsmorpheme:

(17) a. Funktionen der t-Markierung:
  i. Verschiebung von der Person des Sprechers auf eine andere Person.
  ii. Verschiebung von der Gegenwart auf eine andere Zeit.
  iii. Verschiebung von der aktuellen Welt auf eine Alternativwelt.
 b. Funktionen der ə-Markierung
  i. Das Denotat des Prädikats ist Element der Person-Koordinate in der Origo.
  ii. Die Auswertungszeit der Proposition ist Element der Zeit-Koordinate in der Origo.
  iii. Die Auswertungswelt der Proposition ist Element der Welt-Koordinate in der Origo.[33]

In der Übersicht ergeben sich bestimmte Referenzbereiche (m. a. W. ein Zeigefeld), die durch die verschiedenen Funktionen der Tempora und Modi abgedeckt werden:

(18) Funktionen und Verweise der Tempus-Modus-Formen[34]

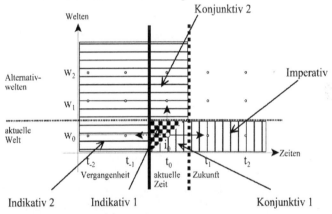

[33] Ebd., S. 232f.
[34] Ebd., S. 238.

Die Analyse stützt sich erkennbar auf eine intentionale Grundannahme eines jeden Sprechaktes: So wird jeder Proposition ein bestimmter Redehintergrund zugeteilt, vor dem sie zu interpretieren ist.[35] Die Autoren beziehen sich stets auf den Default-Fall der Verwendung der jeweiligen Form.[36]

Der Verweis des ‚irrealen' Funktionsbereiches ist auf folgende Weise formalisierbar:

(19) Peter käme.
    i. p = dass Peter kommt
    ii. (Konjunktiv 2)(p) = dass Peter käme
    iii. B= {   p1 = Clara ist da.
                  p2 = Maria ist auch da.
                  p3 = Es gibt genug Bier.}

(20) (Konjunktiv 2)(p) ist an i_0 wahr gdw.
    i. ?i': i' ∈ ∩ ($mb_{fakt}(i_0)$ ∪ B)
    ii. (Indikativ 1)(p) ist wahr an i'.[37]

Als Ergebnis der angeführten Arbeiten Lohnsteins (seit 2000) wird auf einer weiterführenden Abstraktionsebene das Funktionsparadigma des Konjunktivs in direkter Entsprechung zum formalen Aufbau kompositionell rekonstruiert:

---

[35] Die Redehintergründe bei Bredel/Lohnstein unterscheiden sich in der Bezeichnungsweise von denen bei Kratzer, die aber dennoch die Grundlage bilden: Kratzer, Angelika: Modality. In: Arnim von Stechow / Dieter Wunderlich (Hg.): Semantik. Ein internationales Handbuch der zeitgenössischen Forschung. Berlin: de Gruyter 1991, S. 639–650.

[36] In anderen Ansätzen wird diese enge Bindung zu Ungunsten der festen Möglichkeit der Zuordnung in dieser Form nicht angenommen, jedoch mit der Möglichkeit der Berücksichtigung auch der Austauschbarkeit der Formen innerhalb desselben Funktionsbereiches. Vgl. etwa Fabricius-Hansen: Die Geheimnisse der deutschen würde-Konstruktion (Anm. 9).

[37] Bredel/Lohnstein: Zur Ableitung von Tempus und Modus (Anm. 13), S. 241.

(21) Kompositionelle Analyse der Verbmodi[38]

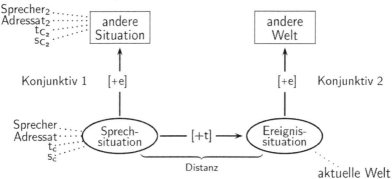

3.3. Zusammenführung

Wie gezeigt, weist die Forschung dem Konjunktiv des Deutschen also eine zentrale Eigenschaft zu: Verschiebung. Auf Basis dieser Beobachtungen möchte ich nun drei Hypothesen formulieren:

H1 Die mit dem Konjunktiv ausgedrückte Verschiebung lässt sich in der folgenden Weise skalieren:

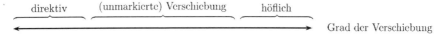

H2 Jede Äußerung im KondK ist vor einer modalen Basis[39] zu interpretieren.

H3 Allen Sprechern ist die modale Funktion des Konjunktivs bekannt; deswegen kann der KondK die höfliche Funktion übernehmen.

Die Typen der Verschiebung sind in den verschiedenen Konjunktivflexemen kodiert.[40] Deswegen gehe ich davon aus, dass neben den Default-

---

[38] Lohnstein/Staratschek: V2, Finitheit, Satztypen (Anm. 29). S. 4.
[39] Wie bei: Kratzer: Modality (Anm. 35), S. 644.
[40] Auf der Basis von Lohnstein: Satzmodus – kompositionell (Anm. 12), Lohnstein/Bredel: Zur Ableitung von Tempus und Modus (Anm. 13) und Lohnstein/Staratschek: V2, Finitheit und die Satztypen (Anm. 29).

Funktionen des Konjunktivs so auch die weniger produktiven Randfunktionen kompositionell erklärt werden können.[41]

(22) Funktionen des Konjunktivs

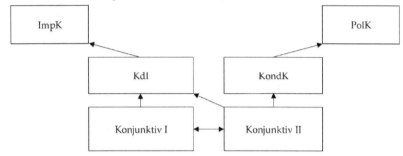

Die Formen Konjunktiv I und Konjunktiv II bilden eine gemeinsame Klasse von Formen, mit denen Verschiebung signalisiert werden kann. Ihre Default-Funktionen sind der KdI (Konjunktiv I) und der KondK (Konjunktiv II). Ferner kann auch der Konjunktiv II im KdI auftreten. Der direktive Konjunktiv (ImpK) ist ebenfalls eine an den Konjunktiv I gebundene Form,[42] wohingegen der PolK ausschließlich im Konjunktiv II realisiert werden kann und eine Unterfunktion des KondK ist.

4. Der dialogische Beitrag des höflichen Konjunktivs

Die aufgestellten Hypothesen werden nun anhand einer verkürzt dargestellten Analyse überprüft (eine Betrachtung des ImpK hat an dieser Stelle keinen Platz).

4.1. Was ist höflich?

Eine feste Definition dessen, was höflich ist, existiert nicht. Praktisch jede Handlung, sprachlich oder außersprachlich, könnte kulturell als höflich

---

[41] Dieser Ansatz wendet sich somit gegen rein pragmatische Annäherungsversuche wie bspw.: Fujinawa, Yoshinori: „Das hätte ich geschafft!" – Zum grenzüberschreitenden Vorkommen von Konjunktiven mit realem Bezug im Gegenwartsdeutsch. In: Neue Beiträge zur Germanistik 5/3 (2006): Germanistische Linguistik heute – anhand von Beispielen aus der Arbeit des IDS, S. 62–76.
[42] Ob er ein Sonderfall des KdI ist, bleibt zu diskutieren.

akzeptiert werden, wenngleich es einige Dinge gibt, die in den meisten Kulturen als höflich gelten. Dazu gehört bspw. die Wertschätzung des Gegenübers, sei es durch die japanische Verbeugung oder die chinesische Sitte, keine klare Ablehnung zu formulieren. Höflichkeit bedeutet, die Integrität des Individuums möglichst unangetastet zu lassen, was bedeutet, dass das Individuum freien Handlungsspielraum hat. Dieser Ansatz wird insbesondere auch von Bredel/Lohnstein vertreten.[43]

Das Deutsche hat einige Möglichkeiten, Äußerungen höflich zu kodieren, wobei dies jedoch graduell zu sehen ist. In unangemessenem Ton oder falschem Kontext könnten selbst diese (abgestuft) höflichen Varianten im Deutschen unhöflich sein:

(23) a. Ich   hätte   gerne   ein Stück   Apfelkuchen
I   have-1SG.SBJV   PARTICLE   a piece   apple pie
'I would like a piece of apple pie'
b. Ich   bekomme   ein Stück   Apfelkuchen
I   get-1SG.IND   a piece   apple pie
literally: ‚I am getting a piece of apple pie'[44]

Stellvertretend für den Diskurs der Höflichkeitsforschung steht an dieser Stelle Schlund (2014).[45] Sie zeigt, dass sprachliche Höflichkeit ein mehrstufiges, kontextabhängiges Konstrukt ist, für das sowohl Satztyp als auch die verbale Kategorie und der Fokus usw. eine Rolle spielen. Mit anderen Worten: Dass der Konjunktiv im Deutschen eine Höflichkeitsfunktion innehat, ist ihrer Analyse zufolge zufällig, da dieselbe Funktion auch auf anderem Wege hätte kodiert werden können.

Dieser Position möchte ich Argumente entgegenhalten, die dafür sprechen, dass der Konjunktiv auf Grund seiner Verschiebefunktion eine besonders gut geeignete Form der Kodierung eines höflichen Sprechakts ist.

---

[43] Bredel, Ursula / Horst Lohnstein: Zur Verankerung von Sprecher und Hörer im verbalen Paradigma des Deutschen. In: Ludger Hoffmann (Hg.): Funktionale Syntax – Die pragmatische Perspektive. Berlin, New York: de Gruyter 2003, S. 122–154, hier S. 148ff.
[44] Schlund, Katrin: On form and function of politeness formulae. In: Journal of Politeness Research 10/2 (2014), S. 271–296, hier S. 291.
[45] Für eine Ausarbeitung des Diskurses oder auch nur der Argumente im Detail bietet diese Arbeit keinen Raum.

4.2. Konjunktiv statt Indikativ

In einem Dialog wie (7) – hier wiederholt als (24) – scheint der höfliche Konjunktiv angesichts der Möglichkeit der Wahl der indikativischen Entsprechung keinen Mehrwert zu haben:

(24) A: Ich bräuchte ein Zimmer.
   B: Wir hätten nur noch die Hochzeitssuite.
   A: In Ordnung, auch die würde ich nehmen.

Zifonun/Hoffmann/Strecker vermuten, dass „es nur so erscheinen [soll], als wäre das Gesagte nicht faktisch".[46] Durch die Verminderung der Faktizität könne eine geringere Verbindlichkeit in alle Richtungen erzielt werden. An dieser Stelle soll jedoch ein Ansatz verfolgt werden, der dieses funktionale Merkmal auf einen anderen grammatischen Ursprung zurückführt.[47]

Das Verb *brauchen* ist an dieser Stelle Ausdruck eines buletischen Redehintergrunds: Sprecher A bevorzugt Welten w_1, in denen er ein Zimmer hat (p) gegenüber Welten w_2, in denen er keines hat ($\neg$p). Die Wünsche des Sprechers (buletischer Redehintergrund) werden durch die ausgedrückte Proposition sortiert (Welten, in denen der Sprecher ein Zimmer hat, sind besser als Welten, in denen er kein Zimmer hat: $[(w_1 \leq_r w_2)]$).

Die höfliche Funktion liegt nun darin, dass die Ordnungsquelle, die normalerweise als Einstellungsausdruck vom Sprecher vorgegeben wird und somit mögliche Welten sortiert, an dieser Stelle der Einschätzung des Gegenübers preisgegeben wird.

(25) **Vorschlag zur informellen Analyse der Bedeutung des PolK**
   a. Ich brauche ein Zimmer.
      → Ein Zimmer zu erhalten, entspricht meinen Wünschen, deswegen bevorzuge ich von der realen Welt aus zugängliche Welten w1, in denen ich ein Zimmer habe gegenüber Welten w2, in denen ich keines habe, und ich weiß, dass B die Möglichkeit hat, meinen Wunsch zu erfüllen.[48]

---

[46] Zifonun, Gisela / Ludger Hoffmann / Bruno Strecker: Grammatik der deutschen Sprache. 3 Bde. Berlin, New York: de Gruyter 1997, S. 1753.
[47] Ein ähnliches Vorgehen findet sich bei Bredel/Lohnstein: Zur Verankerung von Sprecher und Hörer (Anm. 43), S. 148ff.
[48] Voraussetzung: Der Sprechakt ist angemessen.

b. Ich bräuchte ein Zimmer.

→ Ein Zimmer zu erhalten, entspricht meinen Wünschen, deswegen bevorzuge ich von der realen Welt aus zugängliche Welten w1, in denen ich ein Zimmer habe gegenüber Welten w2, in denen ich keines habe, und ich weiß, dass B die Möglichkeit hat, meinen Wunsch zu erfüllen. **Ich übertrage die Einschätzung der Ordnungsquelle der zugänglichen Welten auf B.**

Diese durch den Konjunktiv erfolgte Offenlegung der Sprechermotivation wahrt die Integrität des Gegenübers in höherem Maße, da die Hoheit der Wunschdeutung nicht mehr beim Sprecher liegt. Der Hörer hat nun die Möglichkeit, affirmativ, ablehnend oder auch mit *Das kann ich nicht* zu reagieren, ohne zu stark bedrängt zu werden: „Der Sprecher räumt dem Hörer [...] die Möglichkeit ein, im Falle einer Zurückweisung nicht selbst als ‚unhöflich' zu gelten."[49] Gleichzeitig wahrt dies auch die Integrität des ursprünglichen Sprechers, da bei einer ablehnenden Antwort nicht dessen Wunsch infrage gestellt, sondern nur ausgedrückt wird, dass dieser im Moment nicht erfüllt werden kann.

Sprecher B hingegen verweist auf Welten, die Eigenschaften einer Teilmenge der Welten w_1, also etwa *ein Raum zum Schlafen mit Bett* und *in einem Hotel* beinhalten. Aber auch Eigenschaften einer Teilmenge der Welten w_2 sind vorhanden, wie *eine Suite ist mehr als ein Zimmer*, und so bezieht sich B auf eine Menge von Welten $w_3 = w_1 \cap w_2$. Enthalten ist darin auch: *Wir haben kein Zimmer* – in dem Sinne, in dem Sprecher A mutmaßlich Sprecher B den Begriff Zimmer versteht.

Im Falle des Modalverbs *(nicht) brauchen*[50], ist der Beitrag des PolK der oben beschriebene. Der Redehintergrund als modale Basis ist bereits in der Verbbedeutung kodiert. Im Falle eines nicht-modalen Verbs wie *haben* ist die folgende Äußerung vor einem epistemischen Redehintergrund getätigt. Die Eigenschaft als Antwortsequenz bringt es mit sich, dass hier nicht kontextfrei Bezug darauf genommen wird, dass es eine freie Hochzeitssuite gibt, sondern dass sie sozusagen ein Gegenvorschlag ist, der die Akzeptanz der Wahrheit der initialen Äußerung voraussetzt.

---

[49] Bredel/Lohnstein: Zur Verankerung von Sprecher und Hörer (Anm. 43), S. 147.
[50] Vgl. Ich brauche das nicht zu tun bzw. *Ich brauche das zu tun.

(26) **Vorschlag zur informellen Analyse der Bedeutung des PolK**
   a. Wir haben nur noch die Hochzeitssuite.
   → Gleichzeitig gilt: Es gibt ein Zimmer gemäß einiger Teileigenschaften der Welten w1 und es gibt ein Zimmer gemäß einiger Teileigenschaften der Welten w2. Deswegen biete ich an: Ein Zimmer mit Eigenschaften w1 ∩ w2.
   b. Wir hätten nur noch die Hochzeitssuite.
   → Gleichzeitig gilt: Es gibt ein Zimmer gemäß einiger Teileigenschaften der Welten w1 und es gibt ein Zimmer gemäß einiger Teileigenschaften der Welten w2. Deswegen biete ich an: Ein Zimmer mit Eigenschaften w1 ∩ w2, und **ich übertrage A offen die Einschätzung, ob diese Welten w3 für ihn – auf Grundlage seiner modalen Basis – zugänglich sind.**

Der Indikativ (ohne modal zu verstehendes oder echtes Modalverb) verweist auf die als real eingeschätzte, aktuelle Welt. Der höfliche Konjunktiv verweist im nicht-modalen Fall auf mögliche Welten und überträgt die Einschätzung der Zugänglichkeit auf den Hörer. Im modalen Fall überträgt er die Einschätzung der Ordnungsquelle.

Mit anderen Worten: Dass der Konjunktiv II die Form ist, mit der dieser höfliche Übertrag ausgedrückt wird, kann nicht verwundern. Verschiebung auf mögliche Welten ist in ihm semantisch kodiert, und im Falle des PolK wird nicht darauf Bezug genommen, was denkbar ist, sondern wie sich die denkbare Situation zur aktuellen Welt verhält. Die Offenlegung dessen folgt dem Prinzip: Höflich ist, was das Gegenüber nicht vor eine vollendete Entscheidung stellt.

4.3 Möglichkeit der Formalisierung

Mit dem von Donka Farkas und Kim Bruce vorgeschlagenen Diskursanalysemodell[51] ist eine genauere Explikation der Analyse möglich. Das Modell sieht zwei Sprecherinstanzen (A und B), einen sog. ‚Tisch', der als Raum für geäußerte Inhalte (‚discourse commitments', DC) dient, solange sie noch *at issue* sind, weiterhin den ‚Common Ground' (cg)[52]. Der cg ist

---

[51] Farkas, Donka / Kim Bruce: On Reacting to Assertions and Polar Questions. In: Journal of Semantics 27 (2010), S. 81–118.
[52] Im Sinne von: Stalnaker, Robert C.: Assertion. In: P. Cole (Hg.): Language Typology and Syntactic Description. Cambridge: Cambridge University Press 1978, S. 315–332.

diejenige Menge an Propositionen, die von allen Partizipanten zum Zeitpunkt t des Gesprächs c akzeptiert und anschließend geteilt werden, gemeinsam mit denjenigen Propositionen, die das geteilte Hintergrundwissen der Partizipanten abbilden. Zusätzlich gibt es das ‚projected set' (ps), welches stets die Menge der möglichen Ausgangszustände des cg beinhaltet. Dabei gilt: ps ⊃ cg.

(27) Notation einer Dialogstruktur:

A	Table	B
DC_A	S	DC_B
Common Ground *cg*	**Projected Set** *ps*	

Wird jetzt also (25a) geäußert, geschieht das Folgende: Relativ zum ursprünglichen Kontextzustand s_1 und somit dem Inhalt im ps: $ps_1 = \{s_1\}$ äußert A: *Ich brauche ein Zimmer*. Wie oben beschrieben, geschieht dies vor dem buletischen Redehintergrund r = ich möchte übernachten, weswegen $[(w_1 \leq_r w_2)]$.

(28) K_1: A assertiert ‚Ich brauche ein Zimmer' relativ zu K_1:

A	Table	B
p	„Ich brauche ein Zimmer'[D];{p}'	
cg $s_2 = s_1$	**ps** $ps_w = \{s_1 \cup \{p\}\}$	

Das Ergebnis ist der modifizierte Kontext K_3.

Die Äußerung, die für den angeführten Dialog als Antwort akzeptabel ist, ist ebenfalls eine Assertion. Mit der Äußerung von *Wir haben nur noch die Hochzeitssuite* erkennt Sprecher B die Wahrheit von p an. p wird somit in den cg verschoben bzw. als Teil des cg akzeptiert.

(29) K_3: B assertiert ‚Wir haben nur noch die Hochzeitssuite' relativ zu K:

A	Table	B
	„Wir haben nur noch die Hochzeitssuite'[D];{p}'	q
cg $s_2 = \{s_1 \cup \{p\}\}$	**ps** $ps_w = \{\{s_1 \cup \{p\}\} \cup \{q\}\}$	

Wird stattdessen die Äußerung im Konjunktiv getätigt, so ist, unabhängig von der Verwendung eines Modalverbs, im Falle des PolK die modale Basis Teil dessen, was *at issue* ist.[53]

---

[53] Ob eine im Konjunktiv getätigte Äußerung, sei sie auch im PolK, eine Assertion ist, bleibt problematisch.

(30) A: Ich möchte, dass p.
  → p soll wahr werden in w1, also [(w1 ≤r w2)]

(31) K1: A assertiert ‚Ich bräuchte ein Zimmer' relativ zu K_1:

A	Table	B
p	„Ich bräuchte ein Zimmer'[D];{p ∧ [($w_1 \leq_r w_2$)]}'	
cg $s_2 = s_1$	ps $ps_w = \{s_1 \cup \{p\}\}$	

Das ps dieser Äußerung unterscheidet sich nicht von demjenigen der indikativischen Äußerung, da zwar die modale Basis mit auf den Tisch gelegt wird, aber diese nicht Bestandteil von p ist, sondern nur die Grundlage des Sprechakts. Die Offenlegung, die der Konjunktiv an dieser Stelle signalisiert, hat nur die Funktion des Übertrags der Einschätzung an den Hörer, wie dringend p ist. Diese Machtübertragung bzw. das Überlassen der Entscheidung ist eine sprachliche Anerkennung der Höherrangigkeit oder zumindest eine Wertschätzung des Gegenübers, die als höflich empfunden wird.

Ähnlich verhält es sich bei der Antwortsequenz im PolK. An der Akzeptanz von p als wahr und der Hinzufügung zum cg ändert sich nichts, doch über den Gehalt der indikativischen Äußerung hinaus wird erneut offen auf die modale Basis der initialen Äußerung Bezug genommen.

(32) B: q ist wahr.
  → Es gibt ein Zimmer gemäß einiger Teileigenschaften der Welten w_1 und es gibt ein Zimmer gemäß einiger Teileigenschaften der Welten w2, wie offengelegt in der modalen Basis von p. In Bezug auf die modale Basis von p biete ich an: Ein Zimmer mit Eigenschaften w3 = w1 ∩ w2.

(33) K2: B assertiert ‚Wir hätten nur noch die Hochzeitssuite' relativ zu K2:

A	Table	B
	„Wir hätten nur noch die Hochzeitssuite'[D];{q; [($w_1 \leq_r w_2$)]}'	q
cg $s_2 = \{s_1 \cup \{p\}\}$	ps $ps_w = \{\{s_1 \cup \{p\}\} \cup \{q\}\}$	

Wie im Falle der Antwort im Indikativ kann hier affirmativ oder ablehnend reagiert werden, doch ist der offene Bezug Bs auf eine von A eingeführte modale Basis kulturell ein Zeichen der Wertschätzung As durch B.

Folgerichtig müsste abschließend eine dritte, von der Verschiebung im KdI und im Default-KondK differente, Verschiebeoption angenommen werden, die der bloßen Wunschoffenlegung ein Merkmal verleiht, das die Deutungshoheit des Hörers eindeutig macht. Diese Verschiebung kann ausschließlich im Dialog erfolgen. Eine Ausarbeitung dieses Merkmals muss an dieser Stelle auf zukünftige Arbeiten verschoben werden.

5. Fazit

Für die beiden zentralen Funktionsbereiche des Konjunktivs, den KdI und den KondK, wurde seitens der Forschung gezeigt, dass der Konjunktiv als eine Verschiebeinstanz wirkt. Nach dem vorliegenden Ansatz kommen die beiden Randfunktionen des Konjunktivs, ImpK und PolK, auf Grund der Verschiebeeigenschaften des Konjunktivs zustande und sind Subklassen der beiden Funktionsbereiche.

Der PolK ist nun eine Möglichkeit, das soziale Phänomen der Höflichkeit sprachlich zu kodieren. Ich schlage an dieser Stelle vor, in den grammatischen Eigenschaften des Konjunktivs (Verschiebung) nach dem Grund dafür zu suchen, warum ausgerechnet der Konjunktiv als ein Mittel dafür geeignet ist. Der Verschiebungstyp im KondK erzeugt die Interpretation der Proposition vor einem Redehintergrund. Im PolK (mit oder ohne Modalverb), einer Subklasse des KondK, findet ein Übertrag der Einschätzung des Redehintergrunds bzw. der Ordnungsquelle statt. Dieser Übertrag wahrt die Integrität des Hörers, indem er ihm keine Pflicht auferlegt, sondern ihm im Gegenteil eine Art wechselseitig Integrität wahrende Entscheidungsverantwortung verleiht.

Auf dieser Grundlage muss zu den beiden Verschiebungstypen im KdI und im KonK wahrscheinlich ein weiterer Verschiebetyp angenommen werden. Etwa: ‚Verschiebe die Bewertung meiner Wünsche auf den Adressaten.' Argumente für die Annahme dieses Typs wurden in diesem Papier angeführt.

Die Beiträgerinnen und Beiträger

Janina Beutler, BA-Studium der Fächer Anglistik und Klassische Philologie, MA-Studium der Germanistik mit Schwerpunkt Linguistik an der Bergischen Universität Wuppertal (BUW). Derzeit im Promotionsstudium im Fach Germanistische Linguistik und wissenschaftliche Mitarbeiterin bei Prof. Horst Lohnstein an der BUW, zusätzlich Studium der Musik. Thema der Dissertation: Untersuchung von V1-Sätzen – Syntax und Semantik von V1- und V2-Strukturen im Deutschen. Vorträge im Rahmen des Projekts *IPIW – international promovieren in Wuppertal* und auf der Jahrestagung der *Deutschen Gesellschaft für Sprachwissenschaft (DGfS)* 2017.

Valeria Fernandez Blanco, Diplom-Germanistin der National Universität von La Plata (Argentinien). Wissenschaftliche Assistentin am Lehrstuhl Studienbegleitender Deutschunterricht. Thema der Dissertation: „Literarische Ontologie bei Foucault – der ‚regressus ad infinitum' als Binnenbegriff in den Werken Jorge Luis Borges' und Franz Kafkas." Teilnahme am Graduiertenkolleg „Texte – Zeichen – Medien" und am Kolloquium „Literaturwissenschaft als Kulturwissenschaft" an der Universität Erfurt. Forschungsprojekte zu den Themen „Las expresiones de la violencia. De Grecia a la actualidad" (Die Darstellung der Gewalt von den Griechen bis zur Gegenwart) und „Fronteras, marginalidad y ruptura" (Grenzen, Marginalität und Brüche). Publikation zur Monstrosität in Franz Kafkas Texten.

Caterina Cappuccio, Studium der Literatur und Geschichte an der Università Cattolica del Sacro Cuore (Mailand), an der Ludwig-Maximilians-Universität (München) und an der Bergischen Universität Wuppertal. Seit 2017 Promotionsstudium an der BUW bei Prof. Dr. Jochen Johrendt. Thema der Dissertation: „Die päpstliche Kapelle und ihre Wirksamkeit (1046–1216): Ein Vergleich zwischen den Kirchenprovinzen Mailand und Salzburg." Forschungsschwerpunkte: Papstgeschichte (11.–13. Jahrhundert), Päpstliche Kapelle, Beziehungen zwischen Rom und den Kirchenprovinzen, Geschichte der Kirche in der Lombardei und in der Kirchenprovinz Salzburg.

Myriam Dätwyler, Studium der Germanistik und Kunstgeschichte an der Universität Lausanne (2005–2012). Masterarbeit zum Thema: „Der Walser-Chor. Mehrstimmigkeit in Robert Walsers Werk". Seit 2008 tätig in der Lehre, seit 2012 Assistentin für Linguistik an der Universität Lausanne (Einführungskurse, Masterkurs zur Performanz im Dadaismus, zs. mit Prof. A. Schwarz, transversales Linguistik-Seminar). In ihrem Dissertationsprojekt, betreut von Prof. Peter Utz, befasst sie sich mit dem Gesamtwerk von Robert Walser in Bezug auf den Dialog und die Dialogizität. Publikation: Il était une fois… La compréhension et le malentendu chez Robert Walser. In: Ekaterina Velmezova / Myriam Dätwyler / Alexander Schwarz (Hg.): Le malentendu dans tous ses états, Cahiers de L'ILSL 44 (2016).

Martina Di Stefano, Master in Classics at University of Pavia. Currently enrolled in a joint-PhD program between University of Trento and University of Grenoble, PhD thesis: „Conflicting Harmony. The depiction of Socrates' Interlocutors in Plato's Dialogues." She is a member of C.R.I.M.T.A (http://crimta.unipv.it/) and has collaborated with Osservatorio Permanente sull'Antico. Research stays at University of Paris-Nanterre, University of Heidelberg and InterDaF of Leipzig. Further areas of interest: ancient theatre, the reception of antiquity, the relationship between philosophy and literature, epistemology of human and social sciences (history and anthropology). Publications: I lettori di Platone: l'influenza di Iser sugli studi platonici e alcune nuove prospettive. In: Wolfgang Iser – Verso un'antropologia della letteratura. Enthymema (under review); Review to M. Quijada Sagredo: M. C. Encinas Reguero (a c. di): Retórica y discurso en el teatro griego. Madrid 2013. In: Athenaeum 2 (2017) (forthcoming); Il passato come futuro possibile. Generi letterari e discronia della città nel Crizia. In: La città com'era, com'è e come la vorremmo (Atti dell'Osservatorio Permanente sull'Antico: a. a. 2012/2013, Pavia, Sezione di Scienze dell'Antichità), a cura di E. Corti. Firenze 2014, pp. 119–123.

Ricardo Márquez García, studierte Deutsch als Fremdsprache und Soziologie (B. A.) an der Universität Bielefeld und Interdisziplinäre Lateinamerikastudien (M. A.) an der Freien Universität Berlin. Er unterrichtete, gefördert vom DAAD, Germanistik an den Universitäten in Yaoundé (Kamerun) und Antananarivo (Madagaskar). Für die Ausstellung *Deutscher Kolo-*

nialismus. Fragmente seiner Geschichte und Gegenwart des Deutschen Historischen Museums interviewte er kamerunische Experten und produzierte eine Videoinstallation. Seit 2016 promoviert er an der Universität zu Köln zur Geschichte des Sklavenhandels in der Region des kamerunischen Graslandes. Zurzeit lebt und forscht er in Kamerun. Publikation: Ehemalige Sklaven aus Jamaika als Wegbereiter der deutschen Kolonisierung Kameruns? (im Druck).

Sven Hanuschek, Professor für Neuere deutsche Literatur und Geschäftsführer des Departments für Germanistik, Komparatistik, Nordistik und Deutsch als Fremdsprache an der LMU München. Mitglied des PEN. Vorsitzender der Internationalen Kipphardt-Gesellschaft. Arbeitsgebiete: Verhältnis von Literatur und Sozialpsychologie, Ethnologie, Film; Biographie; deutsche Literatur der frühen Moderne, Nachkriegsliteratur, Neo-Avantgarden, Gegenwartsliteratur. Publikationen (Auswahl): Mithg. von treibhaus. Jahrbuch für die Literatur der fünfziger Jahre (edition text + kritik), neoAvantgarden (edition text + kritik), Johnson-Studien (VR unipress), Hg. von Chironeia (Aisthesis) und InTERventionen. Künste und Wirklichkeiten (Wehrhahn). Bücher u. a. über Elias Canetti, Heinrich Heine, Uwe Johnson, Erich Kästner, Heinar Kipphardt, Laurel & Hardy.

Ursula Kocher, Professorin für Allgemeine Literaturwissenschaft an der Bergischen Universität Wuppertal. Arbeitsgebiete: Editionswissenschaft, Narratologie, Emblematik und Mnemonik, Indien in deutschsprachiger Literatur, Frühneuhochdeutsche Literatur, literarische Semiotik, Geschichte der Novelle und Kurt Schwitters. Veröffentlichungen in diesen thematischen Feldern, z. B. Kurt Schwitters: Die Sammelkladden 1919–1923. Hrsg. von Ursula Kocher und Isabel Schulz. Berlin u. a. 2014 (= Kurt Schwitters. Alle Texte. Band 3).

Johanna-Helene Linnemann, Studium der Deutschen Philologie, Allgemeinen und Vergleichenden Literaturwissenschaft, Indologie, Philosophie und Kunstgeschichte in Tübingen und an der Freien Universität Berlin (2003–2012). Halbjähriger Lehraufenthalt an der University of Delhi mit einem Stipendium des DAAD (2009). Seit 2012 Doktorandin in der Allgemeinen Literaturwissenschaft bei Prof. Dr. Ursula Kocher an der Bergischen Universität Wuppertal. Seit 2012 wissenschaftliche Mitarbeiterin. Die Dissertation befasst sich mit der „Ästhetik des Pflanzlichen" vom 17. bis 19. Jahrhundert.

Drishti Magoo, Master's degree at the University of Delhi. Currently doctoral student in Comparative Studies at the Faculty of Humanities and assistant for international academic relationships to India at the University of Wuppertal. Her field of research lies in the semiotic analysis of the *Diaries* of Franz Kafka (1910–1923).

Pia Martin, Master's degree in English at the University of Wuppertal. Currently doctoral student, teaching and research assistant at the Department of English Studies (BUW). She taught courses on the introduction to Literary Studies and on Gothic Romanticism. Her research interests: adaptation theory, popular literature around 1800 and dramatic adaptations of the Romantic period. Doctoral thesis about dramatic adaptations of the Romantic period, combining recent approaches from adaptation theory and cultural studies. Publications: (with Salman Abbas) Rew. Rüdiger Zymner / Achim Hölter (Ed.): Handbuch Komparatistik: Theorien, Arbeitsfelder, Wissenspraxis. Stuttgart: Metzler 2013. In: Julia Afifi / Rekha Kamath / Thomas Schwarz / Carmen Ulrich (Ed.): German Studies in India. Beiträge aus der Germanistik in Indien. New Delhi: Iudicium 2015, pp. 251–253.

Robert Moscaliuc, holds a BA in English and Romanian Languages and Literature from the University of Cluj-Napoca (Romania), a first-level MA in American Studies from the University of Turin (Italy), and a second MA in Modern Languages and Literature from the same University. Currently, he is PhD student at the University of Turin, conducting research in the field of contemporary American literature, focused on the literature produced and developed in the aftermath of the American ‚war on terror' in both Iraq and Afghanistan. Conducted research at the City University of New York as a visiting research scholar in various fields: ethics of fiction, the AIDS crisis of the 1980s in the United States, representations of Italian culture in American literature and film. Recent publication: The Proximal – Ancillary Coverage Continuum and the Discourse of the American ‚War on Terror'. In: Harbors, Flows, and Migrations: The USA in/and the World. Cambridge: Scholars Publishing 2017.

Valerio Petrucci, Bachelor and Master degree in Classics at La Sapienza University of Rome. For the Bachelor thesis, he focused on the transmission of the Cicero's epistolary ad Brutum, especially on the discovery of its „second book" by the Swiss Andreas Cratander in 1528. For the Master's dissertation, he worked on the textual transmission of the poems of the Greek author Anacreon, with a special interest in the papyrological evidence. Currently, he is PhD student in Latin Philology at the University of Wuppertal with a project concerning the Graeco-Latin bilingualism in the Latin poetry of the 1st and 2nd centuries, namely on the Epigrammaton Libri of Martial.

Benjamin Richarz, Studium der Germanistik und Geschichte (B. A.), angeschlossen M. A. in Germanistischer Literaturwissenschaft an der Bergischen Universität Wuppertal. Seit Oktober 2013 Arbeit am Dissertationsprojekt in Germanistischer Linguistik zur Semantik und Pragmatik des Konjunktivs im Deutschen, betreut von Prof. Dr. Horst Lohnstein.

Martin Schmidt, Studium der Fächer Geschichte, Klassische Philologie und Bildungswissenschaften im Master of Education an der Bergischen Universität Wuppertal. Seit 2015 wissenschaftlicher Mitarbeiter bei Prof. Dr. Stefan Freund in der Klassischen Philologie an der BUW. In seiner Dissertation arbeitet er zu Laktanz, *Divinae Institutiones* Buch 3.

Andrew Smith, graduated with 1st in History from Glasgow University 2013. Awarded three major prizes by Glasgow University in 2012/2013. Commenced PhD on Pope Leo IX in October 2013 which questions whether or not he was a reform pope. Gained AHRC Scholarship in June 2015. Delivered papers at Conferences at the Universities of Stirling, Bristol and Edinburgh; at the University of Mainz; at the IPIW Summer School and IPIW PhD Conference at the University of Wuppertal (July 2015, November 2016) and at the Leeds Medieval Congress (July 2016). Teaching part time at Glasgow University.

Georges Tilly, Ph. D student at the University of Rouen (Normandy) and the University of Naples (Federico II). Fields of study: Neapolitan humanism and its influence on European literature, with special insights on the works of its lead figure Giovanni Pontano (1429–1503). Recently published articles: Il primo agrumeto rinascimentale. Il ‚De hortis Hesperidum' di Giovanni Pontano nella storia culturale ed agraria della Campania. In Giuseppe Germano (Ed.): Per la valorizzazione del patrimonio culturale della Campania. Il contributo degli studi medio- e neo-latini. Napoli: Paolo Loffredo 2017, pp. 95–105; La raison de l'étonnement: Le numerus dans l',Actius' (1507) de Giovanni Pontano. In Dominique de Courcelles (Ed.): La raison du merveilleux. Paris: Classiques Garnier [forthcoming 2017].

Hannah Tischmann, Ostmitteleuropa-Studien mit dem Schwerpunkt Baltikum und Skandinavistik in Münster und Lund. Seit 2014 Universitätsassistentin an der Abteilung Skandinavistik der Universität Wien. Promotion zum Thema: Funktion von literarischen Zeitpraktiken für die Konstruktionen von sozialen Ungleichheiten in schwedischer Arbeiterliteratur aus den 1970er Jahren und nach 2000. Forschungsschwerpunkte: Skandinavische Literaturen ab dem 19. Jahrhundert, neueste Gegenwartsliteratur, Verhältnis von Literatur und Gesellschaft.

Lisa-Marie Teubler, PhD candidate in English Literature at the Centre for Languages and Literature at the Lund University, Sweden. Her main research interest is the study of rhetorical means and strategies of persuasion and legitimization. In her dissertation, she investigates the application of these means in the works of Charles Dickens. Other research interests are in 19th century literature as well as in composition studies. She is teaching literature, writing and rhetoric at Malmö University and at Lund University.

Carmen Ulrich, PD Dr., Studium der Neueren deutschen Literatur, Ethnologie und Philosophie an der LMU München; Promotion 2003; Habilitation 2012; DFG-Forschungsprojekt (2005–09), DAAD-Lektorin an der Universität Daugavpils/Lettland (2003–05) und der University of Delhi (2010–15). Seit 2015 tätig an der Universität Wuppertal im Projekt „International promovieren in Wuppertal". Publikationen: „Bericht vom Anfang". Der Buchmarkt der SBZ und frühen DDR im Medium der Anthologie (2013); Sinn und Sinnlichkeit des Reisens. Indien(be)schreibungen von Hubert Fichte, Günter Grass und Josef Winkler (2004). Aufsätze zur Literatur in der DDR, Reiseliteratur, Diskursanalyse, zu den Autoren Wolfgang Koeppen, Elias Canetti, Bertolt Brecht, Adalbert Stifter, Paul Pörtner u. a. Mithg. der Zeitschrift German Studies in India (2010/2012/2015).